PSYCHOLOGICAL CONTAINMENT IN RELATIONSHIPS:

Converting Experience To Meaning

CAROLLE M. DALLEY

Acknowledgements

It is my good fortune to have Kevin Richard as reviewer of this manuscript. Kevin is a lecturer at the Assisi Institute: The International Center for the Study of Archetypal Patterns. He conducts lectures in Archetypal Pattern Analysis. In reviewing the manuscript, Kevin offered insightful observations about topics in Analytical Psychology that I apply in the biographical chapters. I am responsible for any imperfections in this book.

UPS Store # 4670 did the graphic design work that converted my hand-drawn diagrams into digital images which became illustrations for this book.

Outskirts Press made available a large selection of possible cover designs from which I chose an abstract design. To customize the abstract design, I asked the designer to overlay two overlapping circles that represent a shared reverie, a common mental activity in psychological containment.

Outskirts Press staff members were supportive in the publication of this book. They guided me through the sequence of publishing activities, made recommendations in areas unfamiliar to me, then produced the eBook and paperback formats for selected platforms.

Table of Contents

Introduction

This book is a call to action that invites readers to take away a portable understanding of psychological containment. To facilitate a portable understanding, I have structured the chapters so that sections align with characteristics of a mode of containment. To give readers the freedom to read chapters in any order they choose, I repeat definitions of projection, appropriation, and symbolization in the biographical chapters, because these processes are foundational to psychological containment. An understanding of psychological containment affords an advantage in being able to ascertain whether a relationship includes psychological containment. It also has the advantage of discerning whether a containment has more of a potential for psychological growth or psychological harm.

There are two psychologists who are well known for their publications about psychological containment in relationships. Wilfred Bion developed the containment model, which was later enhanced by Duncan Cartwright. I refer to their work as the Bion-Cartwright containment model, to honor both their contributions. Bion built the model intending it to apply to people who are psychologically well and those who are psychologically ill. Bion identified three modes of containment. He expected that the model would be expanded to accommodate more modes of containment, and that is what Cartwright did. Cartwright added two modes of containment. All of the modes of containment that Bion and Cartwright defined involve the minds of two people. While reading biographies as I conducted research for this book, I saw the need for additional modes of containment. With due respect to Bion and Cartwright, I propose two additional modes of containment. See Chapter 7 for descriptions of the modes of containment.

Psychological containment is a complex topic, so, I offer a layered description:

- **Flows of communication**: In the first layer of information about psychological containment, I focus on the flows of conscious and unconscious communications between the people in a containment. To do that, I use digital images in which there are arrows to show direction in the flows of communication.
- **Two definitions of archetype**: In the second layer, I focus on explaining containment in terms of two separate definitions of archetype. One definition is from the perspective of 20th century psychologists who define archetype as a biological entity. They see the activation of an archetype in terms of an unconscious projection from the psyche. The other definition is from the perspective of 21st century psychologists who define archetype as an emergent phenomenon. They see activation of an archetype in terms of a conscious appropriation from the cultural environment.
- **Symbolization**: In the third layer, I describe the symbolic thought forms that emerge during containments where there is psychological growth. In accordance with "A Critical Dictionary Of Jungian Analysis" I explain each symbol in terms of concept, intent, purpose and content.
- **Biographical examples of psychological containment**: In the last layer, I provide biographical chapters about people — some famous, others infamous — whose lives illustrate the modes of containment.

The goals of this book are informational:

- Advance an awareness of the containment model as developed by Wilfred Bion and enhanced by Duncan Cartwright.
- Explain that the model's relevance to society resides in the fact that relationships and containments are pervasive throughout a lifetime. They can start as early as the mother-infant relationship, and continue throughout life in a series of possibilities that include father-child, brother-sister, friend-friend, teacher-student, worker-coworker, employee-employer, apprentice-expert, girlfriend-boyfriend, husband-wife, and mentor-mentee attachments.
- Provide examples of modes of containment by reference to biographies of people who are known in the public domain.

The scope of this book:
- The lives I select to illustrate modes of containment are of (in)famous people who lead their lives in normal, everyday settings, as different from therapeutic settings. Although the Bion-Cartwright model is relevant to both developmental and clinical settings, I chose to leave clinical settings out of the scope of this book.
- The book covers three modes of containment defined by Wilfred Bion, two modes of containment defined by Duncan Cartwright, and two modes of containment that I propose adding to the containment model.
- Each biographical chapter is centered around the duration of a particular containment, and is not intended to be a complete biography of anyone's life.

The audience for this book:
- I write primarily for an audience of psychology clubs that admit laypeople as members.
- My intended audience extends to associations, societies, clubs and any forum where psychologists engage the public, in the interest of advancing knowledge of psychology for the benefit of society.

The arrangement of this book:
- **Chapter 1** *"How a Mind Depends on Another Mind for Meaning"* This chapter describes the communications between two minds in the Bion-Cartwright containment model. It includes three modes of containment defined by Bion (commensal, parasitic and symbiotic) and two modes of containment defined by Cartwright (autistic and pseudo-containing).
- **Chapter 2** *"How a Mind Depends on Itself for Meaning"* This chapter describes communication within the mind of one person who finds himself / herself in isolation. My proposal is that a reflexive mode of containment be added to the containment model for people who are able to convert their own life experiences to meaning by engaging in internal dialogues. I noticed this in people who withdrew into isolation from society, or on whom isolation was imposed.
- **Chapter 3** *"How a Mind Depends on a Deity for Meaning"* This chapter describes communication between the mind of a human and their perception of deity. My proposal is that a theistic mode

of containment be added to the containment model for people who are able to convert their own life experiences to meaning by interacting with their deity. I noticed this in people who rely on their deity for sustenance, especially in times of difficulty.

- **Chapter 4** *"Archetype: Biological Entity vs Emergent Phenomenon"* While reading the literature about containment, I found the references to 'projection' disembodied, so, I wrote this chapter to explain archetypes as the source of projections. I included the 20th century definition of archetype as biological entity, as well as the 21st century definition of archetype as emergent phenomenon.
- **Chapter 5** *"Characteristics of a Containment"* In this chapter, I explain the basic elements of psychological containment.
- **Chapter 6** *"Symbolization in the Construction of Meaning from Raw Experience of Life"* In this chapter, I explain that, regardless of how psychologists define archetype, they see symbolization as being essential to containments which lead to psychological growth. It is the emergence of symbols that foster the generation of meaning during the dialogue of the containment pair.
- **Chapter 7** *"Modes of Containment "* This chapter explains the modes of containments in detail.
- **Chapters 8 through 11** These chapters are four examples of the commensal mode of containment. This mode was defined by Bion in the original containment model.
- **Chapters 12 and 13** These chapters are two examples of the symbiotic mode of containment. This mode was defined by Bion in the original containment model.
- **Chapter 14** This chapter is an example of the parasitic mode of containment. This mode was defined by Bion in the original containment model.
- **Chapters 15 and 16** These chapters are two examples of the autistic mode of containment. This mode was added to the containment model by Cartwright.
- **Chapter 17** This chapter is an example of the pseudo-containing mode of containment. This mode was added to the containment model by Cartwright.
- **Chapters 18 and 19** These chapters are two examples of the reflexive mode of containment. This is a mode that I propose

adding to the containment model.

- **Chapters 20 and 21** These chapters are two examples of the theistic mode of containment. This is a mode that I propose adding to the containment model.

The chapters of the book do not need to be read in the order presented. Readers who are familiar with topics of projection, appropriation and symbolization may prefer to go directly to the biological chapters.

During my development of the manuscript, Kevin Richard kindly conducted reviews. He thoughtfully reviewed drafts of the chapters and offered insightful comments. I appreciate his candor and his response to what I call my author's angst. His candor came to the fore when I asked him to review a draft of the first chapter. His comment: If you are aiming for an audience of laypeople, you missed the mark ... this draft is too analytical and too academic. In assessing my options, I thought I could either change my target audience, or change my writing style. Since I am not a psychologist, I did not think it appropriate to claim to be writing about containment for any level of formal education. So, I decided to target an audience of psychology clubs that admit laypeople as members. Since then, I have been adjusting my writing with an aim for a style that is informative and conversational. Readers will let me know if I achieved that style.

One instance of my author's angst was related to the chapter about Carl Jung and Sigmund Freud. On my first round of research about the relationship between Jung and Freud, I chose the symbiotic mode of containment as being applicable because there was no psychological growth, nor any psychological harm resulting from their relationship. When I read what I wrote, I experienced author's angst about my interpretation of the disciple-leader relationship between the two men. How could I say there was no psychological harm, when, at the end of their relationship, Freud fell into a neurosis and Jung fell into a psychosis? Kevin and I had a multi-pronged discussion about possible influences that could have contributed to the end of their relationship, after which I embarked on a second round of research. On further research, I found that Jung and Freud were already snowballing their way to psychological disorders long before they met. My interpretation is that their collaboration might have been a tipping point, but neither can be said to have caused harm in the other. Had they been paying closer attention, these two sages of the psyche might have realized that their emotional bond was based on a shared delusion. Neither man could be what the other wanted him to be. Jung could not be a subservient disciple; Freud could not risk his authority as a leader.

In writing about containment, psychologists often refer to the relationship between mother and infant as an example of containment. Most mothers do not have any training in psychology, yet they function as capable containers for their infants. Most infants do not have the language skills to engage in conscious communication. Yet, infants achieve psychological growth from unconscious communications with their mothers. Containment is an everyday activity that occurs among everyday people. Mentor and novice. Religious leader and member of a religion. Romantic partners. Brother and sister. Close friends. Professor and student. Gang leader and gang member. Doctor and patient. Co-workers.

As an introduction to the meaning of psychological containment, I share a hypothetical story that was created by Margot Waddell, a psychologist who works at the Tavistock Clinic in London. She published the story in "Inside Lives: Psychoanalysis and the Growth of Personality" in 2002. Waddell offers hypothetical interactions between a child and three possible mothers as a simplified illustration of containment. While the child is experiencing difficulty fitting together a jigsaw puzzle, a projection of anxiety is cast from the child's mind onto the mother's mind. To explain the notion of containment, Waddell offers different responses from three hypothetical mothers as possible attempts at containment.

1. The first mother feels irritated that her child is unable to assemble a simple puzzle. On becoming aware of the mother's irritation, the child experiences more anxiety, feels less capable of completing the puzzle, and leaves the room crying.

2. The second mother notices that her child is struggling with the puzzle. Assuming that the child's problem will be solved if she just puts the piece of puzzle in the correct place, she does just that, leaving the child no better able to assemble the jigsaw.

3. The third mother encourages her child to persevere with the

puzzle a little longer, and offers hints about fitting the pieces of the puzzle together. She gets a sense of her child's level of distress and helps by turning the piece of the puzzle around the right way so the fit becomes more obvious to the child. By engaging the child and offering hints, the mother helps the child achieve a measure of autonomy and a sense of having the capability to complete the puzzle.

Waddell then describes the effect that each of the three hypothetical mother-child interactions could be expected to have on the child:

1. The first mother fails to function as a container for the anxiety that the child is projecting about not being able to complete the puzzle. This mother lacks the ability to engage the child and transform the feelings of anxiety, with the result that they are returned to the child without any change. The child does not benefit from this interaction. This is a failed attempt at containment because the mother fails to contain the child's anxiety.

2. The second mother demonstrates some capacity to tolerate the child's anxiety and is able to engage the child in a way that she thinks is helpful to the child. However, she does not have the capacity to entertain the feelings that the child has projected for long enough to be able to sift through them and work out what the child is truly trying to say. The child is not trying to communicate that it wants the puzzle to be solved. The child is trying to tell the mother about the intense distress felt when faced with the prospect of having to do something without her. As a container, the mother demonstrates enough tolerance of the frustration to avoid evasion of the child's projection, but not enough to engage the child in the kind of introjection that would foster the development of a sense of autonomy and capability. Repeated cycles of this style of containment can lead to the child developing an internal world that cannot survive without dictatorial moral strictures to give it coherence.

3. The third mother tolerates the child's anxiety long enough to sift through the uncertainty of the situation looking for clues as to what the child is communicating. When she does intervene, it is with an eye on how the child is responding, and in a way that allows the child to discover a sense of his own capacity and she does not impose meaning on him. She engages the child in an

interaction that enables him to convert his experience of anxiety about the puzzle into meaning for himself. Meaning is teased out during the interaction between them.

The third mother offers the child the best potential for psychological growth. Waddell portrays the complexity of the interplay between child and mother as seen through the lens of Bion's containment model. The mother's introjection — her response to the child's projection — can be negative or positive. The first mother had a negative effect. The third mother had a positive effect. I chose Margot Waddell's hypothetical example partly because it involves a child who is not yet fluent in a language. That makes the point that the communication in a containment is partly conscious and partly unconscious. Not yet fluent in a language, the child was not able to articulate his anxiety in words, so he used facial expression and gestures. Another reason I chose Waddell's example is that it indicates that containment happens in normal everyday activities, and is not limited to therapy.

A containment can lead to psychological growth or psychological harm, or neither. It is important to be able to make that distinction because what looks like a happy relationship can involve a containment whose outcome is harmful. An example of what appeared to be a happy relationship, but which had a harmful containment came to public attention in 2021. The story was documented in a book titled "*Vanlife Nightmare: The Gabby Petito Story*" which was independently published by W. G. Davis in July 2022. The story was also aired by Lifetime which released a TV adaptation called "*The Gabby Petito Story*" in October 2022. Gabby and Brian were in love and engaged to be married. In a vehicle customized for van life (a contemporary outdoor lifestyle of living in a vehicle), they were taking a road trip across the United States, stopping at national parks along the way. Gabby was launching her career as a travel influencer, by posting happy, romantic videos on social media to share the couple's travel experiences. It appears that no one in their social circles noticed the toxic nature of their relationship. It took two strangers — who observed the couple in a short period of time — to notice the toxicity of their relationship. The first stranger was a gentleman who saw Gabby and Brian in a physical altercation on a sidewalk. Concerned about the violence that he witnessed, he called the police to report the matter. When the police tracked them down, Gabby and Brian each insisted they were in love and did not want the other to be arrested. The second stranger who noticed the toxic nature of their relationship was a park ranger who accompanied the police during an interview of Gabby. The park ranger told Gabby that she was in a toxic relationship. A few days later Gabby was found dead. The cause of her death turned out to be strangulation. A few weeks later, investigators found Brian's body, with a written confession that he had taken Gabby's life, to put her out of her pain after she fell down. The cause of his death was suicide. After strangling Gabby, Brian left her body outdoors near a park in Wyoming. He did not inform her family. He did not inform the authorities. He drove the van to his parents' home in Florida.

Had anyone in their social circle been familiar with psychological containment, they might have noticed that the relationship had more potential for harm than growth. When Gabby fell in love, she had idealized expectations about Brian as a fiancé. She was striving to establish her career as a travel influencer, and expected him to be supportive. Instead, he undermined her efforts, and expressed doubts about her ability to achieve a successful outcome. In addition, he called her crazy and attached the label of Obsessive-Compulsive Disorder (OCD) – a condition that her parents point out had never been a diagnosis for Gabby. Someone familiar with psychological containment might have noticed that Brian was not yet at a stage in his life where he could become a container for Gabby's projection. Brian was not able to provide the mental scaffolding for Gabby to become an autonomous, independent member of society, because he had not yet established a place for himself in society as an autonomous, independent adult. Gabby was transitioning from being an employee working in a store to a self-employed travel influencer. She was defining a role for herself in society. She established a web site to record her travels, purchased a van, customized it for van life, and set out on a road trip to record and publish her travel adventures. Brian was still living in his parents' home, and he did not appear to have entrepreneurial self-supporting aspirations. He told the police that he did not own a 'phone. He was using Gabby's 'phone. The authorities charged Brian for withdrawing money from Gabby's bank account after her death. A young person builds a career as a means of establishing their place in society. A career becomes an integral part of a person's identity in the transition from adolescence to adulthood. Brian was not able to provide the mental scaffolding necessary to help Gabby process the emotional turmoil she experienced in building her career, because she was trying to do something that he had not yet accomplished. Brian graduated from high school a year before Gabby. Five years later, at the time of their road trip, he had not yet established himself as an independent, self-supporting adult in society. What is worse is that he had been prescribed medication for his diagnosis of anxiety disorder, but he was not taking the medication. Since he did not have the experience of having built a career to establish himself as a functioning adult in society, and was not able to manage his own medication, he could not help Gabby process her career-related emotions. That relationship did not promise psychological growth.

I chose that example because Gabby and Brian lived out much of their road trip on social media where people are selective about what they disclose of themselves. According to the social media postings, Gabby and Brian were living a romantic, adventurous life in a happy relationship. What was not noticeable on social media was the fragility of their psychological containment. Unfortunately for the couple, no one in their families or their social circle noticed the crack in their containment. The people who saw the toxicity of the relationship were strangers. Sadly, after the police arranged a night of separation, the young couple — unaware that nothing was resolved — continued on their path to destruction. If any reader is aware of a situation that warrants an intervention, see Appendix A – Hotlines for Psychological Support.

The research and organization of content for this book were satisfying experiences for me. I hope readers find the book informative enough to respond to the call for action by taking away a portable understanding of the modes of containment.

Carolle M. Dalley
June 2023

Abbreviations

CHAPTER I

How a Mind Depends on Another Mind for Meaning

"A mind is dependent on another mind for meaning: but this necessarily remains ineffable, opaque, and in flux."
— Duncan Cartwright

In human society, relationships abound. Anybody can have a relationship with anyone else. A person can have a relationship with a family member, a spouse, a friend, a co-worker, a neighbor, a religious leader, a mail carrier, a dog walker, and a security guard. While there is a proliferation of relationships, only certain relationships have meaningful impact on our lives. Impactful relationships are the ones that have psychological significance. A word that psychologists use for those relationships is 'containment'. When a relationship has psychological significance, it occurs in the context of a containment, where one person is called the 'contained' and the other person the 'container'. The contained and the container establish a mind-to-mind interaction that enables psychological growth of one, or both of them. What gives the containment its psychological significance is that it has the potential for converting raw life experience into meaning. That potential depends on the narrative dialogue that occurs during the containment. It also depends on the container's ability to provide mental scaffolding for psychological growth. Some containments lead to psychological growth, while other containments can lead to toxic outcomes. It is important to know the difference.

Role of the Narrative Dialogue in a Containment

Psychologist Warren Colman expresses the view that there is always a narrative dialogue going on in a person's life. If the narrative dialogue is not with another person, then the narrative dialogue is internal. A narrative dialogue is a constructive process in which a story is created first by one person, and then taken over and retold on a new level by the other (AAA 147 – 148). A narrative dialogue continues with increasing complexity throughout a person's development. The containment pair engages in a 'reverie' that can give meaning to the contained's experience of life. This involves the container holding a storyline while the contained gradually internalizes the meaningful links made for him / her. In this way the contained gradually acquires an awareness of a sense that their mind is an agent of change (AAA 148). The narrative is then taken over by the contained. A successful narrative dialogue is one that can become meaningful to the contained so that he / she can take it over, use it for themself and adapt it to establish a sense of connection between their intrapsychic experience and the external world.

Humans construct their lives by weaving together relationships with other people into autobiographical narratives. We keep autobiographical narratives up-to-date because we rely on them for a sense of continuity in our lives, and a sense of identity. Relationships are not just about people getting together to share common interests. Relationships sometimes involve establishing emotional bonds. Relationships that have emotional bonds are foundational for psychological growth. Psychologists use different words for relationship. Sometimes they use the word 'attachment' and other times they use the word 'containment'. While they use different words for relationship, they have a general agreement that early relationships are important because they are indicators of future relationships. Early relationships that are formed with caregivers, usually parents, form templates for other relationships later in life. The templates are not fixed; they can change, but a concerted effort is necessary to bring about change. Sometimes we find ourselves in relationships with people we did not choose, a parent, a boss, a neighbor. Other times, we choose the people with whom we want to establish relationships, like a friend, spouse, a mentor. In this book, I use the Bion-Cartwright containment model to explain ways in which people form relationships of psychological significance, then I provide biographical chapters about people in whose lives the modes of containment are illustrated.

Relationship & Containment

A psychologist named Wilfred Bion drew on his experience as a practitioner in the psychoanalytic movement to define the containment model in the 1970's. Another psychologist, Duncan Cartwright, used his psychoanalytic practice as his basis for enhancing the containment model in 2010. I refer to it as the Bion-Cartwright containment model to honor the contributions of both psychologists. By establishing a containment model, these psychologists were portraying how people have been relating to each other in the evolution of human relationships. With the notion of containment, they are distinguishing those relationships that have psychological significance. They are putting labels like 'contained' and 'container' and 'reverie' on human interactions that have been going on for centuries. Relationships between mothers and babies, between best friends, between wives and husbands, and between co-workers have been demonstrating modes of containment long before the discipline of psychology came into existence.

Since the narrative dialogue is central to containment, I think it is important to focus attention on the flow of communications, during a containment. I make drawings to show the flow of communications — both conscious and unconscious — between two minds during a containment. To simplify the description of psychological containment, I show the Bion-Cartwright containment model in terms of lines of communication. In the drawings, the contained and container are shown as stick figures. The arrows indicate the directions in which communications flow between two minds. The figures in this chapter depict my interpretation of the flows of communications in the Bion-Cartwright model. Here are the headings for the figures:

- Communication in Relationship without Containment
- Communication in Relationship with Containment
- Communication in Reverie
- Communication in Dialectical Interaction.

What differentiates a containment from a relationship is that the containment has an emotional bond between two minds, along with conscious and unconscious flows of communication between the two minds. In a relationship without containment, the communication is primarily conscious, that is, verbal communication, spoken or written. In a relationship with containment, there are both conscious and unconscious flows of communication. Unconscious communication refers to nonverbal cues that provide information where an emotional bond exists. It includes body language, facial expression, intuition, hand gestures and shared reverie.

FIGURE 1.1: Communication in Relationship without Containment

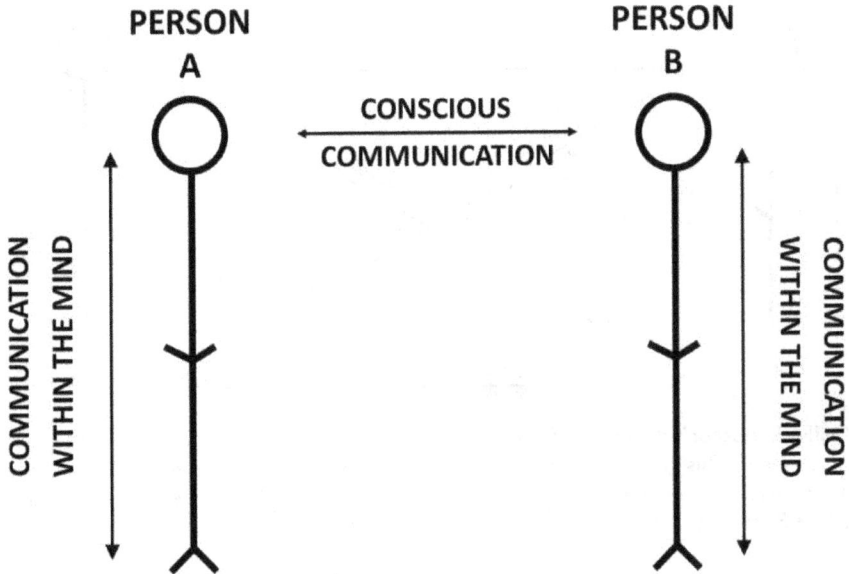

SOURCE: Author's depiction of the lines of communication in a relationship where there is no containment.

Figure 1.1 shows Person A and Person B in a relationship where there is no containment. The two-way arrows indicate that communication can flow in either direction. The horizontal arrow shows conscious communication between the minds of Person A and Person B. Vertical arrows indicate conscious and unconscious communication occurring within the mind of each person. Relationships without containment are about casual interaction, without emotional connection. While a relationship without a containment may be cordial, it has no potential for psychological growth, because the unconscious mind-to-mind connection is missing. There is no emotional bond forming a bridge between the two minds. Examples of relationships without containment are interactions one might have with a dog-walker, a security guard at an office building, or a mail carrier.

FIGURE 1.2: Communication in Relationship with Containment

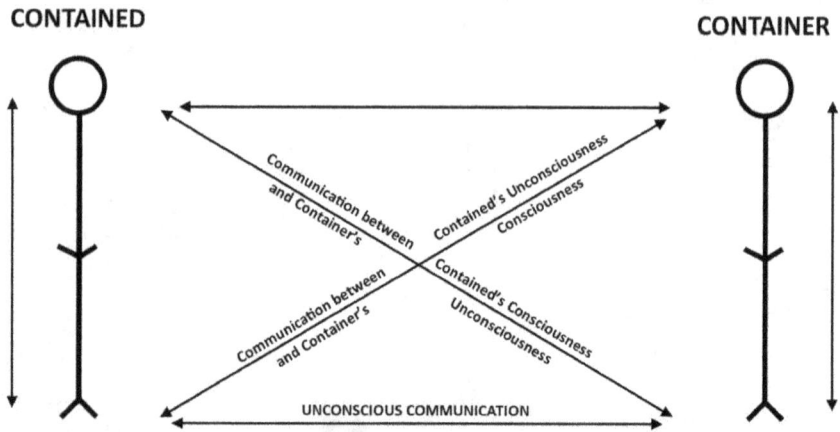

SOURCE: Author's depiction of lines of communication in a relationship where there is a containment. This interpretation is an integration of Wilfred Bion's containment model in *"Attention and Interpretation"* (AI 72 – 82; AI 106 – 124) and Carl Jung's relationship diagram in *"The Psychology of Transference"* (Collected Work 16, paragraph 422).

Figure 1.2 shows a relationship with a containment. The containment involves one person labeled 'Contained' and another person labeled 'Container'. The lines of communication in Figure 1.2 are a combination of the lines of communication in Figure 1.1 plus additional lines of unconscious communication. The horizontal arrow at the bottom of Figure 1.2 shows unconscious communication between the minds of the containment pair. There are two diagonal arrows. One diagonal arrow indicates communication between the contained's consciousness and the container's unconsciousness, while the other diagonal arrow shows communication between the container's consciousness and the contained's unconsciousness. Examples of relationships with containment are those that exist where the interaction has its basis in emotional bonds. For example, containments exist between best friends, mentor and mentee, romantic partners, twins who have a close relationship, psychologist and patient. A relationship with a containment has the potential for psychological growth, because there is an unconscious mind-to-mind connection, and there is an emotional bond forming a bridge between the two minds.

FIGURE 1.3: Communication in Reverie

CONTAINED   CONTAINER

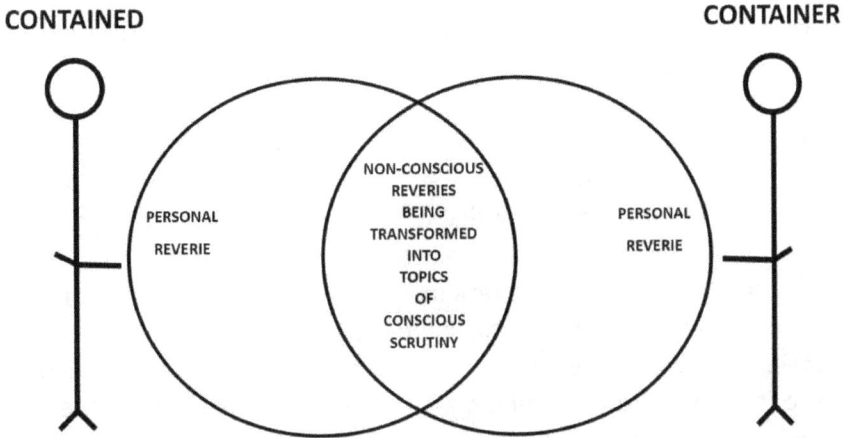

SOURCE: Author's interpretation of communication in the form of reverie being shared by contained and container. This interpretation is based on Thomas Ogden's "*Reverie and Interpretation*" (RI 107 - 124).

Figure 1.3 shows an overlapping of the contained's personal reverie and the container's personal reverie. Each engages in their own private reverie, shown in a circle. Where the circles overlap, there is nonconscious shared reveries that can be transformed into topics which the contained and container can scrutinize consciously. Containment involves an interplay of conscious and unconscious states of reverie (AIE 137). Shared reverie occurs when the containment pair achieves continuity of experiential context and verbal content. Ogden describes the capacity for reverie in terms of communication in a psychological space where two people develop their ability to generate thoughts, feelings and sensations without believing that there is a script which they are expected to follow (RI 51 – 53). During containment, reverie moves towards verbal symbolization of experience (RI 158). Reverie is a private dimension of experience that can involve embarrassing aspects of life. The thoughts and feelings that make up reverie can be so private that they may not be discussed with colleagues. To attempt to hold such thoughts, feelings and sensations in consciousness is to forego a type of privacy that people unconsciously rely on as a barrier separating what is held as private from what is shared.

A reverie is both an individual psychic event and an unconscious, inter-subjective construction (RI 159). The shared reverie is where the containment pair has the opportunity to derive meaning from experience. The shared reverie is the context in which the narrative dialogue plays out the meaning-making imperative of the archetype from which a contained's projection is cast. Although Ogden wrote "*Reverie and Interpretation*" with other psychologists in mind, I find that much of the content of his book can be valuable for laypeople, because it explains reverie as an occurrence in normal everyday life as much as in psychologists' offices. Reveries are moment-to-moment thoughts, feelings and sensations that are instrumental in understanding and metabolizing lived experience. In a containment, reveries are musings from the lives of the contained and the container, also from the world in which they live. Reveries can include ruminations, daydreams, fantasies, bodily sensations, fleeting perceptions, images emerging from sleep, musical notes and literary phrases. During containment, these are the contents that run through the minds of the contained and the container (RI 158).

FIGURE 1.4: Communication in Dialectical Interaction

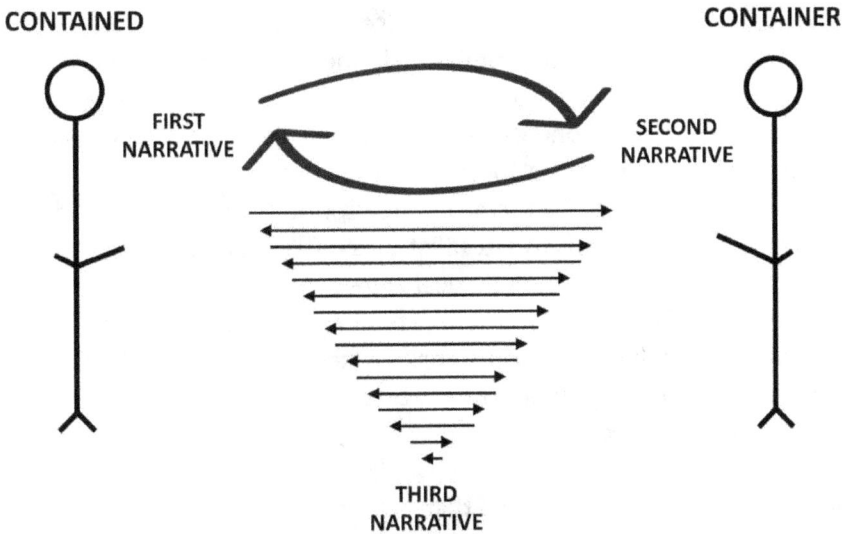

CONTAINED   CONTAINER

FIRST NARRATIVE   SECOND NARRATIVE

THIRD NARRATIVE

SOURCE: Author's interpretation of dialectical interaction based on Duncan Cartwright's bi-directional field (CSM 11 – 15) and Thomas Ogden's dialectical interplay (RI 107 – 133).

Figure 1.4 depicts a dialectical interaction where the lines of communication flow between contained and container in a back-and-forth movement between two narratives. The first narrative (contributed by the contained) and the second narrative (contributed by the container) undergo a series of declarations, negations and modifications to produce a third narrative, or dialectical output (CSM 11 – 15; RI 107 – 133). Arrows show the lines of communication between contained and container. Central to containment is the interplay between conscious and unconscious communications that lead to the creation of a third narrative. Arrows indicate the tension of opposites in the dialectical interplay between the containment pair. Safeguarding the privacy of the contained and container is critical to creating and preserving the conditions for conscious and unconscious communication between the two (RI 137). Maintenance of a psychological frame supports the privacy of the containment pair. As the containment continues, progress is marked by a psychological movement, also known as a psychological shift, that involves change.

A psychological movement is the outcome from dialectical interplay of reveries of the contained and container (RI 108). The psychological movement involves a change that addresses the unprocessed state of mind that initiated the containment. If the containment is successful, there will be two results of the dialectical interaction. There will be an internal change for one or both people in the containment pair, and an external result that is a joint dialectical output. The internal result is private; it may take the form of a new outlook, a flash of insight, an illumination, a resolution to a conflict or a different direction in life. The internal result involves psychological growth for one or both contained and container. The external result of the dialectical interaction is something discernible in the external world, such as a visible problem solved, a research that ends in an invention, or the creation of a joint legacy by the containment pair.

Duncan Cartwright points out that a containment can only take place if the container has an ongoing relationship with the unconscious part of their own psyche, and has already been processing a state of mind similar to the unprocessed state of mind projected from the mind of the contained. He also cautions that the container is at risk of having the contained's unprocessed state of mind undo or compromise their already processed state of mind. Warren Colman informs us that the containment depends on receptivity to states of reverie (AIE 117).

Sources

While writing this chapter, I relied on information in the following sources:
- *"Unrepresented States and the Construction of Meaning"* by Howard Levine
- *"Attention and Interpretation"* by Wilfred Bion
- *"Containing States of Mind"* by Duncan Cartwright
- *"Reverie and Interpretation"* by Thomas Ogden
- *"The Psychology of Transference"* by Carl Jung
- *"Projection and Re-Collection in Jungian Psychology"* by Marie-Louise von Franz.

CHAPTER 2

How a Mind Depends on Itself for Meaning

"Humans now have an imaginative space within which symbols can function in what appears to be an entirely internal way ... it is only through the use of symbols as a means of communication that imagination becomes possible as a solitary function ... in a communicative dialogue with ourselves."

— Warren Colman

The Bion-Cartwright containment model has five modes of containment, each of which involves two people in a mind-to-mind interaction. I am proposing the addition of a reflexive mode of containment to the Bion-Cartwright model. In my studies, I have found the Bion-Cartwright theme that a mind depends on another mind for psychological growth is limited. There is only one mode of containment for the psychologically healthy, while there are four modes of containment for borderline disorders or worse. Wilfred Bion was a British psychanalyst who built the containment model, in which he focused on one mind depending on another mind for meaning. His references are about two minds, for example, mother-infant, wife-husband, and patient-psychoanalyst. Bion built the model with three modes of containment; one mode is conducive to psychological growth ... the other two modes are not. Duncan Cartwright is a South African clinical psychologist who enhanced Bion's containment model. Cartwright also focuses on one mind depending on another mind to achieve psychological growth. His examples are analyst-analysand and patient-psychologist. With Cartwright's enhancement, the model has one mode of containment that is conducive to psychological growth ... the other four modes are not. Their focus on one mind helping another mind is understandable ... they write from their therapist's perspective. They write for an audience of other therapists. While I have a great deal of respect for clinical psychologists Bion and Cartwright, I believe that if the containment model had been built by developmental psychologists, it would be more balanced in terms of modes of containment conducive to psychological growth, and modes of containment that are not conducive to growth.

In proposing the addition of a reflexive mode of containment, I draw on the work of psychologist, Warren Colman, who wrote the book "*Act and Image: The Emergence of Symbolic Imagination*" in which he stated:

> "*Humans now have an imaginative space within which symbols can function in what appears to be an entirely internal way ... it is only through the use of symbols as a means of communication that imagination becomes possible as a solitary function ... in a communicative dialogue with ourselves.*"
>
> – Warren Colman (AI 94)

My interpretation is that with the emergence of symbolic imagination, humanity became capable of psychological growth without a mind being dependent on another mind. To demonstrate that a mind can depend on itself for meaning and psychological growth, I use biographies of Dante Alighieri and Ludwig Beethoven. Each man found himself in isolation, with no one to mirror his life, no one to be a container. Dante was isolated because he was exiled from his home city, Florence. Having run into conflict with his political opponents, who confiscated his resources and threatened his life, he fled Florence, leaving behind his wife and children as well as his network of friends and colleagues. Alone, he travelled in the style of a nomad, accepting food and accommodation from people he met along the way. It was during this isolation, that he composed *Inferno*, the first part of a trilogy that became known as *La Commedia*

(Divine Comedy). I propose that Dante became a container for himself. To become a container for himself, Dante arranged a literary device in which he functioned in two roles simultaneously. In one role, he was flesh and blood Dante-the-poet. In a fictional role, he was Dante-the-protagonist in *La Commedia*. That literary device enabled an ongoing dialogue between Dante-the-poet and Dante-the-protagonist for about twenty years during which he composed the poem *La Commedia*. Dante's isolation was externally imposed by exile, while Beethoven's isolation was self-imposed. As Beethoven was losing his hearing, he retreated from society. He was losing the sense most valuable to a musician, and he was reluctant to acknowledge the loss in public. So, he avoided social gatherings, and he stopped giving public piano concerts. In his self-imposed isolation, he set up a dialogue between Beethoven-the-lover and Beethoven-the-musician. With this ongoing dialogue, he came to terms with his unrequited love for his Immortal Beloved, and focused on composing original, classical music. Even though his hearing got worse, he continued to compose in his mind. For example, he composed his famous Symphony 9 *"Ode To Joy"* without ever hearing it. In biographical chapters, I provide details about my reason for proposing that – counter to the Bion-Cartwright theme that a mind needs another mind for psychological growth — Dante and Beethoven achieved psychological growth during periods of isolation.

FIGURE 2.1: Communication within a Mind

CONTAINED & CONTAINER

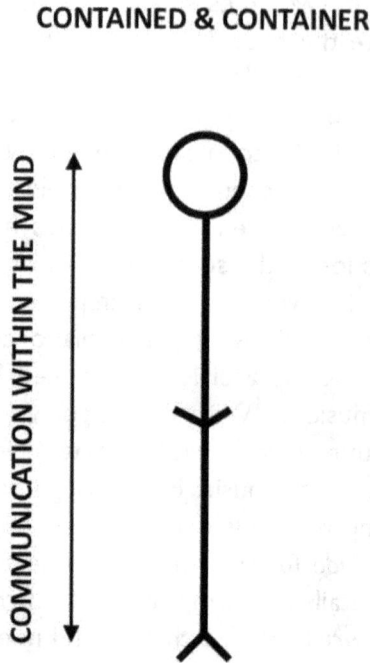

SOURCE: Author's depiction of communication in the internal dialogue during a reflexive mode of containment.

Figure 2.1 shows a stick figure that functions as both contained and container. There is a two-way line of communication between the conscious and unconscious aspects of the psyche. When a person is in isolation, it can have the effect of heightening the internal communication within the psyche. Since there is no one to mirror their life, no other mind to provide mental scaffolding for psychological growth, the person has to rely on himself or herself. If the person has a capacity for symbolic imagination, he or she can construct meaning from their life experience. As examples of the reflexive mode of containment, I offer events in the lives of Dante Alighieri and Ludwig Beethoven. See later chapters for my analyses of their lives.

Sources

In writing this chapter, I drew on the following sources:
- *"Act and Image: The Emergence of Symbolic Imagination"* by Warren Colman
- *"Conversations About Reflexivity"* by Margaret S. Archer (Editor)
- *"Unrepresented States and the Construction of Meaning"* by Howard Levine
- *"Containing States of Mind"* by Duncan Cartwright
- *"Dante: A Life"* by R. W. B. Lewis
- *"Beethoven: A Life"* by Jan Caeyers.

CHAPTER 3

How a Mind Depends
on a Deity for Meaning

"(B)elief in spiritual forces is an expression of affective states
that have become symbolized via collective representations
and thereby transformed, which includes taking on a social
aspect."

— Warren Colman

I propose that a theistic mode of containment be added to the Bion-
Cartwright model. In conducting research for this book, I found the
Bion-Cartwright theme that a mind depends on another mind for
psychological growth has its limits. As it stands, the containment
model has one mode that is conducive to psychological growth, and
four modes that are not. I believe the mode of containment conducive to psychological growth needs to be differentiated. Psychological
growth is not limited to relationships in which one mind depends on
another mind. In building the containment model, British psychanalyst, Wilfred Bion, and South African clinical psychologist, Duncan
Cartwright, both focus on the theme that one mind depends on
another mind for meaning. That may be true for people who find their
way into therapy, where the mind of a patient depends on the mind of
a therapist. That theme also applies to the population at large, where
mother-child, mentor-mentee, apprentice-expert, and wife-husband
historically form containment pairs. However, in my research, I found

that there are people who derive meaning from their life experiences, not just in relation to other minds, but also in relation to their perception of deity. As psychologist Warren Colman points out, the derivation of meaning from life experience involves bringing something into the form of symbolic language through which it can enter the domain of meaning (AIE 249). Colman further explains that meaning is always public and shared, because there is no such thing as a private language (AIE 249). Meaning is not limited to what a mind can learn from depending on a more psychologically mature mind. According to Colman, meaning has its basis in culture, without culture there can be no meaning (AIE 249). Since religious belief systems are part of human culture, I propose that individuals can derive meaning from interaction with their deity.

Colman explains that, in Bion's model, collective representations and their social mediation include mystical experiences that cannot be put into words, but are nevertheless contained within an organized meaning-structure of myth, tradition and disciplined practice (AIE 248). The symbolic rituals of religion provide the containment for deriving meaning from life experiences (AIE 256). Symbolic imagination is a way of deriving meaning in situations of heightened affectivity, such as love, hate, grief or despair. Belief in spiritual forces is an expression of affective states that become symbolized through collective representations (AIE 239) which can achieve transformation by ritualized practice of symbolic imagination (AIE 250). Religious rituals bring the collective representations of shared belief systems into the form of a symbolic language through which it can enter the domain of meaning. It is by engagement with the social-symbolic world that affective states become represented and therefore structured and thinkable (AIE 248).

It is with great respect to Bion and Cartwright that I propose adding a theistic mode to the Bion-Cartwright model. In proposing the addition of a theistic mode of containment, I draw on the work of psychologist, Warren Colman, who wrote the book "Act and Image: The Emergence of Symbolic Imagination" in which he stated:

"(B)elief in spiritual forces is an expression of affective states that have become symbolized via collective representations and thereby transformed, which includes taking on a social aspect."

— Warren Colman (AIE 239)

In describing spiritual forces, Colman references Lucien Levy-Bruhl's definition of 'mystical' as a belief in forces and influences and actions which, though imperceptible to the senses, are nevertheless real (AIE 239). Their reality is demonstrated by the relief that humans experience after divulging their troubled affective states to a deity on whose collective representations they have come to rely for transformation in times of distress. Colman makes the point that containment can be provided in the symbolic rituals of religion (AIE 256). As more humans came to live in social groups, their emotional lives became more developed, and symbolic language became necessary both to reflect this and to organize it (AIE 256).

FIGURE 3.1: Communication with a Deity

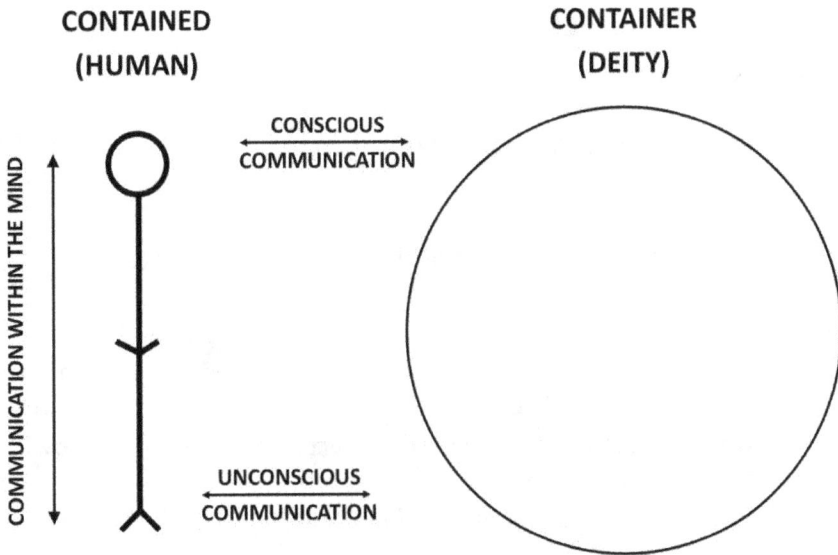

SOURCE: Author's depiction of a person-deity dialogue in a theistic mode of containment.

Figure 3.1 shows lines of communication between a person (the contained) and their perception of deity (the container) during a theistic mode of containment. There is a line of conscious communication that occurs between the conscious part of the person's psyche and the shared, tangible world of sacred scripture that embodies a religious belief system. There is also a line of communication between the unconscious part of the person's psyche and the shared intangible world of symbolic imagination, not known to the physical senses. In this line of communication, the person can engage a higher power in rituals of prayer or meditation. When people who have shared religious beliefs experience a need for psychological containment, they sometimes engage in rituals that invoke meaning in ways that are beyond the world of the physical senses. I offer two examples of the theistic mode of containment. One example is the songwriter, Charles Austin Miles, who explained that he had an encounter with the Christian Son of God, and that encounter produced the hymn "I Come To The Garden Alone". The second example is in the sacred text "Bhagavad Gita" where Prince Arjuna engaged the Hindu Lord Krishna in discourses about whether to wage a righteous war. See later chapters for my analyses of Miles' experience as song-writer and Arjuna's experience as warrior.

Sources

In the preparation of this chapter, I relied on the following sources:
- *"Act and Image: The Emergence of Symbolic Imagination"* by Warren Colman
- *"I Come To The Garden Alone"* by Charles Austin Miles
- *"The New American Bible"* by Catholic Book Publishing
- *"Perennial Psychology of the Bhagavad Gita"* by Swami Rama
- *"GITA: A Timeless Guide For Our Time"* by Isaac Bentwich (translator)
- *"Unrepresented States and the Construction of Meaning"* by Howard Levine
- *"Containing States of Mind"* by Duncan Cartwright.

CHAPTER 4

Archetype: Biological Entity vs Emergent Phenomenon

Archetypes are "innate neuropsychic centers possessing the capacity to initiate, control and mediate the common behavioral characteristics and typical experiences of all human beings irrespective of race, culture or creed."
— Anthony Stevens (Archetype as biological entity)

"(A)rchetypes are the emergent properties of the dynamic developmental system of brain, environment and narrative."
— George B. Hogenson
(Archetype as emergent phenomenon)

At the beginning of the 21ˢᵗ century, Analytical Psychologists were falling into two opposing camps regarding the definition of archetype. There was a contentious debate about archetype in the year 2001, when psychologists from all over the world gathered on the grounds of St. John's College in Cambridge, England, for the fifteenth tri-annual Congress of the International Association for Analytical Psychology (IAAP). Two psychologists with opposing views vigorously defended their definitions of archetype. Anthony Stevens regarded archetypes as biological entities, while George Hogenson viewed archetypes as emergent phenomena. Stevens argued for his biological, evolutionary view that archetypes are innate structures which exist *a priori* in the collective unconscious-ness of the psyche. From a complex systems point of view, Hogenson argued that archetypes are emergent properties of dynamic, develop-mental systems made up of brain, environment and narrative. The 2001 Congress of the IAAP did not produce a conclusive definition of the ori-gin of archetype, but it shone a spotlight on the fact that the definition of archetype is undergoing a bifurcation. After all, an archetype cannot be both a pre-existing biological entity and an emergent phenomenon. The bifurcation in definition of archetype started when psychologists began to notice that the concept of emergence can apply to archetypes. Carl Jung's archetypal hypothesis was yielding to a more contemporary, scientific point of view.

The notion of emergent phenomenon entered the scientific world in 1875 when George Henry Lewes, an amateur physiologist, coined the word 'emergence' in an article titled *"Problems of Life and Mind"* to explain the behavior of complex systems as they evolve to new levels of organization. For several years afterwards, the concept of emergence did not attract the attention of psychologists, perhaps because Lewes was a physiologist. The concept of 'emergence' was not well known when Carl Jung composed his archetypal hypothesis in the 1940's. The 1989 inaugural publication of *Emergence Magazine* provided a forum for scientists to share ideas about emergence. Then, in the March 1999 issue of *Emergence Magazine*, economist Jeffrey Goldstein pub-lished an article titled *"Emergence as a Construct: History and Issues"* in which he defined emergence as *"the arising of novel and coherent structures, patterns and properties during the process of self-organization in complex systems"*. Three years later, scientist Peter Corning elaborated on Goldstein's definition by identifying some common characteristics of a complex system in *"The Re-emergence of Emergence"*. One char-acteristic is that a complex system exhibits an emergent property of novelty, in the sense that new features arise in the system without the influence of cause and effect. Also characteristic of emergence is that the complex system exhibits a coherence of integrated components and maintains it over a period of time. A third characteristic is that the complex system exhibits a global property of wholeness. An additional characteristic is that the emergent property is a product of a dynami-cal process. A fifth characteristic is the presence of a feedback loop for the conveyance of information.

Four years before the 2001 IAAP Congress, Anthony Stevens had published "Archetype Revisited" in which he aligned his definition of archetype to Carl Jung's definition in terms of biological evolution. The widening bifurcation in the definition of archetype would become clear in publications that followed the 2001 IAAP Congress. In the following years, a number of psychologists published books in which they favored the definition of archetype as an emergent phenomenon. In 2003, Jean Knox published "Archetype, Attachment, Analysis: Jungian Psychology and the Emergent Mind". In 2004, George Hogenson published the essay titled "Archetypes: Emergence and the Psyche's Deep Structure" in the book "Analytical Psychology: Contemporary Perspectives in Jungian Psychology" which was jointly edited by Joseph Cambray and Linda Carter. In 2016, Warren Colman published his book "Act and Image: The Emergence of Symbolic Imagination". Knox, Hogenson and Colman all proposed a definition of archetype as an emergent phenomenon.

Two Definitions of Archetype

Analytical Psychologists agree on the existence of archetypes, but they disagree on the definition of archetypes. More specifically, they disagree on how archetypes come into existence. According to Warren Colman, archetypes do exist, because otherwise people would not be able to make sense of the narratives of their lives (AIE 48). Archetypes exist in profusion. In my opinion, archetypes are like Hallmark greeting cards ... there is one for every occasion. Jung's basic definition was that there exists an archetype for every common situation in life. Dictionaries tend to define archetype in terms of roles, but when I read further into the psychological literature, I discern categories of archetypes, such as role, event, organization, mental construct, and human attribute. Examples of archetypes in the role category are mother, father, lover, leader, warrior, innovator, mentor and killer. The event category of archetype includes war and homecoming. Urbanism and the stock market are examples of the organization category of archetype. In the mental construct category, there are archetypes of time and space. Archetypes in the human attribute category are language and intelligence.

The bifurcation in the definition of archetype is about the origin of archetypes. The bifurcation became noticeable in psychological publications at the turn of the century. A generalization that I make from reading their publications is that psychologists who published works in the 20th century favored the definition that an archetype is pre-existent, while an increasing number of psychologists who publish works in the 21st century take the more scientific approach of describing archetypes as emergent phenomena. For opposing definitions of archetype, I draw on the works of the two psychologists who presented their opposing views at the 2001 IAAP Congress. They are Anthony Stevens and George Hogenson. Here is Stevens' definition of archetype:

> Archetypes are "innate neuropsychic centers possessing the capacity to initiate, control and mediate the common behavioral characteristics and typical experiences of all human beings irrespective of race, culture or creed."
>
> – Anthony Stevens
> - Archetype as biological entity (AR 352)

That is Stevens' definition of archetype in the Glossary of his book "Archetypes Revisited". In the book, he explains that his definition of archetype is drawn from Carl Jung's definition. An archetype is not individual, it is universal. It constitutes a common psychic substrate that is pervasive across all humanity (AR 14). Jung believed that all the essential psychic characteristics that distinguish us as humans are with us from birth, encoded in the human genetic makeup (AR 16). Stevens states that archetypes are biological entities that are subject to the laws of evolution, and which evolved through natural selection. They are responsible for coordinating the behavioral and psychic repertoires of our species in response to whatever environmental circumstance we may encounter. Archetypes are not inherited ideas, but rather inherited modes of functioning (AR 17). Archetypes are species-specific patterns of behavior, for example, the behavioral pattern of salmon that swims upstream to reproduce by laying eggs. Examples of human patterns of behavior are marriage, co-habitation and copulation.

Here is Hogenson's opposing definition of archetype:

"(A)rchetypes are the emergent properties of the dynamic developmental system of brain, environment and narrative."
— George Hogenson
- Archetype as emergent phenomenon (AEP 48)

In *"Patterns of Action: Emergence in Complex Dynamic Systems"* Hogenson characterizes archetype as an emergent phenomenon. He also sees an archetype as a pattern of behavior embedded in a complex system that extends beyond the individual mind to include an environmental context (AEP 46). Hogenson points out that sociality is what distinguishes the biological model from the emergent model of archetype. In the biological model, archetypes are structures formed within the psyche, without reference to human sociality in the external environment. In the emergent model, human meaning and intentionality emerge out of multiple generations of human sociality, and cannot do so except through sociality (AIE 47). Hogenson does not believe that archetypes are located anywhere specific such as brain or genes. He sees archetypes as emergent properties of a dynamic, developmental system that is made up of brain, environment and narrative.

Emergence occurs in complex adaptive systems. Some examples of complex adaptive systems are birds, fishes, ants and humans. Complex adaptive systems are capable of exhibiting both emergent behavior and emergent structure. For example, emergent behavior is evident in the flocking of birds. A flock of birds is not guided by any leader or by any central organization. Without any central planning, birds fly in a cohesive flock, often in a "V" formation. Each bird follows a simple rule to stay a certain distance away from neighboring birds. That creates a formation which moves through the air in a cohesive pattern of bird flocking behavior. Fishes demonstrate emergent schooling behavior without any centralized intelligence. When the circumstances are conducive, such as a heightened sense of danger from predators in the environment, fish are driven to be close to each other. They swim in a coordinated elliptical pattern of emergent fish behavior. They maintain the pattern even though individual fish may be leaving or joining the group. Ants exhibit both emergent behavior and emergent structure. When the seasonal climate and the ant population reach a threshold, ants assemble in a group to form a new colony. The group collectively builds a colony without any blueprint to guide them. It is as if a group intelligence kicks in when ants assemble in a group. The ants assume assorted roles such as worker ants, soldier ants, reproductive ants and builder ants. There is no leader ant who makes assignments to other ants. Ants simply adopt roles of their own choosing. Some forage for food sources, some repro- duce creating a new generation of ants, while others build a mound for housing the colony. An emergent architectural structure takes the form of chambers and tunnels built from dirt, sand and vegetation. The ants function as if the colony possesses a collective super-mind. They create a chemical trail on the ground to communicate with each other about location of food sources, disposal of waste, the arrival of intruders, and the care of larvae.

Evidence of both emergent behavior and emergent structure is seen in humans. An example is the emergence of cities. Individuals take on a variety of roles in the emergence of a city. Engineers build roads and bridges. Architects design homes, banks, places of worship and shopping centers. Service providers establish utilities such as water, electricity, waste disposal. Protectors set up a police force and a com- munity watch. Facilitators of communication establish a postal mail service and an Internet service. Suppliers arrange for the delivery of furniture and grocery. And of course, there are city dwellers who consume the accommodations, utilities, supplies and services. There is no centralized intelligence coordinating all the roles. Yet, individu- als function as a collective unit in ways that sustain a city over gen- erations of time. City is an emergent phenomenon. Over time, novel features emerge, for example, the emergence of infrastructure to sup- port broadband Internet service, which came into common usage in the late 20th century. Emergent behavior is seen in novelties such as online shopping and online dating. Over time, cities come into being as emergent phenomena driven by city dwellers' desires for food, safety, convenience, comfort and security.

Comparison of Two Definitions of Archetype

I explain the difference between the two definitions of archetype to help readers understand that psychologists have two different perspectives on how archetypes influence the behaviors and communications of humans. When someone is in the throes of a projection or an appropriation, the definitions hardly matter. What matters is that there is an available container who has the experience of providing mental scaffolding that is conducive to the derivation of meaning from difficult life experiences. In the range of the normal psychology of everyday living, the container may be a grandmother, a best friend or a mentor, as long as they have the mental scaffolding adequate to address the particular life experience. Outside the normal range of psychology, professional help is appropriate.

The central difference between the two definitions of archetype is about how archetypes come into existence. The 20th century writers tend to the view that archetypes are pre-existent heritage that accumulates in the unconscious part of the psyche over generations of humanity, while the 21st century writers lean toward the scientific explanation that archetypes are emergent phenomena which arise from the sociality of a human population that forms a complex adaptive system. In the table below, I compare two definitions of archetype, the biological definition and the emergent definition.

Archetype as Biological Entity	Archetype as Emergent Phenomenon
An archetype is an invisible, **biological entity** whose existence becomes known through human behaviors and communications.	An archetype is an invisible, **emergent phenomenon** whose existence becomes known through human behaviors and communications.
An archetype is made up of an **ancestral heritage** of human experience accumulated over multiple generations.	An archetype is an **emergence** from a complex system that is made up of human actions, the cultural environment and people's narratives of their lives.
Archetypes are located in collective unconsciousness inside the **psyche**.	Archetypes have no specific location; they are pervasive across the **cultural environment**.

Archetype as Biological Entity	Archetype as Emergent Phenomenon
When an archetype is activated, there is a forcible evacuation from the psyche, in the form of a **projection** from an individual mind.	When an archetype is activated, there is an emotional **appropriation** from the archetype in the cultural environment.
The content of a projection is **raw experience** about emotions, images and memories that are incomprehensible and so are evacuated as unbearable states of mind.	The content of an appropriation is **processed experience** about meaningful thoughts of emotions, images and memories that are adopted from the cultural environment.
Introjection involves the construction of meaning from the content of a projection.	**Internalization** involves the construction of meaning from the content of an appropriation.
Introjection is mediated by the help of another mind more skilled in the construction of **meaning from the content of a projection.**	Internalization is mediated by the help of another mind more skilled in the construction of **meaning from the content of an appropriation.**
Archetypes are activated at **critical stages of the life cycle** of individuals, creating opportunities to develop capacity for symbol formation appropriate for the stages.	Archetypes are activated at **levels of psychic complexity** of individuals, enabling a gradual emergence of the capacity for symbol formation appropriate for each level.
Symbolic forms are pre-given (in archetypes in collective unconsciousness) and can be related back to the emotional states they represent.	**Symbolic forms are emergent** (from archetypes in the cultural world) and can be related back to the emotional states they represent.
The **transcendent function** (Carl Jung, Anthony Stevens) refers to the capacity to process symbolic information that arises from archetypes which are defined as biological entities.	The **reflective function** (Jean Knox, Warren Colman) refers to the capacity to process symbolic information that emerges from archetypes which are defined as emergent phenomena.

See Appendix B for characterizations of archetype by each of Carl Jung, Anthony Stevens, Wilfred Bion, Jean Knox, George Hogenson and Warren Colman.

In writing about the containment model, both Wilfred Bion and Duncan Cartwright made reference to projection as the event that initiates a containment. The implication is that a containment starts with a projection from an archetype located in collective unconsciousness. Warren Colman observes that Bion's containment model is compatible with the concept of emergence (AI 222 - 225). The implication is that a containment can be initiated by an appropriation from the cultural environment. My interpretation is that, for the purpose of containment, the origin of the archetype matters less than the availability of a container who provides mental scaffolding to help the contained process difficult emotions, thoughts, memories and images. Even though psychologists are divided on how archetypes come into existence, they are in agreement on the notion that archetypes enable humans to construct meaning from events in their lives and to develop the capacity for symbolization. A feature that both definitions of archetype have in common is that they enable people to construct coherent narratives of their lives. As Warren Colman pointed out, archetypes serve the purpose of enabling people to understand their basic human narratives (AIE 48). The ability to process symbolic information plays an important role in the potential for psychological growth that occurs in relationships. Archetypes enable the symbolization that supports psychological growth when two people engage each other in an iterative dialogue. What the two definitions of archetype have in common is that they enable the use of symbols for construction of meaning from human experience (AIE 3, 30). According to George Hogenson, a theory of archetypes must give rise to a viable theory of symbolization and the amplification of a symbol must enable transformation (AEP 53). That is because an archetype gives access to the symbolic world, and carries the imaginal experience of a person far beyond a sense of containment in a relationship with another. People who derive psychological growth from relationships are those who have developed the capacity for symbolic thinking.

Psychologists who publish works in the 21st century favor the characterization of humans as complex adaptive systems, and they define archetypes as phenomena that emerge from the cultural environment in which humans live. The features of a complex adaptive system that apply to relationships between humans are self-organization, feedback loop, novelty, coherence and a dynamic process.

- **Self-organization:** Complex adaptive systems are self-organized in the sense that they are formed by a process of spontaneous order. They create overall order from local interactions between parts of an initially disordered system. The process does not require design or control by any external agent, nor any centralized control. The rules governing the interactions of constituents of a complex adaptive system are simple and they operate at a local level among individuals. The simple local rules of interaction enable self-organization, without control by any individual.
- **Feedback Loop:** A complex adaptive system has a feedback loop that is made up of a bottom-up process and a top-down process. The bottom-up process involves interaction among the individuals functioning according to basic simple rules. The top-down process is a constraining effect that society has on individuals. Together, the top-down and bottom-up processes make up a reciprocal feedback loop between individuals and society.
- **Novelty:** New features emerge from a complex adaptive system, without having any cause-and-effect connection to earlier versions of the system. The new features cannot be predicted from interactions of individuals in the system.
- **Coherence:** A complex adaptive system sustains a coherent integration of the behavior of individuals, over a period of time.
- **Dynamic Process:** Emergent properties are the products of a dynamical process of interaction among the individuals in a complex adaptive system.

Psychologists who embrace the scientific concept of emergence regard these features as contributors to human behaviors in a complex adaptive system. Psychologists in both the archetype-as-biological-entity and archetype-as-emergent-phenomenon camps interpret Wilfred Bion's containment model as being compatible with their outlook. Bion developed the model using the terms projection and introjection, which are words commonly used by the archetype-as-biological-entity camp. But, Jean Knox, George Hogenson and Warren Colman, who are all from the archetype-as-emergent-phenomenon camp, interpret Bion's model in the emergent sense. The versatility of Bion's model makes it an appealing model for explaining containment for an audience of laypeople who gravitate to psychology clubs.

Bion's Model as a Vehicle for Symbolization that Accompanies Psychological Growth

Wilfred Bion's containment model uses the word 'containment' to refer to a relationship that is based on an emotional bond and has the potential for psychological growth. Regardless of whether psychologists fall in the archetype-as-biological-entity camp or the archetype-as-emergent-phenomenon camp, they tend to see psychological growth in containment as being related to symbolization. For example, Warren Colman sees Bion's model as involving archetypes when unformulated affective experiences are gathered together into a thinkable symbolic form. Culture provides the means that makes this possible by scaffolding basic affective states into forms of affective cognition that are distributed across the social and material world (AIE 225). Psychologists from both perspectives – pre-existent and emergent – regard archetypes as being instrumental in the symbolic process that enables the construction of meaning from life experiences.

The dynamic process of interaction — one of the characteristics of a complex adaptive system – is central to the transformation of unbearable states of mind in the containment model. As the dialogue between contained and container progresses, symbols come up in the dialogue to guide the transformation. What Anthony Stevens and Wilfred Bion have in common is that they both describe interaction between people in terms of a dynamic process that they call symbolization. They both use the terms 'projection' and 'introjection' to explain how people process unbearable states of mind. Although Stevens does not make specific reference to Bion's containment model, he describes the synthesis of the poles of an archetype in terms of symbolization. He points out that if one can bring oneself to bear the psychic tension generated by the polar opposites of an archetype, the transformation is raised to a higher plane where the conflict can be resolved, and a new synthesis between consciousness and unconsciousness achieved. That synthesis is attained, not rationally, but symbolically (AR 277 - 278). Stevens uses

Jung's expression 'transcendent function' as a label for the dynamic process of interaction. It is through the transcendent function that unbearable states of mind are transformed as new symbols arise during the unconscious communication in a containment. Stevens points out that the transcendent function does not proceed through reason because reason does not accommodate ambiguity. When the transcendent function is ongoing, the psyche transcends reason and the rules of logic (AR 278) because the psyche can accommodate incompatibilities. Stevens advises that there is psychic wealth to be had in symbolic forms that arise from the dynamic process that plays out in the transcendent function (AR 278). He states that the transcendent function resides in the mutual influence of consciousness and unconsciousness which have a compensatory relationship with each other (AR 315).

Jean Knox, George Hogenson and Warren Colman all refer to Bion's containment model as a vehicle for symbolization that accompanies psychological growth. They use the expression 'reflective function' as their label for the dynamic process that plays out during a containment. The reflective function and the transcendent function are not equivalent, but they both involve symbolization. Instead of using Bion's language about 'projection' and 'introjection' they use 'appropriation' and 'internalization'. Projection and introjection refer to pre-existent archetypes that reside in the collective unconscious part of the psyche. Appropriation and internalization refer to emergent archetypes that are pervasive across the cultural environment. Despite their differences about the origin of archetypes, psychologists generally describe a dynamic process for managing unbearable states of mind. Those psychologists who incline to the pre-existent view of archetypes call their dynamic process the transcendent function. Psychologists who lean to the emergent view of archetypes call their dynamic process the reflective function. Both camps have the same word for the essence of what happens in their dynamic process ... they call it symbolization. The potential for psychological growth in a relationship is related to the capacity for symbolization and narrative competence.

Reflective Function, Transcendent Function, Alpha Function

The labels 'reflective function', 'transcendent function' and 'alpha function' all involve a dynamic process of which symbolization is a part. In Jean Knox's book "*Archetype, Attachment, Analysis: Jungian Psychology and the Emergent Mind*" she writes that the concept of a reflective function has emerged to explain the vital role of people's capacity to relate to others as mental and emotional beings with their own thoughts, desires, intentions, beliefs and emotions (AAA 10). The capacity for a reflective function has implications for psychological growth and in particular for the construction of meaning from life experiences. Knox identifies four interrelated elements that contribute to the development of the reflective function: narrative competence, intentionality, appraisal and subjectivity (AAA 142 - 143). I explain these elements because they support the symbolization that can occur when one mind opens up a dialogue with another mind in a containment.

- **Narrative competence:** This element of the reflective function enables people to make psychological links among life's events in a meaningful way (AAA 146). That includes making connections across the desires and intentions of the people who play various roles in one's life. It also includes being able to compose a coherent autobiographical story of the past and the present, for a sense of continuity in one's life.
- **Intentionality:** This element of the reflective function forms the basis of desires and appetites (AAA 149 - 150). Appetites and desires help people to know what interests them, and when they have had enough, so that they can maintain a healthy connection between mind and behavior.
- **Appraisal:** This element of the reflective function enables people to become aware of other people as mental and emotional beings. It enables the knowledge of oneself as a person with a mind and emotions, also with the ability to evaluate and make judgements about the quality and meaning of experiences. Development of the reflective function depends on the existence — in a person's mind — of internal working models which contain information about mental and emotional processes in oneself and others. Appraisal may become a conscious process,

but since it arises from the meanings stored in internal working models, it is often an implicit process, operating automatically and in a form that is usually inaccessible to conscious awareness. This process of evaluating the importance of events provides an unconscious basis for a sense of psychological identity, without which people do not feel that they have minds of their own, but always defer to other people's judgement because they feel more real than their own (AAA 153).

- **Subjectivity:** This element of the reflective function enables people to link events into a meaningful narrative. It requires an appetite for appraising the emotional significance of experience. Difficulty in establishing such links is often accompanied by the absence of any real sense of separateness. When that happens, there is no sense of psychic space between people. Hence there is limited opportunity for symbolic communication with another (AAA 156).

The essence of the reflective function is the capacity to experience one's own and other people's psychological separateness and individuality (AAA 143) in the transformation of unbearable states of mind into bearable states of mind via the symbolic process. The reflective function is an interpretative tool that can help people gain an understanding of events, symptoms and patterns in their lives (AAA 145). A well-developed reflective function can be a defense against psychological distress. Without a well-developed reflective function, life experiences can seem non-specific and difficult to comprehend. The reflective function is the center of our sense of meaning and capacity to symbolize. The reflective function, as described by Knox, Hogenson and Colman, translates to Bion's alpha function. The alpha function is about the transformation of meaningless beta elements into meaningful alpha elements, which then become the building blocks of symbolic thought (AAA 163). The alpha function and the transcendent function share a common goal with the reflective function: these functions mediate the transformation of unbearable states of mind into bearable states of mind via a symbolic process. Regardless of whether psychologists align their outlook to the alpha function, the transcendent function or the reflective function, they all define those functions in terms of symbolization. The symbolization occurs during the narrative dialogue that plays out in a containment.

The next chapter provides more details about the symbolization that occurs during containment.

Sources

These are the sources of information that I used in preparing this chapter:

- "*Act and Image: The Emergence of Symbolic Imagination*" by Warren Colman
- "*Archetype, Attachment, Analysis: Jungian Psychology and the Emergent Mind*" by Jean Knox
- "*Archetypes: Emergence and the Psyche's Deep Structure*" by George Hogenson in "*Analytical Psychology: Contemporary Perspectives in Jungian Psychology*" edited by Joseph Cambray & Linda Carter
- "*Archetype Revisited: An Updated Natural History of the Self*" by Anthony Stevens
- "*SYMBOLIZATION: Representation and Communication*" by James Rose
- "*Containing States of Mind*" by Duncan Cartwright
- "*A Critical Dictionary of Jungian Analysis*" by Andrew Samuels, Bani Shorter & Fred Plaut.

CHAPTER 5

Characteristics of
a Containment

"The container function ... refers to part of a set of mental apparatus that enables the creation of thoughts so as to give rise to new meaning."

— Duncan Cartwright

In *"Containing States of Mind"* Duncan Cartwright describes containment as a meeting of two minds that takes place in a bi-directional field where the participants contribute to a field of meaning that is bigger than the sum of their contributions (CSM 12). In the field of meaning, there are cycles of projective and introjective communication that transform unassimilated emotions into bearable states of mind. The participants communicate at conscious and unconscious levels of experience, leading to patterns of psychic organization that do not lend themselves to linear interpretation, but can be interpreted symbolically through language (CSM 14 – 15). During the narrative dialogue between the participants, there is opportunity for the emergence of symbols as conveyers of meaning that permit interpretation through verbal communication. Emergence and interpretation of symbols occur in the context of a psychological frame, where the containment pair has the privacy necessary for shared reverie. Projection and introjection refer to pre-existent archetypes that reside in the collective unconscious part of the psyche. Appropriation and internalization refer to emergent archetypes that are pervasive across the cultural environment. Characteristics of a containment include certain conditions necessary for containment, a projection (or appropriation) that initiates the containment, the existence of a psychological frame for shared reverie, and an ongoing narrative dialogue. If the containment is successful, there will be a psychological movement followed by the emergence of a symbol that can lead to the conversion of meaning from experience.

Conditions for Containment

Cartwright points out that a containment can only take place if the container has an ongoing relationship with the unconscious part of their own psyche, and has already been processing a state of mind similar to the unprocessed state of mind projected from the mind of the contained. He also cautions that the container is at risk of having the contained's unprocessed state of mind undo or compromise their already processed state of mind. In "Act and Image" Warren Colman informs us that the containment depends on the containment pair having receptivity to states of reverie (AIE 117).

Projection (or Appropriation) Initiates Containment

In describing the containment model, Bion and Cartwright focus attention on projection as a marker for the beginning of a containment. That indicates they view the initiation as coming from an unconscious source, the psyche. Other psychologists, for example Colman and Hogenson, see containment as beginning with an appropriation. That indicates they view the initiation as coming from a conscious source in the external environment. Regardless of whether psychologists see a containment as having a conscious or unconscious source, they view the beginning of the containment as the activation of an archetype, that forms a bridge between the containment pair. The sending mind is the contained, while the receiving mind is the container. The activation of the archetype can have a source that is either within the internal world or in the external world of the contained. The activation has a substantial emotional effect on the containment pair. Examples of sources in the external world are the loss of a loved one, or achievement of a long-sought goal. Examples of sources in the internal world are a burden of anxiety, or a dream. If the receiving mind is that of a capable container, the participants set up a psychological frame for a narrative dialogue between contained and container, otherwise the attempt at containment fails.

Psychological Frame

One of the characteristics of a containment is that there is a psychological frame for the containment pair to engage in iterative dialogue. Cartwright describes a containment as having a perimeter around it. In other words, a containment has a psychological frame which includes a purpose, a space boundary and a time boundary (CSM 133). The purpose of a containment is the metabolism of the content of a projection or an appropriation. The time boundary is about the duration and the frequency with which the containment pair interacts to metabolize the content of a projection, or appropriation. The space boundary is the place, physical or virtual, where contained and container interact with each other. The psychological frame acts as a supportive structure for the containment, making it possible for an 'overlapping state of reverie' (RI 116). A psychological frame is a matrix of projection and introjection — or appropriation and internalization — set in an environment with a defined space dimension and a time dimension. This matrix is what makes it possible to have 'overlapping states of reverie' (RI 116). The matrix involves conditions for generating unconscious, creative output from the containment. It also has the potential for harm. The psychological frame sets the conditions for receptivity to states of reverie on the part of both contained and container. The privacy of the psychological frame is conducive to a state of reverie because it allows the containment pair to enter into a state of shared, or overlapping, reverie. Overlapping states of reverie enable a mental space for iterative dialogue, which is a necessary condition for psychological growth.

Narratives in Dialectical Interaction

Together, the projection and introjection (or appropriation and internalization) form a matrix of conscious and unconscious communications between the containing pair. The creation of a matrix depends on the capacity of the containment pair to engage in a dialectical interplay of states of reverie that are at the same time private and unconsciously communicative (RI 108). In the next chapter, I describe the reveries that facilitate the conversion of experience to meaning during a containment.

Going into the containment, there are two narratives. The first narrative is contributed by the contained, as an unassimilated state of mind. The second narrative is the container's retelling of the first narrative at a new level (AAA 147 – 148). The narrative dialogue is an iterative process in which a story is created first by one person, and then taken over and retold on a new level by the other (AAA 147 – 148). The container holds the storyline while the contained gradually internalizes the meaningful connections made for him / her. Gradually, the contained acquires an awareness of a sense that their mind is an agent of change (AAA 148). The narrative is then taken over by the contained. A successful narrative dialogue is one that can become meaningful to the contained so that he / she can take it over, use it for himself / herself and adapt it to establish a sense a connection between their intrapsychic experience and the external world. A narrative dialogue continues with increasing complexity throughout a person's development. The containment pair engages in a 'reverie' that can give meaning to the contained's experience of life. If the efforts of the contained and container are successful, their interaction generates a third narrative. Although it is called a third narrative, it is not composed by any one person. It is the result of the iterative dialogue between contained and container. The psychological frame supports the unconscious generation of a third narrative in the matrix of communication.

An aim of the containment is to transform non-conscious reveries into conscious topics for scrutiny, in the interest of metabolizing the contents of a projection / appropriation. The contained's narrative feeds into their private reverie. The container's narrative also feeds into their private reverie. The psychological space where the two reveries overlap is where the subjective construction known as the third narrative originates. The generation of a third narrative requires receptivity to states of reverie on the part of both contained and container. The frame creates a privacy that is conducive to states of reverie … for each to enter into their own state of reverie, as well as enter into a shared reverie.

Overlapping states of reverie are a necessary condition for elaboration of unconscious communication and generation of a third narrative. The psychological frame creates a mental space for the development of a third narrative, that is partly shared and partly individual, partly conscious and partly unconscious. The frequency of encounter between contained and container enhances the capacity to generate overlapping states of reverie (RI 118). These reveries may be about external sensory experiences that the contained needs help to process. They can also be about internal emotional experiences which the contained needs help to understand. As the containment progresses, the contained and container may switch roles. This is likely to happen in the commensal mode of containment which has the greatest potential for psychological growth. If the containment is successful, a third narrative is generated. The third narrative can include anything of value produced, created, invented, or changed in external reality. It can also include anything changed, such as outlook, knowledge or confidence, in the internal reality of the contained. According to Cartwright:

> "The container function ... refers to part of a set of mental apparatus that enables the creation of thoughts so as to give rise to new meaning."
> — Duncan Cartwright (CSM 8)

The contained's mind is dependent on the container's mind to derive meaning from unprocessed experience. That is why it is necessary for the container to have an ongoing relationship with the unconscious part of their own psyche, and to have already been processing a state of mind similar to the unprocessed state of mind projected from the mind of the contained. The third narrative stands in dialectical tension with the contained and the container as separate individuals with their own subjectivities. Contained and container each participates in the unconscious, intersubjective construction of the third narrative, but do so asymmetrically (RI 109) The experience of contained and container in relation to the third narrative is asymmetrical because each contributes differently to its construction and elaboration (RI 130). Each experiences the third narrative in the context of their own separate, individual personality system which is shaped and structured by their own form of psychological organization, their own linkages of personal meanings derived from the totality of their history, and their unique set of experiences (RI 110). The third narrative is not a single event, but is a jointly, asymmetrically constructed and experienced set of conscious intersubjective experiences in which contained and container participate (RI 110). In a containment, the interaction between contained and container is dialectical. Together, they contribute to and participate in an unconscious intersubjectivity. Their dialectical interaction rests with the capacities of the contained and container for reverie. The dialectical interaction is about tensions such as between love and hate, disclosure and privacy, communicating and not communicating (RI 124). If the narratives in the dialectical interaction progress well, they generate a psychological movement.

Psychological Movement

A psychological movement may take the form of a dream, an image, a synchronistic event, an intuition or a revelation. A marked affective shift occurs during the dialectical interaction. The psychological movement has the effect of recasting the past in the context of a new set of experiences that occurred in shared reverie (RI 96). There is a new narrative, being generated by the containment pair, and it holds a form of coherence of past and present that is less fearful, and less anxious (RI 96) than at the beginning of the containment. What is noticeable about the shift is an improved capacity for reflective thought (RI 97). This marks the beginning of a capacity to contain, or live with, the positive or negative emotions that prevailed at the beginning of the containment. The psychological movement results in a shift of perspective (RI 98). The contained starts to recognize formerly unconscious content of the projection that was split off from consciousness (or the conscious content of an appropriation drawn from the external environment). The shift in perspective is the outcome from the dialectical interplay of reveries of the containment pair (RI 109). Dreams that occur during the course of containment are manifestations of an intersubjective third narrative. Thomas Ogden's view is that dreams which occur within a containment are intersubjective. Since the dream occurs in the context of containment, it is not the contained's dream, but a dream that results from the interplay of the containment pair ... a result of the dialectical tension between the two. Each plays a contributing role. Regardless of whether the psychological movement involves a dream, or an image, or something else, it marks the opportunity for symbol-forming capacities in the containment pair.

Symbols in Conversion of Experience to Meaning

Jean Knox, George Hogenson and Warren Colman all make reference to Wilfred Bion's containment model as a conveyance for symbolization that occurs during psychological growth. 'Reflective function' is their label for the dynamic process that plays out in a containment. Rather than using Bion's language about 'projection' and 'introjection' which implies a biological archetype, they use language about 'appropriation' and 'internalization' which implies an emergent archetype. In spite of their differences about the origin of archetypes, these psychologists describe the potential for psychological growth in a containment as being related to the capacity for symbolization as well as narrative competence.

Anthony Stevens informs us that meaning of life can be derived from experiences obtained in an extraverted quest in the outer world, as well as from an introverted quest within the psyche (AR 37). The extraverted quest involves empirical analysis in the world of material objects. The introverted quest involves the symbol-forming capacities latent within the psyche. To understand the meaning of our lives, modern humans need to be receptive to encounters with life-enhancing symbols (AR 40). The connection between archetypes and meaning of life enables people to comprehend the complexity of their lives in relation to human existence (AR 40). It enables people to establish a connection between themselves and nature. Because of the widespread tendency of people to seek explanations and perceive meaning, it appears to be a characteristic of the psyche. In a containment, the unassimilated experience that forms the content of a projection, or appropriation, can be converted into meaning about life. A containment provides the psychological space in which the meaning-making potential of symbolization can be realized. See the next chapter for more information about symbolization in a containment.

Sources

The sources of information that shape my thinking in this chapter are:

- *"Archetype Revisited: An Updated Natural History of the Self"* by Anthony Stevens
- *"Projection and Re-Collection in Jungian Psychology"* by Marie-Louise von Franz
- *"Containing States of Mind"* by Duncan Cartwright
- *"A Critical Dictionary of Jungian Analysis"* by Andrew Samuels, Bani Shorter & Fred Plaut
- *"Archetypes: Emergence and the Psyche's Deep Structure"* by George Hogenson
- *"ACT AND IMAGE: The Emergence of Symbolic Imagination"* by Warren Colman.

CHAPTER 6

Smybolization in the Construction of Meaning from Raw Experience of Life

"Culture does not arise from ideas in the mind but out of social and material practices which become embedded in symbols as carriers of meaning that can be transmitted to subsequent generations and transformed by future circumstances.

So although ideas cannot be inherited, symbols can be – not biologically, of course, but through the medium of culture, the true medium for the emergence of the psyche."

– Warren Colman

It is the view of George Hogenson that a theory of archetypes must give rise to a viable theory of symbolization (APC 53). Authors of both the pre-existent and the emergent definitions of archetypes refer to symbolization as a way of constructing meaning from the raw experience of life. This raises the question: What is symbolization? Here is an excerpt from "A *Critical Dictionary of Jungian Analysis*" in which Andrew Samuels and others explain the beginning and the end of the symbolic process:

"The symbolic process begins with a person's feeling stuck, 'hung-up', forcibly obstructed in pursuit of his aims and it ends in illumination, 'seeing through' and being able to go ahead on a changed course" (CDJ 145).

Samuels further explains that, from the point of view of Analytical Psychology, a symbol is defined in terms of concept, intent, purpose and content. The following definitions are derived from "*A Critical Dictionary of Jungian Analysis*" and are intended to help readers acquire a basic understanding of the symbolic process, that is referenced in the biographical chapters of this book.

- **Concept:** The concept of symbol is an intuitive idea that cannot yet be formulated in any specific way. The intuitive idea emerges from a dilemma where the alternatives cannot be resolved rationally. A symbol expresses itself in images which are not logical, but which encapsulate the psychological situation of the person for whom they arise. A symbol is the best description or formulation of an unknown outcome, which is assumed to exist.

- **Intent:** The intent of a symbol is the goal behind the intuitive idea. The goal is difficult to verbalize, and it is not readily discernible from the image in which the symbol presents itself. The intent of the symbol is consistent with the principle of enantiodromia, where a strongly held conscious position eventually moves in the direction of its opposite, as if it is being balanced by an unconscious movement in a compensatory way. The attitude of consciousness is being balanced by movement originating in unconsciousness. From the balancing activity there emerges a new outlook that is not subject to logic, but which provides a new perspective. When confronted with this new perspective, the ego is freed from the tyranny of the dilemma, and so is able to exercise reflection and choice in pursuing a new path.

- **Purpose:** The purpose of the symbol is not to find an alternative point of view, or a compensatory point of view, but to attract attention to a new perspective that emerges from the tyranny of the dilemma. If appropriately understood, the new perspective can be an opportunity for psychological growth.

- **Content:** The content of the symbol is in the meaning of the image. A symbol is 'pregnant with meaning' that presents a challenge to thoughts and feelings. The content of the symbol is expressed in unique and individual terms, while at the same time expressed in universal imagery. With reflection, the content of the symbol can be recognized as aspects of those images that control, order and give meaning to human lives. The source of the content can be traced to the archetype from which the symbol emerges.

The symbol is an unconscious response to a conscious dilemma. Analytical psychologists refer to three types of symbols: 'unifying symbols', 'living symbols' and 'symbols of totality'. Unifying symbols are those which draw together disparate elements of the psyche. Living symbols are interwoven with one's conscious situation. Symbols of totality are those that pertain to realization of the self. Symbols can appear in a variety of contexts, such as, in the development of those who are psychologically well, and in the treatment of those who are psychologically ill. Symbols also appear in historical settings across time, as well as cultural settings across the globe. Symbolic images are fascinating pictorial statements that depict the psychic reality of humans. Symbols have no literal meaning. They are not allegorical, because that would imply a comparison with something that has a definition. They are about something that is resolutely alive and stirring in the psyche, but does not yet have an outcome or a means of achieving an outcome. The effort involved in processing symbolic information, such as images, fantasies, words, gestures and ideas, can be stimulating because it is mentally demanding, without being limited to aesthetic or linguistic appreciation. A symbol can play a psychological, mediatory role and a transitional role in the life of a person who has the capacity to process symbolic information.

Symbolic thought is the representation of reality through the use of abstract concepts, such as words, gestures, images and numbers. There is a difference between symbolic thought and rational thought. Symbolic thought accommodates the perception of ambiguities, while rational thought follows rules of logic and does not accommodate ambiguities. In "SYMBOLIZATION: Representation and Communication" James Rose explains that symbols provide clues for understanding what is obscure, and the manner of their formation and usage can offer something important about how and why people communicate with one another

(SRC 7). The formation of a symbol provides a line of approach to how humans create their subjectivity, that is, their sense of self and its attendant sense of reality (SRC 7). Rose sets out to explain the formation of symbols as a means of communication, in particular, in managing the inevitable and unavoidable anxiety about change. The basis of Rose's thinking is that a person can only know their mind through discourse with another mind about something external to both minds. In describing the formation of symbols, Rose considers the temporal dimension of symbol formation to be important because time is significant in the iterative nature of a discourse that allows a repeated examination of a person's experience that progressively deepens and broadens the meaning constructed from their life experience (SRC 8). Rose is referring to a clinical setting, but I believe the iterative nature of discourse is equally applicable to a containment that is in a non-clinical setting, that is, in everyday life. Psychological growth is not limited to clinical settings; people also grow psychologically from interaction in the everyday world. Rose's iterative discourse is compatible with Bion's model because the interaction between minds progresses iteratively in a containment.

Experience & Meaning

In the Bion-Cartwright containment model, there are two minds engaged in an iterative dialogue. The contained is the person who depends on the container for help in processing unrepresented states of mind. The iterative nature of their interaction is central to contemporary thinking about symbolization because it implies a link to the concept of representation (SRC 8). The iterative dialogue occurs in a learning system where two people engage in a communication that involves both conscious and unconscious components. Learning takes place through the work of a progressive triangulation. In psychology, a two-person relationship that is under stress becomes a three-person system, rather like a triangle. The communication becomes something significant in structuring the contained's mind and their relationship with the container. This something — which is potentially disturbing to the contained — is not clearly represented in the contained's mind, and is not easily representable to another mind. By repetitively and progressively working through a series of triangulations, the unrepresented can become represented states. During the iterative dialogue between contained and container, a symbol may appear as part of a representation of an experience that the contained finds difficult to communicate. The symbol serves the purpose of representing an experience for easier communication. A symbol has both a representative and communicative function (SRC 10). Symbols occur in many forms and the iterative nature of the dialogue allows the parties concerned to experience the repetition of process and thus gradually begin to bring the meaning of the symbol into focus (SRC 11).

The concept of symbolization is useful in describing what happens during a containment, because the containment starts with an experience that is unrepresentable and undergoes a series of iterations of dialogue in which the experience can become representable. The containment is about enabling the contained to develop representations from unrepresentable experience … with the help of a capable container. The communication between contained and container is partly conscious and partly unconscious. A containment is a suitable setting for observing the creation of symbols and developing an understanding of what they seek to communicate. The symbolic imagination combines material things and linguistic structures to allow multiple reconstructions of new imaginative possibilities. Imaginal things are freed from the limits of material things, made possible and held in place by the abstract structure of language (AIE 119). The ability to develop a new perspective is the basis for self-reflective consciousness (AIE 119). New ways of relating to self and others slowly emerge from the dialogue between contained and container (AAA 10).

Many people develop crucial skills of language, numeracy, reasoning, a sense of identity, and the ability to form relationships. Central to all of these is the capacity to symbolize, so humans acquire a sense that experience can be meaningful. The notion that the human mind has self-organizing, emergent properties is rapidly gaining ground over a more genetically, deterministic model (John Dupre's 2001 book "*Human Nature and the Limits of Science*"). Developmental research supports the view that new meaning is constantly being created as a central part of the process of psychological development. A crucial feature of this process is that it is highly sensitive to, and dependent on, an interpersonal environment (AAA 52). The development research supports the emergence of symbolic representations out of the self-organization of the human mind in the context of relationships (AAA 53 - 54).

Psychologists like Wilfred Bion adopt an individual perspective when formulating a one-to-one emotional containment by a responsive container, for deriving meaning from experience. Other psychologists like Clifford Geertz adopt a social perspective when formulating a socio-cultural frame for deriving meaning from experience. Warren Colman sees both perspectives as having the same implication: a human cannot develop to maturity without interaction with another in a context in which meaning can be formulated from experience. Colman interprets this to mean that symbols come from the world, not from the mind. Here is his explanation:

> "Culture does not arise from ideas in the mind but out of social and material practices which become embedded in symbols as carriers of meaning that can be transmitted to subsequent generations and transformed by future circumstances. So although ideas cannot be inherited, symbols can be – not biologically, of course, but through the medium of culture, the true medium for the emergence of the psyche." (AIE 89)

Colman's explanation is that a human mind without a symbolic world would hardly constitute a human mind at all (AIE 224). Colman proposes a model of the emergence of symbolic imagination as a collective social phenomenon before it can be a psychological one that is 'internalized' by individuals. The emergence occurs in strata (AIE 236). He sees the psyche and the social world as being part of each other, and he views them as coming into being through the emergence of constitutive symbols (AIE 237). Without public meanings, most of people's perceptions would make no sense. In Colman's view, meaning is always public and shared since there is no such thing as a private language. Without culture there can be no meanings. Meanings are created and made manifest through their public cultural enactment (AIE 249).

Sources

The sources of information that shape my thinking in this chapter are:

- "Act and Image: The Emergence of Symbolic Imagination" by Warren Colman
- "Archetype, Attachment, Analysis: Jungian Psychology and the Emergent Mind" by Jean Knox
- "Archetypes: Emergence and the Psyche's Deep Structure" by George Hogenson in "Analytical Psychology: Contemporary Perspectives in Jungian Psychology" edited by Joseph Cambray & Linda Carter
- "SYMBOLIZATION: Representation and Communication" by James Rose
- "Containing States of Mind" by Duncan Cartwright
- "A Critical Dictionary of Jungian Analysis" by Andrew Samuels, Bani Shorter & Fred Plaut.

CHAPTER 7

Modes Of Containment

"For (Wilfred) Bion, a real human mental connection is like an emotional storm caused by the coming together of minds that crave and resist each other."
— Duncan Cartwright

Containment is a human mental connection between the mind of a person and an 'other'. Often, the other is another person. The other can also be a group, an organization or an inanimate thing. When the connection is between two minds, it involves emotions that can be tumultuous. The two minds alternate between being drawn together and being pulled apart in a dialectical interaction whose aim is to manage unprocessed experience. Unprocessed experience can be external experience of what is going on in the world, such as sensory observations of natural disasters, political influences, social influences or religious influences. Unprocessed experience can also be internal experience of what is going on within the psyche, such as feelings, thoughts, joy, gratitude, beliefs and fears. To categorize the notion of containment into modes of differing psychological effect on people involved in mental connections, psychologist Wilfred Bion developed the containment model, for which he identified three modes of containment. He pointed out that he expected others to identify additional modes. Years later, psychologist Duncan Cartwright added two modes of containment. To honor their work, I refer to the model as the Bion-Cartwright containment model.

While conducting research for this book, I decided to propose two additional modes of containment. The modes of containment described in this book portray different ways of relating, with some being psychologically healthy and others being harmful. Here is the list of modes of containment.

Modes of containment defined by Wilfred Bion:
- Commensal mode of containment
- Symbiotic mode of containment
- Parasitic mode of containment.

Modes of containment defined by Duncan Cartwright:
- Autistic mode of containment
- Pseudo-containing mode of containment.

Modes of containment proposed by Carolle Dalley:
- Reflexive mode of containment
- Theistic mode of containment.

What is notable about the Bion-Cartwright model is that there is just one mode of containment for psychological wellness, the commensal mode. All the other modes are about borderline illness or worse. That is understandable. Bion and Cartwright are clinical psychologists who see the world through the lens of mental health professionals treating patients. As clinical psychologists, their calling is to function as containers for patients who are recovering from psychological disorders. I believe that if the containment model had been built by developmental psychologists, there would be a better balance between modes of healthy containment and modes of unhealthy containment. I am not a psychologist, but after studying a variety of biographies, I propose – with due respect to Bion and Cartwright — the addition of two modes of containment that I believe will enhance the model. Later in this chapter, I explain my justification for proposing these two modes of containment. My guess is that more modes of containment will be identified in the future, as the containment model is applied across a wider spectrum of psychological wellness-illness.

Bion and Cartwright focus on the theme that the mind of a person depends on the mind of another person to achieve psychological growth. A person who has grown psychologically from overcoming a difficult experience in life can become a container for a person who is grappling with a similar life experience. For example, a person who has grown psychologically, from overcoming an experience of trauma, can become a container for someone who is currently struggling with trauma. The more mature person – the container — provides a mental scaffolding that helps the less mature person – the contained - convert difficult life experiences to meaning. This is how Cartwright describes the interaction between contained and container during a containment:

> "For (Wilfred) Bion, a real human mental connection is like an emotional storm caused by the coming together of minds that crave and resist each other."
> – Duncan Cartwright (CSM 3)

In this chapter, I describe each mode of containment and identify the people whose biographies I use in later chapters to illustrate the modes of containment. Bion and Cartwright both use the language of archetype-as-biological-entity, that is, projection and introjection. To honor their work, I use their language to describe the modes of containment. In later chapters, where I describe biographies, I explain containment from the two perspectives of archetype-as-biological-entity and archetype-as-emergent-entity.

Commensal Mode of Containment

The following description of the commensal mode of containment is my interpretation taken from "Containing States of Mind" by Duncan Cartwright (CSM 145 - 151).

In the context of the containment model, the word 'commensal' refers to a relationship characterized by fellowship, where the outcome is psychologically beneficial to both participants. The commensal mode of containment offers the best opportunity for psychological growth for both people in a relationship (CSM 145). This containment begins with a projection. The projection is cast from the mind of the person called the contained, onto the mind of another person called the container. The contained does not set out deliberately to cast a projection. The casting is involuntary; and it originates from the unconscious part of the psyche of the contained. If the person on whom the projection is cast responds with the willingness and capability to become container of the projection, it opens a path for the relationship to become a containment, with the opportunity for psychological growth. The contained and container form an emotional bond and the interaction between them occurs in an iterative inter-weaving of narratives. The first narrative comes from the contained, whose projection is an unconscious communication about a state of mind that is causing anxiety because of an inability to process certain experiences in life. The anxiety may involve sensory experiences from the external world, or it may involve unsettled emotions and thoughts in the mind of the contained. The first narrative can also include conscious communication, expressed in spoken words and perhaps written words. The second narrative comes from the container. This narrative includes both unconscious and conscious communication. It is an iterative development of an introjection that engages the minds of both the contained and the container. An introjection is the opposite of a projection. An introjection is an unconscious process that can help to allay the anxieties experienced by the contained. The conscious part of the second narrative is made up of spoken and possibly written communication that the container uses to help the contained to grapple with anxieties about unsettled emotions and thoughts. The introjection is a way of transmitting information about a state of mind that the container has already processed successfully, and is therefore able to help the contained to process a similar state of mind.

In the commensal mode of containment, the interaction between the contained and container generates a third narrative that is beneficial to both contained and container. This is the mode of relating through which optimal psychological growth can be achieved. The third narrative is a dialectical interaction between contained and container. It represents a symbolic product of the two minds relating to each other. It is described as dialectical because it is a way of arriving at a useful result through a series of opposing arguments. The commensal mode of containment promotes psychological growth when the state of mind that creates anxiety for the contained matches a state of mind that the container already knows how to process. Also necessary for progress is a psychological frame to contain the interaction between contained and container. The frame includes an agreed purpose for the containment, a physical or virtual place where the interaction occurs, and agreed times for interaction. The psychological frame provides an opportunity for individual and overlapping reveries, that is, for shared musings about the contained's unprocessed state of mind. If there is a good fit between contained and container, the shared musings generate new ways of understanding and obtaining meaning from life experiences. The third narrative can be a source of insight and creativity for both the contained and container. In the commensal mode, the container function works toward curiosity about experiencing the unknown. In the commensal mode, it is the formation of symbols that builds the third narrative. Although the commensal mode is synonymous with psychological growth, the realization that the containing mind is also connected with and influenced by other minds can involve anxieties. The commensal mode makes progress when the fit between contained and container has a psychological frame that enables narratives that are meaningful and generative. Neither the contained nor the container is lodged in the mind of the other in reciprocal interaction, but they have overlapping reveries that foster new meanings, and new ways of experiencing. In this mode, symbols and their cultural contexts are entertained by the contained and container as they collaborate in the dialogical interaction that generates meanings from experience. The contained and container interpenetrate each other's internal worlds through mutual processes of projection and introjection in order to understand each other. The creation of a third narrative leads to an expansion of the psychological space, where symbols become generators of meaning.

In later chapters, I choose the following relationships to illustrate the commensal mode of containment:
- Newsroom copyboy Carl Bernstein and newspaper editor Sidney Epstein
- Physicist Albert Einstein and Mathematician Hermann Minkowski
- Political couple Michelle & Barack Obama and their marriage counsellor
- Microbiologist Emmanuelle Charpentier and biochemist Jennifer Doudna.

Symbiotic Mode of Containment

The following description of the symbiotic mode of containment is my interpretation based on "*Containing States of Mind*" by Duncan Cartwright (CSM 139 – 142).

Used in the context of the containment model, the word 'symbiotic' refers to a relationship of mutual dependence, where psychological growth is limited, or inhibited. In the symbiotic mode of containment, a projection is cast from the mind of the contained onto a person, a group, or an organization (CSM 139). The projection is made up of unprocessed emotional and cognitive experiences that create anxiety for the contained. If the projection is cast onto a person with whom the contained establishes an emotional bond, and if the person is willing to become a carrier of the projection, he or she becomes the container by making themselves mentally available to help make the content of the projection more manageable and thinkable.

The connection between contained and container is one of emotional turmoil that is dampened by each seeing the other as an extension of themself. In the symbiotic containment, each becomes a receptacle for the other's sense of identity. The contained may depend on a group for a sense of identity, while the group depends on the contained to be part of the group. If the contained exceeds the limits of group identity, their dependence on the group breaks down. In the symbiotic containment, the contained and container live with a part of their sense of identity existing in the other. Because each has a portion of their identity con-tinually outside of themself, they appear to be balancing on an edge, where their experiences do not feel like their own. Continually living outside of themselves, each appears to be dependent on experiences that belong to another. The contained produces the first narrative, and the container produces the second narrative, but there is no real third narrative because, in the symbiotic mode, the communication between them is one of reciprocity, where each depends on the other.

A third narrative would disrupt the reciprocal containment. The mind of the contained needs another, but the container is so dependent on unprocessed experiences as the primary means of interacting with the contained that they find themselves in a mutual dependence with limited opportunity for psychological growth. For the symbiotic mode of containment, the minds of the contained and container do not connect by mutually exploring each other's interior world for growth. They participate in a complicity that protects the relationship as it stands. Their bond is based on a shared delusion. Their reverie is restricted or contrived. Each may have a curiosity about the other, but only as it serves to maintain the symbiotic union. There is no real third narrative in the symbiotic mode of containment. The reciprocal symbiotic cycle has no product beyond the contained-container. Communication of unassimilated experience is essentially pre-verbal, and therefore not consciously known to the contained and container. If they pay attention to the communication aspects of their relationship, the container stimulates in the contained a curiosity about the psychical nature of the container's mind. This begins as a two-person, two-narrative arrangement, but it does not have the traction of a dialectical interaction that could lead to a third narrative. Each depends on the other to mutual advantage. Because the contained and container are in a reciprocal relationship, dependence works both ways. The mind of the contained needs another, but the containing mind is dependent on unassimilated experience because this is the communication through which the container can connect and know the contained for possible mental growth. Mental growth however, is limited to mutual dependence within the limit of the two-narrative arrangement. Although the two-narrative communication may serve a protective developmental function, curiosity about the container's mind is limited to attention paid to projected content and their pre-verbal nature. Thoughts that allow two minds to connect through imaginative exploration and mutual verbal communication are not available in the symbiotic mode. This creates a blind spot that arises from complicity between the two protagonists to protect an attachment which must not be uncovered. The contained and container may find themselves having a delusion shared by two people in close association.

In later chapters, I choose the following relationships to illustrate the symbiotic mode of containment:
* Psychologist Carl Jung and psychoanalyst Sigmund Freud
* Catholic monk Thomas Merton and Abbot James Fox.

Parasitic Mode of Containment

The following description of the parasitic mode of containment is my interpretation based on *"Containing States of Mind"* by Duncan Cartwright (CSM 143 – 145).

When used in the context of the containment model, the word 'parasitic' refers to an asymmetrical relationship in which the contained feeds off the meaning-making resources of the container. Lacking adequate resources to process their own intolerable emotional and cognitive experience, the contained attempts to parasitize the meaning-making resources of the container. The container may have the resources to process a projection cast from the mind of the contained, but the effort at containment is thwarted because of envy on the part of the contained. With parasitic anxiety, the contained trivializes or attacks the container's efforts at making unprocessed experiences tolerable and meaningful. The first narrative comes from the contained and the second narrative comes from the container. In the parasitic mode of containment, the interaction between the contained and container might generate a third narrative, but it is destructive to the relationship. Any attempt at containment destroys the rapport that exists between contained and container. The relationship between contained and container has asymmetrical qualities and real exchange between them is compressed or denuded of meaning. Meaning-making cannot be tolerated due to destructive attacks on each other. For example, out of envy, the contained may attack the container's ability to process the emotional turmoil communicated by the projection. The third narrative in the parasitic mode is the product of untransformed emotional turmoil that destroys or attacks the emotional bonds between contained and container. In the parasitic mode, the third narrative has the effect of being subtly harmful in ways that weaken emotional bonds between contained and container. The parasitic mode operates within bonds that strip the relationship of emotion, making them feel meaningless, indifferent and lifeless. In the parasitic mode, a creative union between contained and container cannot be tolerated and real exchange between contained and container is compressed or robbed of meaning through destructive attacks against each other.

In a later chapter, I choose the following relationship to illustrate the parasitic mode of containment:
- Serial killer Ted Bundy and his girlfriend Elizabeth Kendall.

Autistic Mode of Containment

The following description of the autistic mode of containment is my interpretation based on "*Containing States of Mind*" by Duncan Cartwright (CSM 151 – 154).

When used in the context of the containment model, the word 'autistic' refers to a relationship in which the contained lacks the ability to participate in a containment. Autistic containment is an attempt at a relationship that is initiated by a projection cast from the mind of the contained to a person, place or thing. This mode of containment occurs when the interaction between contained and container is hindered because a limitation in the mind of the contained prevents active participation in a containment. This mode of containment is not functional because some of the mental operations of the contained are shut down. When a projection is cast from the mind of the contained, it impacts the external aspect of a thing, rather than being projected onto the mind of a person. Because a part of the mental life of the contained is shut down, the means of communicating the projection to another mind are not functional. What occurs instead is a projection to the surface of an inanimate thing in an attempt to avoid relating to another, which would pose a risk of exacerbating the anxiety that caused the projection in the first place. The contained focuses on the surface of things as a means of deriving meaning from their emotional and cognitive experiences. The connection between word and emotion is broken, and in its place, there are meaningless inanimate things that block the processing of experience. It is emotion that enlivens the contained-container relationship. When emotional bonds exist, interaction between contained and container can be established. When stripped of emotion, the bonds between contained and container are reduced in vitality, or become approximations of inanimate things. In the absence of a first narrative, it is impossible for the creation of a worthwhile containing narrative. The inability to introject a good containing narrative retards development of a multi-dimensional internal space. As a result, the contained relates to things as 2-dimensional forms, that is, surfaces in an attempt to hold the self together.

There is no contained-container relationship, only elements that cling together to form a precarious structure of containment surface. This form of relating is driven by phantasies of sticking to an object to gain coherence rather than relying on projecting onto the mind of a person. 'Surface' refers to the external part of an object as different from projecting into the interior. For example, the sound of the voice — as opposed to the meaning found in the words — is clung to as a defining boundary in autistic relation. These attempts at containment can be represented at different levels of psychical experience. All have a common reliance on the 'sensory surface' of the object and the need to block entry into a containing thinking object, whether psychical or external. The autistic mode contributes to the generation of agoraphobic experience by turning internal experience into entrapping inanimate objects. Agoraphobia is a psychological disorder in which a person experiences fear of places or things that induce panic attacks. Obsessive people often use routine and ritual to create boundaries to their experiences as a means of blocking encounters with their own mental world. Preoccupation with the frame and boundaries of psychological space can also be used as an autistic surface to prevent the emergence of new experience. People using the autistic mode tend to nullify background containing experiences by adopting repetitive and preservative strategies that reduce interaction to a near-sensory surface. The psyche generates its own objects by turning psychical functions, processes, and activities into objects in their own right. Preoccupation with the frame and boundaries of psychological space can also be used as an autistic surface to prevent the emergence of new experience.

In later chapters, I choose the following relationships to illustrate the autistic mode of containment:
- Congressman Anthony Wiener and sexting messages sent via Social Media
- Firefighter John Orr and fires he set as a clandestine arsonist.

Pseudo-containing Mode of Containment

The following description of the pseudo-containing mode of containment is my interpretation based on *"Containing States of Mind"* by Duncan Cartwright (CSM 154 – 160).

In the context of the containment model, the expression 'pseudo-containing' refers to a relationship in which the contained and container bypass the emotional turmoil that are a natural part of contained-container relationships. Instead, they mimic the containment and pervert its role. In this mode, unprocessed emotional and cognitive experiences are communicated with what appears to be an assurance and a sense of righteousness. Uncontained mental states take the forms of emotional overload and overly reasoned thoughts. Both contained and container resist containment and emotional growth. In the pseudo-containing mode, the container functions as an apparently well-reasoned person who resists entering a containing relationship and is unable to feel the benefits of being held in mind by another. In the pseudo-containing mode, the narrative of the contained is not derived from raw experience that seeks transformation, but is generated by mimicking the unconsciously perceived intentions, needs or functions of the container. The result is a great deal of pseudo-intelligence and story-making that does not allow genuine components of thought to emerge from the container. Because the pseudo-containing mode short circuits the process of feeling held in another's mind, it leaves the contained with no sense of what is involved in managing unassimilated thoughts and feelings. There exists only a marginal idea that thoughts can be explored or developed, and the containment fails because the contained engages in a manic takeover of the role of the container.

When there is a difficult transition from adolescence to adulthood, it can lead to a sense of omniscience that involves an attempt to triumph over conflicts about dependency. Adolescents triumph over dependency by precociously approximating the adult container function, so as to exclude all other perspectives and meanings. The idea of being 'right' and the adherence to rigid ideas limit the potential of obtaining meaning from another mind because it is cut off by narcissistic phantasies. The container function is nullified. The container fails to respond to the contained's need to identify with the container's role. This serves to obscure the moment-to-moment interaction between contained and container where there are constant reminders of separateness and differences between them. Awareness of difference is usually obliterated by the contained's voracious envy which precludes being dependent on a container. The consequent effect is that the contained is excluded from the more realistic experiences of being contained or held in the mind of another. Without there being any tolerance for difference between contained and container, the ability to make use of a real container disappears from the mind of the contained. This could explain why the contained appears to be going along reasonably well in their containment, with little intervention from the container. Such a relationship may be interrupted by sudden declines that happen unexpectedly. Challenges to the pseudo-containing mode of containment result in the contained's need to hold the sense of self together, but that is not sustainable. Because difference between contained and container cannot be tolerated, the contained feels trapped in a world where a separate containing mind does not seem to be available. Challenges to the pseudo-mentalization can lead to extreme reactions because it gives rise to a terrifying sense that their attempts to think are worthless. This containment has a perverse nature because unprocessed emotional content does not undergo transformation. Instead, there is an attempt to avoid real emotional experience. The pseudo-containing mode often appears to mock the difficulties and struggles that have to be undertaken if emotion is to be made meaningful. To be helpful, the container must oppose the manic takeover of the container by attempting to rescue the contained. Here, the container stamps his / her authority on knowing what is right for the contained and subtly attacks the contained's overly assured attempts to look after him / herself. In short, the container engages in a struggle to win the containership back from the contained. In the pseudo-containing mode, what appears to be reasoned and mature thinking is actually uncontained thoughts that convey very little understanding or meaning. Pseudo-containing occurs when the reality of difference, separateness, and the opaque nature of another's mind is obscured by defensive strategies that attempt to resist entering the containment.

In a later chapter, I choose the following relationship to illustrate the pseudo-containing mode of containment:

- Lawyer Michael Cohen and businessman-politician Donald Trump.

Reflexive Mode of Containment

The following description of a reflexive mode of containment is my proposal for addition to the Bion-Cartwright containment model.

In the context of the containment model, I use the word 'reflexive' to denote a situation where a person depends on their own mind for containment. Reflexive containment occurs when a person in isolation — voluntary or imposed — turns their attention to thinking about their own mental processes. Warren Coleman wrote that Bion's alpha function is going on all the time. When the communication is not going on between two minds, it is going on within the psyche of the individual. I am proposing the addition of a reflexive mode of containment to the Bion-Cartwright model. In my research for this book, I noticed that there are people who, in isolation, achieve psychological growth that is comparable to that achieved by containment pairs with mind-to-mind interactions. I identified two examples of people who had a reflexive mode of containment. One example occurred in the life of Dante Alighieri whose isolation was the result of his being exiled from Florence. Another example occurred in the life of Ludwig Beethoven whose isolation was self-imposed when he withdrew from society due to the loss of his hearing. In the reflexive mode of containment, the contained mirrors their own mind because there is no available container. The person's isolation becomes a psychological frame for processing difficult life experiences, which can involve negative emotions such as unrequited love and regret, or positive emotions such as the personal accomplishment of building creatively on one's artistic ability. The psychological frame is a mental space where the person retreats to engage in searing mind-searching. In the reflexive mode of containment, the contained sets up an arrangement where the mind reflects on itself. That involves a mind which functions in two roles at the same time. One is the mind-of-the-flesh-and-blood-person. The other is the mind-of-an-imaginary-counterpart, who has opposing views. The two engage each other in dialectical interaction about difficult emotions and unsettling thoughts that disrupt the person's life. In iterations of mind-searching, the person can achieve a transformation of outlook that alleviates the emotional turmoil of having to wrestle with difficult life experiences in isolation. The first narrative comes from the mind-of-the-flesh-and-blood-person, while the second narrative comes from the mind-of-an-imaginary-counterpart. If the containment is successful, the iterations of dialogue between the mind-of-the-flesh-and-blood-person and the mind-of-an-imaginary-counterpart generates a third narrative. Part of that third narrative is internal ... it is a new outlook on conducting one's life. Another part of the third narrative is external ... a creative product that has utility for others. During their reflexive modes of containment, Dante and Beethoven each produced creative products that have been useful to humanity.

In later chapters, I describe their reflexive modes of containment in the context of their relationships:
- Italian poet Dante Alighieri and Beatrice Portinari
- German composer Ludwig Beethoven and his Immortal Beloved.

Theistic Mode of Containment

The following description of a theistic mode of containment is my proposal for addition to the Bion-Cartwright containment model.

In the context of the containment model, the word 'theistic' refers to a relationship between a person and their perception of deity. The bond between the person and their deity is a belief system. Examples are the Christian belief system and the Hindu belief system. A theistic mode of containment occurs when a person's mind engages with their perception of a deity. Psychologist Warren Colman explains the notion of 'mystical' as a belief in forces, influences and actions which, although they are not perceptible to the senses, they are nevertheless real. So, belief in spiritual forces is an expression of affective states that have become symbolized and transformed through collective representations, and this includes taking on a social aspect (AIE 239). This means that people can grow psychologically from their relationship with their deity. In my research for this book, I found two instances of theistic modes of containment. One instance is the relationship between gospel songwriter Charles Austin Miles and the Christian Son of God. Another instance is the relationship between Prince Arjuna and the Hindu Lord Krishna.

In the theistic mode of containment, the contained chooses a psychological frame for expressing the burden of unprocessed experience, which can involve negative emotions such as guilt or positive emotions such as gratitude. The frame is a place of worship, which can be physical, for example, a church or a temple. The place of worship can also be mental imagery, for example, an imaginary garden. In the theistic setting, the contained adopts an attitude of prayer to a deity that is believed to be all-knowing and omnipotent. The contained has confidence in the deity as a container. When the contained experiences overwhelming emotions that cannot be resolved alone, a projection is involuntarily cast from the mind of the contained onto their perception of a containing deity. The contained addresses the overwhelming emotion, such as guilt or gratitude, to their containing deity with a prayer for relief from the overwhelming experience. The contained lingers in the psychological frame where there may be a series of prayerful reveries, over a period of time. The first narrative comes from the contained in the form of a prayer for relief from an overwhelming emotion. The second narrative comes from the contained's mental imagery of an anticipated communication from the deity. Over time, there may be a sense of the deity gradually introjecting a metabolized version of the overwhelming emotion, as a response to their prayer. It can be experienced as a blessing, an admonition, a rebuke, a restitution, a forgiveness, a punishment, or some form of counselling.

In the theistic mode of containment, the contained believes themself to have a relationship with their chosen deity, as a source of knowledge, protection, and emotional support. These are some of the same characteristics that patients ascribe to psychologists. What appears to be a dialectical interaction occurs in the prayerful context that the contained sets as a psychological frame for the containment. The contained obtains relief from the interaction with their deity. The relief may be palpable and infused with meaning. A third narrative may have a noticeable internal effect, such as relief from emotional burden, and possibly a revised outlook on the contained's direction in life. There may also be an external result such as a creative product that is useful to the community.

In later chapters, I choose the following relationships to illustrate the theistic mode of containment:

- American gospel songwriter Charles Austin Miles and the Christian Son of God
- Indian Prince Arjuna and the Hindu Lord Krishna.

Sources

In writing this chapter, I drew on the following sources:

- *"Attention and Interpretation"* by Wilfred Bion
- *"Containing States of Mind"* by Duncan Cartwright
- *"Unrepresented States and the Construction of Meaning"* by Howard Levine
- *"The Psychology of Transference"* by Carl Jung
- *"Projection and Re-Collection in Jungian Psychology"* by Marie-Louise von Franz.

CHAPTER 8

A Commensal Mode of Containment Involving: Carl Bernstein & Sidney Epstein

"By the end of that first month, it was clear to me that the best job to aspire to in the world was city editor of the (Washington Evening) Star — and that if and when I ever grew up, I wanted to be Sid Epstein. Substantively, temperamentally, sartorially."

— Carl Bernstein

Carl Bernstein and Bob Woodward were 1973 Pulitzer Prize winners for public service. They got the award for their investigative reporting of the Watergate scandal. Although it was a high journalistic achievement for both men, it had another significance for Bernstein. Bernstein had to surmount a number of obstacles to become a reporter. He had dropped out of university at a time when reporters were required to have a university degree. His university-educated parents were worried that he would not amount to much. He left his first job as a copyboy-turned-city-desk-clerk because, despite earning the respect of his editor and having published many articles, he was not considered eligible to become a reporter, due to his lack of a university degree. Bernstein's award of a Pulitzer Prize sent a clear message to all who had doubted his potential as a reporter. In earning the coveted Pulitzer Prize, Bernstein had demonstrated that he was fully capable of functioning as a professional reporter without a university degree.

The story of Bernstein's striving to become a newspaper reporter began while he was still in high school. My source of information is "*Chasing History: A Kid In The Newsroom*" by Carl Bernstein. Set in the early 1960s, this chapter is an account of a mentoring relationship between Carl Bernstein, aspiring newspaper reporter, and Sidney Epstein, editor of the *Washington Evening Star.* A sixteen-year-old high school student, Bernstein could barely restrain his passion for becoming a newspaper reporter. It far exceeded his interest in formal education. He was elated to be offered a part-time job as copyboy, the lowest position in the newsroom at the *Star.* Sidney Epstein was a respected editor, who may have seen in Bernstein, a younger version of himself. Epstein had been a teenager with unbounded enthusiasm for newspaper reporting and a matching distaste for academics. Seeing potential in Bernstein, Epstein promoted him from copyboy to city desk clerk and assigned him responsibilities that would ordinarily go to a reporter. Over a period of four years, Bernstein applied himself and accumulated a portfolio of newspaper articles, some of which had been published on the first page of the *Star* ... a rare accomplishment for a novice. The *Star* instituted a new policy in the third year of Bernstein's employment: A university degree became a mandatory requirement for anyone wanting to be a reporter. Bernstein pleaded to be accepted as a reporter on the grounds that he had already demonstrated his skills as a reporter, but the hiring manager would not accept experience as a substitute for academic qualifications. Bernstein left the *Star* to take up a position at *Elizabeth Daily Journal.*

My interpretation is that Carl Bernstein and Sidney Epstein had a reporter-editor relationship that morphed into a commensal mode of containment, with Bernstein as the contained, and Epstein as the container. Their weekly meetings presented an opportunity for the experienced editor, Epstein, to function as a container for the eager aspirant Bernstein, who was in the throes of psychological distress about his future. Having been in Bernstein's situation — a teenager who was passionate about becoming a reporter, but was surrounded by obstacles — Epstein knew the kind of guidance his young protege needed. There was a projection from Bernstein's mind to Epstein's mind and Epstein stepped up to the role of container. To help readers become better informed about the interaction between Bernstein and Epstein, I provide background information of Carl Bernstein and Sid Epstein, in the next two sections.

Background Information about Carl Bernstein

Carl Bernstein was born to Jewish parents, Alfred and Sylvia, who lived in Washington, D. C. His birth was in February 1944, three months after Private Alfred Bernstein of the U. S. Airforce departed for an assignment in World War II (CH 42). Father Bernstein was unable to obtain leave to go home for the birth of his son. For the first two years of his life, while his father was on assignment in the South Pacific, Carl lived with his mother and her parents (CH 98). After Alfred returned from the South Pacific, the Bernstein family remained in Washington, D. C. until 1955, when they relocated to Silver Springs in Maryland (CH 34). Alfred and Sylvia Bernstein were civil rights activists, who had been members of the Communist Party in the 1940s. A graduate of George Washington University, Silvia worked as a statistician. She campaigned for desegregation and the end of the Vietnam War. A lawyer who graduated from Columbia Law School, Alfred noticed that his career began floundering after he was accused of being a communist, so, he established a commercial laundromat as a second career (CH 26).

In Maryland, Carl attended Montgomery Blair High School (CH 12) where he relished the role of circulation and exchange manager for the school's newspaper *Silver Chips* (CH 12). That is where he got his first exposure to newspaper publication. An aspect of his academic life that he recalls with pride is attending a typing class with a group of girls (CH 45). He achieved a typing speed of roughly 90 words per minute, a skill that later served him well in obtaining his first newspaper job as copy-boy (CH 45). At age sixteen, Carl Bernstein was concerned about his diminishing interest in high school studies. A son of university-educated parents, he wanted to meet his parents' academic expectations for him, but he was struggling in high school. As his interest in school curriculum diminished, his passion for the newspaper business grew. He was determined to become a newspaper reporter. After reaching out to a number of local newspapers, he secured a part time job as copyboy, the lowest position in the newsroom at the *Washington Evening Star* (CH 8). Although Bernstein put a great deal of effort into reaching out to local newspapers, he gives his father the credit for actually securing a job. Father Bernstein feared that his son would not amount to much because of his low academic performance (CH 7 – 8). The credit Bernstein takes for himself in landing the job of copyboy is that he had one marketable skill. Having studied typing, he was able to type at a speed of about ninety words per minute. The ability to type that fast was a rarity in the newsroom at the time.

On the first day of August in 1960, Bernstein began working as copyboy in the newsroom at the *Washington Evening Star*. That is where copyboy Bernstein met city editor Sidney Epstein. One of Bernstein's assignments at the *Star* was to talk with over sixty members of staff in the newsroom and draft a weekly schedule of their shifts. On Thursdays, Epstein would review the draft, make adjustments if necessary, and approve it for general use. Bernstein looked forward to his Thursday meetings with Epstein. The sessions started at four o'clock in the afternoon, and lasted for an hour, sometimes more. Their discussion expanded to include topics about assignments Carl performed in preparation to become a reporter. He would ask questions, and Epstein would take the time to discuss how he had reported on an event. Sometimes Epstein would comment on Bernstein's work without being asked. On other occasions, Epstein would share a story for tutorial purposes. A good deal of Bernstein's education about newsroom activities took place in the Thursday meetings with Epstein.

Bernstein was doing well as a copyboy. Supported by Epstein's mentoring, he took advantage of any available opportunities to learn his new role. He described his copyboy's responsibility as mediation between the thinking part of the operation and the mechanical part, that is, between writing articles and getting the paper out the door (CH 15). After fourteen months of being a copyboy, Bernstein was promoted to dictationist. Bernstein was learning a lot in the newsroom, but not making much progress at the University of Maryland. In the Fall Semester of 1962, he was suspended from the University for 'accumulating close to a hundred violations' in parking tickets (CH 182 – 183). He called the suspension the happiest fall and winter of his life. He had hoped to return in the Spring because being enrolled at the university provided him a safe harbor from being drafted into the war in Vietnam. Without school to concern him, he worked 40 hours plus overtime in the dictation shifts and occasionally took on additional assignments.

Background Information about Sidney Epstein

I found no record of a memoir by Epstein, or a biography about him. The source of information about him is the library at the *Washington Evening Star*. That is where Bernstein looked to learn what he could about his new profession. While exploring the library behind the newsroom, Bernstein found clippings that were informative about Epstein's background and his sensibilities as a writer (CH 42 – 44). Sidney Epstein was born in Wilmington, Delaware in 1921. He grew up in Washington, D. C. where his parents, Abe and Ida, owned a small restaurant on Seventh Street. Epstein graduated from Central High School in Washington, D.C. (CH 43). At age sixteen, he began his career as copyboy at the *Washington Herald* in 1937, having dropped out of Georgetown Washington University in his freshman year to become a fulltime reporter (CH 43). By the time he reached his twenty-first birthday, he was known among his colleagues as a crack rewrite man (CH 43). He joined the U. S. Marines in 1942, and served two years in the South Pacific before returning home as a captain. On his return, he became city editor of *Times-Herald* (CH 43). In 1954, the *Washington Post* acquired the *Times-Herald* and he went to the *Washington Evening Star* (CH 43). While working there, he married Eleni Sakes, who was the newspaper's fashion editor.

Epstein's physical appearance was commanding. He was taller than six feet, with the body of an athlete (CH 39). With piercing brown eyes and a smile that is unforced, his appearance was set off by custom-made suits and monogrammed shirts (CH 39). The overall effect was too elegant for a newsroom. It was more suitable for a gentleman's fashion magazine than a newsroom. His talents as editor and leader were combined with a single-minded fierceness to be the first to get the story, to get it right, and to write it tight, through the five editions per day (CH 39). He encouraged camaraderie among his staff, though he did not join in. He hovered above the proceedings, aloof but always definite and exacting, pronouncing orders that were ruthlessly clear (CH 39). Not only did Epstein have a way with words, he also had a rigorous insistence on stories being verified from every available angle (CH 42 – 44).

Epstein's personal distance from his staff was part of what made him an effective leader (CH 40). It contributed to his mystery because it was his preference that the reporters know almost nothing about his personal life outside the newsroom (CH 40). Bernstein found Epstein to be calm and self-possessed (CH 41). The greater the pressure and the bigger the story, the more important it became for him to stay calm in the storm, to take the measure of all the howling and to ignore it. He seemed a completely self-possessed man with an air of equanimity. Almost everything he did in the newsroom seemed methodical, but he brought an artistry to his work. It was in the first week of August 1960 that city editor Sidney Epstein first encountered copyboy Carl Bernstein in the newsroom of the *Washington Evening Star*. In the next two sections, I describe the archetype of editor from two perspectives, first from the perspective of archetype-as-biological entity, then from the perspective as archetype-as-emergent phenomenon.

Context of Archetype as Biological Entity: Projection & Introjection

Viewed from the perspective of an archetype being a biological entity, the emotion-laden aspiration that Bernstein announced at the end of his first month at the *Star*, indicated that an unconscious projection had been cast from Bernstein's mind to Epstein's mind. The editor archetype was activated and the contents of the projection were images of an idealized editor. This is Bernstein's statement at the end of his first month at the *Star*:

> "By the end of that first month, it was clear to me that the best job to aspire to in the world was city editor of the (Washington Evening) Star — and that if and when I ever grew up, I wanted to be Sid Epstein. Substantively, temperamentally, sartorially" (CH 44).

Substantively, temperamentally and sartorially are words which indicate that Bernstein idealized his editor. 'Substantively' points to the editor's job as being of considerable importance. 'Temperamentally' is about a disinclination to put changing moods on display, as is appropriate for an editor. 'Sartorially' makes note of a stylish, but professional way of dressing. The words represent an idealization of what Bernstein imagined an editor might be. It was also a fantasy about what Bernstein might become. Since this is a projection, these words convey images arising from unconsciousness, where, as a biological entity, the archetype of editor is located. The editor archetype is made up of an ancestral heritage of human experience in relations between editors and reporters accumulated over multiple generations. Epstein became a willing carrier of the projection. The activation of the editor archetype became known through the behaviors and communications exhibited by Bernstein and Epstein during their weekly Thursday meetings. This is where their editor-reporter relationship was established. The relationship became a containment when Epstein began using the Thursday meetings to address Bernstein's anxieties about becoming a reporter. Activation of the editor archetype indicates a forceable evacuation of a projection from Bernstein's mind to Epstein's mind. The content of Bernstein's projection was raw experience of emotions, images and memories related to the newspaper business. They were incomprehensible to him and were therefore evacuated as an unbearable state of mind, in the form of a projection.

Bernstein's desire to become a newspaper reporter was fueled, not just by his unwavering curiosity about the newspaper business, but also by his anxiety about other matters. The realization that his father did not expect him to 'amount to much' must have injured his pride. He wrote of his ongoing alienation from his parents because they had been members of the Communist Party. To Bernstein, the *Star* was a family that was less fraught with stress and anxiety than the one at home in Silver Springs. He was more comfortable in the newsroom with Sid Epstein and ... (others) ... than he had ever been at home (CH 171). Bernstein was a disappointment to his university-credentialed parents. He was a teenager, on the brink of dropping out of academic life, willing to work hard at becoming a reporter, and very much in need of guidance. Of all the professionals in the newsroom, Epstein was the one he sought as mentoring editor. Bernstein did not explicitly ask Epstein to be his mentor, and Epstein did not explicitly volunteer to be Bernstein's mentor. Epstein was likely mindful of having been in Bernstein's position. Epstein had been a teenager who dropped out of George Washington University to take the job of copyboy in his drive to become a reporter. He had the experience that Bernstein sought to acquire. He understood Bernstein. He could see his younger self in Bernstein. Bernstein's projection found a hook in Epstein. His willingness to become a carrier of the projection is noticeable in the unobtrusive way that he made the four o'clock Thursday meetings into a psychological frame for offering guidance, in other words, for metabolizing Bernstein's projection. Epstein became a willing container for Bernstein's projection. By using the Thursday meetings to coach Bernstein about the newspaper business, he indicated that he was engaging Bernstein in the metabolization of the undifferentiated passion of becoming a newspaper reporter.

In response to the projection, Epstein initiated an introjection that involved the construction of meaning from the content of Bernstein's projection. The Thursday meetings gave Epstein the opportunity to help Bernstein construct meaning from the content of his projection. Bernstein's mind had found another mind upon which he could depend for psychological growth. The two had embarked on a commensal containment with Bernstein as the contained and Epstein as the container. Introjection was mediated by Epstein, whose mind was evidently skilled in the construction of meaning from the content of a projection about navigating the newspaper industry. Through engagement with Epstein, Bernstein's emotional state was metabolized and structured into usable thoughts that could be integrated into consciousness. The editor archetype was activated at a critical stage in the lifecycle of Bernstein, creating opportunities for his transition from an adolescence who is dependent on his parents, to an adult who is an independent self-supporting professional. Later in this chapter, I describe the symbolization that I believe occurred during the dialectical interaction between Bernstein and Epstein.

Context of Archetype as Emergent Phenomenon: Appropriation & Internalization

When considering archetype as an emergent phenomenon, it is seen as an emergent property of a dynamic developmental system. In this context, the editor archetype is an emergence from a complex system that is made up of society's attitudes and actions related to journalism, the cultural environment in which editors function, and the narratives that people compose about their lives as professionals in the newspaper business. With regard to the emergent definition of archetype, the processes identified for converting life experience to meaning are appropriation and internalization. The contents of the appropriation are made up of information drawn from the external world, and internalized into the contained's mental model, where it can be reconstructed to make it useful in creating new information. The processes of appropriation and internalization can be observed in the way that children acquire language skills. At first, children appropriate language from social and cultural sources in the external world, then, with the help of caregivers, they internalize language into their mental models. Then they use the internalized language constructs to compose sentences on their own. The underlying assumption of appropriation is that knowledge is socially constructed. So, when a person adopts an appropriation from society, the contents of the appropriation are reconstructed so that it becomes meaningful for the person, who can therefore use it for new purposes. The content of Bernstein's appropriation was experience made up of meaningful thoughts, emotions, images and memories about an editor's role drawn from the cultural environment of journalism.

Activation of the archetype of editor became noticeable through the behaviors and communications between Bernstein and Epstein during their Thursday meetings. Bernstein had a conscious appropriation about the characteristics of an editor's role in the cultural world of journalism. Bernstein's aspiration, declared at the end of his first month of working at the *Washington Evening Star*, indicated that his appropriation from the culture of the newspaper business was superficial and vague. As a reminder, his observations at the end of his first month at the *Star* was *"I wanted to be Sid Epstein. Substantively, temperamentally, sartorially"* (CH 44). Those words are about the outward appearance of the editor;

they do not address the activities performed in the role of editing. As an emergent phenomenon, the archetype of editor has no specific location; it is pervasive across the culture of the newspaper industry. In his eagerness to become a reporter, Bernstein was focusing on the visible, external editor-like qualities that were observable to him. He wanted to be like editor Epstein, but he evidently had a rather naïve idea of what it took to function as a city editor. He was focusing on external attributes because he had no understanding of the knowledge and skills necessary to function as an editor. His choice of words provides some visibility into how Bernstein saw the role of city editor. His words revealed that he did not have a realistic appreciation of the newspaper business, where he desperately wanted to turn his passion into a demonstrable skill. What he appropriated from the world of journalism was what he could understand at the time.

During the Thursday meetings, Epstein was able to mediate a dialogue that enabled Bernstein to build a more nuanced mental model of newspaper reporting, then reconstruct it to create meanings about what could be relevant for his own life as a novice striving to become a full-fledged reporter. It is because Epstein already had the personal experience of constructing meaning from an appropriation about entry into journalism that he was able to guide Bernstein in the reconstruction of his appropriation into thoughts and emotions meaningful to his own life. During their engagement with the social-symbolic world of newspaper reporting, the dialectical interaction between Bernstein and Epstein enabled the transformation of Bernstein's appropriation into a structured, ordered, state of mind about how he might function in the world of journalism. They rendered Bernstein's passionate communications (Substantively, Temperamentally, Sartorially) into useful emotions and thoughts by providing order and structure. Bernstein learned how to investigate, how to craft a well-written article, and how to get it published.

The editor archetype was activated at the level of psychic complexity where Bernstein was transitioning from adolescence to adulthood. The success of the containment indicates that Bernstein achieved a degree of narrative competence that enabled him to connect past with present experiences and combine them into a meaningful autobiographical narrative about his entry into the world of journalism. After adopting the appropriation about what it takes to become an editor, Bernstein came to adjust his mental model of an editor. He understood and was grateful for Epstein's contribution to his education about the newspaper business. He appreciated the guidance about how to conduct research for an article, how to interview local influencers in the community, how to compose a succinctly written article, and how to interact with other professionals in the newsroom.

The containment came to an end when Epstein yielded to the hiring manager's insistence on the *Star's* new policy that a university degree is a prerequisite for newly recruited reporters. When he left the *Star*, he was still determined to pursue a career in journalism, but some of the sheen of 'Substantively, Temperamentally, Sartorially' had rubbed off. By that time, he had a reconstructed mental model that included a new-found image of what he was capable of doing as a reporter. In the next section, I use quotes from Bernstein's autobiography to describe the symbolization that I believe occurred during the dialogical interaction between Bernstein and Epstein.

Converting Experience to Meaning: Symbolization

Psychologists in both archetype-as-biological-entity and archetype-as-emergent-phenomenon camps acknowledge the value of symbolic thought in a successful containment, that is, a containment in which psychological growth occurs. My source of information about the communications between Carl Bernstein and Sidney Epstein is *"Chasing History: A Kid In The Newsroom"* by Carl Bernstein. My interpretation is that between age sixteen and twenty-one, Bernstein was involved in a commensal mode of containment with Epstein. During that time, their opportunity for symbol formation appears to be captured in the phrase 'shoulder to the wheel' which points to a new state of being without specifying the outcome. When the *Star* decided that a university degree was a mandatory requirement for a reporter, Bernstein was disappointed. Believing that Epstein had not done enough to stand up for him, Bernstein indicated he wanted to speak with the hiring manager. The hiring manager's response was:

> *"Carl, you've really put your shoulder to the wheel and your work has been great. But experience is no substitute for the training program"* (CH 308).

That is when it dawned on Bernstein that he might not be establishing a newspaper career at the *Star* (CH 308). He was putting his 'shoulder to the wheel' but his effort was not bringing him any closer to the status of reporter than when he arrived at the *Star*. He felt he was stuck in a rut, and he had no control over the situation. The effort he put into becoming a reporter had all come to naught. Although his request for reporter status had been rejected, Bernstein noticed that he continued to receive reporting assignments as before the announcement of the requirement for a degree. He described his feeling in terms of 'the wheel':

> *"I continued to be assigned just as many stories as before, and I was treated by my editors as if my shoulder was still on the wheel"* (CH 311).

According to *The Penguin Dictionary of Symbols*, the wheel symbolizes cycles, new beginnings and renewals. The wheel is a symbol of movement and liberation from existing conditions. It is a symbol of ceaseless change under its own momentum. *A Dictionary of Symbols* by J. E. Cirlot states that the wheel refers to the rotational tendencies of all cyclic processes. In choosing the expression 'The Wheel' as title of the chapter about how he came to the realization that there was no future for him at the Star, I believe Bernstein was indicating that the symbol of 'the wheel' had significance for him. My interpretation of the significance 'the wheel' held for Bernstein was one of transition, of movement, of change. As the wheel turns, a person turns to face a new direction. He was putting in the effort and getting praise, but the wheel was not turning. His situation was not changing. He had no prospects.

In "*A Critical Dictionary of Jungian Analysis*" psychologist Andrew Samuels and others, explain that from the point of view of Analytical Psychology, a symbol is defined in terms of concept, intent, purpose and content. Here, I apply the dictionary definition to the symbol – 'shoulder to the wheel' — that emerged in Bernstein's communication, when the *Star's* hiring manager rejected his request to substitute his experience for the new requirement of a university degree.

- **Concept:** The concept of putting one's 'shoulder to the wheel' is about exerting effort, but without any useful information of what that effort might be. For Bernstein, the concept of 'shoulder to the wheel' brought forth images of ambition. He was willing to put in effort to achieve his ambition. He had been putting in effort, but it led nowhere.

- **Intent:** The intent behind the concept of 'shoulder to the wheel' was to accomplish a change from fledgling university student to newspaper reporter, but it was difficult to articulate because the traditional path for achieving that ambition – a university degree — was not accessible to him. He could not imagine himself completing a university degree, but he had no other ambition aside from newspaper reporting. The intent of 'shoulder to the wheel' was to do work, to make an effort, but he was at a loss about how to match up an effort with his goal in a workable combination.

- **Purpose:** The purpose that the symbol 'shoulder to the wheel' served was one of resolving a conflict. The purpose the symbol served was not merely to come up with an alternative ambition, nor to work out a logical derivation of a solution to the conflict between credential and ambition. The purpose was to reveal a new outlook through the back-and-forth interaction of opposing sides of the conflict. To overcome that conflict, Bernstein had to demonstrate to his parents and teachers and editors that he was capable of amounting to something worthwhile. It gradually occurred to him that the symbol 'the wheel' was pointing him in a new direction ... away from the *Star*.

- **Content:** The content of the symbol was meaning that had not yet become available in Bernstein's mind. According to the dictionary of terms in Analytical Psychology, a symbol is 'pregnant with meaning' that presents a challenge to thoughts and feelings. A symbol is expressed in images that control, order and give meaning to people's lives. The chapter in which control, order and meaning all come into question in Bernstein's autobiography is the chapter he named 'The Wheel'. It appears that 'the wheel' – part of the expression 'shoulder to the wheel' — struck an emotional chord with him. In that chapter, after logic and common sense had drained him, a new path came into view. A job offer came to him, unsolicited.

One evening, a couple of co-workers invited Bernstein out to a local bar to commiserate with him about being rejected as a reporter because he had no university degree. They shared their curiosity about why the *Washington Evening Star* was setting up stricter newspaper reporting credentials than *The Washington Post*, when the *Post* was a more successful newspaper. It occurred to Bernstein that if other newspapers did not require a degree, maybe there was an opportunity for him elsewhere. For different reasons, Bernstein's colleagues were leaving the *Star*. One colleague named Jo Anne left the Star and returned to Penn State where she took a job as a teaching assistant in the Journalism Department. Another colleague, Lance, left the Star to accept a job as a writer for TIME magazine. Departures of his colleagues made Bernstein consider his own situation. So, when editor Coit Hendley, Epstein's deputy, asked Bernstein if he is interested in going to work at *Elizabeth Daily Journal* as a reporter, Bernstein was ready. The *Elizabeth Daily Journal* is in New Jersey and Bernstein had never been there, but he accepted the job offer sight unseen.

The development of the symbolic process has something in common with the principle of enantiodromia, according to which, a given conscious outlook eventually gives way to an opposing outlook that emerges from an unconscious source. Bernstein was more comfortable in the relationships he had at the *Star* than the relationships he had at home. The *Star* was a place where intense friendships had developed, where personal and professional lives intermingled in shared labor, stories, politics and gossip (CH 311). Bernstein's conscious outlook had been that the Star was his home and if he put his 'shoulder to the wheel' he would achieve his ambition of reporter status. After more than three years of that hope, he realized the *Star* did not see the situation the same way. Once that conscious expectation reached its limit, an opposing outlook emerged. A job offer came to him without his applying for it. 'The wheel' turned in a new direction. The emergence of the new outlook gives the impression of a compensatory effect at work. The conscious outlook was being balanced by an unconscious movement. The symbol aided the transition, not by logic and planning, but by encompassing his psychological situation.

Bernstein's encounter with Epstein transformed his life experience, that is, his internal dread of possible consequences of academic failure and his ignorant exuberance about newspaper reporting, into meaningful, usable thoughts, leading to growth of personality between teenage years and adulthood. Cartwright reports that, for Bion, a real human mental connection is like an emotional storm caused by the coming together of minds that crave and resist each other (CSM 3). Bernstein craved the mentoring connection he had with Epstein, but he put up a resistance to what he saw as Epstein's tacit acceptance of the hiring manager's refusal to regard him as an existing reporter.

The ability to generate meaning demands that the encounter between contained and container be subjected to a series of transformations. This means finding ways of tolerating the emotional storm for long enough so that it can be thought about and given particular personal meaning. Bernstein tolerated the storm of looming academic failure, alienation from his parents, and lack of knowledge about the career he desired. Cartwright reads Bion as having emphasized the transformative qualities of lived experience always unfolding at the cusp of one's awareness (CSM 3). For Bernstein, the cusp of awareness was that line between school-boy awareness and adult reporter awareness. Bernstein and Epstein engaged each other in an editor-reporter relationship that is a common relationship among humans, with a tradition as old as journalism. Their relationship is an example of the commensal mode of containment, the mode that offers the greatest potential for psychological growth.

The symbolic process began with what society expected of him and what he expected of himself. That continued until he felt he was being obstructed by circumstances beyond his control. The symbolic process ended with a new opportunity opening up, not by logical design, but by the symbol pointing in a new direction. 'The wheel' turned, and a new path came into view. The symbolic process ended with Bernstein being relieved of 'feeling stuck'. The change in employer gave him an immediate recognition as a full-fledged newspaper reporter and a new-found confident state of mind about pursuing a career in journalism.

Call To Action: Take Away A Portable Understanding

The Bernstein-Epstein containment is an interesting story of a young apprentice having a mind-to-mind connection with an older expert who provides guidance about entry into a profession, until the apprentice can progress on his own. My hope is that readers take away from this chapter a portable understanding of the characteristics of the commensal mode of containment. To help readers enrich their awareness of the commensal mode of containment, I offer the following summary of the main aspects of how Bernstein and Epstein functioned as a containment pair in converting Bernstein's experience of adolescent anxieties into meaning, on the way to becoming a newspaper reporter.

- **Mode:** Carl Bernstein and Sidney Epstein had a commensal mode of containment.
- **Roles:** Bernstein, the contained, was an aspiring reporter whose projection was cast onto his editor Epstein, the container.
- **Symmetry:** The containment was asymmetrical in the sense that Bernstein was a teenager aspiring to become a reporter, while Epstein was an adult and an experienced editor. There was a gradient of psychological maturity between them. Epstein was able to help Bernstein achieve psychological growth because Epstein had the successful experience of transitioning from university drop-out to full-fledged reporter, when he was an adolescent like Bernstein.
- **Psychological Frame:** The psychological frame for the containment between Bernstein and Epstein was set in Epstein's office at the *Washington Evening Star.* In a containment, the psychological frame has a purpose, a space boundary and a time boundary. The purpose of the psychological frame in which Bernstein and Epstein worked together was originally intended for Epstein to review Bernstein's draft of the weekly schedule for employees in the newsroom. The original purpose of the meeting morphed into a situation in which Epstein helped Bernstein overcome his anxieties about becoming a reporter. The space boundary was their meeting place in Epstein's office. The time boundary was a weekly Thursday meeting, that was held between 1960 and 1965.
- **Dialectical Narrative:** A successful containment has three

narratives. The first narrative consisted of Bernstein's autobiographical account of a mix of related anxieties with which he
was preoccupied as a teenager. Anxiety about dropping out of
school. Anxiety about being drafted into the Vietnam War if
he dropped out of university. Anxiety that he might not be accepted as a reporter if he dropped out of university. Anxiety
regarding his lack of knowledge about the newspaper business.
Anxiety and hurt pride about his father's expectation that he
would not amount to much. The second narrative was Epstein's
contribution of a well-paced guidance likely borne out of a recognition of his younger self in Bernstein. Having dropped out
of Georgetown University to become a copyboy as a teenager,
Epstein fully understood Bernstein's anxieties. He was receptive
to Bernstein's unspoken need for guidance, and he responded
by using the Thursday meetings to pay attention to Bernstein's
narrative, and facilitate the creation of a serial, pedagogical story
of the newspaper business. Because of his experience as an editor coupled with his own psychological maturity, he was able to
function as container for Bernstein's anxieties. The third narrative was the result of a dialectical interaction between Bernstein
and Epstein. It yielded a visible component and an invisible component. The visible component was a portfolio of published
newspaper articles which provided evidence that Bernstein had
graduated from copyboy status to investigative writer status.
The invisible component was a maturing sense of his capability that enabled him to confidently pursue a new opportunity
when the *Star* established a rule that reporters had to have a
university degree. During the containment, the floundering
sixteen-year-old had matured into a twenty-one-year-old adult
with a grounded sense of being able to establish his place in
the world. He moved out into the world of journalism with the
confidence that the lack of a university degree was not going to
prevent him becoming a full-fledged journalist.

- **Psychological Growth / Harm**: At the end of the containment,
there was evidence of psychological growth for Bernstein. His
unassimilated state of mind about his anxieties was transformed
into an assimilated state of mind about having acquired reporting
accomplishments that demonstrate his capability as a reporter.

During the dialectical interaction with Epstein, Bernstein overcame the psychological distress of not being qualified for the only job he ever wanted. Internally, he had a new-found sense of his own agency as the driver of his path in life. He had acquired the knowledge and the confidence to investigate breaking news, and write well enough to get his articles published. Externally, he was able to leverage the experience he acquired at the *Star* to achieve an award at *Elizabeth Daily Journal* and grow his career to the point of later earning a coveted Pulitzer Prize – the industry's highest journalistic award — at *The Washington Post.*

After the Containment Ended

Bernstein left the *Washington Evening Star* in 1965 to become a full-time reporter for *Elizabeth Daily Journal* in New Jersey, where he won first prize in New Jersey's press association for investigative reporting. In 1966, Bernstein left New Jersey and began reporting for *The Washington Post*, where he covered various aspects of news in Washington D. C. While working at the *Post*, Bernstein earned an award for joint investigative reporting with Bob Woodward, for their coverage of the Watergate scandal in 1973 (CH 335).

Epstein stayed at the *Washington Evening Star* until it ceased publication in 1981 (CH 345). After leaving the *Star*, Bernstein kept in touch with Epstein for many years. They would sometimes get together to catch up on what was happening in each other's lives. In 1997, Epstein asked Bernstein to speak at his funeral and Bernstein agreed. Bernstein delivered the eulogy for his former mentor in 2002, when Epstein died. He was 81 years old.

Years later, when CBS News asked if he had any role models among the many Pulitzer Prize-winning journalists with whom he had worked, Bernstein identified Sidney Epstein by stating:

> "*I owe him a lot. He somehow saw things in me, maybe that I didn't see in myself. And he was a great, great editor*". See CBS News website, article titled "*Carl Bernstein on chasing history*" dated January 9, 2022.

After publishing his autobiography in 2022, Bernstein commented on his formative years in an interview with CBS News:

> *"The formative part of my being a reporter occurred from ages 16 to 21 at a great old-fashioned newspaper, The Washington Star — not (The Washington) Post"*. See CBS News web site, article titled *"Carl Bernstein on chasing history"* dated January 9, 2022.

Sources

My sources of information about Carl Bernstein and Sidney Epstein are:

- *"Chasing History: A Kid In The Newsroom"* by Carl Bernstein
- Carl Bernstein's eulogy for Sidney Epstein:
  <u>Washington Star Editor Sidney Epstein Dies - The Washington Post</u>
- Washington Post investigative reporter Carol Leonnig's interview of Carl Bernstein:
  <u>Transcript: Washington Post's interview of Carl Bernstein</u>
- CBS News web site January 9, 2022:
  <u>Carl Bernstein on chasing history - CBS News</u>
- *"Containing States of Mind"* by Duncan Cartwright
- *"Projection and Re-Collection in Jungian Psychology"* by Marie-Louise von Franz
- *"Symbolization: Representation and Communication"* by James Rose (editor).

CHAPTER 9

A Commensal Mode of Containment Involving: Albert Einstein & Hermann Minkowski

"The years of searching in the dark for a truth that one feels but cannot express, the intense desire and the alternations of confidence and misgiving until one breaks through to clarity and understanding, are known only to those who have themselves experienced them."

Albert Einstein

"Superfluous learnedness" was Albert Einstein's disdainful response when he saw Hermann Minkowski's first draft of a mathematical proof of Einstein's intuition about a theory of relativity. In mocking contempt, Einstein complained about a later draft: *"Since the mathematicians have grabbed hold of the theory of relativity, I myself no longer understand it"* (ELU 133). Gradually, after further rounds of communication with Minkowski, Einstein came to understand and admire Minkowski's final mathematical proof. The 1907 to 1908 collaboration that brought together Einstein's brilliant intuition about relativity and Minkowski's mathematical prowess was not their first encounter. The two men knew each other from their days at the Zurich Polytechnic

when Einstein was a student and Minkowski was a mathematics lecturer. Having little interest in mathematics, Einstein often skipped Minkowski's lectures ... so often, that Minkowski labeled student Einstein a 'lazy dog' (ELU 35). Years later, when Einstein was unable to prove his intuition about relativity, he swallowed his past humiliation, and reached out to Minkowski for help.

Einstein's biographer, Walter Isaacson, provides a basic definition of relativity: *"The theory of relativity asserts that the fundamental laws of physics are the same wherever your state of motion"* (ELU 107). Another way of stating the theory is that the relationship between measurements of space and time is invariant — does not change — regardless of the frame of reference of the observer. For example, when observing a moving train, the relationship between the measurements of space and time remains invariant whatever your frame of reference (ELU 132). Einstein was not the only scientist to have an intuition about relativity. Other physicists also tried to find mathematical grounding for their intuitions about relativity. What made them give up on their search for mathematical proof was that they could not fit their intuitions into Newtonian Physics and Euclidean Geometry, which were the prevailing mathematical structures at the time. Having skipped many of Minkowski's mathematics lectures, Einstein was unencumbered by the solid knowledge of Newtonian Physics and Euclidean Geometry that restrained his contemporaries. So, Einstein approached Minkowski expecting him to produce a proof using existing mathematics. In both those topics, space and time are separate dimensions. According to the prevailing mathematical structures, space was 3-dimensional, and time was 1-dimensional. What Minkowski brought to the exploration of relativity was the novel idea of 'spacetime' ... a concept that combined space and time into a 4-dimension continuum, which is outside the realm of Euclidean Geometry. Einstein had published an article about his theory of relativity in 1905, but it was just a theory until 1908 when his collaboration with Minkowski produced a proof of the theory, based on the development of a new non-Euclidean mathematics. Unfortunately for humanity, that was the only collaboration between Einstein and Minkowski, because Minkowski died soon after proving Einstein's theory. Shortly before he died, Minkowski remarked wistfully *"What a pity that I have to die in the age of relativity's development"* (ELU 133). Hospitalized for internal organ issues at the end of 1908, Minkowski died soon after, at the age of forty-four (ELU 133).

My interpretation is that Albert Einstein and Hermann Minkowski had a commensal mode of containment during their collaboration on the theory of relativity. During the period 1907 to 1908, they collaborated on translating Einstein's intuition about relativity into a mathematically sound contribution to science. Einstein was the contained whose unrepresented state of mind about his inability to prove relativity left him feeling stuck in his career and prompted him to seek help from Minkowski. As an experienced mathematician, Minkowski became the container, who helped Einstein by mediating the transition from a muddled intuition of relativity to a proven theory about relativity. I believe the containment was successful in terms of psychological growth because it not only transformed Einstein's unrepresented state of mind to a represented state of mind, but also because the output from the dialectical interaction between Einstein and Minkowski produced a lasting scientific legacy for humanity. To help readers understand the collaboration, I offer some background information about Einstein and Minkowski, in the next two sections.

Background Information about Albert Einstein

My main reference for the life of Albert Einstein is the biography "*Einstein: His Life and Universe*" written by Walter Isaacson. The birthplace of Einstein was Wurttemberg, Germany, where he was the first child of parents Hermann and Pauline Einstein. The year after his birth in March 1879, his Jewish family relocated to Munich where they established a company that produced electrical equipment. He attended Catholic school until age eight when he was enrolled at the Luitpold Gymnasium. In 1894, following his family's loss in competitive bids to provide the city of Munich with electric lighting, the family moved to Italy in search of business opportunity (ELU 22). With the help of a family tutor, Einstein excelled in physics and mathematics. His academic goal was to study at the Zurich Polytechnic in Switzerland. In 1895, he failed his first attempt at the entrance examination, but passed the following year (ELU 25). He took an interest in playing the violin and was good enough to participate in local concerts. Although he did not claim to be of the Jewish faith, he was happy to be a member of the Jewish people (ELU 30). To avoid military service, he relinquished his German citizenship in 1896 (ELU 29) and remained stateless until he obtained Swiss citizenship in February 1901.

While at Zurich Polytechnic, he befriended classmate Marcel Grossmann who habitually wrote detailed notes in mathematics lectures and who willingly shared them with Einstein. Einstein earned the disdain of mathematics lecturer, Hermann Minkowski, who called Einstein a 'lazy dog' because he often skipped mathematics classes (ELU 35). Einstein's friendship with Grossmann continued several years after they graduated from Zurich Polytechnic. As a student at Zurich Polytechnic, Einstein met his future wife, Mileva Maric. She was the only female student in the physics and mathematics classes. While studying together, they became lovers. The couple took a romantic vacation to Lake Como in Italy, and Mileva soon realized she was pregnant with Einstein's child (ELU 64). After failing her examinations, she returned to her hometown in Serbia where she stayed until the birth of a daughter. Before Mileva left Zurich, Einstein agreed to write her father a letter about plans for their future as a couple, but Einstein did not write her father (ELU 66). Although Einstein wrote Mileva letters of love, he did not visit her during the pregnancy. Baby Lieserl was born in 1902 and there is no evidence that Einstein ever met his daughter face to face. The way that biographer Isaacson describes Einstein's expression of love for Mileva and baby Lieserl is that his love was rather abstract, because it was not enough to induce him to visit them (ELU 75). It is not clear if Mileva gave up baby Lieserl for adoption, or if Lieserl died of scarlet fever. Researchers found no record of a birth, a death or an adoption. The first time that information became available about Lieserl was in 1986 when researchers found reference to her in an exchange of letters between Einstein and Mileva.

In 1900, Einstein graduated from Zurich Polytechnic and was awarded a Federal teaching diploma. He was job hunting for the better part of two years, but was unsuccessful in finding a teaching job. His search was hampered by the fact that none of his lecturers at Zurich Polytechnic thought enough of his scholastic performance to write him a recommendation. Marcel Grossmann came to the rescue by helping Einstein get a job at the Swiss Patent Office, where his role was to process applications about electrical inventions.

Einstein and Mileva married in 1903, had a son Hans Albert in 1904, and a second son Eduard in 1910. By 1914, the marriage came to an end when Mileva discovered that Einstein was involved in a romantic relationship with his cousin Elsa Lowenthal. In exchange for a divorce, Einstein promised Mileva the prize money from a Nobel Prize he expected to win. They divorced in 1919 and Einstein married his cousin Elsa. When he later won a Nobel Prize in 1921, he did give the prize money to Mileva, but he took little interest in the lives of his sons.

In 1905, Einstein earned his PhD and published his proposal for a theory of special relativity based on his brilliant intuition. Unable to prove his theory two years after publishing the proposal, Einstein approached his former lecturer, Hermann Minkowski, with a request for help in working out a mathematical proof.

Background Information about Hermann Minkowski

There are English translations of Hermann Minkowski's scientific publications, but I found no English language biography. My reference for analysis of his drafts of presentations about relativity is *"Minkowski's Space-Time: From Visual Thinking To The Absolute World"* written by Harvard scholar, Peter Galison. Minkowski was born in June 1864 in Russia and his family immigrated to Prussia in 1872. He enrolled in the Altstädtisches Gymnasium in Königsberg where his education included science and classical literature. When Minkowski graduated from the Gymnasium, he enrolled at the University of Königsberg where he earned his doctorate in 1885. He relocated to Zurich for the role of lecturer in mathematics at Zurich Polytechnic where Einstein became one of his students. In 1902, Minkowski was invited to the University of Göttingen, where he worked while collaborating with Einstein on the theory of relativity. In the next two sections, I describe the Einstein-Minkowski relationship first in the context of archetype-as-biological-entity, then in the context of archetype-as-emergent-phenomenon.

Context of Archetype as Biological
Entity: Projection & Introjection

When an archetype is defined as a biological entity, it is regarded as an ancestral heritage of human experience accumulated over many generations, and it is located in collective unconsciousness. When psychologists define an archetype as a biological entity, the processes they identify for converting experience to meaning are projection and introjection. Projection is an evacuation of unconscious content from the psyche due to an unbearable state of mind. Einstein's projection was an unbearable state of mind about his confidence in his intuition about relativity coupled with his inability to prove it mathematically. The mix of emotional certainty and rational uncertainty became an unbearable state of mind, which was evacuated from his mind in a projection. There was an involuntary projection cast from the mind of Einstein to the mind of his former lecturer in mathematics at Zurich Polytechnic. Minkowski was surprised that Einstein, — the former student whom he had labeled a 'lazy dog' — could have such a brilliant idea as a theory of relativity (ELU 132). Challenged by Einstein's intuition, Minkowski agreed to help. Einstein reached out for help as the contained, and Minkowski agreed to help, making him the container.

The archetype of discovery was activated at a critical stage of Einstein's life cycle. He had been trying to make the transition from being a clerk in the Swiss Patent Office, to becoming a university lecturer. His 1905 publications had earned him the attention of academics, and he wanted to follow up on his relativity proposal by providing mathematical proof. It was a time in his life when he felt that he was in a rut. His career was not progressing. The year 1905 had been very productive. That was the year he produced his PhD dissertation along with a number of other publications that brought him recognition in the academic world. Two years later he was still grappling with how to prove his intuition about relativity. At the same time, he was so confident of his intuition about relativity that he could not let it go. As a theoretical physicist, Einstein was disinclined to conduct physical experiments, preferring instead to conduct what he called 'thought experiments'. His thought experiments had previously earned him success, but his thought experiments about relativity left him feeling stuck between his passionate intuition about relativity and his inability to find a mathematical proof. This was a period of disturbance in his life. He had not previously experienced such malaise. After grappling with the mathematics of relativity for several months between 1905 and 1907, he decided to request help from Minkowski.

The containment involving Einstein and Minkowski began when they agreed to collaborate in 1907. The emotionally toned behaviors and communications between them were related to their shared passion about discovering the mathematics of relativity. Together, they set out to discover how mathematics accommodates relativity, indicating that the discovery archetype was activated. The archetype of discovery is made up of an ancestral heritage of human experience in discoveries about the physical world accumulated across the history of humanity. With Minkowski facilitating the introjection process, they examined Einstein's projection, by considering the relation to current knowledge about physics, and possible support by the existing mathematical structures of the day. After engaging in a number of rounds of dialogue and drafts of possible proofs, Minkowski realized that the existing mathematical structures, Newtonian Physics and Euclidean Geometry, were not suitable for proving Einstein's theory. A new mathematical structure was necessary.

Einstein's projection was broken when Minkowski explained that the proof of his theory about relativity could not be achieved with the existing mathematical structures, and would need a new structure. In the throes of the activated discovery archetype, Minkowski and Einstein had worked at finding a proof until they had exhausted logical means at their disposal. Then logic gave way to imagination. Minkowski realized they would have to go outside the realm of traditional mathematics to find a proof of relativity. Minkowski got the insight to combine space and time into one dimension, which he called 'spacetime'. There followed more rounds of dialogue and drafts in search of a new mathematical structure to support Einstein's theory. When Minkowski discovered a new geometry, he then had to further facilitate the introjection process by persuading Einstein that the new geometry was necessary to prove his theory of relativity. Minkowski was able to mediate an introjection by engaging Einstein in a dialogue that enabled him to construct meaning from the content of his projection and integrate the meaning into the conscious aspect of his psyche. Skeptical at first, Einstein gradually came to understand the new geometry, after which he welcomed the proof that Minkowski offered. Through rounds of dialectical interaction, they were able to transform Einstein's unrepresented state of mind into useful thoughts of relativity, based on the new mathematical structure.

Seen from the context of archetype-as-biological-entity, my interpretation is that Einstein and Minkowski achieved psychological growth as a containment pair, because they were able to process the content of Einstein's projection by converting his frustrating life experience about relativity into something meaningful for themselves and humanity. The decision to lean on another mind, that he knew to be a source of academically recognized mathematical skills, created an opportunity for symbol formation and psychological growth. Later in this chapter I write a section on the details of symbolization that influenced the collaboration between Einstein and Minkowski.

Context of Archetype as Emergent Phenomenon: Appropriation & Internalization

In the context of archetype-as-emergent-phenomenon, the discovery archetype is viewed as an emergent property of a dynamic, developmental system that is made up of the human capabilities for discovery, the society's external environment of physical reality, and the narrative competence of scientists in the society. As an emergent property of a complex system, the discovery archetype included society's attitudes and actions related to nature, knowledge of physics and mathematics, the cultural environment in which scientific work was being done, along with the narratives that scientists composed about their experiences as researchers of physical reality. When regarded as an emergent phenomenon, the discovery archetype does not exist in any particular location; rather, it is pervasive across the cultural environment. When psychologists define an archetype as an emergent phenomenon, the processes they identify for converting experience into meaning are appropriation and internalization.

Appropriation is an adoption of conscious content from social and cultural sources in the external environment. It is about drawing information from the cultural and social world and reconstructing it. The information may be taken from disciplines such as science, art, literature, or language. It may also be drawn from images, behaviors, or communications in the society. The contents of the appropriation are adopted from the external world, and internalized into the adopter's mental model so that it can become meaningful to the adopter. Then, it is restructured to make it useful in creating new information. For readers who are unfamiliar with the processes of appropriation and internalization, they can be observed in the way that children acquire language skills. At first, children appropriate language from social and cultural sources in the external world, then, with the help of adults, they internalize language into their mental models. Then, they use the internalized language constructs to compose sentences on their own. The underlying assumption of appropriation is that knowledge is socially constructed. When a person adopts an appropriation from society, the contents of the appropriation are reconstructed so that it becomes meaningful for the person, who can therefore use it for new purposes. The social and cultural sources available to Einstein were those that existed in the early 20th century academic world of Bern, Switzerland, where he was living when he proposed his theory of relativity. In the European academic world, there were other scientists who were sharing ideas about relativity, but none had found a way to prove it mathematically. In his role as contained, Einstein adopted his appropriation from that early 20th century European world of scientific ideas flowing in academia. The source of Einstein's appropriation about relativity came primarily from scientific musings in the scientific milieu. His appropriation was a combination of ideas about relativity flowing in the academic community, plus knowledge of traditional mathematical structures of Newtonian Physics and Euclidean Geometry, in a mix of narratives of the scientists who expressed opinions about relativity.

Internalization is the incorporation of a cultural appropriation into one's mental model. Einstein had a mental model of relativity, but it was an assembly of his appropriation from the scientific community combined with his own intuition derived from his customary 'thought experiments'. That assembly was not enough to prove relativity. When

Einstein and Minkowski began their collaboration, they were trying to use traditional mathematical structures to find a proof. In the role of container, Minkowski facilitated an internalization with rounds of dialogue, drafts of proof, and revisions. Together, they examined Einstein's appropriation, parsed it, interpreted it, and tried to support it with the existing mathematical structure of the early 20th century. When that approach did not result in a proof, Minkowski abandoned traditional mathematics, and advanced a new concept of 'spacetime'. Einstein was miffed that the mathematics had veered away from the traditional mathematics with which he was familiar. He complained that he no longer understood relativity. Over a period of dialectical interactions with Minkowski, Einstein came to accept the notion of spacetime as essential to the proof of relativity. After persuading Einstein of the necessity of the concept of spacetime, Minkowski was able to help Einstein reconstruct the contents of his appropriation, by applying spacetime in working out a proof of the theory of relativity. Information about space and time was adopted from the cultural world, then reconstructed to create the new concept of spacetime, which was then used to prove relativity.

Einstein's decision to seek help from another mind, known to be more accomplished in mathematics, opened him up to an opportunity for dialogue conducive to symbol formation. When they had exhausted logic, they turned to imagination. What helped them overcome their reliance on traditional mathematics was their capacity for symbolic thought. During their iterative dialogue, there emerged a symbol that enabled them to shift attention from a focus on traditional mathematics and to a search for a new mathematical structure that could support relativity. Guided by symbolization, they were able to convert Einstein's appropriation to scientific meaning which was sound enough to satisfy the scientific community. The success of the collaboration indicates that Minkowski and Einstein achieved a degree of narrative competence that enabled them to connect past with present scientific experiences, and combine them into a meaningful new scientific story. Their high level of psychic complexity is seen in the way they successfully engaged in rounds of dialectical interaction that transformed the mix of emotional certainty and scientific doubts into gifts of new knowledge for humanity. They earned the respect of the scientific community for their collaboration in finding a proof of relativity. Viewed from the context of archetype-as-emergent-phenomenon, I believe that Einstein and Minkowski achieved psychological growth as a containment pair because of their capacity for symbol formation, coupled with their openness to being guided by the symbol that emerged during their collaboration. In the next section, I explain the symbolization that occurred during the collaboration between Einstein and Minkowski.

Converting Experience to Meaning: Symbolization

As a containment pair, Einstein and Minkowski, fit the Bion-Cartwright theme that a mind is dependent on another mind for meaning (CSM 2). The mind of Einstein, the contained, was depending on the mind of Minkowski, the container, for help to derive meaning from his unprocessed state of mind about relativity. Regardless of whether psychologists see an archetype as a biological entity or an emergent phenomenon, they agree that symbolization is an aid to psychological growth during a containment. Einstein and Minkowski's capacity for symbolic thought became evident during their collaboration. I do not have access to any direct communication that occurred between Einstein and Minkowski during their collaboration on relativity. What I rely on are *"Einstein: His Life and Universe"* by Walter Isaacson and an article *"Minkowski's Space-Time: From Visual Thinking To The Absolute World"* written by researcher Peter Galison. Galison obtained versions of drafts of presentations that Minkowski made at the University of Gottingen during the Einstein-Minkowski collaboration. Galison analyzed the text of the drafts to assess Minkowski's trend of thought during his search for proof of Einstein's intuition about relativity. The trend of thought is indicative of a changing state of mind while he was working on a mathematical proof of Einstein's theory of relativity.

While looking for Minkowski's trend of thought in the series of draft presentations about relativity, Galison found a repetitive use of the phrase 'pre-established harmony'. My interpretation is that Einstein and Minkowski had an opportunity for symbol formation during the containment and it was captured in Minkowski's repetitive use of the phrase 'pre-established harmony'. 'Pre-established harmony' points to a compatibility between nature and mathematics without specifying anything particular about that compatibility. During the collaboration, Minkowski maintained a confidence in his notion of a 'pre-established harmony' between nature and mathematics. He believed mathematics to be a language for articulating the nature of physical reality. If relativity is a legitimate aspect of nature, Minkowski felt there must be a mathematical structure to express relativity.

The symbolic form of 'pre-established harmony' can be related to the mix of emotional states of Minkowski and Einstein as they collaborated on their search for a bridge between physical reality and the mathematics needed to support the novel idea of relativity. Minkowski's phrase 'pre-established harmony' was a symbolic form that expressed his confidence that they would find a mathematical proof for an existing, if yet undiscovered, fact of relativity in nature. The capacity of Minkowski and Einstein to symbolize was demonstrated by their journey of discovery in finding a proof of the theory of relativity ... one of the more abstract topics in science. They had to adjust their view of mathematics. Euclidean Geometry applies to flat surfaces, such as circles and triangles, but it does not apply to curved surfaces like topographical maps of landscapes. Since relativity involves curved surfaces, a new geometry was necessary.

During their collaboration, Minkowski facilitated rounds of dialogue while he prepared drafts of proof for Einstein's theory of relativity. There were occasions when Einstein expressed dissatisfaction with Minkowski's approach. One source of dissatisfaction was that Einstein saw Minkowski's approach as unnecessarily complex. Einstein countered with his idea that the proof would be simple if relativity is a fact of nature. For Minkowski, the phrase 'pre-established harmony' was a recurring theme that pointed to an emerging idea that he shared with Einstein. They came to a joint intuition that relativity was already a fact of nature, and that there is a harmony between nature and mathematics, so it was just a matter of finding the right mathematical language to demonstrate that relativity exists in nature. The phrase 'pre-established harmony' does not have a literal meaning. In the scientific domain, the phrase had no meaning, but the phrase functioned as a symbol that pointed to something that was emerging in the collaboration of the two scientists. Although they could assign neither definition nor specific outcome to the symbol of 'pre-established harmony', they were confident that it pointed to a real possibility that a mathematical proof could be found.

The flash of insight came to Minkowski in the idea of combining two dimensions, space and time, in a new dimension that he called 'space-time'. In traditional Newtonian Physics, space and time are separate dimensions. Space has three coordinates about geographic location, and time has one coordinate about duration. In relativity, the relationship between space and time does not change, so a combined spacetime dimension was necessary. Although this containment occurred in the domain of science, the search for proof of Einstein's intuition was not a matter that could be resolved in a strictly rational way. These were two experienced scientists, who had received academic awards for their work. If the proof of relativity could have been accomplished by logic alone, they would have done it readily. Logic was not enough to find a proof, partly because proof of relativity required imagination ... the imagination to look beyond existing rules of logic. A serial dialogue of Einstein's narrative and Minkowski's narrative led to a third narrative imbued with the imagination of a new mathematical structure that eventually delivered proof of relativity to humanity. The flash of insight about spacetime was the turning point in the collaboration. Minkowski and Einstein were able to discover the mathematical underpinnings of relativity because they, unlike their contemporaries, were willing to step outside of established knowledge about Newtonian Physics and open themselves up to discovery of a non-Newtonian Physics (ELU 133). To do that, they engaged in a symbolic process that yielded scientific meaning drawn from their emotional and rational investments in a theory that befuddled the scientific community.

In "A Critical Dictionary of Jungian Analysis" psychologist Andrew Samuels and others explain that symbols are captivating pictorial statements ... enigmatic portrayals of movement stirring the psyche. From the point of view of Analytical Psychology, a symbol is defined in terms of concept, intent, purpose and content. Here I interpret Minkowski's symbol of 'pre-established harmony' in terms of concept, intent, purpose and content.

- **Concept:** The concept of the symbol 'pre-established harmony' is about a congruity that already exists between nature and mathematics. The symbol was not an instrument of rationality; it was a summary of the psychological situation in which Einstein and Minkowski collaborated. Minkowski's faith in a 'pre-established harmony' guided the direction, structure and emphasis of his work on relativity (ELU 24). Minkowski believed in the power of mathematics to lead scientists to an understanding of physical reality, of which relativity was a part.

- **Intent:** The intent behind the symbol 'pre-established harmony' was discovery of a mathematical expression for relativity, but it was difficult to articulate because the specifics of the outcome were unknown. There was a general intent to form a link between nature and mathematics, but without any idea of how to accomplish that in a manner that would be acceptable to the scientific community. The intent behind 'pre-established harmony' in Einstein's approach was to find a simple solution. The intent behind 'pre-established harmony' in Minkowski's approach was to discover a new mathematical structure. It took rounds of dialogue for them to integrate their intent.

- **Purpose:** The purpose that the symbol of 'pre-established harmony' served was one of pointing to the discovery of a new mathematical structure to address the conflicting expectations of the two scientists. The purpose that the symbol served was not merely to come up with an alternative point of view. Nor was the purpose of the symbol to work out a logical derivation of a solution to the conflict of emotional certainty and rational doubt about relativity. The purpose the symbol served was to reveal a new mathematical structure through the back-and-forth dialogue of opposing sides of the collaboration.

- **Content:** The content of the symbol of 'pre-established harmony' was a subtle meaning. According to the dictionary of terms in Analytical Psychology, a symbol is 'pregnant with meaning' that presents a challenge to thoughts and feelings. A symbol is expressed in images that control, order and give meaning to people's lives. The symbol of 'pre-established harmony' gave order and meaning to the Einstein-Minkowski collaboration through a number of influential factors. One factor was the integration of sources of influence on their work. They had to take into consideration the University of Gottingen's board of scientists to whom Minkowski presented drafts because the board represented the scientific community, whose endorsement would be necessary for a proof of relativity. Another factor was that Einstein and Minkowski were putting their scientific careers at risk by pursuing spacetime which did not have scientific grounding at the time. They also considered the different views of other scientists who expressed opinions about relativity. Yet another factor in the ordering of the collaboration was that the back-and-forth movement in the dialogue between Einstein and Minkowski fluctuated between two different styles of mental activity. Einstein's style was inclined to a concrete, visual thinking in which he manipulated clocks, rods, light beams and trains. Minkowski's style was inclined to geometric, visual thinking in which he played with grids, surfaces and curves. Their back-and-forth dialogue fluctuated between the concrete and the geometric until something new emerged from unconscious activity … a new mathematical structure. On the one hand, the meaning of the symbol 'pre-established harmony' found unique expression for Einstein and Minkowski in the proof of relativity. On the other hand, the symbol reflected a universal imagery of harmony between nature and mathematics, in the form of a new mathematical structure.

The development of the symbolic process is consistent with the principle of enantiodromia, according to which, a given conscious outlook eventually gives way to an opposing outlook that emerges from an unconscious source. The emergence of the new outlook gives the impression that there is a compensation at work. The conscious outlook is being balanced by an unconscious movement. The symbol 'pre-established harmony' helped the transition from one path to the other, from focus on Newtonian Physics and Euclidean Geometry to non-Newtonian Physics and non-Euclidean Geometry, on the way to finding a proof of relativity. The symbol aided the transition, not by rationality, but by summing up the psychological situation of Einstein and Minkowski. The symbolic process began with them feeling stuck with an unyielding Newtonian Physics. They had built their scientific careers on Newtonian Physics, but it offered no solution. Initially, they could not find a way to prove relativity, but when the symbol of 'pre-established harmony' emerged, it pointed a way to get out of being stuck. The symbolic process ended with Einstein being able to see that his theory of relativity found its scientific grounding in Minkowski's new structure of mathematics, which proved special relativity, and paved a path for going forward with his later theory of general relativity.

Call To Action: Take Away A Portable Understanding

As a containment pair, Albert Einstein and Hermann Minkowski had an interesting collaboration that illustrates one instance of the commensal mode of containment. This chapter is not just a story about the discovery of a new mathematical structure for proving relativity. It also provides an example of the kind of relationship that has the makings of psychological growth, which is characteristic of the commensal mode of containment. This chapter is a call to action for readers to take away a portable understanding of the commensal mode of containment. To help readers, I offer the following summary as a reminder of how Minkowski played the role of container in helping Einstein to convert his experience of scientific anxiety into meaning, in terms of discovering that relativity is evidence of a pre-established harmony between nature and mathematics.

- **Mode:** Albert Einstein and Hermann Minkowski had a commensal mode of containment.
- **Roles:** Einstein, the contained, was a theoretical physicist whose projection was cast onto his former mathematics lecturer, Minkowski, the container.
- **Symmetry:** This was an asymmetrical relationship. There was a gradient of mathematical skill between them. As an experienced mathematician who had earned a number of awards, Minkowski had the capability and the confidence to look beyond traditional mathematics to discover the concept of spacetime, which was necessary to prove Einstein's theory about relativity. Einstein was a brilliant physicist who needed mathematical help because his intuition about relativity stopped at the limit of traditional mathematics.
- **Psychological Frame:** In a containment, there is a psychological frame that has a purpose, a geographic boundary and a

time boundary. The purpose of the psychological frame in which Einstein and Minkowski collaborated was to discover a mathematical structure for the theory of relativity. Geographically, they collaborated across two countries, Switzerland and Germany. Einstein was living in Switzerland, while Minkowski was working at the University of Gottingen in Germany. In terms of time, the collaboration lasted about two years from 1907 to 1908, but the frequency of the communication and the medium of the communication are unknown. Both Switzerland and Germany had telephone service, postal service and railway service in the period of collaboration, so their communication could have used any of those services.

- **Dialectical Narrative:** This containment had three narratives. The first narrative was Einstein-the-contained's narrative about his life as a theoretical physicist who grappled with his unproven intuition about relativity. The second narrative was Minkowski-the-container's narrative about his life as a mathematician who recognized that a new mathematical structure was necessary to prove relativity. The dialectical interaction between those two narratives generated a third narrative. The third narrative had an internal component and an external component. The internal component was their new outlook on mathematics that incorporated the new concept of spacetime in the mental models of Einstein and Minkowski. The external components were their gifts to the scientific community ... a non-Newtonian Physics and a proof of the theory of relativity. The third narrative is neither causally related to, nor derivable from, the first and second narratives.

- **Psychological Growth / Harm:** The containment ended with psychological growth for both Minkowski and Einstein. Minkowski's growth is seen in his ability to reassemble existing mental constructs of space and time to fashion a new mathematical structure in keeping with meaning that underpins the symbol 'pre-established harmony' Einstein's unprocessed state of mind about not being able to prove his theory was transformed into a processed state of mind. He overcame the psychological distress associated with being confident of his intuition while being unable to prove it. Evidence of his psychological growth is seen in his learning a new way of functioning by adaptation to a new outlook in his scientific life. He was able to integrate the new mathematical structure into his mental model about physical reality.

After the Containment Ended

The containment pair, Einstein and Minkowski, ended their collaboration in 1908, with the publication of their proof of the theory of special relativity. Minkowski was hospitalized for complications about internal organs in late 1908, and he died in January 1909. Although Einstein's publications credited Minkowski with discovering the mathematical structure necessary for proof of relativity, a number of 21st century scientific text books identify Einstein as the lone genius who proved the theory of relativity.

After Minkowski died, Einstein was able to use the concept of spacetime to develop and publish a theory of general relatively in 1916. The theory of general relativity differs from special relativity because it takes gravitation into account. Although Minkowski and Einstein worked out a theoretical proof of relativity in 1908, no one had tested the theory experimentally. In May 1919, astronomers set up equipment in countries where the solar eclipse was expectable to be visible, because they wanted to test the theory of relativity. Sir Arthur Eddington led the English expedition to an island off the west coast of Africa to take measurements of the light coming from stars. It turns out that the sun's gravity bends the path of light from distant stars ... just as Einstein had predicted. Measurements taken during the solar eclipse indicated that the locations of the stars appeared to be displaced because their light had to travel to earth on the curved space that formed around the sun due to gravity.

During a 1915 interview by Professor James Overdruin, this is how Einstein described his feelings about the success of the Einstein-Minkowski collaboration:

> "The years of searching in the dark for a truth that one feels but cannot express, the intense desire and the alternations of confidence and misgiving until one breaks through to clarity and understanding, are known only to those who have themselves experienced them". See Stanford University web site.

In the year 2000, TIME Magazine chose Einstein as Man of the Century, for his many contributions to science, including the theory of relativity, photo-electric effect and quantum theory. The magazine characterized him as a genius of the twentieth century.

Sources

The sources of information that shape my thinking in this chapter are:
- *"Einstein: His Life and Universe"* by Walter Isaacson
- *"Minkowski's Space-Time: From Visual Thinking To The Absolute World"* by Peter Galison
- *"Containing States of Mind"* by Duncan Cartwright
- *"A Critical Dictionary of Jungian Analysis"* by Andrew Samuels, Bani Shorter and Fred Plaut
- *"Symbolization: Representation and Communication"* by James Rose (editor)
- Stanford University web site: <u>Stanford University</u>.

CHAPTER 10

A Commensal Mode of Containment Involving: The Obamas & The Counsellor

"We should always have three friends in our lives. One who walks ahead who we look up to and follow, one who walks beside us who is with us every step of our journey, and then one who we reach back and bring along after we've cleared the way."

— Michelle Obama

Michelle Robinson and Barack Obama met in early summer of 1989 when both worked at Sidley & Austin, a corporate law firm in Chicago. By the end of summer, they had fallen in love. Drawn together by romantic interest combined with a mutual passion for public service, they married in 1992. After marriage, they comfortably integrated their roles as professionals-cum-spouses. Then, they decided to start a family. After the birth of two children, recollections of their own childhood experiences loomed into memory and disrupted their lives as a loving married couple. Memories of their childhood appear to have set unflinching expectations of each other as parents. Michelle could not understand why Barack's parenting was not like that of her father. Barack could not understand why Michelle's parenting was not like that of his mother. They had entered into marriage with conflicted assumptions about family life. Despite their deep love and devotion to each other, their marriage was on the brink of divorce. Michelle was dissatisfied because she felt she was doing more than her share of parenting. Barack thought she was being unreasonable. He expected her to understand that his life as a senator required him to be away from home for a number of days each week, and therefore unable to share the parenting as Michelle's father had done. He was dissatisfied that Michelle's parenting was not as flexible as his mother's parenting had been. Michelle and Barack are Ivy League trained lawyers. If their marital problem could have been solved with rationality alone, they would have solved it by themselves. Their problem was more emotional than it was rational. Unable to resolve their conflicting expectations of each other, they sought the service of a marriage counsellor. Michelle was so convinced that Barack's parenting was out of line, that she expected the marriage counsellor to bring Barack around to her way of thinking ... to fix Barack. The counsellor did not do that. He mediated a dialogue between both Michelle and Barack that enabled them to shed assumptions that their spouses should replicate their parents' behaviors, and instead, create workable guidelines to suit the circumstances of their own marriage. With help from the counsellor, they were able to metabolize their unprocessed states of mind about parenting and render them into useful emotions and thoughts for integrating their new roles as parents into the mental models they had already built as professionals-cum-spouses. Their newfound outlook of integrated lives as professionals-cum-spouses-cum-parents served them well in shaping their family life for a promising future. With their new parenting arrangement, the Obamas became a political family, at first devoted to serving communities in the state of Illinois, and later becoming public servants for the nation. In 2017, Barack and Michelle became the 44th President and First Lady of the United States of America.

My interpretation is that Michelle and Barack had a commensal mode of containment with the marriage counsellor functioning as the container. My sources of information are "Becoming" by Michelle Obama and "A Promised Land" by Barack Obama. The Obamas were able to convert their unassimilated marital experience to meaning through the mediation of the counsellor. There was a projection from Michelle to Barack and a projection from Barack to Michelle, but neither became a carrier for the other. The marriage counsellor mediated the processing of the contents of their projections. The commensal mode of containment is the mode that offers the most potential for psychological growth. Although Michelle and Barack did not refer to their marriage in psychological terms, their communications and behaviors pointed to a commensal mode of containment, in which reciprocal exchanges enabled them to conduct their marriage along a transformational path from spouses to parents. In the next two sections, I provide background information about the lives of Michelle and Barack, so that readers can become familiar with their early life experiences.

Background Information about Michelle Obama nee Robinson

Born in Chicago in January 1964, Michelle grew up in a family consisting of her father Fraser, her mother Marian, and elder brother Craig. Fraser was a pump operator in the city water purification plant, while Marian was a secretary. Craig was approximately two years older and devoted to his sister. As a youngster, Michelle attended Bryn Mawr Elementary School, then Whitney Young High School where she graduated in 1981. Michelle's childhood experience was acquired in a stable, middle-class family, in which father and mother worked 9-to-5 jobs and were home in time for a regularly scheduled family dinner. To them, family dinner was not just about satisfying hunger; it was a regular gathering for parents to teach their children about life. After high school, Michelle enrolled in Princeton University to major in Sociology, and she later graduated with a Bachelor's degree in Arts in 1985. At Princeton, she was active in the Third World Center, which is an academic, cultural group established to support minority students. Michelle later earned a law degree from Harvard Law School in 1988.

Michelle's first job was at Sidley Austin LLP in Chicago where she worked as a lawyer in the department that processed cases related to intellectual property. It was there that she met Barack Obama. As their friendship was getting underway, two significant people in Michelle's life died within a short period of each other. In the autumn of 1989, Michelle's close friend Suzanne died from cancer. It was an emotional blow because Suzanne was only twenty-six years old. Michelle had been expecting a life-long friendship, but the death focused her attention on the brevity and uncertainty of life. In early 1991, Michelle's father died at age fifty-five from complications related to multiple sclerosis. In her memoir, *Becoming*, Michelle characterized these two deaths as a turning point in her life. The two deaths affected her deeply. Her attention focused on the brevity of life in general, as she contemplated the specific goals of her own life. She decided that life was too short to be wasted. Since she was less interested in corporate law than public service, she sent out copies of her resume to the legal departments of local community-oriented non-profit organizations, universities and foundations (BC 146). After a number of interviews, she chose a role as assistant to the Mayor of Chicago (BC 151). Her salary was reduced, but her satisfaction was service to the grassroots of her community. Barack encouraged Michelle to pursue her passion for public service. With the transition from corporate law to public service, her career took off on a path that led to her becoming First Lady, wife of the 44th President of the United States.

Background Information about Barack Obama Jr.

In August 1961, Barack Obama Jr. was born in Hawaii as the biracial child of Kenyan Barack Obama Sr. and American Ann Dunham, both of whom were students at the University of Hawaii. Barack Sr. was studying economics, while Ann was studying anthropology. Soon after the birth of their son, Barack Sr. and Ann separated. From September 1961 to June 1962, Ann took her son to Seattle, where she studied at the University of Washington. Barack Sr. graduated in September 1962 and left Hawaii for a tour of the United States, after which he enrolled at Harvard University for graduate work in economics. Ann returned with Barack Jr. to Hawaii in late 1962 to resume her undergraduate studies in anthropology. While studying, she asked her parents to take care of Barack Jr. In January 1964, Ann divorced Barack Sr. He received a Master's degree in economics in May 1964, and returned home to work as an economist for the Kenyan government. In the following year, Ann married an Indonesian fellow student named Lolo Soetoro. Ann, Lolo and Barack Jr. relocated to Jakarta, Indonesia in 1967, when Barack Jr. was six years old. While in Jakarta, Ann trained teachers at the Institute for Management Education and Development. Ann and Lolo welcomed a baby girl named Maya into the family in August 1970. By late 1980, Ann and Lolo were divorced. Lolo died in 1987 due to health issues related to his liver.

Because Ann valued education as an important influence in life, she sought the best schooling for her son. In 1971 she sent ten-year old Barack Jr. back to Hawaii to live with her parents because she believed there was a better opportunity for his education in America than in Indonesia. He was enrolled in Punahou School in Hawaii while he lived with his grandparents. In December 1971, Barack Sr. visited Hawaii and spent some time with Barack Jr. who was ten years old. That was the last time Barack Jr. saw his father. Barack Sr. experienced setbacks in his career due to conflicts with political leaders in Kenya, took solace in drinking, and sustained injuries while driving under the influence of alcohol. He later died in a car crash in Kenya in 1982.

Ann remained in Jakarta to work on her dissertation in economic anthropology. Her fieldwork in Indonesia earned her a Master's degree in anthropology in 1975. She conducted further research from 1986 to 1988 in Pakistan, where her work earned her a PhD in 1992. Ann relocated to New York in 1992 to apply economic anthropology to microfinance in the banking industry. Following a diagnosis of uterine cancer, she died in Hawaii in 1995.

Over his lifetime, Barack Jr. had intermittent contact with his mother and very limited contact with his father. After his father returned to Kenya, Barack Jr. saw him just once when the older Obama visited Hawaii. Barack's mother took care of him in periods between marriages, divorces, university studies and anthropological research. His maternal grandparents filled the gaps when his parents were not available. Having graduated from Harvard Law School in early 1991, Barack Jr. returned to Chicago to take up residence and prepare for the bar examination. After graduation, he entered public service as a senator in the state of Illinois. From there, his political career proceeded on a path that led him to become the 44th President of the United States.

Marriage & Parenting

Michelle and Barack got married in October 1992 at the Trinity United Church in Chicago (BC 163). At the time, he had two jobs. He was teaching law at the University of Chicago, and working as a senator in the state of Illinois. She had a job as assistant to the Mayor of Chicago. The couple lived in Hyde Park, while he worked in Springfield, Illinois. As senator, his work in Springfield kept him away from home half a week and sometimes more. Michelle was comfortable with that. While there were just the two of them, each accommodated the other's schedule. If he was late coming home for dinner, it did not bother her. When he was away from home, she pursued her own interests. When they had children, it turned out they had very different expectations and assumptions about parenting. The first daughter Malia arrived in 1998 and Sasha followed in 2001. With two children to care and Barack away from home for days at a time, Michelle felt she was functioning as a single mother. She felt overloaded and pointed out to Barack that he needed to be more involved in the family. She was expecting him to function like her father, who had been consistently home for family dinner as an essential part of raising a family. Michelle projected images of her father's behavior onto her husband. Barack thought she was being unreasonable. He projected images of his mother's behavior onto Michelle. His mother lived in a loose arrangement of being in and out of face-to-face family life. Barack grew up with the assumption that affection can be dispensed at a distance and grandparents can be substitutes for parents. Barack expected Michelle to understand that the nature of his political role as a senator required him to be away from home.

In her biography, Michelle states that people live the paradigm they know (BC 204). The paradigm she knew was one where marriage would be like her parents' marriage in Chicago. Two middle-class parents working 9-to-5 jobs and consistently being home in time for dinner with the children. Dinner was not just about consuming food to satisfy hunger. It was a regularly scheduled time for family interaction, expressions of affection, praise for accomplishments and opportunities to work out issues. It was a time when parents were present and emotionally available to provide children with guidance about life. The paradigm he knew was the extended family life that he experienced with biological parents in Hawaii, with stepfather and mother in Indonesia, and with grandparents in Kansas. For him, family love was not based on being in the same place geographically, or on time spent together. He had learned to fit his childhood needs into the schedules of which ever parent, step-parent or grandparent happened to be available at the time. Growing up with a biological father living in Kenya and a mother often away from home on anthropological adventures, his impression was that parental care and parental love can be dispensed at a distance. Unable to resolve the conflicting expectations of each other, the Obamas decided to obtain the service of a marriage counsellor. In the next two sections, I describe the processes that underpin the interaction between the Obamas and the marriage counsellor. First, I describe their interaction in terms of archetype as biological entity, then, I describe their interaction in terms of archetype as emergent phenomenon.

Context of Archetype as Biological Entity: Projection & Introjection

Psychologists from the discipline of Analytical Psychology regard human interaction as being influenced by archetypes. Those who define archetype as a biological entity regard it as an ancestral heritage of human experience that is accumulated over multiple generations and located in collective unconsciousness, that is, in the psyche. When psychologists define an archetype as a biological entity, the processes they identify for converting life experiences into meaning are projection and introjection: Projection is an evacuation of unconscious content from the psyche due to an unbearable state of mind. There were two projections in the Obamas' relationship. One projection was from Michelle's mind to Barack's mind. The contents of that projection were compelling images of idealized masculine behavior, indicating that the animus archetype was activated. Because of those images, she expected that Barack would behave toward the family as her father had done. Loving one's family was accomplished in a stable marriage, with the husband being home every night for a dinner ritual that was not just about food, but also about being a resource for guiding the children through life. Love was dispensed by being physically present. The other projection was from Barack's mind to Michelle's mind. The contents of that projection were equally compelling images of idealized feminine behavior, indicating that the anima archetype was activated. He expected that Michelle would be like his own mother, Ann. Loving one's family was an activity that weaved its way through marriages and divorces, university study and research work, all without having to be physically present. Parental love was sometimes available via physical presence, and sometimes was provided remotely.

Introjection is a transformation of an unbearable state of mind to a bearable state of mind, followed by its integration into conscious content of the psyche. Neither Michelle nor Barack became a carrier for the other's projection. They never questioned each other's devotion to the marriage, but Michelle found herself functioning as a single parent and regarded the situation as unsustainable. Barack did not understand why she could not be more accommodating, considering that his job as a politician required him to be away from home while working with other senators in the state's capitol. Michelle could not get Barack to fit her projection of spousal behavior. Barack could not get Michelle to fit his projection of spousal behavior. To help them determine how to fit parenting into their marriage, they reached out to a marriage counsellor.

The marriage counsellor was able to mediate a three-way dialogue that enabled Michelle and Barack to recognize their projections as unconscious assumptions, construct new meanings from the content of their projections and integrate the new meanings into the conscious aspects of their psyches. The marriage counsellor guided Michelle and Barack in the construction of meaning from their projections. The minds of Michelle and Barack were engaged with the mind of the counsellor, who helped them to process their confused emotional states and structure them into useful thoughts. The animus and anima were activated at the critical stage of the Obamas' life cycle when they were transitioning from a comfortable marriage partnership to the new, perplexing roles of motherhood and fatherhood. The Obamas' projections were broken when they experienced flashes of insight into their own behaviors during symbol formation. For the Obamas, symbol formation appears to be captured in Michelle's word 'becoming' which points toward a new state of being without specifying what that state would be. In a later section of this chapter, I describe the symbolic form of 'becoming' and relate it to the Obamas' transition from marriage partners to parents.

Context of Archetype as Emergent Phenomenon: Appropriation & Internalization

Those psychologists who define archetype as an emergent phenomenon, regard it as an emergent property of a dynamic, developmental system that is made up of human brains, human activities, society's external environment and the narrative competence of humans in the society. When viewing archetype as an emergent phenomenon, the processes for converting life's experience to meaning are appropriation and internalization. Appropriation is an adoption of conscious content from social and cultural sources in the external environment. The Obamas' containment involved two appropriations. What Michelle appropriated from the society in which she grew up were societal expectations of parenthood in middle-class Chicago. What Barack appropriated from the society in which he grew up were societal expectations of flexible parenthood in Hawaii and Indonesia. The Obamas are well educated people, capable of working out solutions to logical problems, but they could not fit their appropriations into their family life. That is because it was not just a logical problem; the problem was also fraught with charged emotions. Knowing that the recurring conflict posed a risk to the marriage, they decided to obtain the service of a marriage counsellor.

Internalization is the incorporation of a cultural appropriation into one's mental model. The marriage counsellor was able to mediate a three-way dialogue that enabled Michelle and Barack to understand their appropriations and use the content of the appropriations to construct meanings relevant to their own lives, and internalize the meanings into their mental models of family life. The marriage counsellor guided Michelle and Barack in the construction of meaningful thoughts and emotions from their appropriations. Michelle and Barack were able to transform their unrepresented, emotional states of mind into represented states of mind and structure them into useful thoughts about guidelines for parenting. The Obamas' opportunity for symbol formation was captured in Michelle's word 'becoming' which points to a new state of being without identifying any particular outcome. In the next section, I describe symbolization in detail.

Converting Experience to Meaning: Symbolization

Psychologists in both archetype-as-biological-entity and archetype-as-emergent-phenomenon camps agree that the capacity to symbolize is essential to a successful containment, that is, a containment in which psychological growth occurs. I do not have access to the direct communication that occurred during the Obamas' marriage counselling. I rely primarily on Michelle's autobiography in which she describes her states of mind going into and coming out of marriage counselling. She used the word 'Becoming' as the title of the autobiography, and the phrase 'Becoming Us' as title for the chapter about her and Barack's transition from married couple to parents. This is the chapter where she describes marriage counselling. She writes that chapter with a sense of emergence of a new outlook for her and Barack. So, I see 'becoming' as the symbol that emerged for the Obamas' communication during their reflection on their life as a married couple grappling with the vicissitudes of parenting. For the Obamas, the word 'becoming' functioned as a symbol that pointed to something unknown that was emerging in the couple's life.

During counselling, their projections were broken by flashes of insight into their own behaviors. What broke Michelle's projection was her flash of insight into her own behavior. It occurred to Michelle that by making her satisfaction with parenting contingent upon Barack's physical presence, she was conveying to her daughters the old patriarchal notion that life begins when the man of the house arrives home. That was a revolting idea for her as a woman who values independence. To avoid perpetuating that patriarchal limitation on her daughters, she discovered that she could undo the knot that blocked her 'becoming' a happy mother, by rearranging resources to support her lifestyle without being reliant on Barack being available on a regular basis to participate in family activities. Since that patriarchal attitude did not fit with her goal of raising her daughters to become independent women, she was willing to adjust her parenting style.

What broke Barack's projection was a flash of insight which he described in "A Promised Land". His insight came when he reflected on a promise he had made to himself that he would not be like his own father:

"I thought now about the promise I'd made to myself after Malia was born, that my kids would <u>know</u> me, that they'd grow up knowing my love for them, feeling that I had put them first" (PL 36).

To make sure that his children know him, he would have to give them priority in his life.

The marriage counsellor helped Michelle and Barack to turn their attention away from blaming each other to reflection on their own assumptions, and reconstruction of their outlooks. That enabled them to withdraw their projections and gradually work out an agreeable arrangement about how to conduct their family life by carving out roles that suit their particular family and by setting boundaries in which to function. They reconstructed their unrepresented states of mind to create a family structure suitable for accomplishing the goals they had for their family. The counsellor's mediation of their conflicted expectations led them to realize they had to restructure their states of mind, and work out the parameters of their own parenting styles to suit the circumstances of their life together.

In *"A Critical Dictionary of Jungian Analysis"* psychologist Andrew Samuels and others explain that symbols are captivating pictorial statements ... enigmatic portrayals of movement stirring the psyche. From the point of view of Analytical Psychology, a symbol is defined in terms of concept, intent, purpose and content. What follows is my interpretation of Michelle's symbol of 'becoming' in terms of concept, intent, purpose and content.

- **Concept:** The concept of 'becoming' is about passing from an old state into a new state, but without any specific articulation of what that state may be, or any logical path for getting to the new state. For the Obamas, the concept of 'becoming' was expressed in images of blending parental roles into married life. The symbol of 'becoming' was not an instrument of rationality; it was a summation of their psychological situation as new parents.
- **Intent:** The intent behind the concept of 'becoming' was to accomplish a change, but it was difficult to articulate because the Obamas had no idea what might be a mutually agreeable

solution to their conflicted expectations about parenting. They had a general intent to integrate parenting with marriage and careers, but without any idea of how to accomplish that in a manner that would be satisfactory to both.

- **Purpose:** The purpose served by the symbol of 'becoming' was to shift attention toward a new outlook on how to incorporate parenting into marriage. The purpose the symbol served was not merely to come up with an alternative point of view. Nor was the purpose of the symbol to work out a logical deriva- tion of a solution to the conflict. The purpose was to reveal a new outlook through the back-and-forth interaction of oppos- ing sides of the conflict.

- **Content:** The content of the symbol of 'becoming' turned out to be a new meaning of parenting that would bring order to the Obamas' family life. According to the dictionary of terms in Analytical Psychology, a symbol is 'pregnant with meaning' that presents a challenge to thoughts and feelings. A symbol is expressed in images that control, order and give meaning to people's lives. The symbol of 'becoming' guided the Obamas' passing from unprocessed states of mind to processed states of mind about parenting. At the point when they entered marriage counselling, their 'becoming' had been interrupted by a knot in their relationship. At the center of the knot were two sets of expectations that did not mesh with each other. To undo the knot, they had to take into consideration their daughters, child- care, kindergarten, their spousal roles, their careers, plus their household responsibilities. During the counselling, each had a flash of illumination that enabled adjustment of their outlooks on parenting.

The meaning of the symbol 'becoming' was not obvious at first. It gradu- ally found unique expression for Michelle and Barack in terms of the roles they defined for themselves as parents, along with the guardrails, rules, schedules and boundaries they worked out for the circumstances of their family life. The symbol was instrumental in controlling, ordering and giving new meaning to the Obamas' family life.

The development of the symbolic process is compatible with the psychological principle of enantiodromia. According to that principle, a given position eventually moves in the direction of its opposite, and gives evidence of a compensation at work, that is, being balanced by movement from within. The conscious attitude is being balanced by an unconscious movement. The conscious attitude and the unconscious activity are opposing sides of a compensatory relation out of which a new outlook emerges. The new outlook was not logically deduced from either of the opposing sides. The symbol of 'becoming' guided the transition from the old to the new outlook on parenting and marriage by navigating a back-and-forth movement until a synthesis of their opposing outlooks was achieved. The symbol helped the transition from old outlooks to a new outlook, not by rationality, but because it was a summing up of the Obamas' psychological situation at the time. The symbol provided a perspective from which a synthesis of the opposing outlooks on parenting could be produced. When confronted with the paradox of the symbol, the Obamas' egos were freed from the knot of their conflicting outlooks, and they were able to reflect on new possibilities from which to generate a new outlook. The symbolic process started with the Obamas 'feeling stuck' in their roles as parents. The symbolic process ended with Michelle and Barack being relieved of 'feeling stuck'. A loosening of the knot of conflicted expectations that had obstructed their parenting activity gave way to a feeling that their dissatisfaction with their psychological situation had cleared. They had created a new way of parenting that fit their particular family life. To use Michelle's word 'becoming' they set about organizing their own family life without a prescribed goal, without knowing the outcome of their 'becoming'. The outcome was a joint reconstruction of their outlook on marriage and parenting. They created a collection of guardrails, schedules, privileges that took into consideration their young children, their marriage and their life goals of public service. The marriage counsellor helped them to acknowledge and reconstruct their unconscious projections — or their conscious appropriations — and integrate the content into consciousness.

In her biography, Michelle makes an observation that appears to be a metaphor for containment:

"We should always have three friends in our lives. One who walks ahead who we look up to and follow, one who walks beside us who is with us every step of our journey, and then one who we reach back and bring along after we've cleared the way." - Michelle Obama (BMO 216)

Michelle's observation about friendship can be interpreted as a psychological metaphor for the containment model. The theme of the containment model is that a mind needs another mind to grow psychologically. The mind of the contained depends on the mind of the container for growth. Michelle's three friends can be characterized in terms of their psychological maturity and capability to function as container. The friend who walks ahead of her has already developed the capacity to function as a container. The friend who is travelling beside her is currently functioning as a container. The friend who walks behind is someone for whom she will become a container. Michelle's observation is telling because it communicates the message that containment is a normal activity that is common across humanity. People who are more psychologically mature tend to act as ladders for pulling up those who are less psychologically mature. Parents. Mentors. Teachers. Pastoral guides. Coaches. They may not use the language of psychology, but they have strong intuition about the principles, and they know how to function as containers.

Call To Action: Take Away A Portable Understanding

The Obamas-Counsellor containment is a story as old as the human species. A young married couple engages in a mind-to-mind connection with an experienced marriage counsellor about a conflict they cannot resolve by themselves. The counsellor mediates a dialogue about the transition from marriage to parenthood until a solution emerges. This chapter is a call to action for readers to take away a portable understanding of the commensal mode of containment. To help readers, I offer the following summary of how the marriage counsellor interacted with the Obamas in converting the Obamas' experience of parental anxieties into meaningful thoughts and emotions about family relationships.

- **Mode:** The Obamas and the counsellor had a commensal mode of containment.
- **Roles:** Michelle and Barack were the contained, while the Marriage Counsellor was the container. They did not switch roles during their containment.
- **Symmetry:** The relationship between the Obamas and the counsellor was asymmetrical. There was a gradient of psychological maturity about parenting. The Obamas were novices at parenting, while the counsellor was an expert in the matters related to parenting and marriage.
- **Psychological Frame:** In a containment, the psychological frame is made up of a purpose, a time boundary and a space boundary. The purpose of the frame was the provision of counselling to help the Obamas manage their unrepresented states of mind related to the mix of parenting and marriage. The space boundary of the frame was the marriage counsellor's office in Illinois. The time boundary, that is, the frequency of meetings and the duration of the counselling were not stated in the Obamas' biographies.
- **Dialectical Narrative:** At the beginning of marriage counseling, Michelle and Barack had their parenting roles lodged in their heads. As the counselling progressed, the containment became an activity that happened less in their heads and more in the psychological space between the participants. Their minds inter-penetrated each other's internal world. One contained narrative came from Michelle; another contained narrative came from Barack. The container's narrative came from the marriage counsellor. The third narrative indicated that both external reality and internal reality changed for the Obamas. Their external reality changed from conflicting behaviors to a jointly prepared blueprint for their parenting style, complete with guidelines, schedules and new parental behaviors. Their internal reality changed in the sense that they relinquished outlooks about their parents behaviors being prototypes for their own marriage. They developed a sense of their own agency as parents. They came to regard parenting in their marriage as an arrangement that they had to work out for themselves. Family life was their responsibility to craft.

- **Psychological Growth / Harm**: The psychological frame proved to be adequate for psychological growth because it enabled them to convert unrepresented states of mind about the responsibilities of parenthood into structured represented states of mind regarding the incorporation of parenting into their marriage. The marriage counsellor helped the Obamas to achieve psychological growth from their relationship. They developed a new sense of agency that enabled them to craft a style of parenting that fit their particular family life. The new parenting arrangement that emerged freed Michelle from the generational tyranny of expecting to have all family members present at fixed dinnertimes as a prerequisite for acceptable parenting. It also freed Barack of the guilt about not being physically present at prescribed times, and allowed him the flexibility to pursue a political career which required him to be away from home to function as a senator.

After the Containment Ended

After the containment, Michelle adjusted to being a political wife by actively supporting Barack in campaigns, while he adjusted to family life defined by guardrails and boundaries which they had jointly established for their family. Barack progressed from Illinois senator to United States senator. Later, he became President of the United States and served two terms from 2008 to 2016. Michelle served as First Lady of the United States. When they left the White House, each wrote a memoir. The Obamas are joint founders of the Obama Foundation which is a non-profit organization established in Chicago in 2014. That Foundation established the Barack Obama Presidential Center which operates a scholarship program in the Harris School of Public Policy at the University of Chicago.

Years after the containment, this is what Barack said to Essence magazine about the result of his and Michelle's parenting:

> *"The great thing about the girls is they've got a wonderful role model in their mom. They've seen how Michelle and I interact – not only the love but also the respect that I show*

to their mom. So I think they have pretty high expectations about how relationships should be, and that gives me some confidence about the future."

– Essence magazine 2013

Talk show host, Oprah Winfrey, interviewed the Obamas 2017, when she asked about their secret to a successful marriage. Here is Barack's response:

"Obviously I couldn't have done anything that I've done without Michelle... not only has she been a great first lady, she is just my rock," he said. *"I count on her in so many ways every single day."*

– Oprah interview 2017

Once the Obamas adjusted to the reality that they have the latitude, and the responsibility, to craft the boundaries and guardrails suitable for parenting within the parameters of their particular family, their marriage has been a source of inspiration for others.

Sources

The sources of information that contribute to this chapter are:
- *"Becoming"* by Michelle Obama
- *"A Promised Land"* by Barack Obama
- *"Barack and Michelle: Portrait of an American Marriage"* by Christopher Andersen
- *"Barack and Michelle Obama: Biography of the Ultimate Power Couple"* by Matthew Wesley
- *"Containing States of Mind"* by Duncan Cartwright
- *"Projection and Re-Collection in Jungian Psychology"* by Marie-Louise von Franz
- *"A Critical Dictionary of Jungian Analysis"* by Andrew Samuels, Bani Shorter and Fred Plaut
- *"Symbolization: Representation and Communication"* by James Rose (editor).

CHAPTER 11

A Commensal Mode of Containment Involving: Emmanuelle Charpentier & Jennifer Doudna

"By studying a phenomenon that evolution had taken a billion or so years to perfect in bacteria, they turned nature's miracle into a tool for humans."

— Walter Isaacson

Many thousand years ago, bacteria became proficient at defending themselves against attack from viruses. Humans are only recently catching up with that proficiency. Two people involved in the catching up are Emmanuelle Charpentier and Jennifer Doudna. One day when Charpentier was a young girl growing up in France, she and her mother were walking past the Institut Pasteur, a research center for infectious diseases. She informed her mother that she would work at the Institut when she grew up. About that time, Doudna was a young girl growing up in Hawaii, when her father gave her a book about the double helix shape of DNA written by James Watson. The book inspired her to pursue studies about DNA and RNA. Charpentier and Doudna grew up to become scientists. They met for the first time in Puerto Rico, at the 2011 American Society for Microbiology Conference, where they agreed to combine their knowledge in a research project aimed at protecting humans from viruses. That was the beginning of a professional relationship that set in motion a series of scientific experiments which led to the development of a viral-defense system, known as CRISPR-Cas9, a gene editing tool capable of changing the genome of humanity. In the year 2020, Charpentier and Doudna met in Stockholm, Sweden, to accept the jointly awarded Nobel Prize in Chemistry for their invention of the viral-defense system.

My reading of Walter Isaacson's book "The Code Breaker" is that Emmanuelle Charpentier and Jennifer Doudna engaged in a scientific collaboration that had the psychological underpinnings of a commensal mode of containment. The relationship was symmetrical because Charpentier and Doudna were both respected scientists, about the same age. They chose to work with each other, and neither was dependent on the other. During the containment, they switched roles. In the first set of experiments, Charpentier was the contained and Doudna the container. In a later set of experiments, Doudna became the contained. In the final round of experiments, Doudna was back to being the container. The commensal mode of containment is the mode that offers the most potential for psychological growth. Although they did not refer to their collaboration in psychological terms, their communications and behaviors point to a commensal mode of containment, in which reciprocal exchanges enabled them to conduct their project along a transformational path from scientists to inventors. To prepare readers for their scientific collaboration, I provide background information about the lives of Charpentier and Doudna, in the next two sections.

Background Information about Emmanuelle Charpentier

Emmanuelle Charpentier was born in 1968 in Juvisy-sur-Orge, a city in northern France. She grew up in a suburb on the river Seine, south of Paris (CB 119). She studied microbiology and genetics at the Pierre and Marie Curie University in Paris. Her father was in charge of the neighborhood park system and her mother was an administrative nurse in a local psychiatric hospital (CB 119). In school, Charpentier liked studying science subjects as well as the arts. She felt at home in a scientific laboratory because it provided a quiet temple for her individual persistence and contemplation. Isaacson quotes her as having said:

"I wanted to create knowledge, not just learn it" (CB 121).

For a career, Charpentier considered two alternatives: either becoming a professional dancer or a scientist. What those two professions have in common is that both require a combination of rigorous discipline, persistence and creativity. Because the career of a dancer is limited in years, she chose to become a scientist (CB 119). Her childhood prediction to her mother was realized when, as a graduate student of the Pasteur Institute, she was awarded a research doctorate for a PhD project in molecular biology.

Charpentier leads a wanderer's lifestyle. Between the years 1992 and 2011, she had lived in seven cities in five countries. Frequent moving made her feel like a foreigner most of the time. In her view, the sense of detachment or slight alienation made her better at figuring out the forces at play. That helped her to be prepared for the unexpected. In 2009 she was moving from a laboratory in Vienna, Austria to a laboratory in Umea, Sweden (CB 123). At the time, there were several scientists conducting research about Clustered Regularly Interspaced Short Palindromic Repeats (CRISPR), which is a biological system found in bacteria. They were interested in Cas9, a protein that plays an important role in how bacteria defend themselves from viruses that attack them. While developing a project about CRISPR-Cas9, Charpentier was invited to make a presentation at a scientific conference. At the time, Charpentier was looking for someone with knowledge of RNA structure. She had been working on CRISPR and she could not figure out the role of tracrRNA, but she realized that it was located in the vicinity of the CRISPR spacers (CB 125). She had a hypothesis that the tracrRNA directs the creation of short crRNAs, but she had not conducted experiments to test that hypothesis. The researchers in her Vienna laboratory had informed her that the absence of tracrRNA meant that crRNAs were not produced. According to Isaacson, Charpentier stated:

"I became obsessed with this tracrRNA, I am stubborn. It was important for me to follow up. I said 'We have to go for it! I want someone to look at it.'" (CB 125).

There was no one in her Vienna laboratory who had the time and the inclination to pursue tracrRNA. That is the drawback in being a wandering professor ... she leaves her students behind, and they move on to other projects. Charpentier considered doing the experiments herself, but at the time, she was busy moving from a laboratory in Vienna to a laboratory in Sweden. Working with a small team that included Krzysztof Chylinski, she discovered that the CRISPR-Cas9 system accomplished its viral-defense mission using only three components: tracrRNA, crRNA and the Cas9 enzyme (CB 125). The tracrRNA took long strands of RNA and processed them into small crRNAs that were targeted at specific sequences in an attacking virus. Charpentier's team prepared a paper for *Nature* magazine which was scheduled to be published in March 2011 (CB 126). She also presented her findings at a CRISPR conference in October 2011 in the Netherlands.

Carpentier had been stressed during her presentation because she had not yet figured out what happened to tracrRNA after it helped to create crRNA. Was the work of tracrRNA done by then? Or did the two little RNAs stick together when it came time to guide the Cas protein to cut up an invading virus? One member of the audience asked her directly, *"Do the three elements stay together as a complex?"* Charpentier tried to deflect the question. *"I tried to laugh and be very confusing on purpose,"* she told Walter Isaacson (CB 126). The issue of what Charpentier knew when she conducted her experiments might seem trivial. However, it led to a set of disputes that shows how CRISPR researchers can be very competitive about who deserves credit for each small advance in science (CB 126). The fact that the tracrRNA did in fact stick around and play an important role in cleavage would be among the discoveries published in the seminal 2012 paper that Charpentier would write with Doudna. But to Doudna's annoyance, Charpentier would sometimes imply, years later, that she already knew this fact in 2011 (CB 126). Charpentier admitted to Walter Isaacson that the 2011 *Nature* paper did not describe the full role of the tracrRNA: *"It seemed clear to me that the tracrRNA needed to continue to be associated with the crRNA, but there were some details we didn't fully understand, so we didn't put this in the paper."* (CB 126). Instead, Charpentier decided to save writing about the full tracrRNA function until she could find a convincing way to prove it experimentally. Charpentier had studied the CRISPR system in living cells. To get to the next step would require a biochemist who knows how to isolate each chemical component in a test tube and figure out precisely how each one works. That is why Charpentier wanted to meet Doudna, who was scheduled to speak at the March 2011 conference of the American Society for Microbiology in Puerto Rico. *"I knew we were both going to attend, ... and I put in my mind that I would find a chance to talk with her"* (CB 127). Emmanuelle Charpentier met Jennifer Doudna in March 2011, in San Juan, Puerto Rico, where they were both scheduled to make presentations at the annual American Society for Microbiology Conference.

Background Information about Jennifer Doudna

Jennifer Doudna was born in February 1964 in Washington D. C. Her parents, Martin and Dorothy, moved the family to Hawaii when she was seven years old. Feeling like an outsider among the Polynesians in the town of Hilo, Doudna retreated into books and developed a defensive layer (CB 4). A turning point came for her when her family relocated from Hilo to the mountain slopes of Mauna Loa. She was more comfortable with the racial mix of students in the new school. She made friends and began exploring plants and insects in the environment. She enjoyed horse-riding, hiking, soccer and exploring nature. To encourage her interest in science, her father gave her a copy of James Watson's book *"The Double Helix"* which aroused her scientific curiosity (CB 7).

Doudna's career was influenced by the realization that the shape and structure of chemical molecules determine the roles they can play in science (CB 8). Motivated by a curiosity about how nature works coupled with a sense of competition about inventions, she decided to become a scientist. Undeterred by her high school guidance counsellor's opinion that girls do not do science, Doudna enrolled in Pomona College in California in 1981, to take advantage of their well-developed chemistry program (CB 29 - 31). In 1985, Doudna was accepted in Harvard's

Department of Molecular Biology. Realizing that she would need to learn more about structural biology, in order to understand how RNA molecules reproduce, she decided to do her doctoral work at Harvard University, where the research focus was shifting from DNA to RNA. Specifically, the focus was on whether RNA had the chemical ability to replicate itself (CB 45). Having earned her PhD in 1989, Doudna decided to do postdoctoral work on the structure of the RNA molecule at the University of Colorado, where she conducted research to figure out the three-dimensional structure of RNA (CB 55). There she encountered a colleague who was using X-ray crystallography to study the structure of proteins. He joined her research to focus on the structure of RNA. Another colleague showed her how to plunge crystals into liquid nitrogen to preserve the RNA structure when the crystals are exposed to X-ray (CB 57).

In 1995, her father's death brought her great sadness because he had been very supportive of her development of a scientific career. His death coincided with a major scientific success. She and her colleague Jamie Cate discovered how a molecule allows RNA to pack helices together to create a three-dimensional shape that enabled the RNA to be self-splicing (CB 60). Just as the DNA double-helix structure enables it to transmit genetic information, the RNA structure enables it to slice, splice and replicate itself (CB 60). This discovery led to the speculation, in the scientific community, that RNA could be used to build a tool to edit genes. In the summer of 2000, Doudna and her colleague Cate were married in Hawaii and soon afterwards, they moved to California, where Doudna's study of RNA structure led her to take an interest in viruses (CB 63 – 65). She was interested in how the RNA in some viruses allow them to hijack the protein-making machinery of cells, and how RNA is used to fight off viruses. She published her results in 2006, in *Science* journal. That led to the speculation that RNA might have the virus-fighting capacity to fight off infections in humans. In March 2011, Doudna was scheduled to make a presentation at the annual American Society for Microbiology Conference in Puerto Rico. That is where she met Emmanuelle Charpentier. In the next section, I describe the activation of the inventor archetype in the context of archetype as biological entity, to explain how Charpentier and Doudna engaged each other through the processes of projection and introjection to convert their laboratory experiences into scientific meaning in the area of human defense against viruses.

Converting Experience to Meaning: Projection & Introjection

When psychologists define archetype as a biological entity, they regard it as an ancestral heritage of human experience accumulated over many generations and located in collective unconsciousness. When an archetype is defined as a biological entity, the processes identified for converting life's experiences into meaning are projection and introjection. A projection is an evacuation of unconscious content from the psyche due to an unbearable state of mind. Initially, there was a projection of an idealization of a scientific inventor from Charpentier to Doudna. The unconscious projection arose from the inventor archetype, that is, an ancestral heritage of human experience about scientific invention that humans have accumulated over multiple generations.

When they met, Charpentier informed Doudna "*I've been thinking about contacting you about a collaboration*" (CB 127). Doudna told biographer Isaacson that when they met in the coffee shop at the hotel where the conference was being held, "*I was instantly struck by her intensity but also her sly humor. I immediately liked her*" (CB 127). Next day, Charpentier and Doudna had lunch together and went for a walk in the streets of San Juan. When the discussion turned to the Cas9 protein, Charpentier became excited, "*We have to figure out exactly how it works … What's the exact mechanism it uses to cut DNA?*" (CB 127). Charpentier was taken by Doudna's seriousness and attention to detail. She told Doudna "*I think it's going to be fun to work with you*" (CB 127). Doudna was moved by Charpentier's intensity. "*Somehow, just the way she said that it would be fun to work with me made a chill run down my back,*" Doudna recalled (CB 127 -128). One enticement was that it was just the sort of detective project that gave Doudna a sense of purpose: the hunt for the key to one of life's basic mysteries (CB 128).

The behaviors and communications between Charpentier and Doudna were related to their expectations of inventing a scientific tool to manage change of the human genome, indicating that the inventor archetype was activated. Located in collective unconsciousness, the inventor archetype is made up of an ancestral heritage of human experience related to the acquisition of knowledge about the science and art of invention over multiple generations. Activation of the inventor archetype indicates a forceable evacuation of a projection from Charpentier's mind to Doudna's mind. The content of Charpentier's projection was raw experience of emotions, images and memories about the connection between viruses and the human genome. They were incomprehensible to her and were therefore evacuated as an unbearable state of mind. Doudna became a willing carrier of the projection. She was eager to participate in the scientific project whose goal was to invent a defense for humans against viruses.

In that early encounter, a projection was cast from Charpentier's mind to Doudna's mind. It was the Swiss psychologist Marie-Louise von Franz who wrote that wherever known reality stops, where we touch the unknown, there we project an archetypal image. Charpentier wanted to create new knowledge, not just learn existing knowledge. (CB 121) She had reached the edge, not just of her personal known reality, but also the known reality of the scientific community, with regard to viruses. At the time, humanity had no viral defense system; the scientific community was researching possibilities. Charpentier's obsession was about finding out how RNA works and putting it to use in fighting viruses. She had published results of her 2011 CRISPR experiments, but when asked about the mechanism for splicing DNA, she acknowledged to Isaacson that she deliberately offered an evasive answer. She had a hypothesis, but deflected the question because she had not conducted any experiment to test her hypothesis. Moreover, she did not believe she had sufficient knowledge of RNA to compose adequate experiments. Her scientific angst about RNA led her to seek out Doudna, who was known for her RNA expertise. What triggered the projection was Charpentier's anxiety about her desire to invent a viral-defense tool coupled with the uncertainty about whether she had enough of a background in RNA structure to be able design relevant experiments to adequately test her hypothesis. Charpentier described herself as being 'obsessed with tracrRNA' (CB 125). When Charpentier met Doudna, the two scientists soon realized that they have expertise about topics, microbiology and biochemistry (CB 183), that both have bearing on viral defense. They bonded on a shared passion about inventing a way for humans to defend themselves against viral attack. They agreed to collaborate on CRISPR experiments. They began their collaboration with Charpentier in the role of contained while Doudna played the role of container. Charpentier's experience in cellular biology and Doudna's experience in biochemistry complemented each other and formed the scientific basis of their collaboration. CRISPR research needed a combination of the two topics (CB 183). Doudna identified Martin Jinek, a structural biologist, as her laboratory assistant. Charpentier identified Krzysztof Chylinski, a molecular biologist, as her laboratory assistant. Together, these four people were able to invent a tool for viral-defense.

In the context of archetype as biological entity, projection is followed by introjection, if the containment is to be successful. Introjection is a transformation of an unbearable state of mind to a bearable state of mind, followed by its integration into the conscious realm of the psyche. The process of introjection occurred in a back-and-forth dialogue between Charpentier and Doudna, across a number of experiments. The dialogue involved both conscious and unconscious communication that together enabled a recognition of the unprocessed state of mind about viruses and a gradual transformation to a bearable state of mind of how to defend humans against viruses. To explain how introjection occurred during the collaboration, I describe the three rounds of experiments in which Charpentier and Doudna changed roles in a back-and-forth exchange of being supportive and critical of each other's scientific hypotheses. For those readers who do not care for the scientific explanation of the three rounds of experiments, I suggest skipping the next three sub-sections.

First Round of Experiments: Charpentier is Contained & Doudna is Container: In the first round of experiments, Charpentier played the role of contained, while Doudna played the role of container. From her location in Berkeley, Doudna initiated a series of Skype calls that included Charpentier, Chylinski and Jinek to work out a strategy for figuring out the mechanisms of CASPR-Cas9. Isaacson likened the collaboration to a miniature United Nations: a Berkeley professor from Hawaii, with her post-doctoral researcher from the Check Republic, and a Parisian professor in Sweden with her Polish-born, post-doctoral researcher working in Austria (CB 129). The CASPR project became a 24-hour per day operation, divided into two 12-hour shifts. Jinek would do an experiment in Berkeley, and at the end of his shift, he would send results via e-mail to Chylinski in Vienna. Chylinski would start his shift by reading Jinek's e-mail. Then, there would be a Skype call for the team to decide the next step. Chylinski would perform the next experiment during his shift and send Jinek the results while Jinek was sleeping. When Jinek awoke there would be results in his inbox. At first Charpentier and Doudna joined the Skype calls once or twice per month, but the pace quickened in July 2011, when Charpentier and Chylinski flew to Berkeley for the annual CRISPR conference. They had bonded in Skype meetings, but this was the first time that Jinek and Chylinski met in person (CB 129). In Berkeley, the four scientists used their face-to-face meeting for a brainstorming strategy to figure out exactly what molecules were necessary for a CRISPR system to cut the DNA of a virus. Doudna informed Isaacson:

> "There's nothing like sitting in a room with people and seeing their reactions to things and having a chance to bat around ideas face to face. That's been the cornerstone to every collaboration that we've had, even those where we are conducting a lot of the work by electronic communication" (CB 131).

Jinek and Chylinski were initially unable to make CRISPR-Cas9 chop up the DNA of a virus in a test tube. They had been trying to make it work with just two components: the Cas9 enzyme and the crRNA. In theory, the crRNA would guide the Cas9 to the virus target, which would then get chopped up. But the experiments did not produce the expected results (CB 131). Doudna had been invited to collaborate on the CRISPR project because of her expertise in the structure of RNA. Although the team members jointly brainstormed a strategy for discovering the role of RNA, it seems reasonable that Doudna would have had a significant influence on the choice and construction of the experiments. When that first round of experiments did not work, Doudna must have been befuddled. She had not offered an alternative experiment. The scientific doubt and uncertainty that initially plagued Charpentier must have shifted to Doudna when that first round of experiments failed to produce expected results. That is when the team decided to take a new approach. Doudna is a seasoned researcher, who at a logical level in her mind, would know that experiments are just that ... trials which may or may not work. However, Doudna must have wondered if her RNA expertise — for which she was invited to participate in the project — was adding any value to the team.

Second Round of Experiments: Charpentier is Container & Doudna is Contained: For the second round of experiments, Charpentier and Doudna switched roles. Doudna became the contained and Charpentier became the container. The team turned its attention to the experiment Charpentier had conducted in 2011. At that time, Charpentier had a hypothesis about the role of RNA, but she had not tested it. The team turned its attention to exploring Charpentier's 2011 hypothesis. Her untested hypothesis was brought to the fore and the team used it as the point of departure for designing their second round of experiments. This was when tracrRNA entered the project. In Charpentier's 2011 paper, she had shown that tracrRNA was required for producing the guide. She later said she suspected it played a larger, ongoing role, though that possibility had not been part of her experiments. The team used Charpentier's hypothesis to build a second round of experiments. As a preliminary test of her hypothesis, Chylinski decided to throw tracrRNA into his test tube mix. It worked ... the three-component complex chopped up the target DNA. Jinek told Doudna about the result: "*Without the tracrRNA, the crRNA guide does not bind to the Cas9 enzyme*" (CB 131). After that breakthrough, the team composed detailed experiments to demonstrate the mechanism by which the DNA was targeted and sliced. Doudna and Charpentier became more involved in the daily work. The team was mindful that it was headed to an important invention: determining the essential components of a CRISPR viral-defense system (CB 131). During the second round of experiments, Chylinski and Jinek sent e-mail results back and forth, progressively adding small features to the viral-defense tool. Charpentier and Doudna joined the increasingly frequent strategy calls. They were able to discover the precise mechanism of each of the three essential components of the CRISPR-Cas9 complex (CB 131 – 132). The crRNA contained a 20-letter sequence that acted as a set of coordinates to guide the complex to a piece of DNA with a similar sequence.

The tracrRNA, which had helped create the crRNA, then had the additional role of acting like a scaffold that held the other components in just the right place, when they attached to the target DNA. Then the Cas9 enzyme began slicing the DNA (CB 132). This is how Doudna described the results. The protein, an enzyme called Cas9, can be programmed to find viruses and cut them up. Over billions of years, bacteria evolved this weird way to protect themselves against viruses. And it was adaptable; every time a new virus emerged, the bacteria learned how to recognize it and beat it back (CB 132). It became clear that this little system, had enormous potential application: the crRNA guide could be modified to target any DNA sequence. It was programmable. It could become an editing tool. Isaacson quotes Doudna as saying:

> "Once we figured out the components of the CASPR-Cas9 assembly, we realized that we could add a different crRNA and get it to cut any different DNA sequence we chose. ... It wasn't just some gradual process where it slowly dawned on us. It was an oh-my-God moment" (CB 133).

When Jinek showed Doudna his data demonstrating that it is possible to program Cas9 with different guide RNAs to cut DNA wherever one desired, she declared:

> "Oh my God, this could be a powerful tool for gene-editing" (CB 134).

The scientists realized they had developed a means to rewrite the human genome ... the code of life. The second round of experiments, which was based on Charpentier's hypothesis, worked well. That round of experiments created new knowledge. It also raised a new question: what is the minimum RNA necessary to cut up DNA? The next step was to figure out if the CASPR system could be made simpler. If so, it might become not just a gene-editing tool, but one that would be much easier to program and cheaper than existing methods (CB 134). Jinek was experimenting to determine the minimum requirements for the crRNA that served as a guide to the tracrRNA that clamped it to the target DNA. He asked Doudna: What RNA is essential for cutting up DNA? Doudna had a profound understanding of the structure of RNA and an almost childlike joy in figuring out the ways it worked (CB 134). The question intrigued her. That was the kind of question that aroused her scientific curiosity. She delighted in figuring out nature's mysteries. That would become the topic of the third experiment.

Third Round of Experiments: Charpentier is Contained & Doudna is Container: In the third round of experiments, they switched roles. Charpentier was back to being the contained and Doudna became the container. Doudna's realization that the team could add a different crRNA and get it to cut any different DNA sequence put her back into the role of container. The team continued to strategize in Skype meetings, while working shifts that alternate between Europe and the U. S. A. As the team brainstormed, it became clear they could link two RNAs together fusing the tail of one to the head of the other in a way that would keep the combined molecule functional. Their goal was to engineer a single RNA molecule that would have the guide information on one end and the binding handle on the other end. That invention is what they ended up calling 'single-guide RNA' or sgRNA (CB 134). This is how Doudna describes the occasion:

> "It was one of those moments in science that just comes to you. I had this chill and these little hairs on my neck standing up. In that moment, the two of us realized that this curiosity-driven, fun project had this powerful implication that could change the direction of the project profoundly" (CB 134 – 135).

Doudna urged Jinek to begin work right away on fusing these two RNA molecules to work in a single guide for Cas9. Jinek rushed to order the necessary chemical supplies. Jinek had discussed the idea with Chylinski and they quickly designed a series of experiments. Once they had figured out what parts of the two RNAs could be deleted and how they could be connected, it took only 3 weeks to make the single-guide RNA that worked (CB 135). It was immediately obvious that the single guide RNA would make CRISPR-Cas9 a more versatile, easy-to-use and reprogrammable tool for gene-editing. What made the single guide system particularly significant was that it was a human-made invention, not merely a discovery of a natural phenomenon (CB 135). With those three rounds of experiments, the Charpentier-Doudna collaboration had produced two important results: (CB 135).

- The first was the finding that tracrRNA played an essential role, not just in creating the crRNA guide, but more important, holding it together with Cas9 enzyme and binding it all to the target DNA for the cutting process. In other words, they had invented a gene-editing tool that can be programmed to find viruses and cut them up.
- The second finding was the invention of a way to fuse two RNA molecules together into a single-guide RNA. The implication of this invention was that they were able to make the gene-editing tool function faster and cheaper.

Isaacson's observation was apt ... Doudna and Charpentier were able to turn nature's miracle into a tool for humans (CB 135). To write the scholarly paper about their CASPR-Cas9 experiment results, the four scientists used the same round-the-clock collaborative methods they had employed in their experiments. Jinek worked during the day in California, handed things off with a late-night Skype call as dawn was breaking in Europe, and then Charpentier and Chylinski would take the lead for the next 12 hours. On June 8, 2012, Doudna e-mailed the manuscript to the editors of Science journal. Doudna and Charpentier were listed as the principal investigators leading the laboratories. Although there were other researchers working on CASPR-Cas9, this was the first time researchers had isolated the essential components of the viral-defense system and invented their biochemical mechanisms. In addition, the manuscript contained another potentially useful invention: the single-guide RNA. The paper suggested that CASPR-Cas9 could be useful for gene-editing in humans. (CB 137).

During their 14-month period of containment, Charpentier and Doudna had reversed roles twice. Their project marked a period of alternating projection and introjection as they took turns at being the lead designer of experiments. My interpretation is that by switching roles, each round of experiments got the best of scientific knowledge that each had to offer. In each round of experiments, Charpentier and Doudna engaged each other in a dialogue that allowed them to convert their unprocessed states of mind to processed states of mind about a viral defense system.

They engaged each other in an ongoing dialogue about differing scientific points of view, with the result that there was a shift of attention from each preceding round of experiments to the next round of experiments. Throughout the project, the involuntary casting of projections followed by introjections harnessed their desire for creating new knowledge and channeled it into scientific invention. Charpentier and Doudna were able to mediate dialogues that enabled them to construct meanings from the contents of their projections and integrate the meanings into the conscious aspects of their psyches. It is because the two scientists were capable of constructing meanings from projections that they were able to guide each other in the construction of scientific meaning as the rounds of experiments progressed during their project. The minds of Charpentier and Doudna were engaged in helping each other to metabolize their unprocessed emotional states about viral-defense and structure them into useful gene-editing thoughts. In the next section, I describe the activation of the inventor archetype in the context of emergent phenomenon. Then I explain how Charpentier and Doudna used the processes of appropriation and internalization to convert their laboratory experiences into scientific meaning as they invented a viral-defense system to protect humans from viruses.

Context of Archetype as Emergent Phenomenon: Appropriation & Internalization

When an archetype is defined in the context of emergent phenomenon, the archetype is seen as an emergent property of a dynamic developmental system that is made up of the human brains, human actions, the society's external environment and the narrative competence of humans involved. When viewing an archetype as an emergent phenomenon, the means for converting life experience to meaning are appropriation and internalization. The behaviors and communications between Charpentier and Doudna were related to their scientific research aimed at inventing a viral-defense system. This indicates that the inventor archetype was activated. The inventor archetype emerged from a complex system that was made up of scientists' brains, scientists' actions, the scientific community's knowledge of viruses and humans, as well as the narratives that researchers composed about their lives as scientists. In the context of archetype as emergent phenomenon, the inventor archetype has no specific location; it is pervasive across society's cultural environment. Activation of the inventor archetype indicates that Charpentier and Doudna had conscious appropriations from the inventor archetype located in the external world. The contents of their appropriations were processed experience made up of meaningful thoughts, emotions, images and memories about a scientist's role in research drawn from the cultural environment. In the three rounds of experiments, Charpentier and Doudna were able to sustain a dialectical interaction that enabled both to use the content of their appropriations to construct scientific meanings relevant to their own lives, and internalize the meanings into their mental scientific models. In using their appropriations to design rounds of experiments in search of a viable viral-defense system, they demonstrated their capabilities in the construction of meaning from the contents of their appropriations. They were able to guide each other in the construction of scientifically meaningful thoughts from the contents of their appropriations. Through their engagement with the social-symbolic world of science, they were able to transform their appropriations and structure them into useful thoughts about inventing a viral-defense system. With each round of experiments, one scientist helped the other wade through the images of an appropriation, parse unprocessed states of mind, and internalize processed states of mind. The inventor archetype was activated at the level of psychic complexity where Charpentier and Doudna were transitioning from researchers to inventors. The success of the research project indicates that the scientists achieved a degree of narrative competence that enabled them to connect past and present scientific experiences, and combine them into a meaningful dialogue about protecting humans from viruses. In the following section, I offer my interpretation of the symbolization that occurred in the communication between Charpentier and Doudna during their project.

Converting Experience to Meaning: Symbolization

While I do not have access to transcripts of communications between Charpentier and Doudna, I do have access to their communications with biographer Walter Isaacson, who interviewed both scientists about their interaction during the project. After interviewing them about their interaction during the project, Isaacson makes the following observation:

> "By studying a phenomenon that evolution had taken a billion or so years to perfect in bacteria, they turned nature's miracle into a tool for humans" (CB 135).

I believe the expression 'they turned nature's miracle into a tool for humans' captures the symbol that emerged during the interaction between Charpentier and Doudna. The symbolic process is an experience in images. Before the project began, Charpentier and Doudna had mental images of how bacteria are able to ward off invading viruses. Over the course of about a billion years, bacteria evolved the ability to protect themselves from viruses. Scientists regard that as nature's miracle because bacteria evolved the capability on their own, without help from scientists. Charpentier and Doudna hoped that science could provide humans with a tool for their own defense against viruses. Their opportunity for symbol formation was captured in images from the expression 'they turned nature's miracle into a tool for humans' which points to a new state of being without specifying what the outcome will be, or the means of achieving an outcome. The symbolic form of the expression 'turn nature's miracle into a tool for humans' can be related to their raw emotional states that represented their confused ideas about defending humans against viruses, when the project began. In "A Critical Dictionary of Jungian Analysis" psychologist Andrew Samuels explains that, from the point of view of Analytical Psychology, symbol is defined in terms of concept, intent, purpose and content. Here, I interpret the symbolic expression 'they turned nature's miracle into a tool for humans' in terms of concept, intent, purpose and content.

- **Concept:** The concept behind the symbol 'they turned nature's miracle into a tool for humans' is one of rendering nature's miracle into something new, but without any specific notion of what the new thing may be, or any logical route to achieve something new. For Charpentier and Doudna, the concept was expressed in images of scientific utility for humanity. The symbol of 'turned nature's miracle into a tool for humans' was not an instrument of rationality; it was a summation of the psychological situation of Charpentier and Doudna at that point in their lives.

- **Intent:** Behind the symbol 'turning nature's miracle into a tool for humans' was an intent to accomplish a change in how humans fight off viruses, but it was difficult to articulate because the end state of the change was unknown. There was a general intent to experiment with DNA and RNA, but without any specific idea of how to invent a tool to defend humans from attack by viruses.

- **Purpose:** In the interaction between the two scientists, the symbol of 'turning nature's miracle into a tool for humans' served the purpose of focusing attention on collecting the relevant knowledge and experience necessary to invent a tool for addressing the conflict between humans and viruses. The purpose the symbol served was not merely to come up with a new version of something that already existed. Nor was the purpose of the symbol to work out a logical derivation from nature's way of warding off viruses that attack. The purpose was to invent something new through the back-and-forth interaction between the scientific knowledge contributed by Charpentier in the area of microbiology, and by Doudna in the area of biochemistry.

- **Content:** The content of the symbol was a collection of universal scientific images. Some of the images were in the projections cast from the minds of Doudna and Charpentier, while others were images from the scientific community. The content of symbols are enigmatic images of something stirring in the psyche. The source of these images was traceable to the archetype of inventor. The symbol found a unique expression for Charpentier and Doudna as they engaged in three rounds of experiments which enabled them to harness the energy of the inventor archetype and direct it to the invention of a tool that performs a new service for humanity. According to the dictionary of terms in Analytical Psychology, a symbol is 'pregnant with meaning' that presents a challenge to thoughts and feelings. The meaning of the symbol of turning nature's miracle into a tool for humans was not immediately obvious. The meaning derived from the symbol came into view as Charpentier and Doudna switched roles of being contained and container during rounds of experiments. The scientific images of the symbol guided Charpentier and Doudna from unprocessed states of mind to processed states of mind about how to defend humans from viruses. By taking turns at being the lead in designing experiments, they took turns at leading the introjection. They took turns at sorting out and finding expression for each other's unprocessed state of mind. The symbol was instrumental in guiding the transition from the path of research to the path of invention, not by rationality, but by containing the psychological situation of Charpentier and Doudna. They invented the means to rewrite the human genome ... the code of life. They invented a tool that is scientifically sound, has the capability to defend humans from viruses, as well as the potential for changing the genes of future generations. In the process of inventing the viral-defense tool, they transformed their roles from researchers to inventors.

The symbolic process began with the two scientists feeling stuck in a research project. They wanted to compete in the scientific race for viral defense, but they did not have an immediate solution. They would have to conduct experiments to explore the hypotheses they had in mind, and there was no guarantee the experiments would work. The symbolic process ended with them harnessing the energy of the activated inventor archetype in collaboration to take a new path going forward as inventors. The relationship between Charpentier and Doudna is an example of the commensal mode of containment, the mode that offers the greatest potential for psychological growth. During a 14-month scientific project, they engaged each other in a relationship as co-inventors. These two people demonstrate Cartwright's endorsement of Bion's view that the mind is always in transit and in a state of becoming something else (CSM 2). Their interaction epitomizes the notion that reality is mediated through the mind of another. During the period of containment, they switched roles. Without planning to do so, they naturally took turns at being contained and container. The switching indicates that they were mediating each other's reality. Each mind was dependent on the other mind for scientific meaning, and the derivation of scientific meaning was always in flux.

Charpentier and Doudna used their encounter to transform their passion for creating new knowledge, their sense of competition, and their combined expertise into meaning, not just for themselves, but for all of humanity. The gene editing tool that they invented has the potential to enhance the germline of future generations. As scientific researchers, they pushed the cusp of their awareness and were transformed by the experience. They demonstrated what Cartwright points out as Bion's emphasis on the transformative qualities of lived experience always unfolding at the cusp of our awareness (CSM 3). The cusp of awareness for Charpentier and Doudna was the edge of human knowledge about defending Homo Sapiens against invading viruses.

Call To Action: Take Away A Portable Understanding

This chapter is the story of how two researchers, Emmanuelle Charpentier and Jennifer Doudna, invented a scientific tool that not only defends humans against viruses, it also has the capability of modifying genes of one person in a way that replicates that modification in the genes of future descendants. This chapter is a call to action for readers to take away a portable understanding of the commensal mode of containment. To help readers, I provide the following summary of how the two scientists interacted with each other in converting their experiences of scientific anxieties into meaningful thoughts and emotions about using a gene-editing tool to help humanity fight off viral attacks.

- **Mode:** Charpentier and Doudna had a commensal mode of containment.
- **Roles:** In the first round of experiments, Charpentier was the contained, while Doudna was the container. They switched roles in the second round of experiments, and switched back to their original roles in the third round of experiments.
- **Symmetry:** The relationship between Charpentier and Doudna was symmetrical. They were able to switch roles readily because they were co-equals, who had chosen to work with each other. Both were managers of scientific laboratories, and both were established researchers. Each respected the expertise of the other, and neither was dependent on the other. There was no power gradient in the interaction between Charpentier and Doudna.
- **Psychological Frame:** The psychological frame of a containment has a purpose, a space boundary and a time boundary. For Charpentier and Doudna, the purpose of the psychological

frame was to encapsulate the scientists in a defined time and space for conducting experiments in the viral-defense project. The space of the frame had a physical component and a virtual component. The physical component was about geographic location. Geographically, the containment took place in two research laboratories: Charpentier's laboratory located in Umea, Sweden, and Doudna's laboratory in California, U.S.A. The virtual component was about communication. They communicated using Skype meetings and e-mails. The experiments were conducted in the laboratories in Sweden and USA, while the brainstorming and strategy-making activities occurred virtually via Skype telecommunications connecting the two countries. The time boundary of the psychological frame was an interval of 14 months of containment, during which the team worked 24 hours per day, in two 12-hour shifts. That psychological frame supported the collaboration between the two laboratories located nearly half-way across the world from each other. The laboratories provided space for quiet contemplation while conducting experiments. From the perspective of the containment model, the laboratories can be regarded as spaces for engaging in individual scientific reverie. The scientists also had the opportunity for overlapping reverie, during Skype meetings.

- **Dialectical Narrative:** The commensal mode of containment has three narratives. In the relationship between these two scientists, the first narrative was the account of scientific angst about RNA that came from Charpentier, the contained. The second narrative was from Doudna, the container. It offered a scientific dialogue and suggested experiments to address the scientific angst of the contained. Since Charpentier and Doudna switched roles during the containment, the first narrative took the form of threads of scientific angst coming from each of them in turn. Similarly, the second narrative was made up of offerings of specialized knowledge and ideas for experiments contributed by each of them in turn. The dialectical interaction between Charpentier and Doudna generated a third narrative. The third narrative was the interweaving of scientific knowledge that culminated in their invention of a viral-defense system. Another result of their dialectical interaction was that their genetic-engineering invention provided a service to humanity that earned Charpentier and Doudna the 2020 Nobel Prize for Chemistry.

- **Psychological Growth / Harm**: Doudna and Charpentier helped each other to achieve psychological growth from their containment. They developed a new sense of their ability to create new scientific knowledge and use it to invent a tool that fosters a healthier humanity by editing the human genome. Their psychological growth is seen in the increased confidence and sense of agency that led them from researchers to inventors, and later to becoming entrepreneurs.

After the Containment Ended

On hearing the CRISPR-Cas9 presentation by Doudna and Charpentier at a 2012 CASPR conference, there was a general acknowledgement in the scientific community that they had taken the CRISPR research to a new level (CB 148). The *Science* editors published the Doudna-Charpentier paper on June 28, 2012. It galvanized an entirely new field of biotechnology, that is, making CRISPR work in the editing of human genes (CB 149).

For commercializing the CASPR-Cas9 editing tools, Charpentier and Doudna became co-founders of separate companies (CB 213). Charpentier and a colleague founded CRISPR Therapeutics in 2012. Doudna and colleagues founded Intellia Therapeutics in 2014. Over the years, Charpentier and Doudna shared many prizes for their work together. The most prestigious prize was the 2020 Nobel Prize in Chemistry (CB 469).

With the realization that the gene editing tool they co-invented can be used for ethical practices such as prevention of genetic disease, as well as practices of questionable ethics, such as designer babies, Doudna and Charpentier are actively promoting public awareness of the tool, and pursuing a code of ethics to be determined by society about what are acceptable uses of the tool. Concerned about whether CRISPR would do more harm than good, Doudna and Charpentier actively support the creation of a societal code of ethics to distinguish what is acceptable gene-editing. In *"Editing Humanity"* Kevin Davies reports that there was a conference on the ethics of genome-editing at the National Academy of Sciences in Washington, D. C. in 2015, when Doudna and Charpentier were among the scientists, physicians, ethicists, philosophers and members of the public, who participated in discussions of the advantages and the dangers of human germline-editing (EH 255).

Sources

The sources of information that shape my thinking in this chapter are:
- *"The Code Breaker"* by Walter Isaacson
- *"A Crack In Creation"* by Jennifer Doudna and Samuel Sternberg
- *"Editing Humanity"* by Kevin Davies
- *"Containing States of Mind"* by Duncan Cartwright
- *"Projection and Re-Collection in Jungian Psychology"* by Marie-Louise von Franz.

CHAPTER 12

A Symbiotic Mode of Containment Involving: Carl Jung & Sigmund Freud

"Freud had a dream. ... I interpreted it as best I could, but (requested) some additional details from his private life. Then he said, 'But I cannot risk my authority.' At that moment he lost it altogether."

— Carl Jung

Decades before they knew each other, Carl Jung and Sigmund Freud had life experiences which they believe influenced their relationships later in life. In *"Jung: A Biography"* biographer Diedre Bair quotes from a letter Jung wrote stating that, as a boy, he had been the victim of a sexual assault by a man whom he once worshiped (JB 71). When he became an adult, Jung noticed the effect of that assault on his life. He explained that his feelings were hampered considerably after the assault ... any man who tried to become a close friend, who offered friendship in the platonic sense, always became disgusting (JB 71). Jung outlined the route most of his friendships with men would follow throughout the rest of his life: all would begin positively, but most would end badly, in bitterness, rejection, and recrimination (JB 71).

Freud also had a boyhood experience that had lasting effects. In *"FREUD:*

An Intellectual Biography" psychologist Joel Whitebook reports that, as a young boy, Freud developed a love-hate relationship with his nephew, John. The boys loved each other, but fought each other constantly. In adulthood, Freud came to believe that his relationship with John was so important that it determined all his later feelings in his interactions with persons his own age (FIB 33). Whitebook believes the relationship was 'irradicably fixed' in his 'unconscious memory' and provided a template for the many intensely conflicted relationships that Freud had in later life. Whitebook quotes from Freud's book "*The Interpretation of Dreams*":

> *"My emotional life has always insisted that I should have an intimate friend and a hated enemy. I have always been able to provide myself afresh with both, and it has not infrequently happened that the ideal situation of childhood has been so completely reproduced that friend and enemy have come together in a single individual"* (FIB 33 – 34).

As an adult, Freud established friendships with men, then pushed them away as enemies. The implication of their disclosures is that the disciple-leader relationship between Jung and Freud had its precursors in their early lives. Although their relationship started with enthusiastic declarations of friendship and professional respect, I found no indication that their relationship generated psychological growth in either. Despite the fact that their friendship ended in enmity, I found no evidence that the relationship resulted in psychological harm to either. They were playing out patterns of relationship that originated in their early lives ... unhealthy patterns which each man acknowledged, but did not have the wherewithal to disrupt and modify. It took these two sages of the psyche several years of friendship and collaboration to realize that neither man could be what the other wanted him to be. Jung could not be a subservient disciple. Freud could not risk his authority as a leader.

My interpretation is that Jung and Freud had a disciple-leader relationship that became a symbiotic mode of containment, in which Jung was the contained and Freud was the container. Having emerged from an activated leader archetype, a projection was cast from the mind of Jung to the mind of Freud. The content of the projection was Jung's idealization of a leader. Since Freud did not become a carrier of Jung's projection, the containment ended without psychological growth. This was an asymmetrical containment with Jung, the younger man, seeking something that Freud, the older founder of the psychoanalytic movement, had to offer. Although Jung was an established psychiatrist, a respected lecturer, and a published author when he met Freud, he yearned for the opportunity to spend his time primarily on research. Freud was willing to offer that opportunity by making Jung heir apparent to the psychoanalytic movement ... exclusively on Freud's terms. Throughout their symbiotic containment, their roles remained unchanged; Jung remained the contained, while Freud remained the container. The internal outcome of the containment was that there was neither psychological growth nor harm. The external outcome of the containment was that, after years of collaboration, these two venerable sages of psychology produced no joint contribution to psychology. To understand the nature of the relationship between Jung and Freud, it is necessary to examine the circumstances and the cultures in which they grew up. Not only do their relationships in early lives show influence on their later relationships as adults, but the relationships they formed as adults followed repetitive patterns. First, I start with a biographical account of Jung's life. Then I do the same for Freud's life.

Background Information about Carl Jung

This is a brief account of Jung's early life taken from Diedre Bair's biography titled "*Jung: A Biography*" which is my source for background information leading up to the time of his first encounter with Freud. Carl Jung's parents were Paul Jung and Emilie Preiswerk who married in 1869. Paul was twenty-six years old and Emilie was twenty-one. Paul was a well-educated, but poor, Protestant pastor in the Swiss Reformed Church (JB 7 - 8). Emilie had married below her social status, but she was a pastor's daughter who understood the spartan way of pastoral life (JB 17) and she assumed her role as a pastor's wife. After three pregnancies, in which the babies did not survive (JB 18), she became sickly and a certain lethargy came over her. She would go to her bedroom and stay there for hours. In her next attempt to produce a child, she gave birth to Carl (JB 18). Carl was born in 1875 in the vicarage of Kesswil in Switzerland, where Paul provided pastoral guidance for the rural village. At first, Emilie was very attentive to Carl when she was unsure about his survival, but when he became a robust toddler, she relaxed her attention, leaving little Carl in the care of a maid. Then, Emilie assigned Carl to share a bedroom with his father, while Emilie reserved a bedroom for herself. After Carl's third birthday, Emilie abruptly left the vicarage for the first of several long stays at a rest home near Basel (JB 21). Paul's explanation to the parishioners gave the impression that her absence was related to complications which arose from the birth of Carl. Father and son were rarely separated, but Emilie had absences of varying durations away from home (JB 21). When Emilie was away from home, a young woman named Bertha would take care of Carl. On those occasions when Emilie's fragile health necessitated long stays in a rest home, Paul occasionally took young Carl to spend time with Emilie's sister, his Aunt Gusteli in Basel (JB 21). When Emile later needed hospital stays of several months, Paul kept Carl at the vicarage. During Emilie's hospital stays, the pretty blue-eyed girl named Bertha sometimes came to play with Carl and take him for walks along the banks of the Rhine. Bertha would later become his mother-in-law (JB 21).

Emilie had grown up believing that visionary experiences were common to people in general because she and the other Preiswerk family members were accustomed to seeing ghosts, getting visits from spirits and speaking in tongues (JB 17). Emilie had two personalities (JB 20 – 21). One personality was the outgoing Emilie who enjoyed sharing stories about apparitions with her relatives (JB 27). The other personality was a morose, withdrawn person inclined to retreat to her bedroom for long periods of time. After she married Paul, Emilie seemed truly happy only when telling the local parish women about ghosts that roam the vicarage, and listening to their stories. Paul and Emilie did not have a harmonious marriage. They quarreled with each other in the presence of little Carl (JB 20).

The marriage of his parents was troubled — young Carl found the hostile communication between his parents so toxic that he broke out in eczema which he attributed to the disharmony in the marriage (JB 21). For Carl, the word 'father' became synonymous with reliability and powerlessness (JB 21). Villagers gossiped about the pastor's unhappy marriage. Village children avoided Carl because they thought his parents to be peculiar (JB 22). Often left to play by himself, Carl learned to rely on the power of his imagination for entertainment (JB 22). To outward appearances, Paul and Emilie did not seem to enjoy each other's company as much as they enjoyed the company of others. Emilie took little interest in the life of her husband's parish (JB 25). She often spent time with her relatives, the Preiswerk clan (JB 26), while Paul retreated into the sentimental idealism of his former university student days. He adopted the mannerisms of his student days and smoked the long clay pipe favored by students. His parishioners considered him good at matters related to spiritual welfare, but they avoided him otherwise because his conversation was inclined to the repetition of stories from his past (JB 26). Paul spent his time attending to his parishioners in Laufen, where the vicarage had a scenic view of the Rhine rapids (JB 19). There, his pastoral role took on additional responsibilities and he became known as a pastor who specialized in spiritual guidance for those with psychiatric disorders and mental impairment (JB 31). Paul took such great satisfaction from conversing with doctors and ministering to patients that his clinical duties became more prominent than his pastoral duties. Biographer Bair makes the observation that Paul's interest in psychiatric literature and practice was connected to the crisis of faith he experienced, as well as an event in Carl's life at about the same time, while he was a student of the local Gymnasium.

At age 11 years, Carl matriculated to the Humanistisches Gymnasium in Basel (JB 29). He was a tall, sturdy boy, often odorous, with shabby clothes and run-down shoes (JB 29). Ready to fight, he would get into brawls as a result of which teachers would scold or punish him for his aggressive behavior. It was while Carl was at the Gymnasium, that his father was appointed counsellor at the Basel Psychiatriche Universitatsklinik, the University's mental hospital, where he counseled people experiencing crises of faith (JB 30 – 31). One day at the Gymnasium, a classmate knocked Carl to the ground where he became semi-conscious (JB 31). Bystanders took him to the home of his Preiswerk aunts. He seemed to recover, but on returning to school, he began fainting daily between 11:00 AM and 12:00 Noon (JB 31). When he became an adult, he wondered why no one attributed his fainting to hunger. As a schoolboy, he would often leave home with just a cup of milk for breakfast. For a while he stayed home from school, but his recovery was slow, so his father decided to board him with a Catholic priest at a farming community called Entlebuch (JB 32). For the better part of a year, he was supervised by a country doctor who catered to people convalescing from various illnesses. In later life, Jung claimed that a Catholic priest sexually molested him, but he did not identify the priest. When he became an adult, Jung confessed in a letter to Freud that he had been the victim of a sexual assault by a man he once worshiped (JB 71). He further explained that his feelings were hampered considerably afterwards. He explained that his relationships with any man who tried to become a close friend, in the platonic sense, would always become disgusting to him. Jung pointed out that his friendships with men would follow a similar path during the course of his life: they would begin positively, but most would end in bitterness and rejection. Jung's biographer's observation: "*With this admission, Jung outlined the route most of his friendships with men would follow throughout the rest of his life*" (JB 71). The identity of the man who molested Jung is unknown, but there is speculation that he may have been a Catholic priest who became Paul's friend during Carl's boyhood (JB 71). One day while eavesdropping, Carl heard Paul express despair about the future of a son who could not support himself. Carl's reaction was to resume his studies with a vengeance. He made a vow to himself that he would not allow anyone to get the best of him or pity him (JB 32 – 33). When he resumed school attendance, his grades improved and he achieved better relationships with his classmates.

By the time Carl reached his fifteenth birthday, his mother was treating him as an equal. In Carl's presence, Emilie expressed disdain for Paul (JB 35). Carl did not share her disdain, but he did not argue with her because he did not want to insert himself in the conflict between his parents. As he grew older, Carl became more intellectually curious and sought to engage his father in discussions about his Protestant faith, but Paul was disinclined to participate in such discussions. Jung came to believe that his father's repeated reluctance to engage him in intellectual religious discussion was because Paul was consumed by inward doubts (JB 37). His father would encourage him to believe in religious doctrines such as the Trinity, rather than attempt to think them through. Jung started attending Basel University in 1895 (JB 37) when he enrolled in the Faculty of Natural Sciences, to study medicine. Not having the money to pay for tuition, Paul petitioned parish officials for a stipend to pay for Carl's first year of university education (JB 37). The stipend would be available each subsequent year of study, as long as Carl maintained acceptable grades. Carl found the sight of blood unsettling, and the examination of bodies revolting. With that awareness and the realization that the study of medicine would take several years, and therefore be costly, he chose to pursue psychiatry, which was a relatively new discipline at the time.

Carl had the view that his father, a Christian minister, had been trapped in a dead theology, a victim of profound spiritual suffering. His father's bondage to traditional church doctrine caused fits of depression and led to the deterioration of his father's health and his eventual death. Jung once had a dream in which he believed that he experienced God's grace first hand. He wanted to tell his father of the 'miracle of grace' that he discerned from the dream, but he could not tell his father. That inability opened an abyss between them. Jung believed that, for his father, church doctrine blocked what could have been a direct route to God. While Carl was at university, his father grew silent, bitter and his body shrunk. He died of cancer in 1896 (JB 38). After Paul's death, Emilie became deferential to Carl who, in Swiss tradition, had become the man of the family (JB 40). Emilie, along with her two children Carl and Trudi, had to leave the vicarage. Carl's maternal relatives felt he should drop out of university, but his paternal uncle Ernst Jung agreed to provide Emilie and her two children with financial support until Carl completed his studies (JB 41). Carl flourished intellectually at the university, in the study of his chosen specialty, psychiatry (JB 41). He submitted his dissertation "*On the Psychology and Pathology of So-Called Occult Phenomenon*" to the University of Zurich. It was based on seances that the Preiswerk extended family had conducted as entertainment using a homemade ouija board (JB 52). After graduation, he accepted a low-level role at the prestigious Burgholzli Mental Hospital in Zurich, under the direction of Dr. Eugen Bleuler (JB 52). By December 1900, Carl had passed the *Staatsexamen* to obtain a medical certification and was settled into housing accommodations for psychiatrists at the hospital (JB 53 - 55). He continued to pay household expenses for his mother and sister in Basel until 1904 when he moved them to Zurich (JB 54).

In my view, Bleuler turned out to be a father figure to Jung. Jung was a new graduate when Bleuler hired him in a low-level position. Bleuler guided Carl's career as he rose to the position of Assistant Director of the Burgholzli Hospital in just a few years. Bleuler's caring, fatherly attitude was on display from their first meeting. He was waiting for Jung in the doorway when he arrived at the hospital to start work in Zurich (JB 55). As director of the hospital, Bleuler had the option of assigning a senior member of staff to help Jung get settled into hospital life. What he chose to do, in his fatherly way, was to personally help Jung get settled into housing accommodation and escorted him on a tour of the hospital (JB 55). Bleuler also made a point of sitting next to Carl at teatime, as he introduced patients and doctors, all of whom usually took tea together (JB 55). Bleuler offered opportunities, set rules and guardrails and rewarded Jung's good work. When Jung's dissertation was accepted by the medical faculty at the University of Zurich in 1901, Bleuler endorsed Jung's application for a position as lecturer at the University of Zurich (JB 64). Bleuler was generally helpful in guiding Jung's career. Jung was allowed to go to France for training in Jean-Martin Charcot's Salpetriere school in Paris. Bleuler supported Jung in experiments about the Word Association Test. In addition, Bleuler allowed Jung to take time away from work at the hospital for travelling to conferences, and to conduct research.

Bleuler had strict rules about running the Hospital. He expected Carl to dedicate himself to serving the needs of the patients, but he did not expect anything he was not prepared to do himself (JB 55 – 56). Jung described Burgholzli as 'the monastery of the world' (JB 55) and Bleuler as being motivated solely by a Christian ambition to help others (JB 56). Born of peasant stock that was considered socially inferior, Bleuler was the first in his family to be educated beyond elementary school (JB 56). Bleuler was a disciplinarian in the sense that he required all psychiatrists at the Hospital to see all the patients everyday so they would be prepared to treat any patient at short notice (JB 57). He encouraged the psychiatrists to keep up to date on current research as well as treatments in the health care industry. He gave them the opportunity to update their training. Bleuler also insisted that psychiatrists learn the dialects of patients to converse with them on a co-equal social standing (JB 57). He required abstinence from alcohol and made a rule that the hospital grounds were locked at 10:00 PM (JB 60). Bleuler was highly regarded throughout Germany and Switzerland for his work at the Burgholzli Hospital, which hosted about four hundred patients, and was seen as a prestigious institution (JB 58).

For the first six months, Jung remained at the hospital because he had few clothes, was too poor to socialize and was sending his salary to support his mother and sister in Basel (JB 58 – 59). During this time, he blamed his parents for the spiritual tension and burden he experienced while growing up in their home (JB 59). He blamed his family's poverty for the shame he felt about his lack of experience in life. He went to the theatre for the first time at age twenty. His primary emotion was guilt because he could not really afford it. His colleagues thought he might be psychologically abnormal because he lived like a hermit (JB 59). During this reclusive six-month period, Jung worked industriously, and acquired a confidence that never deserted him afterwards (JB 59). During his first year at Burgholzli, Jung worked on his dissertation, while Bleuler expressed an interest and offered comments. The subject of the dissertation was spiritualist activity such as seances conducted by the Preiswerk clan. When the dissertation was published in 1902, the Preiswerk clan was outraged because it implied degrees of insanity in their families (JB 64). Later generations blamed Jung for the fact that young Preiswerk daughters in his generation were deprived of the opportunity to marry, due to the impact of his dissertation in Basel, where the society regarded insanity as being connected to heredity (JB 61).

Jung felt that the environment at the Burgholzli Hospital lacked intellectual stimulation (JB 61), and he missed the intellectual stimulation he found at the University of Basel. What interested Jung most was not the practice of psychiatry, but opportunities for research within the profession (JB 61). The director of the Burgholzli Hospital always held the chair in psychiatry at the University of Zurich (JB 92). As Bleuler's first assistant, Jung was entitled to become a lecturer if his credentials warranted it (JB 92). Jung wanted the honor and set about completing the research on the Word Association Test to qualify himself to become a lecturer. Between 1901 and 1904, Jung and colleagues from Burgholzli worked on the Word Association Test. Carl's research was accepted by the University of Zurich in October 1905 (JB 93) and he became a lecturer.

A poor psychiatrist working to support his mother and sister, Jung longed for the opportunity to do research instead of the drudgery of treating patients. His fortune changed when he renewed his acquaintance with Bertha, who had taken him on walks along the Rhine on occasions when his mother had to be away at a rest home. Bertha had a beautiful daughter, Emma, with whom Jung fell in love. Jung married Emma Rauschenbach from Schffhausen, a town located on the German side of Switzerland. As heiress to a Swiss watch-making empire, Emma received an annual allowance from her family, and later an inheritance when her father died. According to Swiss law, Emma's money was under the control of her husband (JB 82). With Emma's wealth at his disposal, Jung did not need to rely on his hospital salary. So, he was able to take advantage of Bleuler's willingness to approve time away from the hospital without pay, for travelling to other countries and conducting research. When Emma joined Jung in the Burgholzli Hospital's living accommodations, Bleuler's wife became a good friend and mentor for Emma (JB 81).

By 1906, Jung was developing an international reputation (JB 97). Doctors from other countries came to consult with him. He was publishing articles in journals. Following the publication of the Word Association Test in 1904, local Swiss authorities began consulting him about law enforcement matters related to whether suspects were being truthful during interrogations. The year 1906 marked the start of enmity between Jung and Bleuler (JB 97). Jung was paying more attention to his activities outside the hospital than to treatments of patients inside the hospital. Jung and Bleuler were both lecturers at the University of Zurich. Jung was the more popular lecturer because he made himself available to his audience, both students and visitors, for discussions before the start of lectures. He was eager to share his ideas and his presentation style was more appealing than the dry, statistical style of Bleuler. Another factor contributing to the enmity was the frequency with which Jung requested leave from the hospital without pay. Although Bleuler approved all his requests, Bleuler believed that Jung was abusing the privilege. Moreover, other psychiatrists in the hospital came to resent Jung because he was able to get a great deal of time away from the hospital. With Emma's wealth available to him, Jung did not need to rely on his hospital salary, while the other psychiatrists were limited by their dependence on their hospital pay for financial support. What further heightened their enmity was that Jung reached out directly to Sigmund Freud about his 'talking cure' bypassing Bleuler who had been corresponding with Freud for years (JB 99).

While Jung was treating Sabina Spielrein, a young Russian woman for hysteria, Bleuler mentioned a new 'talking cure' developed by Freud. Curious about the talking cure, Jung contacted Freud. Carl Jung first reached out to Sigmund Freud in 1906, when he sought Freud's opinion about the possibility of using the talking cure for Spielrein, a patient at the Burgholzli Hospital. That patient would play a pivotal role in Jung's life. Intelligent, outspoken and beautiful, she was an aspiring medical student. Bleuler was so impressed with her that he allowed her to accompany psychiatrists on their rounds at the hospital. Jung invited her to participate in experiments about the Word Association Test. In a letter requesting supervision about the talking cure treatment, Jung reported to Freud:

> "During the treatment the patient had the misfortune of falling in love with me. Now she always raves ostentatiously to her mother about her love, [and takes] a secret spiteful joy in her mother's terror. ... That's why her mother now wants someone else to treat her" (JB 90).

Jung informed Freud at the time that he agreed to have someone else treat her. However, it was Jung who used the talking cure to help Spielrein overcome hysteria. When she recovered, she enrolled as a medical student at the University of Zurich. The patient-psychiatrist relationship between Spielrein and Jung morphed into a friendship which led to questions about ethical boundaries being breached. Years later he told Freud that his relationship with Spielrein continued after her discharge from the hospital because he "knew from experience that she would immediately relapse" if he withdrew his friendship (JB 90). Jung further explained to Freud: "I prolonged the relationship over the years and in the end found myself morally obliged, as it were, to devote a large measure of friendship to her" (JB 90). Biographer Bair explains that, in one sense,

Jung was relieved that Spielrein had recovered enough to lead an independent life in Zurich, but he was intrigued by her as a woman because she was unlike any he had known in his emotionally restricted life.

After being discharged from Burgholzli, Spielrein continued to have meetings with Jung for consultation. When Spielrein openly proclaimed her feelings for Jung, it left those within earshot to believe they were having an affair (JB 154). That created a rumor which became a scandal that reached Bleuler as well as Spielrein's mother. When Frau Spielrein questioned Jung about the matter, his response was that the relationship progressed from doctor to friend, and because he had "never charged a fee" he did not feel "professionally obligated" to keep anything personal out of the friendship. Biographer Bair points out that hospital records show that Spielrein's father paid for her Friday afternoon sessions with Jung (JB 155). Jung's response to Frau Spielrein implied that money alone would set the boundaries that could restrain his behavior as a psychiatrist. Bleuler's response to the scandal was to ask for Jung's resignation, but he did not demand that Jung leave his post immediately. Instead, he phased out the departure so Jung could complete assignments at the Hospital and finish work on students' dissertations at the University of Zurich. Jung's ambivalent attitude about fidelity in marriage came to the fore later when in 1909 he was assuring Emma that her concerns about the scandal were groundless, while at the same time, Jung wrote to Freud: "the prerequisite for a good marriage ... is a license to be unfaithful" (JB 181).

In January 1907, Jung agreed to be the subject of the Word Association Test conducted by a colleague at the Burgholzli Hospital, Ludwig Binswanger, as part of the research for Binswanger's medical dissertation (JB 109 - 114). Since Binswanger obtained answers directly from Jung, Bair regards the findings as (auto)biographical. Jung designed the Word Association Test to identify complexes that influence the lives of people who take the test, so, the answers that he provided to Binswanger are an indication of Jung's own complexes. As a colleague of Jung at the Burgholzli, Binswanger already knew much about Jung's personal life prior to conducting the test, so his analysis was a better picture of Jung's life than if a stranger had conducted the test. However, Bair notes that Binswanger puts a positive gloss on the results, possibly out of respect for Jung. After the test, Jung commented to Binswanger that he feared he had exposed all his complexes, and "*now everything will come out*" (JB 112). When interpreting Jung's emotional response to stimulus words, Binswanger found that Jung had a high emotional response to the words 'divorce' and 'money' (JB 112). Bair expands on that by pointing out about that time, the marriage of Carl and Emma had veered toward divorce, because rumors about Carl's infidelity plus Emma's discomfort with living in the Burgholzli fishbowl threatened the marriage. Emma's family was so concerned about the humiliation and social embarrassment Carl had heaped upon the Schaffhausen clan that Bertha, his mother-in-law, had given Carl an ultimatum to dissociate himself from the Burgholzli Hospital by finding or building a home (JB 113). At the time, Carl's salary was paltry compared with the annual allowance that Emma obtained from her wealthy family. If Emma had divorced Carl, he would not have been able to continue taking unpaid leave from the hospital for participating in conferences and conducting research. It was maddening to Carl's masculine pride that he was not the main provider for his family. The Word Association Test revealed conflicts in Carl's mind about his marriage and money. Another conflict revealed by the Word Association Test was Carl's response to the words 'fame' and 'money' (JB 131). Binswanger noted that Jung had a strongly pronounced striving for 'knowledge, work and recognition'. Binswanger connected that to frequent accusations by Jung's family that he was striving for public approval far more aggressively than a man of his social standing should do (JB 111). Bair's elaboration is that Jung thought he was seeking professional respect, while Emma's family thought he wanted to thrust himself into the public limelight (JB 111). Binswanger identified Jung's strongest responses as being 'the will to power' and a 'money' complex, and he related them to Jung's dissatisfaction with the monotony of work at the hospital as well as concern about his future way of living (JB 111). What came out of the test was that Jung was conflicted about two main topics: the life he had not yet lived as a lover to women other than the one he married, and the life he was missing due to not being the principal financial provider for his family (JB 113 - 114). Bair points out that Jung could not hope to become the principal provider because Emma's fortune was enormous. It would be easier to find power through approval and affection elsewhere. The conflict for him was knowing that Emma was ready to curtail his search for approval and affection elsewhere. He knew that from her declaration that she would divorce him rather than suffer further humiliation about his infidelities. At the time when Binswanger used Jung as a subject in conducting the Word Association Test, Jung had not yet met Freud face-to-face. The results of the test give some insight into Jung's own psychological biography before he met Freud. His conflicts were related to ambition, the will to power, and desire for the life not yet lived. In March 1907, Jung, Emma and Binswanger went to Vienna, at Freud's invitation. That was the first face-to-face meeting between Jung and Freud.

Three months after Jung met Freud, Dr. Otto Gross arrived at the Burgholzli Hospital with a letter from Freud requesting that he be treated by Jung (JB 136). It was June 1907. After obtaining a medical degree, Gross had worked as a doctor on a ship, then as a psychiatric intern before being previously admitted to the Burgholzli Hospital, where he had been Bleuler's patient. Now, Gross refused to continue treatment with Bleuler, so he had gone to Freud. Freud was too busy at the time to accommodate Gross in his private practice. In deference to his prestigious father, Hans Gross, who felt that his son should be committed to a mental asylum, Freud referred Gross to Jung. A habitual user of morphine, cocaine and opium, Gross was an advocate of political, cultural and sexual revolutions (JB 136). Handsome in appearance, and erratic in behavior, he had been a meandering traveller while he roamed Austria, Germany and Switzerland (JB 136). To get a better understanding of Gross, Jung interviewed his wife Freida, who informed Jung that long before Gross' addictions began, he was unable to adjust to ordinary routines of life because he believed himself to be super-extraordinary (JB 139). Gross insisted that other doctors should pay homage to him as a prophet. Jung's primary observation of Gross was one of having a delusion of grandeur (JB 139). Having been both doctor and patient, Gross was recognized as a gifted analyst and theoretician, but also a dangerous lunatic (JB 140).

Jung expressed sadness that a man with such an intelligent head could be "such a psychopath" (JB 137). Jung and Gross had much in common. Both were psychiatrists, both had published articles about psychiatry, and both were professionally ambitious. There was a mere two-year difference in their age. Both were married. Both liked the outdoor activities and enjoyed travelling. Jung saw in Gross a kinship, so much so that he referred to Gross as being "... *like my twin brother*" (JB 136). Gross had published articles in medical journals and Jung found him a stimulating conversationalist. Jung had experience about the behaviors of patients with psychotic disorders, but Gross was so knowledgeable and articulate about his condition that Jung obtained a "*deeper clarity*" into dementia praecox, a psychotic disorder, while working with Gross. During their time together, Jung saw something of himself in Gross. I believe Jung saw in Gross a psychological mirror reflection of himself. Gross gave voice to psychotic disorder that Jung had only seen in the behaviors of other patients, who lacked the knowledge to articulate their psychic experience as well as Gross did. By calling Gross his twin brother, Jung was acknowledging that he was predisposed to the same disorder that afflicted Gross. Jung noticed that he, an intelligent psychiatrist like Gross, could fall into the same disorder. Mental illness is influenced by genetics and environment. Twin brothers share genes and often grow up in the same environment, and therefore share similar psychological predispositions. By calling Gross his twin brother, I believe Jung was calling out something he had noticed in himself. Jung was expressing a there-but-for-the-grace-of-God-go-I sentiment. Gross offered Jung an insider's view into psychotic disorder for which he had seen external behaviors on display at Burgholzli. And Jung saw himself reflected in Gross' depiction of psychotic disorder. According to Bair, Jung's main interest in the Gross case lay in determining how the excesses of Gross' personal life could be brought under control, at least long enough to harness his intellectual ability in the hope it would permit him to do further important research (JB 141). Jung's intellectual discussion must not have reached a level of stimulation satisfying to Gross because, after two weeks of treatment, Gross absconded, never to return. Gross escaped from the Burgholzli Hospital by climbing over the fence. The relationship between Jung and Gross provides insight into Jung's predisposition before he established collaboration with Freud. My opinion is that Jung saw himself as predisposed to psychotic disorder, similar to his twin brother, the gifted analyst and theoretician, Dr. Otto Gross.

By the time Jung and Freud established a collaboration, Jung was exhibiting signs that the trauma and conflicts of his life experiences were leading him toward the boundary between psychological health and psychological illness. His life experiences included the effects of homosexual assault as a young boy; his conflicted relationships with men; his attempt to avoid the futility of the life that his father had lived; his openness to marital infidelity; his willingness to risk his dual career as psychiatrist and lecturer while acting out the unlived life; and his recognition of a psychological reflection of himself in the talented but psychotic Otto Gross. The conflicts that accumulated in Jung's life before he formed a relationship with Freud suggest that their collaboration was not the main cause of Jung's psychotic episode that followed the breakup of the Jung-Freud relationship.

Background Information about Sigmund Freud

Psychoanalyst, Joel Whitebook, wrote a biography of Freud titled *"FREUD: An Intellectual Biography"* in which he describes childhood relationships that influenced Freud's adult relationships. The biography describes the Freud clan as having a complicated multi-family structure. Jacob and Amalie married in 1855 when he was forty-one and she was twenty-one years old. The following year, their first son Sigmund was born. Jacob and Amalie were a Jewish couple who lived in the Catholic town of Freiberg, Moravia, which later became the Czech Republic. Amalie was Jacob's third wife. Jacob had two sons from his first marriage, Emanuel and Phillipp. Those two sons were close to the age of Amalie. Emanuel was married with a son, John, who was about the same age as Sigmund. Phillipp was a bachelor. The Freud relatives lived in close proximity to each other in the same neighborhood. Jacob's profession was wool merchant. Whitebook describes Jacob as an enticing father for a young child ... gentle, devoted, jocular, and sympathetic (FIB 28). Jacob was an intelligent man who actively educated himself, and whose childlike qualities made him able to delight children with his love of telling jokes and reading stories (FIB 29). Whitebook views Jacob as having idealized his son while Sigmund idealized his father.

Amalie doted on Sigmund and called him *"my golden Sigi"* partly because of a prophesy that having been born with a caul on his head, he was destined to become a great person. Based on the accounts collected by

Whitebook, Amalie was a difficult, dependent, demanding, infantile and self-centered woman (FIB 4). She was also beautiful, lively, sociable and a good housekeeper. Although German was the primary language spoken among the Freud families, Amalie did not learn to speak the language. A descendant of Galician Jews, she spoke a Yiddish dialect all her life. Very emotional and inclined to get carried away by her feelings, Amalie could see herself in her children, but could not see them for themselves. Before Sigmund reached his second birthday, a brother, baby Julius was born, but he died shortly afterwards. His death threw Amalie into a depression. A nanny was hired to take care of young Sigmund, but she was soon dismissed.

Sigmund developed a love-hate relationship with his nephew, John (FIB 33). John was nine months older than Sigmund. John and Sigmund were inseparable and they loved each other, but constantly fought with each other. According to Whitebook, Sigmund believed that his relationship with John was so important that it "*determined all [his] later feelings in [his] intercourse with persons his own age*" (FIB 33). Whitebook reports that the relationship was "*irradicably fixed*" in his "*unconscious memory*" and provided a template for the many intensely conflicted relationships that Sigmund had in later life. To elaborate on that, Whitebook quotes from Freud in "*The Interpretation of Dreams*":

> "*My emotional life has always insisted that I should have an intimate friend and a hated enemy. I have always been able to provide myself afresh with both, and it has not infrequently happened that the ideal situation of childhood has been so completely reproduced that friend and enemy have come to-gether in a single individual – though not, of course, both at once or with constant oscillations, as may have been the case in my early childhood*" (FIB 33 – 34).

An enduring effect of his love-hate relationship with nephew John is seen in Freud's declaration about the patten of his adult emotional life in which he always needed both an intimate friend and a hated enemy. As an adult, Freud established friendships with men, then pushed them away when he realized he could not control them.

The Freud families that were located in Freidberg separated in 1859 in search of better economic opportunities. The breakup of the Freud clan presented a significant loss for young Sigmund because his nephew John, a close playmate, and Sigmund's two half-brothers relocated to Manchester, England. Sigmund's parents left the Jewish orthodox community of Freidberg and settled in the cosmopolitan city of Vienna. In the 2005 edition of Sigmund Freud's book "*The Interpretation of Dreams*" the publisher included a section at the beginning titled "*The World of Sigmund Freud*" which is a chronological outline of Freud's life (ID xi – xix). The outline lists a declining economy and anti-Semitism as the reasons that Jacob and Amalie moved their family to a Jewish community in Vienna, Austria (ID xi). In 1865, young Freud entered secondary school in Leopoldstadt, where he demonstrated a talent for languages.

As Sigmund grew older, he became aware that Jacob's childlike qualities were a mask for his inability to deal with the realities of life, and his shortcomings as a father. Jacob abdicated his parental function and was an inadequate provider. There is no record of Jacob making a living independently. When partnering with others, he was able to achieve a measure of success, but not on his own. According to Whitebook, Jacob abdicated his paternal function in two ways (FIB 30). First, Jacob failed to act as a psychological barrier between Sigmund and his mother, so that the young boy could dis-identify and separate himself from his mother (FIB 30). Second, Jacob failed to be a "*good enough Oedipal adversary*" to enable young Sigmund to contain and shape his aggression and tame his sense of omnipotence (FIB 30). As a consequence of these failures, Amalie remained a frightening figure with whom Sigmund was not able to come to terms and integrate into his psychic life. As an adult, Sigmund continued to struggle with his sense of omnipotence, and he developed an excessive tendency for idealization, which launched him on a repeated quest to find an ideal father (FIB 30). As Freud grew out of his boyhood, his realization that his puerile father was not up to the task of being an emotionally strong father or financial provider weighed on him for years, up to the time in his life when he had to delay his own marriage because he was supporting his parents financially.

Freud enrolled in the University of Vienna to study medicine in 1873 (ID xii). After earning a medical degree, he began a career at Vienna

General Hospital as a clinical assistant in the area of neurology. In 1884, he studied the medicinal properties of cocaine and became a consumer of the drug. He accepted a scholarship in 1885 to study hysterical symptoms and treatment under the direction of Jean-Martin Charcot at the Salpetriere Clinic in France (ID xii). When he returned to Vienna in 1886, he established a private practice in the treatment of nervous disease (ID xii). Over the next few years he established relationships and shared medical cases with fellow-doctors.

In 1895, Freud came to the realization that sickness is not always attributable to physical causes, but can include a psychological cause. That represented a complete reversal of his professional training (ID xiii) as a neurologist. When he found that some sickness has no organic or physiological cause, he turned his attention to psychiatry. In 1896, he began to use the expression 'psychoanalysis' to refer to his clinical method for evaluating health and treating pathology in the psyche. As the founder of psychoanalysis, he developed what would later be called the 'talking cure' which is a treatment that is conducted via an ongoing dialogue between a patient and a psychoanalyst. Freud began his self-analysis and development of his theory of Oedipus complex in 1897. He also came to the conclusion that what people regard as childhood memories are likely to be their earliest fantasies, because the unconscious psyche cannot distinguish between reality and fantasy. In 1899, he published "*The Interpretation of Dreams*" as an introduction to psychoanalysis and his theory about the unconscious aspect of the psyche. Then, in 1902 he founded the Wednesday Psychological Society, as an intellectual circle of fellow doctors to participate in the development of the theories of psychoanalysis. In 1905, he developed his theory about transference and countertransference, which he related to how infantile attachments play formative roles in subsequent therapeutic relationships.

As an adult, Sigmund Freud's reported feelings of being unlovable probably stemmed from his sense that his mother loved him not for himself, but for being her creation. Well into adulthood, Sigmund would dutifully go to Amalie's house for Sunday lunch (FIB 36). He found the lunch visits so anxiety-inducing that he usually arrived late and often experienced gastrointestinal distress (FIB 17). Freud's response to Amalie's mandatory Sunday lunches, showed a disabling dependence on his powerful mother. His narcissistic mother left him feeling unlovable well into his adult years. He was aware that people did not warm to him the way they warmed to Jung. Jung had charisma. That was part of the reason, he wanted Jung to function as a public relations person for the psycho-analytic movement.

Freud fell in love with Martha Bernays in 1882. He lived in Vienna and she lived in a neighboring city. The courtship was conducted mostly by letters, of which Freud wrote over nine hundred. The nature of Freud's romantic behavior when he fell in love with Martha was demanding, jeal-ous and controlling. His inability to tolerate separation was seen in his demand for total compliance and for her complete identification with himself, his feelings, and his opinions. He attempted to control Martha omnipotently (FIB 123). He demanded that Martha renounce her fam-ily's orthodox brand of Judaism, because he wanted an atheist fiancée (FIB 124). Martha complied, but he continued to be plagued by uncer-tainty about his attractiveness and lovability. He experienced severe separation anxiety and fear of losing Martha. When one of her letters arrived, it would restore his psychic equilibrium and elevate his mood (FIB 126 - 127). Theirs was a four-year engagement before they married in Hamburg in 1886. The delay was due to the fact that Freud's savings were dwindling because he was supporting his parents financially, and Martha had a modest dowry. According to Whitebook, there was a pat-tern of dependency on things that Freud used to repair the gaps in the fabric of his sense of self: letters from Martha, cocaine from Fliess, and cigars Freud obtained for himself (FIB 127).

In 1887, Freud established a friendship with Wilhelm Fliess who was a German colleague. Between 1887 and 1901, Freud had what biographer Whitebook called a 'grande passion' with Wilhelm Fliess (FIB 122). As with Martha, Freud experienced a repeat of low tolerance for separa-tion in his relationship with Fliess (FIB 127). He described his separation anxiety by comparing Martha's letters and Fliess' letters with narcotic substances such as the cocaine or the cigars on which Freud depended (FIB 127) because they repaired his sense of separation and restored his sense of self (FIB 127). Freud reacted to Fliess in much the same way he reacted to Martha – love at first sight. Fliess provided the right kind of screen onto which Freud projected his idealizations (FIB 189). When

Freud met Fliess, he was in the process of separating from Josef Breuer (FIB 140). Breuer was being cast off as 'hated enemy' when Fliess was being elevated to the role of 'beloved friend'. Breuer was being cast off because he did not agree with Freud's belief that sexuality was the cause of all hysteria. As with Martha, Freud required unequivocal acceptance from Breuer (FIB 140). Martha complied, but Breuer did not. In letters to Fliess, Freud shared his positive view of homosexuality by commenting on the 'androphilic current' as having a potential for creativity (FIB 230). In his erotic transference to Fliess, Freud wrote letters about the power of homosexual libido. This material disturbed Fliess. Fliess' wife decided that the homosexual bond between the two men threatened the Fliess marriage (FIB 231). Fliess agreed with his wife and brought the friendship with Freud to an end. For Freud, Fliess's role changed from 'beloved friend' to 'hated enemy'. Years later when Freud fainted in the Park Hotel in Munich, he shared with his friend Ernest Jones that he associated his fainting with Fliess in whose presence he had fainted, in the same hotel. Freud also acknowledged to Jones that his androphilic libido was involved in the fainting episode (FIB 304). Freud exhibited a repetitive pattern of behavior toward his colleagues. He attracted colleagues into his orbit. He would share ideas about psychoanalysis. Many would find his ideas appealing. Whenever they disagreed with him, he would adopt the stance that they would come around to his way of thinking as soon as they understood enough about psychoanalysis. When he found that he could not control them, he would end the relationship. That happened repeatedly with a number of colleagues including Joseph Breuer, Alfred Adler, Wilhelm Fliess, Wilhelm Stekel and later, Carl Jung.

At the time Freud and Jung began their collaboration, Freud was showing signs that the trauma and the conflicts he experienced before meeting Jung, were leading him toward the edge of neurosis. There was the loss of brother Julius, who died when he was a baby. Later, there was the loss of a strong attachment with nephew John, whose parents relocated to England. Freud noticed that he had a tendency to form love-hate relationships. He was also aware that Jacob's inadequate fathering left him with Oedipal shortcomings. Sigmund's mother's domineering approach to parenting continued to influence him well into his adult life. His illicit relationship with his sister-in-law curtailed his ability to participate in dream interpretation that involved disclosure of his personal information. His fainting spells along with what he called his unruly homosexual feelings affected his interaction with male colleagues. Freud acknowledged to Ernest Jones that he had a bit of neurosis which he felt needed attention. The trauma and the conflicts that accumulated in Freud's life, before his relationship with Jung got underway, suggest that their collaboration was not the main cause of Freud's neurotic illness that followed the breakup of the Freud-Jung relationship.

Context of Archetype as Biological Entity: Projection & Introjection

This section examines the disciple-leader relationship between Jung and Freud in the context of archetype as a biological entity. When viewed from this perspective, Jung's emotional reaction to Freud is characterized as an unconscious projection from the mind of Jung to the mind of Freud. That emotional reaction, coupled with Jung's willingness to accept the mantle of heir apparent to Freud's psychoanalytic movement, indicate that they had entered into a disciple-leader relationship. The leader archetype was activated and the contents of Jung's projection were images of an idealized leader. Freud had more experience in terms of years in his private practice, while Jung had more experience in treating a variety of mental illness at the public Burgholzli Hospital. Jung looked to Freud as an ideal leader because Freud had the freedom to establish the psychoanalytic movement and the ingenuity to invent the 'talking cure'. Freud saw in Jung the ideal disciple because Jung came into his life as an experienced psychiatrist, a Christian and a Swiss national at a time when Freud was trying to prevent the psychoanalytic movement becoming a Jewish national movement, confined to Austria.

Jung's projection was about his struggle to convert his professional anxiety into meaning about the future of his career. His unprocessed experience pertained to the environment at the Burgholzli Hospital. Jung wanted to recapture the intellectual stimulation he experienced as a student at the University of Basel. At the Burgholzli Hospital, the emphasis was on the daily routine and was strictly oriented to observing patients, keeping track of their treatments and being always prepared to attend to any patient, at short notice. The career path Jung wanted for himself was not compatible with his job. He felt that the rigid routine of treating and monitoring patients at the Burgholzli Hospital did not offer an opportunity for his intellectual flowering. What interested Jung was not the practice of psychiatry, but the opportunity to conduct research in psychiatry (JB 61).

It was the publication of the Word Association Test that first brought young psychiatrist Carl Jung to the attention of the well-established neurologist-turned-psychiatrist, Sigmund Freud. Freud welcomed the Word Association Test because it provided scientific validation for his hypothesis of repression, about which he had not conducted any scientific experiments. The two men began their correspondence in 1906 when they bonded on shared interests in the psyche. Their professional collaboration and personal friendship spanned the years 1906 through 1913, when they shared professional opinions and clinical findings about the interaction between the conscious and unconscious aspects of the psyche. Freud was known for his 'talking cure' as a treatment for patients suffering from repressed fears and conflicts. At the time, the talking cure was not readily accessible because it was not available as a documented procedure. To get access to the talking cure, it was necessary to reach out to Freud. Jung was interested in finding out how to administer the talking cure, but he was in Zurich while Freud was in Vienna. When Jung reached out by letter, Freud invited him to Vienna. The two men met face-to-face for the first time in Vienna, in March 1907. Carl and Emma had lunch with the Freud family. After lunch, Jung and Freud retreated to Freud's study, where they spent thirteen hours discussing various topics related to their profession. Their conversation included a discussion of Freud's theory of sexuality. Jung's later comment was that when he advanced his reservations, Freud attributed them to his lack of experience (FJ 104). Already, in their first meeting, they were having disagreements. After that meeting, it took them years to realize that Jung could not be the subservient disciple Freud wanted, and Freud could not be the non-authorian leader Jung expected.

Years after visiting the Freud family in 1907, Jung gave an account of meeting the family (JSF 151). He noted that the relationship between Freud and his wife Martha seemed superficial and Martha seemed to have no understanding of Freud's career in psychoanalysis. Jung also reported that Martha's sister Minna, who was a member of the household and who was interested in psychoanalysis, pulled him aside and confided her guilt about having an intimate relationship with Freud (JSF 151). From their first meeting, Jung was aware of that conflict in Freud's life. Jung agreed to make a presentation in August 1907 in Amsterdam at the First International Congress for Psychiatry, Psychology, and the Assistance to the Insane, but he had 'unpleasant presentiments' about presenting Freud's unpopular theories of hysteria and sexuality (FJ 112 - 113). Jung's presentation attempted to defend Freud's theories, but was met with contempt for Freud from those present. In April 1908, Freud and Jung attended the Salzburg Congress. There, Freud attributed sexual causes to schizophrenia, while Jung explained schizophrenia in terms of toxins in the brain. At the end of the Congress, Freud told Jung "... *after having moved a few steps away from me you will find your way back, and then go far with me*" (FJ 131). Freud was demonstrating his low tolerance for colleagues who have dissenting opinions. In 1909, Freud and Jung were invited to lecture at Clark University in Massachusetts, USA. By that time Freud's publication of "The Interpretation of Dreams" was already in the public domain, and it had made dream interpretation contingent upon disclosure of private information. While on the seven-week trip together, Freud related a dream and requested Jung's interpretation. When Jung asked for additional private information to aid the interpretation, Freud refused to disclose private details, with the explanation that he was unwilling to put his authority at risk by disclosing private information (MDR 158). Here is an excerpt from "Memories, Dreams, Reflections" in which Aniela Jaffe quotes Jung:

> "Freud had a dream. ... I interpreted it as best I could, but (requested) some additional details from his private life. Then he said, 'But I cannot risk my authority.' At that moment he lost it altogether."
>
> — Carl Jung (MDR 158)

Diedre Bair's biography of Jung explains that the private matter which posed a risk to Freud's authority was the revelation of Freud's alleged sexual relationship with his sister-in-law (JB 164). By the time of the dream interpretation, Jung already knew of the relationship between

Freud and Minna because Minna had confessed to Jung. Jung felt that Freud was giving his personal authority greater priority than psychoanalytic truth. My interpretation is that when Jung realized that Freud prioritized his own authority above psychoanalytic truth, his idealization of Freud was punctured ... it broke Jung's projection. Freud's protection of his authority was particularly stunning to Jung because Freud's own book made dream interpretation contingent upon disclosure of private information. The discrepancy between Freud's published dream interpretation and his private insistence on being the not-to-be-questioned authority in psychoanalysis marked a line in intellectual dishonesty which Jung refused to cross.

Context of Archetype as Emergent Phenomenon: Appropriation & Internalization

This section examines the disciple-leader relationship between Jung and Freud in the context of archetype as an emergent phenomenon. When viewed from this perspective, Jung's emotional reaction to Freud is characterized as a conscious appropriation from the external world. Jung's appropriation was a collection of images, thoughts and emotions drawn from the external environment, including the profession of psychiatry, where practitioners had opportunities to conduct research, perform experiments, make presentations to colleagues and publish their theories in journals. Jung saw Freud as a practitioner leading the league of professionals who were coming up with new theories and new techniques for treating patients. That is what Jung yearned to do ... research. The leader archetype was activated by Jung's appropriation from the external world of leadership including societal expectations of the profession of psychiatry.

The two processes that characterize archetype-as-emergent-phenomenon — appropriation and internalization — are processes that can be readily seen in the way that children acquire language skills. Children appropriate language consciously from social and cultural sources in their community, and with the help of caregivers, they internalize language into their mental models. That is similar to how Jung appropriated idealized leadership from the external world, which included the community of health care professionals. Jung adopted conscious content primarily from the world of psychiatry. The content of his appropriation included societal expectations of leaders in general and psychiatrists in particular. Internalization is the incorporation of a cultural appropriation into one's mental model. An opportunity for internalization of Jung's appropriation was lost when Freud asked Jung to interpret his dream, but refused to provide information about his personal life. When Jung realized that Freud placed his own authority above psychoanalytic truth, his idealization of Freud crumbled. That opportunity for internalization was lost because the idealization of leadership had no basis in psychoanalytic truth. Freud's prioritization of his personal authority above psychoanalytic truth was especially disappointing to Jung because Freud's definition made dream interpretation contingent upon disclosure of private information.

Jung's appropriation was deflated partly by Freud's refusal to risk his authority by disclosing personal information, after having asked Jung to interpret his dream. Another contributing factor to dissolving the appropriation was that, over a period of exposure to Freud's views about the psyche, Jung lost confidence in Freud as a credible leader in their profession. For example, Freud's insistence on the sexual nature of libido was viewed with skepticism among psychiatrists. The dissolution of Jung's appropriation became clear in his 1912 publication of "Psychology of the Unconscious" which precipitated the end of their relationship, because it revealed that his disciple-leadership interaction with Freud was not sustainable. That publication revealed that the two psychiatrists had opposing views about topics like libido, dreams, repression and the unconscious aspect of the psyche. A third contributing factor in the disintegration of the appropriation was their fundamental difference in what each expected of the other. Freud expected Jung to be a compliant disciple who does not question his authority about psychoanalysis. Jung expected Freud to be a leader open to his disciples having different views about psychoanalysis. Neither man fit the expectations of the other.

Since Jung's appropriation was dissolved, the containment generated no new meaning for internalization into his mental model. The containment provided no opportunity for psychological growth. What is remarkable about the relationship between Jung and Freud is that these were two psychiatrists who dedicated their professional lives to helping other people achieve psychological growth, but neither seems to have achieved any discernable psychological growth from their seven-year professional collaboration. It is also remarkable that despite seven years of voluminous correspondence, sharing of ideas, and joint travels to lectures and conferences in several cities … the intense communication between Jung and Freud produced no joint legacy of psychological value. The International Psychological Association (IPA) had been established by Freud and his fellow doctors, including Jung. They had chosen Jung to be the president for three years: 1910, 1911 and 1913. Yet, when Jung resigned in 1913, he walked away from an IPA that remained strictly Freudian. Once Freud realized he could not persuade Jung to adopt the psychoanalytic model, he lost interest in any kind of relationship with Jung. When Jung realized that Freud would not have his authority questioned, Jung lost interest in being Freud's disciple. Jung and Freud had their last meeting at the 1913 International Psychoanalytical Congress in Munich, where Jung made a presentation about psychological types. At the Congress, Jung explained his ideas about the distinction between extraverted types and introverted types. That presentation was a clear departure from Freud's psychoanalysis. It launched Jung's career as founder of a new school that would come to be known as Analytical Psychology. In the next section, I explain my search for evidence of symbolization in the interaction between Jung and Freud.

Converting Experience to Meaning: Symbolization

In my reading of their biographies and the exchange of letters between Jung and Freud, I found nothing that I regard as the emergence of a symbol as described in "A Critical Dictionary of Jungian Analysis" where psychologist Andrew Samuels and others define symbol in terms of concept, intent, purpose and content. In my view, the communication between Jung and Freud never gained the psychological traction of a dialectical interaction. I think their voluminous conscious communications crowded out their unconscious communication, so there was no viable psychological output from their seven-year containment. Jung's unconscious projection of idealized leadership was broken when Freud refused to risk his authority by supplying personal information. There was no evidence of metabolization of the unassimilated content of Jung's projection. Jung's conscious appropriation of idealized leadership was dissolved when the two men failed to establish common ground in their views of the psyche. There was no evidence that Jung's appropriation was internalized into his mental model. Their collaboration began with them disagreeing on the topic of libido and ended with disagreements on the nature of the psyche as a whole. After years of collaboration and friendship, neither had a change of outlook, and they produced no joint legacy.

In relation to the Bion-Cartwright containment model, the word 'symbiotic' refers to an interaction of mutual dependence, where psychological growth is curtailed, or does not exist. Although Jung and Freud had an emotional bond of friendship, and there was a projection cast from the mind of Jung to the mind of Freud, I do not see any indication that Freud functioned as a container. I believe the symbiotic mode of containment applies to their relationship because of what I see as complicity in their mutual dependence. Each had a part of his sense of identity remain underdeveloped because he relied on the other, in whom that sense of identity was better developed.

Jung admired the autonomy and personal freedom that Freud exhibited in establishing the psychoanalytic movement, which included the International Psychanalytical Association (IPA) and the Jahrbuch journal. In addition, Freud had made original contributions to psychiatry in the areas of a published book about dream interpretation, the development of a new procedure called the talking cure, the performance of a self-analysis from which he defined the Oedipus complex, a hypothesis about the influence of libido on psychological disorders, a theory of repressed memories, and hypotheses about the nature of interaction between conscious and unconscious components of the psyche. The psychoanalytic movement was Freud's contribution to psychiatry. Having created it, he could populate it, manage it and shape it as he pleased. Freud had the autonomy and personal freedom to use the psychoanalysis movement for whatever purpose he chose. In addition, Freud was the financial provider for his family. During his time in the psychoanalytic movement, Jung had not yet developed his own autonomy and personal freedom. In his role as heir apparent to the psychoanalytic movement, Jung had been elected editor of Jahrbuch journal and president of the IPA. Although he chafed under Freud's leadership of the psychoanalytic movement, he relied on Freud's autonomy and personal freedom. Jung's sense of autonomy was limited by the fact that he could not be financial provider for his family because his wife's wealth far exceeded what he could earn. His sense of personal freedom was limited by the fact that he spent much of his work life treating patients in a hospital, when he yearned to conduct research. During their collaboration, Jung benefited from the autonomy and personal freedom that Freud exhibited in establishing the psychoanalytic movement, but Jung did not develop his own autonomy and personal freedom during the containment.

Characteristics that Freud admired about Jung were his strong intellect combined with an aptitude for scientific research. Jung was a lecturer at the University of Zurich, where his presentations were popular with students as well as members of the public. He also supervised students' dissertations. As the principal developer of the Word Association Test, Jung demonstrated an aptitude for research that Freud found appealing. Freud found Jung's work on the Word Association Test appealing because it provided validation of Freud's theory of repression ... for which Freud had offered no scientific evidence or hypothesis, despite his desire to give the psychoanalytic movement scientific respectability. When Freud met Jung, the older man immediately designated Jung his scientific son and heir (JB 115). Biographer Bair points out that their first meeting took place at a time when Freud lusted for academic significance (JB 115). During the time they collaborated, Freud did not develop his intellectual, scientific skills. Instead he relegated to Jung the intellectual activities such as editor of the Jahrbuch journal, and role as president of the IPA. Instead of developing his own intellectual and scientific potential, Freud chose to rely on his self-analyses, from which he made admittedly unscientific generalizations about the population at large. The complicity that I see in their symbiotic containment is that Jung depended on Freud's autonomy and personal freedom instead of developing his own, while Freud depended on Jung's intellectual and research skills instead of developing his own.

During their containment, Freud's attention was not on metabolizing the unassimilated emotional and cognitive experiences that created anxiety for Jung. He was mentally available to Jung for the purpose of having Jung's personal assets become assets of the psychoanalytic movement. When they met, Jung was an established psychiatrist at the prestigious Burgholzli Hospital with experience in treating a variety of disorders. He was also a respected lecturer at the University of Zurich, where he supervised dissertations. Jung had credentials and experience that Freud found valuable in expanding the psychoanalytic movement, but the friendship did not include Freud functioning as a container for Jung's projection. Their mind-to-mind connection was not about dialectical interaction. The friendship generated emotional turmoil that was dampened by each seeing the other as an extension of himself. In this symbiotic containment, each man became a receptacle for a part of the other's sense of identity. Freud had a well-developed sense of autonomy and freedom, upon which Jung relied. That made Freud an extension of Jung. Jung had a well-developed intellect and aptitude for scientific research, upon which Freud relied. That made Jung an extension of Freud. There was an unstated complicity between them to be dependent on each other for parts of their identity they were not yet ready to develop for themselves.

Freud and Jung did not undergo formal psychological analysis. In the early 20th century, analysis was not yet a requirement for their profession. However, they both knew of psychological projection. In my opinion, Freud did not become a container of Jung's projection. In spite of voluminous communication between the two men, I found no indication of Freud initiating any effort at introjection. My impression is that their conscious communication crowded out their unconscious communication, leaving little opportunity for either to be psychologically supportive of the other. During the years of their friendship, each expected the other to be an extension of his own desire. Their expectation of reciprocal extension could not be sustained because they had fundamental disagreements about the psychoanalytic movement. Another reason their expectation of reciprocal extension was unsustainable was their secrecy under the guise of collaboration. During the containment, each man was writing a book and mentioned the fact to the other, but they were secretive about the contents of their books. Freud was writing "Totem and Taboo" at about the same time that Jung was writing

"*Psychology of the Unconscious*". Despite claims of collaboration, neither man discussed the content of his book with the other. When published, the views expressed in the two books were so widely divergent that it precipitated the end of their collaboration. The positive beginning of their friendship, followed by acrimony at the end echoed the pattern that each man acknowledged having established as a template for relationships in his early life.

During the years of their friendship, Jung and Freud did not connect by mutually exploring each other's interior world in the interest of psychological growth. As the contained, Jung produced the first narrative about his conflict between his routine treatment of patients in the hospital and the research he yearned to do. As the container, Freud produced the second narrative about his desire for a scientific son and heir to bolster the psychoanalytic movement. However, there was no real third narrative, because the communication between them was one of reciprocity, where each was depending on the other to be something he could not be. This is indicative of the symbiotic mode of containment, which has no product apart from the contained-container interaction. Freud demonstrated little interest in helping Jung process an unassimilated state of mind, because he was busy using Jung's personal assets to enhance the psychoanalytic movement. Jung's mind needed another mind to help him process his projection, but Freud's mind was preoccupied with shaping and controlling Jung to fit the role of heir to the psychoanalytic movement. In the symbiotic mode of containment, the minds of the contained and container do not connect by mutually exploring each other's interior world for psychological growth. Jung and Freud participated in a complicity that protected the relationship as it stood. Their bond was based on a shared delusion ... a delusion of collaboration. Their collaboration was a delusion because they had no common goal and they produced no joint legacy. Their reverie appears to have been restricted to mostly conscious communication. Each was curious about the other, but only as it served to maintain the symbiotic union. Thoughts that allow two minds to connect through imaginative exploration and mutual verbal communication are not available in the symbiotic mode of containment. This created a blind spot that arose from complicity between the two protagonists to protect a shared delusion from discovery. Jung and Freud were two people in close association, but they found themselves in a shared delusion that could not be sustained.

The ability to gather up thoughts and emotions and generate new meaning demands that an encounter be subjected to a series of transformations. This means finding ways of tolerating the emotional storm for long enough so that it can be given particular personal meaning. Jung and Freud grappled with their storm of disagreements about libido, regression, dreams and authority. Cartwright reads Bion as having emphasized the transformative qualities of lived experience always unfolding at the cusp of one's awareness (CSM 3). During their collaboration, both Jung and Freud had their cusp of awareness where meaning is derived from unconscious content of the psyche, but they had divergent ideas about the nature of unconscious content and how it related to consciousness. Their professional knowledge of projection combined with their intense camaraderie were not enough to equip them to manage a projection. If they recognized Jung's projection onto Freud, they did not act on it.

Although the relationship ended in an abrupt and decisive loss of interest in each other, my research did not reveal any psychological harm caused by either. After the relationship ended, Freud experienced a neurotic disorder and Jung experienced a psychotic disorder. I found no indication that either man caused any psychological harm in the other. What I did find is that each was heading toward disorder due to personal conflicts and trauma that they experienced before they met. By their own acknowledgements, relationships in their early lives set a pattern of elevated-friend becoming rejected-enemy in later life. Their relationship fit that pattern.

Call To Action: Take Away A Portable Understanding

In this chapter, I offer the seven-year interaction between Carl Jung and Sigmund Freud as an example of the symbiotic mode of containment. It is a story of a relationship between two people who regarded each other as friends and collaborators, but the relationship left them as it found them, unable or unwilling to engage in an exploration of each other's interior world. Initially, the relationship between Jung and Freud held great promise, but as a containment, it did not result in psychological growth or a joint legacy. As a call to action, I invite readers to take away a portable understanding of the symbiotic mode of containment. Here is a summary of the interaction between Jung and Freud, and the outcome of their containment:

- **Mode:** Jung and Freud had a symbiotic mode of containment.
- **Roles:** Jung was the contained and Freud was the container. They did not switch roles during the containment.
- **Symmetry:** The relationship between Jung and Freud was asymmetrical. They had chosen to work with each other, but they were not co-equals. Jung, the younger man, was an established psychiatrist working in a hospital where he was required to spend most of his time treating patients. Freud had a private practice and was founder of the psychoanalytic movement, which he could fashion as he wished. Each respected the expertise of the other, and to some extent, depended on the other. Jung depended on Freud's autonomy and personal freedom that rendered the psychoanalytic movement an opportunity for research. Freud depended on Jung's intellectual skills and aptitude for research to help put the psychoanalytic movement on a scientific footing. Their relationship had a gradient of power. Jung wanted to participate in the innovations of the psychoanalysis movement, but Freud would only allow that on his own terms.
- **Psychological Frame:** In a containment, the psychological frame is made up of a purpose, a time boundary and a space boundary. The psychological frame of this symbiotic containment did not have a jointly agreed purpose; it held a different purpose for each man. Jung's purpose was finding a path from a career of drudgery in treating patients, to a career of intellectual stimulation in research and experimentation. Freud's purpose was to prepare Jung to take over the psychoanalytic movement by embracing Freud's ideas about the psyche, without question. The time dimension of the frame spanned the years 1906 to 1913 when the two men interacted. Their means of communication included letters, visits to each other's homes, travelling together to lecture in the United States among other countries, and attendance at conferences in several European cities, including Munich. The space dimension connected Jung's home city of Zurich, Switzerland and Freud's home city of Vienna, Austria.

- **Dialectical Narrative:** The first narrative came from Jung as the contained. His narrative was about his yearning to change his career from the mundane activities of treating patients to breaking new ground by conducting research. The second narrative came from Freud as the container. His narrative was about preparing a future for his psychoanalytic movement. My opinion is that the interaction between Jung and Freud did not gain the kind of psychological traction that would have enabled a third narrative. I believe their conscious communication crowded out their unconscious communication, making it impossible to sustain the type of dialogue that could generate a third narrative. If there had been a third narrative, there would have been evidence of it in their internal reality or their external reality. From the point of view of internal reality, their relationship left them as it found them: two individuals bent on pursuing their divergent ideas about the psyche. From the point of view of external reality, there was nothing of jointly created psychological value ... no joint theory, no joint publication, no joint legacy.
- **Psychological Growth / Harm:** There is no indication that either Jung or Freud experienced psychological growth from their relationship, and no evidence that either brought about psychological harm in the other. Before they met, both men had a history of forming friendships with other men, then later pushing them away as enemies. Both men attributed that pattern in their behavior to experiences of conflict and trauma in their lives as young boys.

After the Containment Ended

Following the end of their relationship in 1913, the only contact between them was Jung's reference of a patient to Freud in 1923. After the friendship ended, Jung and Freud each experienced a psychological disorder. Freud experienced a neurotic disorder and Jung experienced a psychotic disorder. Freud's neurotic disorder led him to a deep self-analysis. On recovering from the disorder, he used the knowledge gathered in self-analysis to enhance the psychoanalytic movement. Freud continued to publish books about psychoanalysis, treat patients, build the IPA and expand his group of fellow-doctors to support the IPA. The outbreak of World War II interrupted his career. When Vienna was occupied by Nazi Germany in 1938, his books were burned and he was investigated by the Gestapo. Freud fled from Austria to London, where he wrote his last book *"Moses and Monotheism"*. After suffering from oral cancer, Freud requested a lethal dose of morphine, from which he died in 1939.

After the separation from Freud, Jung lived out the rest of his life in Zurich. Jung experienced a psychotic disorder which led him to analysis by one of his colleagues, as well as a deep self-analysis. On coming out of these analyses, he used the knowledge he gleaned to establish an area of study that he named Analytical Psychology. He treated patients in a private practice, travelled to explore different cultures, published a number of books on Analytical Psychology, and cultivated colleagues to carry on his legacy. Following complications including gastric distress, impaired speech and a stroke, Jung passed away in his sleep in Zurich in 1961. His last book was his memoir titled *"Memories, Dreams, Reflections"* which was published posthumously in 1963.

Sources

The sources of information that shape my thinking in this chapter are:
- *"Jung: A Biography"* by Diedre Bair
- "*FREUD: An Intellectual Biography* by Joel Whitebook
- *"Jung's Struggle With Freud"* by George B. Hogenson
- *"Freud and Jung: Years of Friendship, Years of Loss"* by Linda Donn
- *"Memories, Dreams, Reflections"* recorded and edited by Aniela Jaffe
- *"The Interpretation of Dreams"* by Sigmund Freud
- *"Containing States of Mind"* by Duncan Cartwright
- *"Projection and Re-Collection in Jungian Psychology"* by Marie-Louise von Franz
- *"Symbolization: Representation and Communication"* by James Rose (editor).

CHAPTER 13

A Symbiotic Mode of Containment Involving: Thomas Merton & James Fox

"(B)oth Merton and Dom James ... continued their broken dialogue through much of 1967 ... nothing had changed for either of them. They were fixed in place, as if some dance had long since ended but they had nowhere to go. ... James continued to confine Merton, to fend off even the most sensible invitations to him . On his side, Merton couldn't back far enough away even at the hermitage to be thoroughly free of the abbot's hold."

– Roger Lipsey

Having taken the same religious vows for entering the Cistercian Order for Catholic monks, two men of different temperaments, different backgrounds, and different outlooks, came together at a single place and time. The place was the Abbey of Gethsemani in a remote location in Kentucky. The year was 1948. Both were Catholic monks who had taken vows to conduct their lives in accordance with the rules of the Cistercian Order. They were both rather contrary individuals. Although they came to respect each other's spiritually noble aspirations, they did not respect each other's conduct. Yet, they sustained a 20-year relationship in the Abbey of Gethsemani. The Cistercian Order is a Catholic monastic profession, in which monks balance contemplation with work. They cultivate an atmosphere of silence, while practising vows of obedience, celibacy, and poverty. When they began their relationship, Thomas Merton was thirty-three years old and James Fox was fifty-two. Merton had been living in the abbey for seven years when Fox arrived to assume responsibilities for guiding the monks who live in the abbey. As abbot, Fox was responsible for providing spiritual guidance to the monks and he was expected to make the abbey financially self-sufficient.

My interpretation is that Thomas Merton and James Fox had a relationship that provides an example of a symbiotic mode of containment. In the context of the Bion-Cartwright containment model, the word 'symbiotic' refers to a relationship of mutual dependence, where psychological growth is limited. Their relationship was asymmetrical. They did not choose each other and they were not co-equals. There was a power gradient between them. Fox was an older, more experienced monk, who was in charge of monks at the Abbey of Gethsemani. Merton was subject to the rules of the Catholic monastery, as administered by Fox. To help readers understand the relationship between Merton and Fox, I offer some background information in the next two sections. The background information is about their early lives leading up to their meeting at the Abbey of Gethsemani.

Background Information about Thomas Merton

According to biographer Michael Mott, Thomas Merton's parents, Owen and Ruth Merton produced baby Tom in Prades, France in January of 1915, during the winter of the First World War (SM 5). His parents were artists who met at a Parisian art studio named Tudor-Hart. Ruth was an American pursuing interests in dance and visual arts. A New Zealander, Owen was a water-color painter and a pianist (SM 5). She was Episcopalian, he belonged to the Church of England, and their wedding had been conducted according to Anglican rites (SM 6). In keeping with French law, they registered young Tom as a French national. With the limited funds available to her, Ruth read all the childcare literature she could borrow, and she recorded as much as she could of little Tom's growth, appearance, and the power of observation he displayed, such as his ability to identify soldiers passing in the streets. Medical doctor Tom Izod Bennett, a New Zealander friend of Owen, became godfather when Tom was about a year old (SM 8).

In August 1916, Owen, Ruth and Tom moved to America where they took up residence near the home of Ruth's parents, Samuel and Martha Jenkins (SM 13). World War I was underway. At that time in America, art was not considered important, so Owen found it difficult to support his family from his earnings as an artist. To become independent, Owen and Ruth joined an experimental farming community in Maryland, but that was unsuccessful because their intellectual skills were not a good fit for farming activities (SM 14). Little Tom continued to be the center of his mother's attention until age three when his new-born brother, John Paul, became the new focus of her attention (SM 17). When John Paul was six months old, the boys' paternal grandmother, Gertrude, came from New Zealand to visit. On realizing that Tom had not been taught to pray, she prayed the Lord's Prayer with him each night until he could pray on his own.

Owen was not earning much money and Ruth's wealthy father offered financial help, but Owen and Ruth decided not to accept help unless it was needed for medical reasons. A medical reason arose when Ruth was diagnosed with cancer of the stomach. Tom was six years old when she died in 1921. When Owen went to visit Ruth in the hospital, he left Tom in the car. On his return from the hospital, Owen brought Tom a note from Ruth. In the note, Ruth informed Tom that he would never see her again (SM 20). Later in life, Tom characterized the communication by note as a form of rejection.

In search of opportunities to market his art in 1922, Owen took Tom to stay with friends in Bermuda, but that did not work out and Tom was unhappy. Grandfather Sam turned up in Bermuda to take his grandson back to New York, while Owen moved on to Europe (SM 25) in search of opportunities to market his paintings. In summer of 1925, Owen became gravely ill and returned to see his sons at the Jenkins family home in New York. There were disagreements between him and the Jenkins family. Owen wanted his two sons with him, but he could not support them. He refused financial assistance from Sam. They worked out an arrangement in which Owen took Tom to France, while leaving John Paul with the Jenkins family. Merton was ten and a half years old (SM 25 - 26). In Europe, Owen took his son to art galleries and museums. Young Tom enjoyed the father-son relationship that developed during their time together in Europe.

On the advice of Tom's godfather, Owen registered his son at the French school Lycee Ingress in Montauban (SM 31). While Tom was at Lycee in 1927 and 1928, Owen was able to sell his paintings in galleries in London with the help of friends, though not as many paintings as he hoped (SM 40). By June 1928, Owen had given up hope of becoming a successful artist in France. He arrived at Lycee and took Tom out of school (SM 40), then relocated to England, where he enrolled Tom in the Ripley Court boarding school. On holidays, Tom spent time with his paternal Aunt Maud and Uncle Ben who were living in Ealing, a district in west London (SM 40 – 42). When Owen fell ill, he was hospitalized at Middlesex Hospital (SM 41). In 1929, Tom enrolled in Oakham School in England. That was the year of the Stock Market Crash. At the end of the year, his maternal grandfather Sam, who had survived the Market Crash, arrived in England to set about arranging trusts for his two grandsons (SM 51 – 52). The trusts contained stocks and land in America. Godfather, Tom Izod Bennett, would manage young Tom's trust until he reached age twenty-one (SM 53). At the time that Sam was arranging the trusts, Owen was at Middlesex Hospital under the care of Dr. Tom Izod Bennett (SM 53). On Tom's fifteenth birthday, Sam's gift to his elder grandson was a pipe for smoking, which he encouraged Tom to do while they were arranging the trusts (SM 53).

Tom began to spend his holidays in London with his doctor-godfather and wife, Iris. The Bennetts helped to shape Tom's tastes in music and good manners (SM 54). Tom's world opened up to a new lifestyle with new ideas, and a developing sense of his own powers of mind (SM 54). With the allowance at his disposal, he enjoyed movies and musical records (SM 55). By the end of 1930, he also became aware of the effects of the Depression, from the many soldiers who stood on the sidewalks selling matches and pencils (SM 55). In the soldiers, Tom noticed a terrible sickness, the same sickness that was killing his father, who was still in Middlesex Hospital. Owen's memory was fading. His memories were no longer of the times he shared with Tom; they were of the times he shared with Ruth. In January 1931, Tom became an orphan when Owen died of a brain tumor at age forty-four (SM 55). He was an accomplished water-color and oil painter, but he had struggled to maintain a self-supporting lifestyle.

Merton described his life as lacking in structure and direction, just as his father's life had been lacking in structure and direction. Having noticed Owen's driven quest for recognition as an artist, coupled with the paltry results, Merton attributed it to a lack of what he called family structure and direction. Owen did have family, some in New Zealand and others in England. For most of his life, Owen led a nomadic existence teetering at the brink of poverty, always hoping to get satisfying results from his next artistic effort. Success proved to be illusive. Owen's death left Tom with the impression that his own life might turn out to be just as directionless as his father's life, unless he acquired some guardrails in his life.

Thomas Merton won a scholarship to study modern languages at the University of Cambridge where he started in October 1933 at age eighteen (SM 66). At Cambridge, he was indifferent to religion, according to Mott's quotes from Merton's autobiography (SM 77). Within a year, Merton was in debt, drinking too much, and he was not doing well academically (SM 78). His debts were owed mainly to booksellers, tobacconists, and wine merchants. He and his landlady were in conflict about having women in his room (SM 83). One of the women announced that she was pregnant and she was sure Merton was the father (SM 84). At the time, Cambridge was considering withdrawing Merton's scholarship because his grades were not as high as expected (SM 85). His godfather summoned him to London for a review of his situation, during which he recommended that Merton withdraw from Cambridge and remain in America after the summer holidays. Merton agreed to stay in America. He felt relieved about leaving his Cambridge problems behind, but he felt his godfather had rejected him (SM 85).

Biographer Mott is not sure if what godfather Bennett settled was a breach-of-promise case or a paternity case. Anyway, Bennett arranged a legal settlement and promised not to reveal the legal settlement to Merton's grandfather, Sam (SM 84). Glad to have Merton remain in the

United States, Sam encouraged him to pursue a degree in journalism and helped him enroll at Columbia University in New York (SM 86). In January 1935, Merton entered Columbia University with the intention of obtaining a degree in one of the social sciences, after which he planned to get a job as a newspaper reporter (SM 95). The friends Merton made at Columbia were to become lifetime friends (SM 97). They would later develop careers in the publishing industry, and they were willing to publish his written works before and after Merton became a monk.

Merton experienced additional losses of family members. Grandfather Sam died in October 1936 and about a year later, grandmother Martha passed away (SM 104). In the Spring of 1937, Merton bought a book to pass the time while on a journey by train. The book was Etienne Gibson's "*The Spirit of Medieval Philosophy*" which aroused his curiosity about religion and motivated him to go to church (SM 109). This book marked a turning point in Merton's life. It describes Etienne Gibson's view that medieval philosophy is about the Greek tradition infused with the spirit of Christianity. The book aroused Merton's curiosity about Christianity. By the Spring of 1938, Merton had started graduate work on an English literature program (SM 112). He later changed his thesis to a study of the 18th century English poet and artist, William Blake, who is known for his commitment to Christianity coupled with his disdain for orthodox Christianity. Blake looked down on the Christian separation of body from soul, because he saw each as an extension of the other. He also regarded the concept of sin as a trap set by orthodox Christianity to inhibit natural human desires.

Curious about Eastern religions, Merton asked an Eastern monk, a fellow student at Columbia University, what he should read to gain an understanding of spiritual and mystical life. In a surprising response, the Eastern monk referred to Western books: "*St. Augustine's Confessions*" and "*The Imitation of Christ*". In 1938, after reading books about Catholicism, Merton found the concepts of forgiveness of sins and service to fellow humans appealing. After discussions of Catholicism, Merton took a tentative trip to a local Catholic Church in Corpus Christi. On returning to his room, he experienced a feeling of peace, which he thought would diminish swiftly. The feeling diminished, but did not go away. Something inside him felt settled from the knowledge that he could go back on other Sunday mornings (SM 118). In November 1938, Merton became a Catholic. He felt that the old 'unfixed, frenzied aimlessness' was behind him and a new beginning in front of him (SM 121).

On the first day of September in 1939, hopes of there being no war in Europe were dashed when Germany invaded Poland. That was the start of the Second World War. During that year, Merton wrote a novel, which was rejected by Farrar and Rinehart publishing house (SM 137). However, that rejection did not discourage his interest in writing. By the end of 1939, Merton had decided to enter a seminary in preparation for becoming a Catholic priest (SM 143). He wanted to choose a Catholic order that would allow him to pursue his interest in becoming a writer. His 1940 application to the Franciscan Order was rejected without an explanation. Biographer Mott conjectures that the rejection could be due to Merton's own sense of his unfitness, and the possibility that an English legal settlement regarding Merton's illegitimate English child may be binding in American court (SM 156).

On receipt of his draft card in November 1940, Merton replied by requesting a non-combatant role, while outlining his reason for being a Conscientious Objector (SM 169). During Holy Week of 1941, Merton attended a retreat at the Abbey of Gethsemani (SM 172). In wondering about his desire to become a priest, Merton thought of his beloved father. He believed that, despite his father being a good man, he had floundered because he had no structure in his life. Merton reflected on the fact that he also had no family structure and no direction. Now that he had become a Catholic, the Church was providing him with structure (SM 182). By December 1941 Meron was back at the Abbey of Gethsemani, this time to be interviewed as part of his application to join the Trappist Order (SM 201). He was accepted and given permission to pursue his writing ambition (SM 202). The Abbey of Gethsemani is where Thomas Merton began his relationship with James Fox in 1948 (SM 244).

Background Information about James Fox

The available information about James Fox is limited. I found no record of Fox having written a memoir, nor any biography written about him. Perhaps this is in keeping with his view of monastic life as being about anonymity. My main source of information about Fox is *"Make Peace Before the Sun Goes Down"* by Roger Lipsey. Fox was born in December 1896 in Boston, Massachusetts, where he grew up in a devout Catholic family. His parents, Patrick and Mary, were immigrants from Ireland. He attended Dedham High School where he earned a scholarship to Harvard College to pursue a liberal arts education, majoring in history (MPS 10). By the time he was twenty years old, he had earned a Liberal Arts degree. He completed post-graduate work at Harvard Business School, before going to serve in the U. S. Navy during the First World War. Lipsey quotes Fox's description of his entrepreneurial aspiration when he was a student at Harvard University:

> *"I never went to a Catholic school all my life. And when it came time to choose a university for undergraduate work, I chose a non-sectarian university. I finished the four year undergraduate Liberal Arts course in three years and graduated when twenty years old. Then I went to the graduate school of Business Administration, also there at Harvard. ... I was making plans to become a man of power and influence in the great business world of the United States"* (MPS 10).

At Harvard Business School, Fox studied marketing, accounting, contracts, factory management and military supply (MPS 11). These are the skills on which he focused when he later became abbot at Gethsemani. After World War I ended, he worked at the Internal Revenue Service, where he functioned as an auditor of corporate returns (MPS 11). Fox identified a retreat at the Passionist Monastery in Boston as the occasion when he decided on a religious vocation:

> *"It was on this ... retreat that Grace overcame Nature and I at last surrendered to our dear Lord. I was then twenty four years old. ... Once I entered religious life – the inexorable logic of my mind was now concentrated on things spiritual and eternal"* (MPS 11).

When he joined the Passionist Order in Pittsburgh in 1921, Fox found life at that monastery not compatible with his desire for silence, solitude and seclusion (MPS 12). He obtained permission to transfer to the Trappist-Cistercian Order in 1927 and was ordained a priest in 1930 (MPS 12). The Order of the Cistercians is a contemplative religious order that emphasizes silence and prayer. While a monk in the Monastery of the Holy Ghost in Georgia, he was elected abbot in the year 1946. Two years later, he was assigned the role of abbot of the Abbey of Gethsemani, to replace an abbot who had died. In 1948, James Fox and Thomas Merton began a relationship that would last about 20 years.

The containment model was built by psychologists Wilfred Bion and Duncan Cartwright on the principles of projection and introjection. Since projections occur when archetypes are activated, I describe the relationship between Merton and Fox as mediated by an archetype. To do that, I rely on the two definitions of archetype that are current in the early 21st century. In the next two sections, I describe the Merton-Fox relationship first in the context of archetype as biological entity, then in the context of archetype as emergent phenomenon.

Context of Archetype as Biological Entity: Projection & Introjection

When an archetype is viewed as a biological entity, it is regarded as an ancestral heritage of human experience accumulated over many generations and located in collective unconsciousness. When psychologists define an archetype as a biological entity, the processes they identify for converting life experience to meaning are projection and introjection. Projection is an evacuation of unconscious content from the psyche due to an unbearable state of mind. There was a projection cast from the mind of Merton to the mind of Fox. Having become a Catholic monk, Merton had secured Catholic guardrails for his life, but he still harbored an unsettled state of mind about his ability to live within those guardrails and about his direction in life. His projection was an idealization of a spiritual father that he needed to help him make sense of his life as a monk pursuing a role as a writer in a contemplative monastery. Introjection is a transformation of an unbearable state of mind to a bearable state of mind, followed by its integration into conscious content of the psyche. Fox's behaviors showed no indication that he was capable of introjection; he did not become a carrier of Merton's projection.

Merton had been in the Abbey of Gethsemani for about seven years, when Fox arrived to take up responsibility for the monastery in 1948. As the abbot, Fox was in a position of authority over Merton and the other monks at the abbey. Merton's vow of obedience set him in a situation where Fox was responsible for oversight of his behavior, and for censoring his written works. In the first few years of their relationship, Fox was Merton's confessor, so Fox was responsible for spiritually guiding Merton. In the Catholic Church, 'confessor' is a title used to designate a priest who is granted the authority to hear confession of a penitent and pronounce absolution. A confessor is like a spiritual father. Merton had become a monk because he was in search of structure and direction for his life. So, it was understandable that he would look to the new abbot with hopes of finding a spiritual father. The content of Merton's projection was an idealization of spiritual fatherhood in the form of unprocessed emotions and thoughts about spiritual direction for his life. Fox's authority over Merton and their difference in age put them in a monastic father-son relationship. Fox's title was 'Dom' which is an abbreviation of the word 'dominus' which is Latin for master. Dom is a title used by the Catholic Church to designate a high-ranking monk. When writing to Fox, Merton addressed him as 'Rev. Father'. The monks at the abbey, including Merton, referred to each other as 'Brothers'. There was a power gradient between Merton and Fox for the duration of their 20-year encounter. Having taken a vow of obedience in keeping with the rules of the Trappist subdivision of the Cistercian Order, Merton was duty-bound to submit to the authority of abbot Fox.

The behaviors and communications between Fox and Merton were those of a monk looking to an abbot for fatherly guidance, indicating that the father archetype was activated. Activation of the father archetype indicates a forceable evacuation of a projection from Merton's mind to Fox's mind. The contents of Merton's projection were raw experiences of emotions, images and memories related to fatherhood in terms of direction in life. Because those experiences were incomprehensible to him, they were evacuated from his psyche as an unbearable state of mind. The projection from Merton's mind to Fox's mind created an opportunity for Fox to help Merton metabolize his unassimilated emotional states and structure them into useful thoughts. The father archetype was activated at an important stage of Merton's life. At the time, monks were only allowed to write 4 letters per year. Having been given permission to pursue his writing, Merton published his autobiography in 1948 — the same year Fox arrived at Gethsemani Abbey — and it became a bestseller. Merton was making a transition from contemplative monk in residence to bestselling author and revenue-generator for the abbey. What made this such an ironic transition for Merton was that the Abbey of Gethsemani was a Trappist monastery dedicated to silence and a contemplative lifestyle.

In the context of the Bion-Cartwright containment model, the word 'symbiotic' refers to a relationship of mutual dependence, where psychological growth is limited. In the symbiotic mode of containment, a projection is involuntarily cast from the mind of the contained onto another. Merton's projection was made up of unprocessed emotional and cognitive experiences that created anxiety for him. The projection was cast onto Fox, but Merton felt 'there was no meeting of minds' between himself and Fox, except on a superficial level (MPS 173). This means the containment was not functional. Fox was not mentally available to help Merton render the content of his projection more manageable and thinkable. In his role as the contained, Merton produced the first narrative about his unassimilated state of mind regarding lack of structure and direction in his life. As the container, Fox produced the second narrative about his perception of his role as financial administrator for the abbey. There was no real third narrative from their symbiotic containment because their communication engendered no meeting of minds. Merton's mind needed another mind, but Fox was so focused on mundane experiences as the primary means of interacting with Merton that they found themselves in a mutual dependence with limited opportunity for psychological growth. In the symbiotic mode of containment, the minds of the contained and container do not connect by mutually exploring each other's interior world for growth. They participate in a complicity that protects the relationship as it stands. My opinion is that their bond was based on a shared delusion that by keeping their monastic vows and participating in Catholic rituals, they could achieve spiritual growth. Their shared reverie was limited to the mundane and the secular. Each may have had a curiosity about the other, but only as it served to maintain the symbiotic union.

At the beginning of their encounter, Fox was Merton's confessor, a role commonly associated with being a spiritual guide, or spiritual father. At that point, their relationship had the potential for becoming a containment with Merton as the contained and Fox the container. I believe Merton might have been hoping for a spiritual father-son type of relationship with the older, more experienced abbot, because Merton had entered the Abbey in search of some structure and direction for his life. He believed that he lacked structure and direction in his life, just as his father had been without those qualities. Mindful of what he believed to be a similarity between his own life and his father's life, he sought a source of structure and direction in the Catholic Church, known for its abundance of rules with emphasis on obedience to authority. Merton believed that his father, despite good intentions and a great deal of effort, had floundered in life because there was no family structure to provide direction. He dearly loved his father, but was aware that Owen had not managed his life in a constructive manner. Not wanting to fall into the same splintered, nomadic lifestyle that he had observed in his father, Merton had chosen the Catholic Church, as a source of guardrails and rules ... confessions and forgiveness.

The Catholic Church has an abundance of vows and rules, with many layers of authority to provide support and to enforce them. The Catholic outlook also includes confession and forgiveness, which Merton found appealing. There is structure to be found in all of that, but Merton needed something more personal. He needed a mind to become a container for his unprocessed states of mind. His journals indicate that he had a flourishing interior life. He questioned himself, his thoughts, his behaviors, his outlook, and his critique of himself was not flattering. The Catholic Church has a Sacrament of Confession, which is about self-reflection to determine which thoughts, emotions and behaviors are compatible with the Catholic way of life. As another layer of self-scrutiny, the Catholic Church sets aside 40 days of Lent per year, for the purpose of atonement. Merton had a penchant for soul-searching that would, in time, fill many journals. While reflecting on his interior life, Merton experienced self-doubt and a feeling that his soul might be empty. During confession, he shared his self-reflection with Fox, expecting to get fatherly advice. Instead, there was a gross misunderstanding. As Merton's confessor, Fox was privy to Merton's candid self-reflection about the condition of his soul. Apparently unfamiliar with the depth of self-scrutiny that attends the Sacrament of Confession, Fox leveraged Merton's self-scrutiny against him by labeling him uncured of childhood trauma, unstable, impetuous and neurotic (MPS 85 – 87). In addition to labeling Merton a neurotic, Fox arranged for Merton to see a Catholic psychologist who simply echoed Fox's opinion, without a proper analysis. From there, the relationship between Merton and Fox took off on a downward trajectory of conflicts, suspicion, and resentment.

Fox and Merton had opposing views on a number of topics that were significant in their impact on monastic living. Here are some of them. They had opposing outlooks on war. Fox was proud of the fact that he had served in the U. S. Navy during the First World War, while Merton took pride in being a Conscientious Objector during the Vietnam War. Fox interpreted monastic life as living in anonymity, while Merton was a bestselling author whose publishing friends promoted his writing. Fox wanted to use his Master of Business Administration (MBA) training to make the abbey financially profitable, while Merton saw entrepreneurship as incompatible with the monks' vows of poverty. Fox took pride in changing the abbey from a pastoral farming community to a profit-oriented food processing organization, while Merton worried that royalties from his books were being turned into noisy tractors that disturbed the serenity of monastic life at the abbey, thereby compromising the contemplative aspect of the monastic vocation. Fox did not take much interest in promoting the Second Ecumenical Vatican Council, while Merton wanted to actively promote the ecumenical movement by arranging and attending conferences with leaders of different faiths.

Merton and Fox were contrary individuals. Each exhibited outright contradictions in their behaviors. To name some: When Fox was a younger monk, he had transferred from one monastic order to another because he wanted to find an environment more compatible with his vocation. However, when Merton made a similar request, for the same reason,

Fox refused permission on the specious argument that God sent Merton to Gethsemani, therefore he should stay there. In communications with his superiors external to the abbey, Fox repeatedly referred to Merton as neurotic, but within the abbey Fox was comfortable assigning Merton to be Master of Novices. The contradiction here is that Fox was disparaging about Merton's psychological wellness, while assigning Merton to be a teacher of young novices with impressionable minds. While Fox's communications to his superiors characterized Merton as an impulsive, neurotic miscreant, Fox asked Merton to be his confessor. The contradiction there is that Fox had enough spiritual respect for Merton to value him as a spiritual guide, while downgrading Merton's capabilities to his superiors. An ongoing contradiction was that Fox welcomed the income stream that came from Merton's writing, but was restricting in his censorship of Merton's work. He did not want Merton to write journals, or at least not publish them while he was alive. One of Merton's contrary behaviors is that over a long period of time, he repeatedly asked for permission to live a solitary life in a hermitage, but when he finally got permission, he soon began asking permission to travel to other countries for the purpose of ecumenical conferences. The incompatibility of a solitary hermit life and participation in international ecumenical conferences did not seem to matter to him. Another stark example of Merton's contradictory behavior was his relationship with a nurse. Merton fell in love with a young nurse who was assigned to care for him when he was hospitalized for spinal surgery. In spite of having taken a vow of celibacy, Merton actively courted her affection by arranging telephone calls and outings to social events. He struggled to choose between his vocation and his feelings for the nurse. Eventually, the decision was made for him when she distanced herself from him, by relocating to a different city. Overall, the difference between the two men was that Merton was striving to lead a life as a contemplative monk and a writer, while Fox was striving to make the abbey a profitable farm. They were so far apart in outlook that Merton came to regard Fox more as a business administrator than as a spiritual director.

About five years into their relationship, Fox assigned Merton to be his confessor. My view is that was the point in their containment when Merton's projection was broken. That is when Merton realized Fox was not going to be the spiritual father he needed. By assigning Merton the role of confessor, Fox was handing over to Merton a responsibility for which he saw Merton as being more capable than himself. I believe Merton's projection was broken when he realized that Fox was assigning him the responsibility for spiritual direction. The reassignment of the confessor role from Fox to Merton pointed to the symbiotic nature of the relationship in the sense that each man was avoiding the development of a part of his identity which the other had already developed. Fox was not interested in developing that part of his identity which would make him a competent spiritual father, so he assigned Merton to be his confessor and to be Master of Novices. Merton was not interested in developing that part of his identity which would strengthen his ability to structure and direct his own life, so he engaged in behaviors that were unbecoming to a monk, leaving it up to Fox's authority to rein him in.

My interpretation is that when Merton realized he had no one to help him transform his unprocessed state of mind into meaning, he turned inward and resorted to writing journals. I believe that in the first few years of their relationship, Fox and Merton bonded on a shared delusion that keeping their vows (poverty, celibacy and obedience) and participating in rituals (Mass, sacraments) would result in spiritual growth. Fox kept his vows and organized elaborate rituals of Mass, but he exercised his authority over the monks at the abbey by engaging in practices that were small-minded and petty, under the guise of having a pure intention. He read their mail, and sometimes withheld the mail for trivial reasons. He paid more attention to the economic activities of the abbey than the spiritual development of the monks. He claimed to love simplicity, but he was prone to contrive Masses involving elaborate pontifical vestments and participation of several monks (MPS 189). Lipsey quoted Merton's Journal, volume IV, where he commented on how Fox conducted his life as abbot:

> "His deviousness, his ambivalence, his trickery, his business manipulations are to him pure guileless simplicity because, while he does these things, he does them 'with a pure intention'. ... And he does the same to everybody" (MPS 172).

Merton struggled to keep his vows, and found the rituals to be spiritually wanting. In his second decade at the abbey, Merton stated that while strictness and fervor were common at the abbey, inner growth was lacking (MPS 185). Strictness in compliance with vows and fervent recitation of prayers did not seem to deepen the spiritual lives of the monks (MPS 185). He saw the abbey as:

> "... enveloped in dense spiritual and intellectual fog. ... A community of men dedicated to the contemplative life without too much sense of spiritual things.... Earnestness cannot compensate for such a lack" (MPS 186).

My view is that Merton and Fox shared a delusion that keeping their vows and participation in rituals would obtain inner growth, but it did not. In the sixteenth year of his relationship with Fox, while still trying to come to terms with injustices inflicted by Fox, Merton lamented that he had no model to follow (MPS 195). Merton was trying to be non-judgmental about Fox, while making adjustments in his own life to be tolerant of Fox's injustices, but he had no pattern to follow. Since the space between Merton and Fox fostered no inner growth and no meeting of minds, Merton created a space in his own mind for inner growth. In that space, he studied ancient writers like the desert fathers and mystics, for his spiritual sustenance. Ancient writers were Merton's source of spiritual development. In his encounter with Fox, the father archetype was activated, and the monk-abbot relationship offered the promise of structure and spiritual direction, but Merton's projection did not find a carrier in Fox. Like his biological father, Owen, Merton's monastic father, abbot Fox, was consumed with survival in a world where success is determined by financial measures.

Another way in which Merton relied on his own resourcefulness for inner growth was to secure some solitude for himself. To do that, he left the communal living quarters inside the abbey and chose to live in a makeshift shack on the grounds of the abbey. Merton achieved psychological growth, but it was not the result of any guidance by Fox. The factors that contributed to Merton's psychological growth were his turning inward by writing copious journals, his studies of the spiritual works of mystics and desert fathers, his solitude achieved by living in the makeshift shack, along with his intellectual assessment of the Catholic Church's response to social issues of the 1960's.

The 20-year interaction between Merton and Fox yielded nothing of joint significance. Although each monk learned and grew from his own experience at Gethsemani, neither monk facilitated any significant change in the other. That relationship was a failed containment. At the end of 1967 when Fox resigned from his role as abbot and became a hermit, his interaction with Merton was reduced to occasional communications. Their relationship ended when Merton died a year later at the end of 1968. In this section, I described the Merton-Fox relationship in the context of archetype as biological entity. In the next section, I will describe the relationship in the context of archetype as emergent phenomenon.

Context of Archetype as Emergent Phenomenon: Appropriation & Internalization

If an archetype is defined in terms of emergent phenomenon, it is viewed as an emergent property of a dynamic, developmental system that is made up of human brains, human activities, society's external environment and the narrative competence of humans in the society. When regarding archetype as an emergent phenomenon, the means for converting life's experience to meaning are appropriation and internalization. Appropriation is an adoption of conscious content from social and cultural sources in the external environment. Merton's appropriation was an idealization of spiritual fatherhood drawn from the external world of the Catholic religion. What appealed to Merton were the Catholic guardrails, rules, vows, and sacraments. These are factors that Merton believed would enable him to secure for his life the structure and direction that his father lacked. Internalization is the incorporation of a cultural appropriation into one's mental model. Merton was not able to internalize his appropriation of idealized spiritual father because he did not find in Fox a mind willing or able to provide the psychological containment necessary to incorporate an appropriation.

Appropriation and internalization are processes that can be observed in how children acquire language skills. They appropriate language consciously from social and cultural sources in their community, and with the help of adults, they internalize language into their mental models.

Then, they use their mental models to construct sentences on their own. That is similar to how Merton appropriated idealized spiritual fatherhood from the Catholic world. He adopted conscious content from the Catholic community including the Trappist-Cistercian Order. The content of his appropriation included societal expectations of the role of an abbot, or spiritual father for monks. He adopted processed experience made up of meaningful thoughts, emotions, images and memories about an abbot's role as father, or spiritual guide, drawn from the culture of the Catholic community. The activation of the archetype of father was evident in the behaviors and communications between Merton and Fox as they settled into a monk-abbot relationship. In the context of archetype as emergent phenomenon, the archetype of spiritual father had emerged from a complex system that is made up of thoughts, actions and attitudes that prevailed in Catholic monastic life, plus the religious beliefs in the Catholic community, along with the narratives that Catholics composed about their lives. In the psychological camp, where archetype is defined as emergent phenomenon, the father archetype has no specific location; it is pervasive across society's habits and institutions in the cultural environment. Merton and Fox established a containment in the Catholic tradition of regular confessions. However, Fox was not mentally available to help Merton by engaging in the mind-to-mind connection necessary to enable him to internalize his cultural appropriation of spiritual father.

Between 1962 and 1965, the Catholic Church organized the Second Ecumenical Vatican Council, known for short as Vatican II, as a means of updating the Church for 20th century living. The main intention was to restore unity among Christian denominations, by starting a dialogue with the contemporary world. Some of the activities for improving relations with other religions included the conduct of Mass in the vernacular language of the local population, rather than in Latin. A central focus of the Vatican II was the movement aimed at emphasizing commonalities among faiths by arranging inter-faith dialogues with different religions. Another example of change was the elimination of communication by sign language in monasteries. Vatican II was not a topic of shared interest between Fox and Merton. When Merton wanted to pursue the main, ecumenical innovations set forth in Vatican II, Fox was only willing to implement the lesser innovations, such as the elimination of sign language in the monastery. Merton wanted to promote the ecumenical movement by participating in conferences with leaders of different denominations. Fox was focused on preserving the existing monastic lifestyle and he had little interest in the innovations of Vatican II, while Merton was futuristic and eager to promote the ecumenical movement which was central to Vatican II.

Fox established 'Gethsemani Farms' to support the abbey and he arranged a direct mail business to sell cheese, fruitcake and pork to the public. This business grew to exceed the financial needs of the monastery. When the monks involved asked Fox to stop expanding the business in view of their vows of poverty, Fox disagreed. In my opinion, Fox was doing what he knew how to do, what he was comfortable doing, and what he was successful in doing. He gave a higher priority to financial well-being of the abbey than to the spiritual well-being of a monastery whose mission was a contemplative lifestyle. The contemplative Merton chaffed under the authoritative leadership of the entrepreneurial abbot Fox. Their outlooks on profitability of the abbey were as different as their views on monastic lifestyle. The Trappist monks lived a communal life. Merton shared dormitory style accommodations with the novices who were his students. Merton wanted to become a hermit, to lead a solitary, contemplative life. Fox did not think Merton had the vocation of a hermit. Merton experienced Fox, not so much as a fatherly advisor, but as leader of a capitalist, food-processing plant. Fox experienced Merton as an impulsive, neurotic miscreant who needed the restrain of a strong authority figure. The two monks did not have enough of an overlap of shared interest to establish a worthwhile psychological containment.

Converting Experience to Meaning: Symbolization

In my reading of the biographical literature about Merton and Fox, I found nothing that fit the emergence of a symbol as described in "A Critical Dictionary of Jungian Analysis" where psychologist Andrew Samuels and others define symbol in terms of concept, intent, purpose and content. There was a lot of communication between Merton and Fox, in their confessions, and in their letters to each other. Although there was an abundance of opportunity for conscious and unconscious communication, the interaction between them did not gain the psychological traction necessary to achieve psychological growth. I found no discernable emergence of any symbol in their communication. According to psychologist Duncan Cartwright, a mind is dependent on another mind for meaning (CSM 2). There was an unusual potential for meaning-making in the relationship between Merton and Fox. They were both Catholics, they had taken the same vows, they lived in the same abbey, and each spent years being confessor to the other. Merton and Fox had the opportunity for a mind-to-mind connection with a potential for deriving meaning about their lives based on their experiences. However, neither became the kind of container who facilitated psychological growth in the other. While each man regarded the other with a mix of respect and disdain, their interaction brought no psychological harm to either.

I believe they bonded on a shared delusion that keeping their vows and participation in sacramental rituals would generate inner growth. That did not come about because they carried out their vows in very different monastic activities. Fox focused primarily on economic activities. Merton focused on writing about social issues of the day and contemplative life. Although each spent years being confessor for the other, they did not develop the shared reverie necessary to support the kind of containment that offers psychological growth. Although they had a long relationship that covered two decades, conducted many regular meetings regarding confession, and lived in close proximity to each other, they never developed a bond strong enough to support a dialectical interaction. Their communication lacked the joint impetus necessary to mount a collaborative endeavor. There was not enough common ground between them to generate a third narrative.

According to Duncan Cartwright, a containment can only take place if the container has an ongoing relationship with the unconscious part of their own psyche, and has already been processing a state of mind similar to the unprocessed state of mind projected from the mind of the contained (CSM 3). That raises questions. Did James Fox have an ongoing relationship with the unconscious part of his own psyche? Had Fox already been processing a state of mind similar to the unprocessed state of mind projected from Merton's mind? Fox's handling of the confessor role suggests the answer to both questions is no. If he had an ongoing relationship with the unconscious part of his own psyche, he would have seen the value of the confessor role as an opportunity for unconscious communication. If he had already been processing a state of mind similar to Merton's state of mind, he might not have been so quick to characterize Merton's soul-searching confession as neurotic behavior. He would have understood that the Catholic sacrament of Confession, involves searching one's interior life for belief, doubt, motivation, trauma, lapses in judgement, and so on. The fact that Fox asked Merton to become his confessor suggests that he saw in Merton the spiritual maturity to function as a spiritual guide. Rather than develop his own capability as a spiritual guide, Fox chose to depend on Merton to function as confessor.

Cartwright explains that, for Bion, a real human mental connection is like an emotional storm caused by the coming together of minds that crave and resist each other (CSM 3). The monastic relationship between Merton and Fox had elements of craving and resisting each other. Merton craved the emotional and spiritual support that he desired from a confessor, but he put up a resistance to Fox's characterization of him as neurotic. Fox craved the availability of Merton in the abbey as a source of royalties from his writing, but he resisted Merton's writings that made the Catholic leaders look conscience-free in the face of the war with Vietnam. The capacity to generate meaning from gathering up thoughts and emotions requires the encounter of contained and container be subjected to a series of transformations. This involves finding ways of tolerating the emotional storm for long enough so that it can be given a particular personal meaning. Merton and Fox certainly tolerated an emotional storm for 20 years, but their containment failed because they did not generate meaning from each other's thoughts and emotions. Their interaction did not result in a series of transformations. The two men had a symbiotic containment, in which there was no noticeable impact on the psychological growth of each other.

Fox turned out to be rather similar to Merton's biological father, Owen. Both men struggled for their survival in a capitalistic sense in the material world. All his life, Owen struggled to sell his paintings, but never became a capable provider for his sons. Fox was so devoted to capitalistic goals that even when his subordinate monks pointed out that he should stop striving for money because the abbey had become profit-able, and money-making was not compatible with their monastic vows of poverty, Fox refused because he was functioning in a survival mode. Merton's biological father and his spiritual director were both unable to provide the mental scaffolding that Merton needed for inner growth. Both were preoccupied with survival in a capitalist sense. Merton's rela-tionship with Fox was an echo of his relationship with his father. So, Merton turned inward. He developed his narrative competence by writ-ing personal journals. He sought spiritual direction in what had been written about the desert fathers and mystics. He found inner growth by isolating himself from the communal life inside the abbey. First he lived in a makeshift shack, then later in the hermitage on the grounds of the abbey. Merton's psychological growth and spiritual maturity resulted from his turning inward, as seen in his personal journals and his pub-lications. Merton and Fox had separate legacies, but no joint legacy. Merton's legacy is his collection of spiritual publications in the archive at the Thomas Merton Center, Bellarmine University. Fox's legacy was financial as seen in his establishment of Gethsemani Farms as a profit center for the abbey.

Call To Action: Take Away A Portable Understanding

This chapter is a story about two monks who held common spiritual aspirations. It is also a story of their years of symbiotic containment based on a shared delusion. Their spiritual aspirations were about liv-ing a contemplative life shaped by vows and sacraments. My opinion is that, for the first five years, they shared a delusion that diligent compli-ance with vows and prayerful rituals about sacraments could bring inner growth. At the five year mark when Fox delegated the confessor role to Merton, the projection was broken and Merton turned inward to achieve inner growth, while Fox continued to build Gethsemani Farms into a retail outlet for fruitcake, cheese and pork. This chapter is a call to action for readers to take away a portable understanding of the sym-biotic mode of containment. To help readers, here is a summary of the symbiotic mode of containment involving Thomas Merton and James Fox.

- **Mode:** Merton and Fox had a symbiotic mode of containment.
- **Roles:** Initially, Merton was the contained and Fox was the container during the years when Fox was Merton's confessor. They switched roles when Fox assigned Merton to be his confessor.
- **Symmetry:** Merton and Fox had an asymmetrical relationship. They did not choose each other. There was a power gradient between them, because Merton had taken a vow of obedience, and as the abbot, Fox was responsible for overseeing Merton's compliance with those vows.
- **Psychological Frame:** For Merton and Fox, the purpose of the psychological frame was spiritual development by compliance with religious vows and celebration of the sacraments, in particular, the Sacrament of Confession. The space boundary of the frame was the abbey itself, where a good deal of the interaction between Merton and Fox occurred in Abbot Fox's office. I think it is safe to say that the time boundary was their regular meetings, because throughout the relationship, one was confessor for the other. Confession in the Catholic world is about regular, private encounters, so it is reasonable to think they had regular meetings. Some of the interaction also occurred in an exchange of letters. For example, Merton would write letters unburdening himself about the reasons he thinks Gethsemani is not the right place for him, put the letters in Fox's mailbox, and Fox would respond by writing letters explaining why he thinks Merton should stay at Gethsemani.
- **Dialectical Narrative:** As the contained, Merton produced the first narrative. His narrative was about spiritual growth by searing soul-searching, development of a social conscience, speaking out against war, and promoting the ecumenical movement in line with the Second Vatican Council. In his role as container and confessor, Fox produced the second narrative. His narrative was about the financial profitability of the monastery and the practice of rituals associated with the sacraments. There was no real third narrative from their interaction. Merton's mind needed another mind for psychological growth, but Fox was so dependent upon unprocessed experiences as the primary means of interacting with Merton that he could not function as a container for Merton. In their symbiotic mode of containment, their

minds did not connect by mutual exploration of each other's interior world for psychological growth. They participated in a complicity that protected the relationship as it stood. Their bond was based on a shared delusion that compliance with vows and celebration of the sacraments would result in inner growth. Their reverie focused on conscious communication. Each may have had a curiosity about the other, but only as it served to maintain the symbiotic union.

- **Psychological Growth / Harm:** Since they maintained the reciprocity of each relying on the other for development of an aspect of his personality that he did not care to develop, I do not believe they achieved psychological growth from the containment. Although they were suspicious of each other, resented each other and from time to time frustrated each other, I do not see any indication of psychological harm resulting from the containment.

After the Containment Ended

When Thomas Merton gave up on finding a spiritual father in James Fox, I believe Merton turned inward. At about the fifth year of their long encounter, Fox delegated the confessor role to Merton. That is when I believe Merton started turning inward. He created a communication with himself by writing a profusion of personal journals. After the failure of the Merton-Fox symbiotic mode of containment, Merton had what I propose, in this book, as a reflexive mode of containment. That containment enabled him to produce a volume of literature about his contemplative life as a monk, his spiritual practices and his observations about the ecumenical movement. Merton died in December 1968, while attending an ecumenical conference in Bangkok, Thailand. After his death, the Thomas Merton Center was built at Bellarmine University to archive Merton's writings.

James Fox retired from the role of abbot in December 1967 to become a hermit on the grounds of Gethsemani Abbey. For the 10 years, from 1967 to 1977, he lived as a hermit at the Edelin hermitage a few miles from the abbey grounds. While resident at the Edelin hermitage, two intruders assaulted him. He moved to the abbey infirmary, where he lived until his death in 1987.

In 2015, biographer Roger Lipsey published *"Make Peace Before the Sun Goes Down"* about the long encounter between Thomas Merton and James Fox. He observed that there was a great opportunity for Merton and Fox to collaborate on implementing the pronouncements of the Second Vatican Council 1962. It contained innovations for moving the Catholic Church into a modern era, by updating rules and practices that were centuries old. They did not take advantage of the opportunity. My characterization of their interaction as a symbiotic mode of containment is supported by Lipsey's comments on the unchanged nature of the interaction between the two men, nineteen years into their relationship:

> *"(B)oth Merton and Dom James ... continued their broken dialogue through much of 1967 ... nothing had changed for either of them. They were fixed in place, as if some dance had long since ended but they had nowhere to go. ... James continued to confine Merton, to fend off even the most sensible invitations to him, even from a cardinal; he stopped reading Merton's mail and that of all others for a time, owing to a collective demand to cease and desist, but then resumed doing so. On his side, Merton couldn't back far enough away even at the hermitage to be thoroughly free of the abbot's hold. He was writing, corresponding, praying, meditating, meeting friends from time to time, all of this freely and creatively. But his thoughts and resentment returned often to Dom James"* (MPS 245).

Lipsey further observed:

> *"Their encounter here on earth had terrible aspects, that can no longer be doubted: coercion over many years, resentment over many years, such grave misunderstandings. Yet they were bound by religious obligation and perhaps even by Providence to live it, and they learned from and through each other. Dom James, the monastic entrepreneur and world traveler, became in the end a hermit with nowhere to go except within himself. Father Louis (name given to Merton when he entered the monastery), the contemplative and writer and man of*

conscience, became in the end a world traveler who drew East and West together. His vision is still unfolding" (MPS 260).

Sources

The sources of information that I accessed to write this chapter are:
- *"Make Peace Before the Sun Goes Down"* by Roger Lipsey
- *"The Seven Mountains of Thomas Merton"* by Michael Mott
- *"States of Containment"* by Duncan Cartwright
- *"Projection and Re-Collection in Jungian Psychology"* by Marie-Louise von Franz.

CHAPTER 14

A Parasitic Mode of Containment Involving: Ted Bundy & Elizabeth Kendall

"There is something the matter with me. It wasn't you. It was me. I just couldn't contain it. I've fought it for a long, long time ... it got too strong. We just happened to be going together when it got underway. I tried, believe me, I tried to suppress it. It was taking more and more of my time. That's why I didn't do well in school. My time was being used trying to make my life look normal. But it wasn't normal. All the time I could feel that force building in me."

— Ted Bundy

Ted Bundy was executed in 1989 after being found guilty of serial murder of young women across the United States. After the execution, retired neuropsychologist, Robert DePaolo, published a clinical analysis of the internal dynamics and significant relationships in Bundy's life. DePaolo's observation is that, given the trajectory of Bundy's early life experiences, the chance of him becoming a normal person was rather low from the beginning (BCD 100). The beginning of Bundy's life was in a home for unwed mothers in Vermont. He grew up in a home where the girl he assumed to be his sister, Louise, turned out to be his mother. When Ted became a teenager, he was shocked to discover, from his cousin, John, that he was illegitimate, but despite his anger toward Louise for not telling him, he never confronted her about the circumstance of his birth. Ted grew up to become a handsome, intellectual, young man with a promising future as a lawyer-politician, but he did not live long enough to fulfill that promise. While still a law student, he was arrested for serial murder and later executed. In "The 1976 Psychological Assessment of Ted Bundy" prison psychologist, Dr. Al Carlisle, remarked that Bundy's girlfriend, Elizabeth Kendall, was a breadth of fresh air for Bundy because she provided stability in his life (PA 187). She supported him financially when he had no job and she was always by his side when he needed emotional support (PA 188).

My interpretation is that Ted Bundy and Elizabeth Kendall had a parasitic mode of containment during their romantic six-year relationship from autumn of 1969 to 1975. The relationship was parasitic because Kendall's effort to function as a container was thwarted by Bundy's repeated refusal to address his anti-social behaviors, while continuously depending on her for emotional support, financial support and stability in his life. He was defiant about changing his anti-social behavior and he often trivialized the relationship. He was also envious of her financially comfortable situation. They had chosen each other, but theirs was not a symmetrical relationship. Their relationship had asymmetrical qualities, in terms of socialization, economic achievement, as well as academic and career aspirations. Driven by an internal force he could not control, he parasitized her meaning-making resources. He lacked adequate resources to process his own intolerable emotions and thoughts With parasitic anxiety, he attacked her efforts at making his unprocessed experiences tolerable and meaningful. The parasitic interaction between them generated a third narrative that was destructive to the relationship. Her attempt at containment had the effect of diminishing the rapport that existed between them. Real exchange between them was limited in meaning. Out of envy, he attacked her efforts to process the emotional turmoil communicated by his projection. As an aid to a better understanding of the relationship, I provide background information about the lives of Ted Bundy and Elizabeth Kendall leading up to the time when they met in Seattle.

Background Information about Ted Bundy

At the Elizabeth Lund Home For Unwed Mothers in Vermont, Theodore Robert Cowell was born in 1946. His mother Louise Cowell left him there for three months while she figured out whether to put up her illegitimate child for adoption, or take him home to Philadelphia (SBM 422). Theodore grew up in the Cowell household in Philadelphia, where he believed the two adults, Samuel and Eleanor, to be his parents, and their daughter, Louise, to be his older sister. Samuel was a horticultural- ist by profession and he functioned as a deacon at the local Methodist Church, while Eleanor was a secretary. When Louise grew up and mar- ried Johnny Bundy, they moved to Tacoma, Washington, where Johnny took a job as a cook at an army hospital (PP 22). Louise took Theodore with them to Tacoma. Johnny adopted Theodore, who became known as Ted Bundy. Some biographers portray Ted as the product of incest between Samuel and his daughter Louise. Other biographers explain Louise's claim that she was seduced by a war veteran who abandoned her when she became pregnant. At that time, DNA testing was not yet available, so the question of Ted's biological father remained unanswered.

One day when Bundy became a teenager, he was engaged in a bragging match with a cousin (PP 27). Each was trying to outdo the other in predicting fame and fortune for themselves when they became adults. Suddenly, the cousin informed Bundy that he would achieve neither fame nor fortune because he is illegitimate. Bundy registered shock and disbelief. To prove his point, the cousin took Bundy up to the attic, and searched for a document that demonstrated Ted's illegitimacy. Ted was surprised and disappointed, but he was even more angry with Louise for not telling him about his illegitimate status and for not talking to him about his father. He was also furious that his mother had left him unpre- pared for the humiliation at the hands of his cousin (PP 25).

Ted graduated from Woodrow Wilson High School in 1965 and later enrolled at the University of Washington to study psychology. While an undergraduate, he met Elizabeth Kendall who was working as a secre- tary at the University of Washington School of Medicine. They met in 1969 at a bar where they embarked on a romantic relationship. In 1971, while an undergraduate, he worked at the Harborview Mental Health

Center, Seattle's crisis clinic, where he met ex-policewoman, Ann Rule, who became a friend and confidante. The clinic offered hotline services to patients who had mental illnesses such as anxiety, depression and schizophrenia. Years later, Rule wrote *"The Stranger Beside Me"* a true-crime documentary about Ted's crimes (SBM 9). Rule makes the observation that once arrested by police, Bundy must have known that he would not be free for a relationship for years, yet he bound Kendall to him with love letters, poems and telephone calls from prison (SBM 187).

Background Information about Elizabeth Kendall

Elizabeth Kloepfer was born to middle-class parents in 1945. She grew up in Ogden, Utah where her father was a medical doctor. When she graduated from high school, she continued her education at a college where she earned a Bachelor's degree in Business & Family Life. Elizabeth got married soon after and had a daughter, Molly, who was born in 1966. She divorced her husband when she discovered he was a felon. Struggling with alcoholism and feeling out of place as a single mother in her hometown of Ogden, Kendall decided to relocate so that she could have a fresh start in life. In Seattle, she got a job as a secretary in the medical department at the University of Washington. Seattle is where Elizabeth began a romantic relationship with Ted Bundy at a bar in 1969. In the memoir she later published, Elizabeth describes herself at the time of her relocation, as being a shy, insecure and lonely single mother, who was struggling with alcoholism. She wanted very much to have a family life with a man who would be a good father for her daughter Molly. When Elizabeth Kloepfer wrote her book *"The Phantom Prince: My Life With Ted Bundy"* in 1981, she published under the pseudonym Elizabeth Kendall. Since I rely on that book as a source of information about her relationship with Ted Bundy, I use the pseudonym when referring to her.

Wilfred Bion and Duncan Cartwright built the containment model based on the principles of projection and introjection. Because projections occur when archetypes are activated, I describe the relationship between Ted Bundy and Elizabeth Kendall as being influenced by archetypes. To explain that influence, I rely on the two definitions of archetype that prevail in the early 21st century. In the next two sections, I describe the Bundy-Kendall relationship in the context of archetype as biological entity, then in the context of archetype as emergent phenomenon.

Context of Archetype as Biological Entity: Projection & Introjection

In the literature about Analytical Psychology, some authors define an archetype as a biological entity. When viewed as a biological entity, an archetype is regarded as an ancestral heritage of human experience accumulated over many generations and located in collective unconsciousness. When psychologists define an archetype as a biological entity, the processes they identify for converting experience to meaning are projection and introjection. Projection is an evacuation of unconscious content from the psyche due to an unbearable state of mind. There was a projection cast from the mind of Ted Bundy to the mind of Elizabeth Kendall. The content of the projection was Ted's unassimilated state of mind about his idealized lover. Introjection is a transformation of an unassimilated state of mind to a bearable state of mind, followed by its integration into conscious content of the psyche. This containment failed because Kendall's attempts to function as container were repeatedly thwarted by Bundy's parasitic behaviors.

Ted Bundy and Elizabeth Kendall met in 1969 at the Sandpiper Tavern in the area of the University of Washington. She had gone there with friends to celebrate her relocation from Ogden, Utah to Seattle, Washington, and the start of a new life (PP 8). When Bundy came over and asked her to dance, she was impressed. He was well dressed, handsome, and had a distinctive way of speaking. As the evening wore on, she was hoping he would ask her to dance again, but he did not. Seeing him looking sad and alone at his table, she decided to go over and talk with him. They talked about their relocations to Seattle (PP 9 – 10). A couple at an adjacent table was getting ready to leave and offered them an unfinished pitcher of beer. As they sipped the beer, Bundy offered to show Kendall around Seattle, starting with the public market. He let her know that he missed having a kitchen because he loved to cook. That is when she first thought of him as her Prince, her ideal man, with whom she was already imagining a future (PP 10). Since Bundy had no car, she offered him a ride in her car. Soon they were spending time getting to know each other, dining, drinking and talking about the cities where they grew up, enjoying the sights of Seattle, and taking care of Molly. Elizabeth felt they had become like a family because Ted chose outings that young Molly could enjoy (PP 21). Their projections were cast. Ted saw Elizabeth as an idealized lover … sexually available, financially giving, and forgiving of infidelities. For him, the archetype of lover was activated. Elizabeth saw Ted as her Prince Charming, an idealization of a future husband … a good provider, faithful partner and good father to Molly. For her, the archetype of husband was activated. She thought his extraverted social skills would compensate for her comfortable role of introvert.

Aspiring to become a lawyer-politician, Bundy was already regarded as having a promising future by those he encountered when he did volunteer work in political campaigns. What Kendall did not know and Bundy might not have been ready to acknowledge to himself is that he had a split personality, a socially-sanctioned personality and a socially-forbidden personality. The content of the archetypal image in his projection to her appeared to be unprocessed emotional experience that had two aspects. From the societally-sanctioned side of his mind emerged images about the female companionship he needed to sustain him while he prepared for a career in politics. From the societally-forbidden side of his mind emerged images about hiding and restraining what he called the internal 'force' that was driving him to murder young women. The content of the archetypal image in her projection to him was unprocessed emotional experience about needing someone who could become both a husband for her and a father for Molly.

The behaviors and communications between Bundy and Kendall were related to his expectations of her as an idealized lover and her expectations of him as an idealized husband. Viewed from the perspective of archetype as a biological entity, these archetypes of lover and husband are made up of an ancestral heritage of human experience in relations between the opposite sex accumulated over multiple generations, and are located in the collective unconscious aspect of the psyche. Activation of the lover archetype indicates a forceable evacuation of a projection from Bundy's mind to Kendall's mind. Activation of the husband archetype indicates a forceable evacuation of a projection from Kendall's mind to Bundy's mind. The content of Ted's projection was raw experience of emotions, images and memories related to a lover. They were incomprehensible to him and were therefore evacuated as an unbearable state of mind. The content of Kendall's projection was raw experience of emotions, images and memories related to a husband. They were incomprehensible to her and were therefore evacuated as an unbearable state of mind. Bundy and Kendall were not able to have the kind of dialogue that would enable them to construct meanings from the content of their projections and integrate the meanings into the conscious aspects of their psyches. Kendall tried to be a container for Bundy, but he was not receptive. Since he thwarted her efforts, there was no construction of meaning from his projection. She was trying to help him shape his life into behaviors that fit his aspirations … stop stealing merchandise from stores, quit playing the field with multiple lovers, and pay serious attention to university studies in preparation for a life as a lawyer-politician. He was trying to come to terms with a force he could not control. He was not amenable to metabolizing his unprocessed emotional states, or structuring them into useful thoughts.

The archetypes had been activated at critical stages in their lives. Bundy was preparing for the transition from university student to professional lawyer-politician. Kendall was preparing for the transition from single mother to wife. When Kendall made efforts to be a container and help him understand his unprocessed state of mind, he would thwart her efforts by being defiant. Rather than process the contents of his projection, he preferred to justify his behavior and rely on her to be a source of stability in his life. Lover and husband are archetypes that form bridges between conscious and unconscious aspects of the psyche, and processing projections from these archetypes requires paying particular attention to the images that arise from them. These archetypes present themselves to the ego as an 'other' that represents the opposite sex. The emergence of projections from the archetypes of lover and husband opens up a mental space where members of both sexes can meet in imagination. When they fell in love, Bundy and Kendall opened up a mental space where they could interact. He saw the relationship as a temporary filler in his life, while he prepared for a future that did not include her, despite his words to the contrary. She was emotionally and financially invested in the relationship; while he just wanted her companionship and financial support until graduation, when he would find himself someone he considered more suitable to be a politician's wife. He desired her as an idealized lover … sexually available and financially generous, but not jealous. She desired him as an idealized husband … emotionally available, faithful and receptive to fathering Molly. They enjoyed each other's companionship, but they did not achieve psychological growth from the relationship. He offered his companionship under the false pretenses that he was willing to marry her and carve out a future together, when in fact, he regarded her as unsuitable to be the wife of a politician, the profession to which he aspired. She offered her companionship, her emotional support, and her financial support to the Prince Charming she imagined him to be. Having earned a degree in psychology at the University of Washington, Bundy quite likely had at least an intellectual understanding of projection, but he did not appear to become a carrier for Kendall's projection. It was Kendall who tried to become a carrier of Bundy's projection.

Kendall's attempts to function as a container for Bundy extended to helping him understand his mother's failure to inform him of his illegitimacy. When Bundy expressed anger at Louise for failing to inform him of his illegitimate status, Kendall tried to explain, from a woman's point of view, that his arrival in Louise's life was probably a difficult and painful event for which she might have lacked the emotional skills to cope because she was so young at the time. When Kendall noticed that the unemployed Bundy periodically acquired expensive possessions that she knew he could not afford, she cautioned him about jeopardizing his future by shoplifting. She continued to try to help him understand that he could ruin his life as a lawyer or a politician because of his kleptomania. He thwarted her efforts to become a container by threatening to break her f****** neck if she told anyone about his propensity for shoplifting. With her efforts to discourage his shoplifting blocked, she turned her attention to his other areas of neediness. She paid for his university tuition, gave him a key to her apartment, and generally provided a stable homelife for him. They cooked, shared meals, went sight-seeing, and enjoyed sharing life in Seattle. After a four-month infatuation, she proposed marriage as a stable union from which to build a life together. He acquiesced. She was forthcoming about her expectations, but he was not. While she was looking for marriage and a permanent family life, he was looking for temporary companionship and financial resources to sustain him on his way to becoming a lawyer-politician. They obtained a marriage license, but soon after, he ripped it to pieces during a domestic squabble. She was available to him throughout most of their friendship ... emotionally available and financially available. She made her apartment available to him not just by giving him a key, but by including him in aspects of her life ... sleeping over at her place, visits to her workplace, and visits to her parents' home. He derived satisfaction from hoping that maintaining a societally-sanctioned relationship with her would be enough to keep at bay what he called the 'force' hidden in the socially-forbidden side of his personality. The force was a growing addiction to luring young women into his car, then killing and sexually assaulting them, in that order. Although Kendall was aware of stretches of time when he would be evasive about his whereabouts, she was unaware of his socially-forbidden side. They connected well on a superficial level of relationship, but could not muster the kind of rapport necessary to sustain a containment where two people help each other to grow psychologically. Theirs was an asymmetrical relationship. They had chosen each other, but they were not co-equals. Bundy was mindful, and envious, of the fact that Kendall's family was of a higher socio-economic status than his family. For most of the duration of the containment, Bundy was financially dependent on Kendall. Although Bundy was not emotionally invested in the containment, he managed to solicit from Kendall an enduring willingness to put his interests above her own. Kendall was so emotionally invested in the containment that she found it diffi cult to separate herself from Bundy, even after he confessed that he tried to kill her.

When he graduated from the University of Washington in June 1972, he decided to work a year before going to law school. Bundy got a full-time job at Harborview Hospital Mental Health Center (PP 38), then moved on to campaign for Governor Dan Evan's re-election (PP 42), then later worked at the King County Budget Office (PP 43). He was also appointed Assistant Chairman at the Washington State Republican Central Committee (PP 43). It bothered Kendall to realize that although he was now making a good salary, he continued to steal merchandise from stores, for example, a tool chest from a hardware store (PP 43) and a television from an appliance store. She was unable to help him overcome his kleptomaniac behavior. When he decided to start law school at the University of Utah, he prepared to relocate to Salt Lake City, but did not invite her to go with him. When she asked if she should stay in Seattle or go with him to Salt Lake City, he said it was up to her. When she accused him of taking her for granted; he accused her of being insecure (PP 48). He failed his LSAT test twice before being accepted by the University of Utah Law School in 1972, and about that time, she became pregnant (PP 35 – 36). She got an abortion because, according to her thinking, she needed to be working so that she could pay his law school tuition.

In 1974, the newspapers, radio and TV stations were filled with news about a man named 'Ted' on crutches being a suspect in the disap-pearance of a female student from the University District (PP 64). The news caught Kendall's attention because she had seen crutches in Ted's apartment. Uncertain about what to do, she continued to spend time with him, while feeling afraid that he might figure out that she was con-sidering reaching out to the police, because she wondered if her Ted was the Ted being sought in connection with the disappearance of the student. Then she found out there were reports of young women dis-appearing both in Seattle, where Ted had spent a lot of time with her, and Salt Lake City, were Ted was living as a law student. Kendall called the Seattle police, supplied details about Ted and asked the police to call the Salt Lake City police to find out if there are similarities in the cases of missing young women in both cities. The police assured her that they had already checked out Ted Bundy because his name had appeared on a list of possible persons of interest (PP 70 - 71). Nevertheless, the police asked to meet with her, and during the discussion of Ted's habits, they showed her a psychological profile of characteristics a killer would likely possess. Few of the characteristics fit Ted. The police collected snapshots from her photograph album to find out if the witness could recognize Ted (PP 75). The witness did not positively identify Ted and the police put Ted on the list of excluded possible suspects. When more women continued to disappear in Salt Lake City, Kendall became more concerned about the safety of Molly and herself, but was afraid to go back to the police because they had ruled out Ted twice, so she went to her bishop (PP 79 – 81). The bishop offered to accompany her to the police, and she accepted his offer, but she found him more inclined to rely on prayers than on facts, so she contacted the police herself, this time reaching out to the police in Salt Lake City (PP 85). Again, she was told they had ruled him out.

In the summer of 1975, Elizabeth felt she had come to a turning point ... she and Ted were either going to break up or get married (PP 89). She was in Utah visiting her parents, and Ted, on a break from his studies at the University of Utah, was visiting her at her parents' home. She told him she was tired of their long-distance Washington-Utah relationship and wanted to get married. He suggested they get married at Christmastime (PP 90). They went to the kitchen to tell her parents and their announcement was met with silence. Back in Seattle, she told her friend Angie who expressed caution. When she told her boss at work, he advised her against it because he felt Ted was too much of a social climber to pay attention to her needs. The people who cared about Kendall had deep reservations about her getting married to Ted. Before Christmas, she found out Ted had made a gift of a stolen bicycle to his brother. She was angry because she had been encouraging him to stop shoplifting, but he was not making the effort. Rather than making an effort to change his ways, he tried to justify his behavior on the grounds that she could not understand his need because she had never known need. She countered that she was not in need because she worked. She informed him she could not marry him if he continued his thievery. He did not consider changing his shoplifting behavior. Instead, he seemed to be relieved to call off the wedding. In my opinion, that broke Kendall's projection of an idealized husband. She could not accept an unrepentant kleptomaniac as a husband. After the break-up, each acknowledged their love for the other, but they knew their lives would go in separate directions. Even so, they kept in touch and Elizabeth continued to be supportive for the remainder of Ted's life. He continued to regard her a lover at his disposal and a provider of money, stamps, and free telephone calls, well into the time of investigation for kidnapping and murder. When he was imprisoned, he kept her on an emotional hook by sending her poems and love letters.

In August 1975, Kendall found out from the Seattle police that Ted had been arrested for trying to evade a police officer and for burglary tools being found in his car (PP 94). As more women disappeared, the police put Ted back on the list of possible suspects. On the second day of October 1975, when Kendall found out that Bundy was arrested for kidnapping and attempted homicide, she felt that she had betrayed him by providing the police with information about him (PP 106 - 107). Kendall was experiencing such a tumultuous mix of emotions that she started seeing a psychiatrist, who advised her to stop talking to the police and stop communicating with Bundy (PP 112). She stopped talking to the police, but kept up telephone and letter communication with Bundy. When Bundy turned up uninvited at her apartment, she welcomed him and allowed him to stay several days. Even after Bundy's attorney informed him that the police were surveilling them, Kendall continued to allow Bundy to stay in her apartment, and to go out on dates with him. Intellectually, she knew she was taking a significant risk, but emotionally she had such a tight bond with Bundy, she could not give up on him. Bundy had offered apologies, poetry, letters of undying love, but continued to play the field. Although Kendall expressed her anger at Bundy's deception, she continued to allow him to stay in her apartment … she felt that he needed her desperately, and she was evidently more concerned about his despair than her own safety.

When his trial started in Salt Lake City in February 1976, Bundy's Salt Lake City girlfriend testified on his behalf, but Kendall declined to attend (PP 125). She flew to her parents' home in Salt Lake City for the last day of the trial (PP 129). Bundy asked Kendall to be at the court, but when she got there, he did not introduce her to anyone in his entourage (PP 129). Her parents were horrified that she continued to see him, but she stayed in his apartment for days until the verdict was read in court: guilty (PP 132 – 134). The psychiatric evaluation was inconclusive because Bundy did not fit any specific model of pathology (BCD 63). He did not fit the profile of a psychopath (BCD 69). He was sentenced to spend 15 years in Utah State Prison for abduction of a young woman (PP 148). On appeal, the sentence was reduced because he had no prior conviction. Six months after Bundy's conviction, Kendall was on her way to visit him in prison (PP 150). About a year after being convicted of kidnapping in Utah, he was charged with murder of a woman in Colorado (PP 157). When Kendall declined to go to the trial in Colorado, Bundy sent her an anguished poem:

> "Into a raging river you and I were tossed.
> Separately, we are swept along, trying desperately to save ourselves.
> I understand survival, I practice it myself
> Neither of us has the strength to pull the other to the shore."
>   — Ted Bundy (PP 158)

With that poem, he was denigrating her by dragging her down to his level of depravity. She was not a criminal. She was trying to drag him to shore. He thwarted her efforts and she was not strong enough to help him overcome the internal force that consumed him. In her memoir, she wrote:

> "Ted's letters made me feel loved. I knew the words were only words, but they could still make me feel good" (PP 160).

He called collect at least once a week, and she accepted the calls knowing that maintaining a connection with him robbed her of the motivation to get out in the world and make some real friendships with people who were part of her day-to-day life (PP 162). In one of those collect telephone calls, he confessed that he was not normal, that an internal force was controlling his behavior. He told her that he escaped from prison in Colorado and was captured in Florida, where he was charged with murder. This is how he informed her that he was not normal:

> "There is something the matter with me. ... I just couldn't contain it. ... I've fought it for a long, long time ... it got too strong. ... I tried to suppress it. It was taking more and more of my time. That's why I didn't do well in school. My time was being used trying to make my life look normal. But it wasn't normal. All the time I could feel that force building in me. ..." (PP 176).

In that conversation, Bundy also confessed that he tried to kill Kendall one night while she was sleeping. There was fire in the fireplace, and he closed the damper so smoke would not go up the chimney. She remembered the night when she awakened coughing, eyes running, struggling to breathe. She had gotten out of bed, opened the windows and broken up the fire in the fireplace. Ted had told her he was leaving the apartment to bring back a fan, but he did not return that night (PP 176 – 177). Despite the confession, Kendall could not bring herself to believe that he tried to kill her. As the conversation continued, he offered further explanation for the internal force he could not control:

> "The force would just consume me. Like one night, I was walk-
> ing by the campus and I followed this sorority girl. I didn't want
> to follow her. I didn't do anything but follow her and that's how
> it was. I'd be out late at night and follow people like that...I'd
> try not to, but I'd do it anyway" (PP 177).

The next morning, newspapers and TV stations announced that Bundy was charged with murdering a 12-year-old girl ... same age as Molly. Kendall finally accepted that Bundy was a murderer, but then she started agonizing over whether she had done anything to trigger his rampages (PP 180). The next time he called, she was ready to tell him she no longer wanted him in her life, but she was not strong enough to do that, so she told Bundy not to call anymore because her new boyfriend does not approve of the calls (PP 181). The conflict Kendall experienced was difficult to overcome. Even when her loyalty to him made no sense to her, she continued her support for him. Letters. Collect telephone calls. Gifts of money and stamps. She felt concerned enough to report his suspicious behaviors to the police, but when he was found guilty, she felt she had betrayed him (PP 139). Kendall's counselor told her she had an obsessive-compulsive disorder, a condition that often develops in people who experienced trauma (PP 185). The counselor pointed out that her obsessive mental review of 'Ted and Liz' as a relationship with a future was indicative of denial. Kendall wrote that she was making an effort to protect herself from an unfathomable truth (PP 185). After his execution, she made the observation that during the trials, he only told the truth when he thought it would be a bargaining chip for extending his life (PP 187). After several appeals, Bundy was executed on January 24, 1989 in Florida for multiple murders. Kendall thought "The Phantom Prince" a perfect title for her memoir because in the early years of the relationship, she was so blindly in love that she overlooked his shortcomings, and tossed her values aside. It took her years to realize he was more of a phantom than the Prince Charming she imagined him to be (PP 197).

In this containment, Bundy as the contained, contributed the first narrative, which was about his unassimilated state of mind regarding how to have his socially-sanctioned personality relate to Kendall as a lover, while keeping at bay his socially-forbidden personality whose internal force led him to kill and assault young women. In her attempts at containment, Kendall contributed the second narrative, which was about persuading Bundy to become a law-abiding law-student by relinquishing his kleptomaniac behaviors, to forgive his mother for not telling him about his illegitimacy, and to become a Prince Charming by changing his philandering ways. The third narrative had no substance; it consisted of frequent arguments regarding the couple's disagreements about habitual shoplifting, and degree of commitment to marriage. The lack of a substantive third narrative was the result of Bundy consistently thwarting Kendall's efforts at containment. He preferred to try to justify his behaviors rather than subject his unassimilated state of mind to the scrutiny that would enable a useful containment. In this section, I have described the Bundy-Kendall relationship in the context of archetype as a biological entity. In the next section, I will describe the relationship in the context of archetype as an emergent phenomenon.

Context of Archetype as Emergent Phenomenon: Appropriation & Internalization

This section examines the relationship between Bundy and Kendall in the context of archetype defined as an emergent phenomenon. When considering archetype as an emergent phenomenon, it is seen as an emergent property of a dynamic, developmental system that is made up of human brains, human activities, society's external environment and the narrative competence of humans in the society. When viewing archetype as an emergent phenomenon, the processes for converting life's experience to meaning are appropriation and internalization. For readers who are unfamiliar with these processes, appropriation and internalization can be observed in the way that children acquire language skills. They appropriate language consciously from social and cultural sources in their community, and with the help of adults, they internalize language into their mental models. Then they use the language constructs in their mental models to compose sentences of their own. That is similar to how Bundy appropriated his idealization of a lover from his external world of family life, university life, political campaign life and life of the mentally distressed. Appropriation is an adoption of conscious content from social and cultural sources in the external environment. Bundy's cultural appropriation was a collection of images, thoughts, and emotions drawn from his external environment where lovers are temporary resources to be used for pleasure and entertainment. Internalization is the incorporation of a cultural appropriation into one's mental model. The opportunity for internalization of Bundy's appropriation was lost because he repeatedly thwarted Kendall's efforts to help him process his unassimilated mental state of mind.

There were two appropriations in the relationship between Bundy and Kendall. From the society in which he grew up, Bundy appropriated conscious content about societal expectations of a lover. From the society in which she grew up, Kendall appropriated conscious content about societal expectations of a husband. The activation of the archetypes of lover and husband was evident in the behaviors and communications between them as they tried to fit the content of their appropriations into their mental models. Each had their own expectations about behavior in the opposite sex, but their expectations did not mesh with each other. The content of Bundy's appropriation was processed experience made up of meaningful thoughts, emotions, images and memories about a woman's role as lover drawn from the cultural environment. The content of Kendall's appropriation was processed experience made up of meaningful thoughts, emotions, images and memories about a man's role as husband drawn from the cultural environment. Bundy and Kendall were not able to achieve the kind of dialogue that would enable them to use the content of their appropriations to construct meanings relevant to their lives. There was no internalization of new content into their mental models. They were not able to transform their unassimilated emotional states into useful thoughts. Their opportunity for symbol formation was lost because Kendall's efforts at being a container were thwarted by Bundy's parasitic anxiety.

Cartwright explains that, for Bion, a real human mental connection is like an emotional storm caused by the coming together of minds that crave and resist each other (CSM 3). The romantic relationship between Bundy and Kendall had elements of craving and resisting each other. Bundy craved the emotional support and the financial support he got from Kendall, but he put up a resistance to her attempts to curtail his shoplifting. Although he agreed to marry Kendall, Bundy resisted her expectations of a monogamous relationship. Kendall craved his companionship, his protection and his promise of a future together, but she put up a resistance to his reluctance to give her a place in his life as his fiancée.

The capacity to generate meaning from gathering up one's thoughts and emotions requires the encounter to be subjected to a series of transformations. This involves finding ways of tolerating the emotional storm for long enough so that it can be given particular personal meaning. Bundy and Kendall struggled with their storm of disagreements about the possibility of marriage, long-distance intervals in the relationship, infidelities, and degrees of commitment to each other. Cartwright interprets Bion's containment model as giving importance to the transformational qualities of lived experience always unfolding at the cusp of one's awareness (CSM 3). Bundy's cusp of awareness was that line between what he knew about the socially acceptable side of his personality and the mysterious 'force' of the hidden side of his personality. Kendall's cusp of awareness was the line between her desire for a husband in her life and the figment of her imagination about a Prince Charming. Bundy and Kendall engaged each other in a tumultuous romantic relationship, which provides an example of the parasitic mode of containment. There was no psychological growth. Bundy engaged in psychologically harmful behavior with insincere declarations of endearment — poems, letters and telephone calls – intended to keep Kendall supplying emotional and financial support, even though he had no intention of building a future with her. Psychologically ill-equipped to separate herself from Ted, Kendall continued to supply emotional and financial support even after she came to the realization there could be no future with him. The interaction between Bundy and Kendall produced no third narrative of any consequence. Instead, it resulted in arguments and bickering that were destructive to the relationship.

Converting Experience to Meaning: Symbolization

In my reading of biographies, the poems, and the exchange of letters between Ted Bundy and Elizabeth Kendall, I found nothing that I could regard as the emergence of a symbol as described in "*A Critical Dictionary of Jungian Analysis*" where psychologist Andrew Samuels and others define symbol in terms of concept, intent, purpose and content. There was a lot of communication between Bundy and Kendall. When they were in the same city, they spent a lot of time communicating in each other's company. When they were in different cities, they exchanged numerous letters and telephone calls. So, there was a lot of opportunity for conscious and unconscious communication. However, there was no indication of any symbol formation in the communications between them.

According to psychologist Duncan Cartwright, a mind is dependent on another mind for meaning (CSM 2). With projections cast on each other's minds, Bundy and Kendall had a mind-to-mind connection with a potential for deriving meaning about their lives based on their experiences. However, neither lived up to the challenge of becoming a container who facilitates psychological growth in the other. She tried to be a container for him, but he thwarted her efforts. What he described as an internal 'force' was consuming his energies, making it increasingly difficult for him to appear normal. He did not have the wherewithal to be a container for Kendall. An encounter between two people can transform unprocessed internal and external experience into meaning about life, leading to the growth of personality. For a while, Bundy and Kendall felt that they were satisfying each other's needs. But it turned out the greater part of that satisfaction was entertainment. They enjoyed exploring their new surroundings as they settled into making Seattle their home ... the ferry, the restaurants, the river, taking Molly to a theme park. Four months into their relationship, they obtained a marriage license, but shortly afterwards, Bundy ripped it up during a domestic squabble. That action initiated the slow slide from a relationship with a potential for containment to a relationship without a containment.

Call To Action: Take Away A Portable Understanding

The story in this chapter is about how a serial killer parasitized the meaning-making resources of his girlfriend who tried to become a container for his unassimilated state of mind. To help readers take away a portable understanding of the parasitic mode of containment, I offer the following summary of the containment in the relationship between Ted Bundy and Elizabeth Kendall.

- **Mode:** Bundy and Kendall had a parasitic mode of containment.
- **Roles:** Kendall attempted to play the role of container, but her efforts were thwarted by Bundy, who preferred to try to justify his anti-social behavior rather than convert his experience to meaning. They did not switch roles.
- **Symmetry:** Bundy and Kendall had an asymmetrical relationship. They chose each other, but they were not co-equals. Bundy was financially dependent on Kendall, who was so emotionally invested in the relationship that she found it difficult to let go even when Bundy confessed that he tried to kill her.
- **Psychological Frame:** The purpose of the psychological frame in this parasitic mode of containment was to sustain a romantic relationship. The physical boundary of the frame was Kendall's apartment, where they initially conducted most of their interaction. The time boundary of the frame, in the early years of the containment, was daily interaction as a couple. Over the six-year relationship, the psychological frame degraded, first when they began to live in separate cities, then later because he was under investigation for kidnapping and assault of women.
- **Dialectical Narrative:** The first narrative was Bundy's narrative. It was a two-fold construction of a socially visible narrative and a socially hidden narrative. The socially visible narrative was about processing the content of the projection of lover that was cast onto Kendall. At the same time, the socially hidden part of his narrative was being constructed around an internal force that was gaining control of his life. The force was an impulse to kill. The second narrative, Kendall's narrative, was about a transparently needy woman seeking to transform a Phantom Prince into her ideal Prince Charming. As the relationship was ending, Kendall struggled with the conflict between her intellectual

awareness of Bundy's shortcomings and her emotional devotion to him. The semblance of a third narrative was the product of unprocessed emotional turmoil that had the effect of being psychologically harmful in ways that weakened emotional bonds between them, and was destructive to the relationship. The parasitic mode of containment operated within bonds that strip their relationship of emotional connection, making it feel meaningless, indifferent and lifeless. They did not achieve a creative union.

- **Psychological Growth / Harm**: The relationship resulted in no psychological growth. Bundy succumbed to his internal force that drove him to kill. Kendall became a recovering alcoholic who sought the service of a psychiatrist to help her manage the conflicted emotions she experienced from interacting with the incarcerated Bundy as well as the police in Seattle and Salt Lake City. Kendall's gallant but psychologically feeble attempts at containment were no match for the emotional drain that Bundy's parasitic anxiety placed on the containment.

After the Containment Ended

In 1981, Elizabeth Kendall published the first edition of her memoir "*The Phantom Prince: My Life With Ted Bundy*" while Ted Bundy was in prison. Bundy was later executed for murders in the state of Florida in 1989. Investigators believed Bundy committed over thirty murders in multiple states including Washington, Utah, Colorado, Oregon and Florida. Some of the murders had been committed during his relationship with Kendall, but without her knowledge.

Sources

The sources of information that shape my thinking in this chapter are:
- "*The Phantom Prince: My Life With Ted Bundy*" by Elizabeth Kendall
- Cable TV Channel HLN: "*How It Really Happened*" serial documentary
  - Ted Bundy: Ted Escapes
  - Ted Bundy: The Murder Trials
  - Ted Bundy: The Death Row Confessions

- *"The 1979 Psychological Assessment of Ted Bundy"* by Al Carlisle
- *"The Stranger Beside Me"* by Ann Rule
- *"BUNDY: A Clinical Discussion of the Perfect Storm"* by Robert DePaolo
- *"Containing States of Mind"* by Duncan Cartwright
- *"Projection and Re-Collection in Jungian Psychology"* by Marie-Louise von Franz.

CHAPTER 15

An Autistic Mode of Containment Involving: Anthony Weiner & Digital Images

> *"These destructive impulses brought great devastation to my family and friends, and destroyed my life's dream of public service. … (I) came to grips for the first time with the depths of my sickness last fall and entered intensive treatment. I have a sickness, but I do not have an excuse."*
>
> — Anthony Weiner

U. S. Congressman Anthony Weiner was doing all the things that society expected him to do. High school ... university ... career ... public service ... marriage ... fatherhood. He knew how to successfully make his way in the world. But he did not know himself. He was unaware that he had a predisposition for addiction. By the time he became aware of it, his obsession with sexting digital images was outside of his control. The first time Weiner's sexting behavior became public was in 2011, when he told his wife that it was just a virtual game. He explained that he would log on to Social Media, play his virtual game of trading sexually explicit photographs with women, many of whose identities were unknown to him, then he would log off and return to reality (BL 298). That public revelation of his sexting cost him his seat in Congress. The second time his sexting came to public attention, he had to terminate his campaign for mayor of New York City. The next time his sexting became public, it was about a sexted image of himself aroused in bed with his baby son sleeping next to him ... an image published for all the world to see. His wife filed for divorce. In 2017, Weiner's sexting with a 15-year-old girl cost him his freedom ... 21 months in federal jail. By that time, he had reconstructed his opinion of sexting. He no longer regarded it as merely a virtual game. He asked the judge for leniency by stating: *"I was a very sick man for a long time, I have a disease but I have no excuse."* He acknowledged to the U.S. District Judge that he is an addict attending therapy for his condition (U. S. NEWS, September 25, 2017).

My interpretation is that Anthony Weiner was in an autistic mode of containment involving a stream of digital images of women in the period 2011 to 2017 when he compulsively exchanged sexually explicit communications, known as sexts, with online avatars, most of whose identities were unknown to him. I do not know Anthony Weiner. My interpretation is based on materials found in the public domain, and listed at the end of this chapter. Social Media was not the cause of his compulsion; Social Media merely facilitated his sexting. The interaction between Weiner and the stream of digital images was one of him walling off experience with actual women by avoiding the multi-dimensional qualities of women. To explain the relationship that Weiner had with digital images, it is useful to have some background information about his life. In the next section, I provide background information about Weiner's life. In the section after that, I offer background information about the sexting of digital images.

Background Information about Anthony Weiner

In my research, I found news articles about Anthony Weiner, but it appears that he has not written a memoir, nor has anyone written a biography about him. His wife, Huma Abedin, wrote her memoir, which includes information about him. I rely on news articles, web sites and Abedin's memoir for background information about Weiner. He was born in September, 1964 in Brooklyn, New York. His father, Mort was a lawyer and his mother, Frances, was a teacher of mathematics. The Weiner family is of Jewish descent. Young Weiner graduated from Brooklyn Technical High School in 1981. Then, he went on to the State University of New York at Plattsburgh, where he graduated with a political science degree in 1985. At age 29, he became a councilman in New York, and continued that role for seven years. See *"Anthony Weiner"* on TheFamousPeople web site. In 1999, he became a congressman for New York. The following year, he married Huma Abedin, who was born in Michigan and raised in Saudi Arabia. By the end of 2011, they had a son, whom they named Jordan.

When Weiner began sexting, he saw it as a virtual game. He was a single man at the time. He was curious about the technology that made sexting available. It presented an opportunity for a light social pastime. He probably did not have a clear idea of what kind of game he was getting into, or the possible risk to himself. Even if he pondered those topics, answers would not have been available. Sexting was new. There was not enough data about sexting behavior for psychologists to make interpretations about the benefits and the risk of the technology. There was no information about what draws certain people to those communications. He knew nothing about how to monitor his behavior or detect poor impulse control. I doubt that he considered why sexting appealed to him. He certainly did not know when his sexting left the zone of light social pastime and crept into addiction. It took a few scandals to alert him to the fact that his focus on nudity was regarded as pornography in certain social circles, that his behavior had crossed the line of healthy impulse control, and that he was engaging in illegal behavior with a minor.

Weiner resigned from his position as congressman due to a sexting scandal in 2011, when he admitted sending sexually explicit content to women he met online via his Twitter account. His sexting behavior continued out of control until 2017 when he pleaded guilty to sexting a minor and was sentenced to spend 21 months in federal prison. When being sentenced, he asked the judge for leniency on the grounds that he acknowledged being an addict and that he was having regular professional treatment. Weiner had been doing all that society expected of him. He completed high school. He graduated from university, having acquired a degree in political science. He established a career as a politician and became a responsible, law-abiding member of society. Somewhere along the way, some life experience made him susceptible to addiction, but he did not know. There was probably nothing that prepared him to manage a predisposition to addiction. Parenting usually does not include preparation for addiction. Although the education system aims at the lofty goal of preparing students for life, its most notable achievement has been the stratification of the labor force. Weiner's education clearly did not prepare him to recognize, let alone manage a predisposition for addiction. He was building a life for himself with the knowledge and skills at his disposal. His intellect led him to imagine that sexting was just a virtual game, but he evidently lacked the emotional wherewithal to realize that sexting was becoming a compulsion which aggressively drew him into cyclical behaviors of sexting, feeling guilty and experiencing shame. Those activities continued until his behavior came to public attention. By the time he understood what was happening, his sexting was already beyond his control. See "Anthony Weiner Sentenced to Nearly Two Years in Prison for Sexting Scandal" on the U. S. NEWS web site.

Background Information about Sexting Digital Images

The word 'sexting' is a linguistic contraction of the words sex and texting. Sexting is a social pastime of exchanging sexually explicit images and messages with others using Social Media communication portals, like Twitter and Facebook. Sexting began early in the 21st century when communication portals such as Twitter and Facebook came into common usage. Prospective romantic partners and existing romantic partners began using the Social Media portals to share information with each other. Sexting is a legal activity unless the communication is sent to anyone under the legal age required to give sexual consent. Sexting can be an addiction if it becomes an impulse that the sender of the sexts cannot control.

Robert Weiss, senior Vice President of Clinical Development at Elements Behavioral Health, is the author of "Sex Addiction 101: A Basic Guide to Healing from Sex, Porn and Love Addiction". He oversees treatment for people who have addictive sexual disorders including sexting. He defines addiction as loss of control, which can be seen in a person repeating the same behavior despite negative consequences. Weiss has not met Weiner and does not express an opinion about Weiner. However, Weiss does express sympathy for Weiner because his addiction is so compulsive that he included his young son in a picture he sexted to a woman to whom he wanted to appear attractive. Weiss points out that the high that comes from sexting does not necessarily come from engaging in sex, but from the 'anticipatory fantasy excitement' of imagining the next nude picture, or the next raunchy message. See the U.S. News web site for article titled *"One way to understand Anthony Weiner's compulsive sexting"*. Weiss also points out that the technology of Social Media does not cause addiction. The convenience of technology merely facilitates addiction. The easy accessibility of the technology, coupled with the anonymity of online partners, make sexting appealing. The cause of the addiction is much deeper. According to Weiss, sex addiction is a dysfunction defined by preoccupation to the point of obsession with the behavior, and loss of control over the behavior as evidenced in failed attempts to quit, as well as directly related negative consequences, for example, issues at work, in relationships, or legal troubles (SA 2 – 9).

Charles Samenow is a psychiatrist and associate professor at The George Washington University School of Medicine & Health Sciences. His view is that a pattern of emotional and psychological factors contributes to the risk of addictive behavior. Examples are unhealthy relationships, difficulty forming attachments, as well as underlying mood and anxiety disorders. People who are predisposed to addiction are more vulnerable to compulsive sexting. He observes that the public was inclined to dismiss Weiner's behavior and label him a pervert because his addiction involves sex. They did not realize that Weiner was distressed. Samenow's model of treatment is to require responsibility and accountability but provide support.

Sexting is a flirtatious exchange of sexually explicit photographs, videos and messages between people who are sexually curious about each other. Sometimes they know each other, other times they communicate by pseudonyms so their identities remain unknown. They communicate by digital devices such as smartphones. Sexting is a relatively new type of communication that became popular when the Internet came into common usage. Some couples engage in sexting as harmless, romantic activity. Because sexting is such a recent phenomenon, there are no laws about it. However, some people get into trouble about sexting because it borders on pornography. There is not enough data about sexting for psychologists to distinguish between normal sexting behavior and sexting disorder. The availability of the Internet in the early 21st century coupled with the proliferation of mobile devices made sexting widespread. It appears that weak impulse control may be one of the distinguishing factors. Although there is no definition of sexting as a psychological abnormality and no legislation about sexting, there are treatments for sexting addiction. Inability to control sexting behavior is the criterion for addiction. Symptoms of sexting addiction are poor self-image, sexual dysfunction, and inability to control sexting impulse even after it negatively impacts career and family life.

Psychologists Wilfred Bion and Duncan Cartwright built the containment model on the principles of projection and introjection. Because projections occur when archetypes are activated, I describe the relationship between Weiner and digital images as mediated by an archetype. To do that, I rely on the two definitions of archetypes: first in the context of archetype-as-biological-entity, then, in the context of archetype-as-emergent-phenomenon.

Context of Archetype as Biological Entity: Projection & Introjection

This section is about the interaction that Weiner had with digital images in the context of archetype-as-biological-entity. When an archetype is viewed as a biological entity, it is regarded as an ancestral heritage of human experience accumulated over many generations and located in collective unconsciousness. When psychologists define an archetype as a biological entity, the processes they identify for converting experience to meaning are projection and introjection. Projection is an evacuation of unconscious content from the psyche due to an unbearable state of mind. There was a projection cast from Weiner's mind to a stream of sexting images. The projection was about an unbearable state of mind related to interaction with the opposite sex. Introjection is a transformation of an unbearable state of mind to a bearable state of mind, followed by its integration into conscious content of the psyche. There was no introjection because the sexting images are inanimate, and therefore incapable of helping Weiner process his unbearable state of mind.

I do not know Anthony Weiner. My interpretation of his relationship with digital images is based on my understanding of sexting, plus my understanding of Cartwright's autistic mode of containment, plus Wiener's comments taken from the public domain. Weiner's interaction with the stream of digital images of women appears to be an autistic mode of containment. Duncan Cartwright uses the phrase 'autistic mode of containment' in reference to a relationship where the contained does not have the ability to participate in a containment (CSM 151 – 154). This mode of containment occurs when the interaction between contained and container is hindered because a limitation in the mind of the contained prevents active participation in a containment. This mode of containment is not functional because certain mental operations of the contained are shut down. In an autistic mode of containment, a projection is cast from the mind of the contained and it impacts the external aspect of a thing, rather than being projected onto the mind of a person. Because a part of the mental life of the contained is shut down, the means of communicating the projection to another mind are not functional. What occurs instead is a projection to the surface of an inanimate thing in an attempt to avoid relating to another, which would pose a risk of exacerbating the anxiety that caused the projection in the first place. My reason for labeling this an autistic mode of containment is that the containment involved a projection to the outward aspects, or the surface areas, of the women, rather than a projection to the minds of the women. Another reason for calling the interaction an autistic mode of containment is that the eventual outcome was not psychologically beneficial to Weiner or the women. Weiner's sexting activity involved a projection being involuntarily cast from his mind. Instead of being cast from his mind onto the mind of another person, the projection was cast onto a stream of digital images of women. As it turns out, the projection had a profound effect on his life. That raises questions. What led him to sexting? How did his sexting, which began as a casual virtual game, morph into a scandalous addiction that threatened his career and his marriage? Why was Weiner, a well-educated and law-abiding congressman, not able to restrain his sexting impulse after the first scandal broke? Why did it take multiple scandals for him to come out of denial about his addiction? Those questions require research into details of what shaped his prior relationships. Since there is no detailed biography about Weiner's life, I leave that to future researchers. Certain questions can be answered by connecting Weiner's projection to the relevant archetype, that is, the anima archetype. It is useful to ground the description of a projection in the relevant archetype. According to psychologist Marie-Louise von Franz, a projection always originates in an archetype (PRJ 24).

Weiner's sexting behaviors were related to his expectation about the opposite sex, indicating that the anima archetype was activated. The anima is made up of an ancestral heritage of experience in relations with the opposite sex accumulated over multiple generations. The anima archetype is located in the collective unconscious part of the psyche. Activation of the anima archetype indicates a forceable evacuation of a projection from Weiner's mind to the digital images. The content of Weiner's projection was raw experience of emotions, images and memories related to the opposite sex. More specifically, the content of his projection was a fascination with images of women's bodies, that is, the outer view, the surface view, not actual interaction with women. A collection of emotions, images, thoughts and memories was incomprehensible to him and was therefore evacuated as an unbearable state of mind. Because they are inanimate, digital images lack the ability to function as carrier of Weiner's projection. Having no mind, the digital images were unable to help Weiner to construct meanings from the content of his projection. The digital images could not help him to metabolize his unassimilated emotional states and structure them into useful thoughts.

The anima was activated at the critical stage of Weiner's life cycle, when he was transitioning from bachelorhood to spousehood and fatherhood. At that critical stage of psychological development, his capacity for emotional interaction between contained and container had not yet fully formed, or was partly shut down. As a substitute, digital images were used as psychic surfaces in an effort to hold his sense of self together. Attention to development of the interior aspect of psychic life was either inadequate or evaded, so phantasies that would — in the form of a projection — be cast onto another mind, as a means of communication, were not transmitted to another mind. Instead, the projection was transmitted to the psychic surface, or digital images, of women. Projection relies on communication to an internal mental space. Digital images have no internal mental space. In the autistic mode of containment, ideas or conceptions about an internal mental space bring about anxiety and contribute to fragmentation of the sense of self. In the autistic mode of containment, sensations, thoughts and emotions are used to block mind-to-mind connection or relating to another. The result is a diminishment of vitality in the experience of life. For Weiner, the digital images were inanimate surfaces used to wall off the experience of his emotions.

According to Duncan Cartwright, emotion is the fabric which animates contained-container relations (CSM 152). Containment is a way of relating that is driven by reliance on projection unto the interior, that is, the mental space of another. For Weiner, the purpose of the projection was evaded. Instead of projecting onto another mind, Weiner had phantasies of sticking to the surface of inanimate digital images in an effort to achieve a coherent biographical narrative. He clung to the two-dimensional, digital images instead of getting to know any of the multi-dimensional, flesh and blood women with whom he communicated by sext. Clinging to digital images not only blocked encounter with his own internal world, but also blocked engagement with a containing – thinking – mind. He adopted a repetitive strategy of reducing relationship to interaction with a sensory surface. With that obsessive action, he blocked the processing of experience that would otherwise be jointly constructed in a containment that involves another person. Genuine interaction between contained and container could not occur because it was limited by the level at which his psyche operated.

In his role as contained, Weiner contributed the first narrative, which was a communication made up of a series of sexts that included digital images of himself in sexually provocative poses, accompanied by messages intended to solicit sexually explicit responses. The second narrative was a series of digital images and messages from women, many of whom he did not know. Since the digital images from the women did not form a containment, there was no opportunity for the generation of a third narrative. The first and second narratives did not form a dialectical interaction, so there was no containment. Weiner's narrative did not reach the mental space of the women. The women did not provide containment.

In Analytical Psychology, the anima represents the inner feminine side of a man. Initially, it is about the emergence of a man's object of desire. When a projection first emerges from the anima archetype, its content is about attraction to the opposite sex, and love. As the man matures psychologically, the contents of later projections shift to topics of virtue and wisdom. It makes up the unconscious feminine, psychological qualities that a man possesses. The anima makes itself known by influencing a man's attitude toward the opposite sex. Anima development is about a man opening up to his emotionality, and expanding his consciousness to include love, creativity, intuition and imagination. Weiner's difficulty with impulse control regarding sexting images indicates there was an interruption in his anima development. With his limited impulse control, Weiner lost his grip on reality and was unable to manage a balance of attention to reality with attention to escape from reality. Weiner was increasingly drawn into the escape world of sexting. He also lost his ability to manage boundaries, as seen in his willingness to include his young son in a pornographic digital image. He was willing to justify involving his son by his need to find the next sexual stimulation. He wanted to be physically attractive to women, but did not care for the emotional effort necessary for a person-to-person relationship. He pursued sexual arousal without the involvement of getting to know another. He did not want to handle the intensity of emotional interaction. He lost himself in the pursuit of sexual pleasure, sacrificing himself for the images of his desire. He caved in to his autistic side because he could not control his impulses. The virtual game of sexting gave way to obsession, and the obsession overwhelmed him. His passion led him to neglect his own well-being, his career, his family and his marriage. Overcome by the impulse to acquire a steady stream of sexted images, he neglected his reputation as a congressman, and his responsibility to protect his young son.

Social Media platforms are inanimate; they are not capable of being carriers of projections. However, they are convenient vehicles for compulsive sexting behavior because they enable communication among many people, whose identities can be hidden. Weiner's projections were not cast to physical, flesh-and-blood women. His projections were cast onto digital images of women. In the language of autistic containment, Weiner's projections were cast onto surfaces of women. His goal was not biological sexual intercourse, or establishing intimate relationships by getting to know any woman. His goal was autistic interaction, that is, surface interaction, with pictures of unidentified women for the immediate purposes of sexual arousal and performance, in a digital interaction that he thought of as a virtual game. Initially, Weiner believed sexting was just a virtual game, until he lost his job as Congressman, had to terminate his campaign for mayor of New York, put his marriage at risk, and lost his freedom. I believe that Weiner's projection was broken when he was sentenced to spend time in prison following the scandal of his sext to a minor. That is when he realized that his virtual game had become an addiction which he could not control.

Unfortunately for those who come of age in the 21st century, the education system, the legal system and psychological institutions are all lagging technological development, in terms of discerning impact on humans. Socialization is not keeping abreast of technology. People like Weiner use Social Media portals for entertainment without any guidance about the potential risks because there is not yet enough data on which to base recommendations for assessing the risk that technology poses, and determining which humans are vulnerable. In this section, I described Weiner's interaction with digital images in the context of archetype-as-biological-entity. In the next section, I will describe the interaction in the context of archetype-as-emergent-phenomenon.

Context of Archetype as Emergent Phenomenon: Appropriation & Internalization

This section is about the interaction that Weiner had with digital images viewed in the context of archetype-as-emergent-phenomenon. When considering archetype as an emergent phenomenon, it is seen as an emergent property of a dynamic, developmental system that is made up of human brains, human activities, society's external environment and the narrative competence of humans in the society. In viewing archetype as an emergent phenomenon, the means for converting life's experience to meaning are appropriation and internalization. Appropriation is an adoption of conscious content from social and cultural sources in the external environment. Weiner's appropriation was a 2-dimensional view of womanhood drawn from society's external environment. Internalization is the incorporation of a cultural appropriation into one's mental model. There was no internalization in this autistic mode of containment because sexting images are inanimate and therefore not able to function as a container.

For readers who are unfamiliar with the processes of appropriation and internalization, they can be observed in the way that children acquire language skills. At first, children appropriate language from social and cultural sources in the external world, then with the help of adults, they internalize language into their mental models. I offer that well-known example as a segue into discussion of Anthony Weiner's interaction with digital images in the context of archetype as emergent phenomenon. Weiner appropriated a 2-dimensional view of womanhood drawn from society's external environment, shaped by narratives of humans in the society, and facilitated by the technology available at the time.

The behaviors and communications between Weiner and the unidentified women encountered on the Internet were related to society's expectations of womanhood. The anima archetype was activated at the level of psychic complexity where Weiner was making his way from being a single man to becoming a husband and a father. In the context of archetype as emergent phenomenon, the anima emerged from a complex system that is made up of society's attitudes and actions related to relationships between men and women, the cultural environment in which relationships occur, and the narratives that people compose about their relationships. In this context, the anima archetype has no specific location; it is in the relationship habits and institutions that permeate relationships in the cultural environment. Weiner had an appropriation from the anima in the cultural environment. The content of his appropriation was conscious experience made up of emotions, thoughts, images and memories about a woman's role in society drawn from the cultural environment. When the anima archetype is activated, it is important to distinguish its influence on outer reality from its influence in inner reality, because the anima plays a role in social life as well as a role in personal life. Anima is the archetype which enables a man to establish a bridge between the larger collective of the external world and his inner world. The formation of the bridge depends, not on the functions of ego consciousness such as rationality, but on psychological development. The conscious role of the anima is in social life, while the unconscious role is in interior life. It appears that Social Media was a forum for Weiner's social life. That is where he encountered, not just any women, but those who play the role of seductress by sexting images of their bodies along with flirtatious messages. His desire was not for the women themselves. He had an obsessive fantasy about the images of women's bodies that came in a stream of sexts from online encounters.

In establishing a bridge between a man's exterior and interior life, the anima mediates psychological development by enabling the man to cultivate an independent sense of self as different from socially accepted sense of self. A man becomes more internally aware of what he believes and feels, and becomes more capable of expressing these beliefs and feelings. The man's psychological maturity involves engagement in a series of internal dialogues which help him understand how he relates to the external world. Through those dialogues, the man comes to understand how not to be controlled by the anima. As a man becomes aware of the anima archetype, it allows him to overcome thoughts of who he ought to be and to accept himself for who he really is. The anima can enliven a personality with development and creativity, or it can make the person's outlook solidified and compulsive. When the anima archetype was activated, Weiner's behavior became compulsive. He was in search of the romantic thrill of sexual arousal, without the intimacy of in-person interaction. Searching for experiences of arousal to make him feel alive and energized, he settled for interactions with digital images of women, rather than interacting with actual women. He was not able to find what he was searching for. Maybe he did not know what he was searching for. He engaged in a stream of sexting to find serial sexual arousal rather than a multi-faceted relationship with a real woman. He was constantly looking for the next arousal from the next female image in his next attempt to escape from reality. Unable or unwilling to connect with another at an intimate level, he sought a source of stimulation that would bring him pleasurable satisfaction without the burden of having to satisfy another. He sought an experience that the moment can bring as an escape from reality. Maybe he was trying to avoid the possibility of rejection and damage to self-esteem. Perhaps he found it difficult to cope with existing damage to his self-esteem. In his search for sexual fulfillment, he went from one stream of sexting to another, seeking one feature that satisfies the desire for escape, but not the full range of romantic features of a full-blown containment. He stopped at initial arousal based on physical appearance, and did not move on to engaging the mind of the other. Without another mind to function as a container, Weiner did not have the kind of dialogue that would enable him to use the content of his appropriation to construct meanings relevant to his life, or to internalize the meanings into his mental model of relationship with someone of the opposite sex.

Anthony Weiner created a cyberspace-based psychological frame whose purpose was sexual arousal with online avatars to sustain his developing addiction. The communication portals of Social Media provided the space boundary of the psychological frame for sexting. In particular, his Twitter account was the vehicle for exchanging sexts with online partners. The time boundary the psychological frame may have started in 2011, when the first public scandal occurred, or it could have begun earlier. The time frame ended in 2017 when Weiner went to jail for illegal sexting with a minor. During the period 2011 to 2017, the frequency of his sexting shifted from occasional, social pastime to addiction in the face of diminishing impulse control. Smartphone and Twitter provided a convenient, virtual frame for his addictive behavior because it was hidden, that is, until he inadvertently labeled one of his sexts as 'public' instead of 'private'.

Weiner had become dependent on sexting of digital images in online encounters with women, most of whom were unknown to him. In this asymmetrical relationship, Weiner was a human while the digital images were inanimate entities. Since there was no mind-to-mind connection between Weiner and the digital images, or any mind-to-mind connection between Weiner and the women, there was no opportunity for psychological growth. However, there was psychological harm. Social Media presented a form of communication that was useful and entertaining for Weiner, but it also presented an allure which was so subtle that he hardly knew he was slipping into an addiction. His source of entertainment became a compulsive activity over which he had no control. From an internal point of view, the interactions between Weiner and the stream of digital images resulted in psychological harm brought by gradual loss of impulse control. The external results were public scandal, loss of respect of his political constituents, loss of his position as Congressman, divorce proceedings by his wife, and prison time. He had to face the humiliating situation of requesting leniency from a federal judge, with the explanation that he was an addict obtaining treatment from a health care professional.

Converting Experience to Meaning: Symbolization

In my reading of Huma Abedin's biography and news articles about Anthony Weiner, I found nothing that I could regard as the emergence of a symbol as described in "A Critical Dictionary of Jungian Analysis" where psychologist Andrew Samuels and others define symbol in terms of concept, intent, purpose and content. I had no access to the sexts that Weiner exchanged with women online, but my opinion is that the sexually suggestive communications that accompanied the sexts probably did not provide an opportunity for symbol formation. Raunchy communication did not help Weiner achieve the degree of narrative competence that would enable him to connect past and present experiences and combine them into a coherent and meaningful story of his life. In the absence of a mind-to-mind connection, or not having a tolerance for a mind-to-mind connection, he had limited opportunity for symbol formation.

Since he exchanged digital images with women – whom he did not know — via the Internet, it appears that he did not find a mind-to-mind connection that would entail symbol formation. Symbolic meaning has to be scaffolded by the container's recognition of the contained's gestures, images, and verbal communications, thus enabling the contained to enter a world of meaning, that is, a space of symbolic imagination, previously experienced by the container. The scaffolding helps the contained to make meaning from their affective states, as well as from the shared symbolic world of culture. Weiner did not find an opportunity for making sense of his experience during his sexting communications. Compulsive repetition of sexting gave him stimulation for sexual gratification, but it did not have the effect of psychological containment.

In the autistic mode of containment, Weiner used the digital images as psychic surfaces of the women to bolster and hold together his sense of self. Because he avoided the minds of the women, his appropriations were not communicated by normal social interaction. Containment relies on internal space, that is, the mind of another. In autistic containment, internal space invokes anxiety, with the potential for fragmentation of the sense of self (CSM 151). Relating to another mind is blocked by the adoption of an anti-relational stance that inhibits sensations, thoughts, and emotions. Contained-container interaction is restricted by a narrow-mindedness that focuses on the surface of the other as a means of obtaining a cohesive sense of self. The autistic mode of containment has a deadening effect on psychic experience as others are treated like inanimate surfaces to wall-off experiencing emotion. The relationship between word and emotion is severed, and in its place, are meaningless things that block experience. Cartwright points out that it is emotion which animates the contained-container relation (CSM 152). As long as there are emotions linking the contained and container, there can be a relation between them. However, when the relationship is deprived of emotions, the connection between contained and container reduces the vitality of the relationship. Since Weiner was not interacting with full-fledged human women, the development of a multidimensional internal space between him and the women was inhibited.

In his role as the contained, Weiner saw the other as two-dimensional forms, as surfaces, that he used to hold his sense of self together. There was no real containment, only elements that cling together to form containment surfaces. This attempt at containment, or attempt at relating, is driven by an attempt at sticking to another to gain coherence rather than making a mind-to-mind connection. This mode of relating to another aims to generate a sense of coherence (CSM 152). It relies on the sensory surface of the other and on the need to block entry into a containing, thinking, feeling other. People in the autistic mode of containment tend to adopt repetitive and perseverative strategies that reduce interaction to a near-sensory surface (CSM 153). Weiner's adoption of repetitive sexting became a preservative strategy when he could no longer control it. Weiner found digital images of women to be non-conscious but useful entities. Preoccupation with the digital images made them into autistic surfaces that blocked the processing of emotional experience which would otherwise have been jointly constructed during a containment that involves a real woman.

Call to Action: Take Away A Portable Understanding

This chapter offers an account of the life of a successful public servant who began an innocent virtual game that subtly morphed into an addiction. In the public arena, he adroitly navigated his way through the layers of societal achievements of education, career, marriage and fatherhood. In the management of his private life, he was not so skillful. He thought his virtual game of sexting was a playful occasional escape from reality, but the allure of Social Media gradually seduced him into addiction. Until he was found guilty of illegally sexting a minor, he did not realize that he had a psychological disorder. This chapter is a call to action for readers to take away a portable understanding of the autistic mode of containment. To help readers, I offer the following summary as a reminder of how Anthony Weiner came to realize that his sexting had become more than just a casual pastime.

- **Mode:** There was an autistic mode of containment involving Weiner and a stream of digital images exchanged with women via Social Media.
- **Roles:** Weiner was the contained and the digital images took the place of a container.
- **Symmetry:** This was an asymmetrical relationship. Weiner was a human while the digital images were inanimate entities. Weiner had become dependent on the stream of digital images as a source of periodic escape from reality.
- **Psychological Frame:** The interaction between Weiner and the digital images occurred in a cyberspace-based psychological frame whose purpose was escape from reality in the form of sexual pleasure. Social Media provided the means of communication. The time boundary of the frame was the period 2011 through 2017, while the space boundary was the Internet.

- **Dialectical Narrative:** The first narrative was Weiner's communication of a series of sexts made up of digital images of himself in stages of undress, combined with sexual messages. The second narrative was a collection of digital images and fragmented messages from multiple women, many of them un-identified. There was no third narrative because the first and second narratives did not have the dialectical interaction to support a containment. Weiner's narrative did not reach the mental space of the women. His narrative was not intended to actually engage others. Weiner's narrative was about his role in a virtual game ... an escape from reality. It was a substitute for actual containment. There was no dialectical narrative. Weiner's fragmented narrative did not reach another mind with which to engage in a dialectical interaction.

- **Psychological Growth / Harm:** The interaction between Weiner and the digital images resulted in psychological harm for Weiner. What began as a sexting pastime became a compulsive activity that he could not control. The external reality of the interactions between Weiner and the stream of digital images resulted in nothing meaningful. Instead, it brought him public scandal, loss of support by political constituents, loss of job, divorce proceedings, and alienation from his son. The internal reality of those interactions had no potential for psychological growth because they did not impact his knowledge, his outlook, nor his confidence in relating to women. The internal reality is that he did not recognize that his virtual game had become an addiction until investigators presented evidence and the jury found him guilty of lewd behavior, which is unacceptable to the society in which he lives.

After the Containment Ended

When ordered by a U. S. District Judge to spend 21 months in federal prison for sexting obscene material to a minor, Weiner acknowledged his addiction and informed the judge that he was already in therapy. Weiner served time in the Federal Medical Center Devens in Massachusetts, where his sentence was reduced by three months for good behavior. He was required to register as a sex offender for a minimum of 20 years.

Having lost his job as a U. S. Congressman, he developed a post-prison career in media by becoming a host of a weekly radio show at WABC radio in 2022. He also launched a podcast "*The Middle with Anthony Weiner*" where he offers his analyses about news of the day in New York City.

Weiner's wife, Huma Abedin, filed divorce proceedings in 2017. Later, they decided to settle privately to avoid embarrassment for their son, Jordan. To share the parenting of their son, they live in separate apartments in the same building in New York City. In the aftermath of Weiner's incarceration for lewd behavior with a minor, Social Services made regular visits to the home to check on young Jordan's wellbeing.

Sources

The sources of information that shape my thinking in this chapter are:
- "*BOTH / AND: A Life In Many Worlds*" by Huma Abedin
- "*Sex Addiction 101*" by Robert Weiss
- "*Containing States of Mind*" by Duncan Cartwright
- "*Projection and Re-Collection in Jungian Psychology*" by Marie-Louise von Franz
- TheFamousPeople web site:
  Anthony Weiner Biography – Facts, Childhood, Crimes (thefamouspeople.com)
- U. S. News web site:
  Anthony Weiner Sentenced to Nearly Two Years in Prison for Sexting Scandal (nbcnews.com)
- U. S. News web site:
  One way to understand Anthony Weiner's compulsive sexting (mashable.com).

CHAPTER 16

An Autistic Mode of Containment Involving: John Orr & Serial Fires

"Although attractively, and athletically built, (he) found himself insecure and unable to initiate relationships. His conversations were inept and usually self-centered, causing normal people to avoid him. He had no regular friends. ... The only time he could talk to people was around fires after they were burning. He could then share his knowledge of firefighting and fire equipment and fit in with the scene where he could be the center of attention."

— John Orr

California prosecutors called Glendale Fire Captain, John Orr, the most prolific arsonist of the 20th century, because he is believed to have set more than 2,000 fires between 1984 and 1991. After interviewing Orr, criminal profiler, Anthony Meoli, referred to Orr as a pyromaniac, because the fires were sexually motivated (FF 71 - 72). The fact that Orr had written a fictional book about two characters, a respectable firefighter and a dysfunctional arsonist, did not help his case when investigators closed in on him as the prime suspect. His own behavior was so closely aligned to the fictional arsonist that prosecutors regarded the book as a confession. However, Orr continues to maintain his innocence as he lives out his life in jail. The way Meoli explains Orr's insistence on his innocence, despite all the evidence, is that an admission of guilt would render his life meaningless. All the public service he provided to his community, as a firefighter, would be overshadowed by the shameful acts of an arsonist. The few family members and friends who still believe in him would give up on him. The decreasing brotherhood of firefighters who still have some professional respect for him would abandon him. His 3-decade defense mechanism of rationalization would crumble.

My interpretation is that John Orr was in an autistic mode of containment with serial fires. I do not know John Orr. My interpretation is based on the psychological analyses and biographies published about him, and listed at the end of this chapter. I rely on the Diagnostic and Statistical Manual of Mental Disorders (DSM-5) for a definition of pyromania, and I apply my understanding of Cartwright's definition of the autistic mode of containment. John Orr maintains his innocence because that is the façade that he constructed to maintain a sense of himself as a cohesive whole. It is a fragile façade. He hangs onto it to sustain his sense of self as a functioning human being. When he enrolled in Glendale Community College for an eight-week course in fiction writing in 1990, I think he was looking for something to mirror his life. Having had many roles in the workplace, he has many colleagues. Having had four wives, he has many family members and in-laws. But there was no one he allowed to get close enough to mirror his life back to him. He set out to write *"Points of Origin"* as a fictional story, but it turned out to be a close reflection of his own life. Here are excerpts from *"Points of Origin"* that indicate what is going on in the mind of the antagonist, Aaron Styles, as he observes from a distance the fire that he set in Los Angeles:

> *"Aaron lifted up the binoculars to marvel at the flames. He wanted to be closer. It was his and he needed to be near it, but fear kept him still. ... Police cars arrived and started diverting traffic around the hoses and Aaron decided to move on. He pulled back onto Sunset (Boulevard) and felt his erection straining against his shorts. He cupped his hand over it as he drove, shuddering at the prospect of another fire. The thought made him feel better. ... He drove slowly ... and took out*

several cigarettes. He set them on the seat beside him and constructed several of his (time-delayed fire starting) devices. His sexual excitement continued to build. ... It was unlikely that Aaron would ever become a suspect and he knew it. ... He occasionally walked into the area where his fire was burning, but only well after it was discovered and there were other people watching. He was a loner and insecure. 'His' fires gave him the much-needed attention he craved providing him with feelings of importance and recognition. ... Although attractively, and athletically built, Aaron found himself insecure and unable to initiate relationships. His conversations were inept and usually self-centered, causing normal people to avoid him. He had no regular friends. ... The only time he could talk to people was around fires after they were burning. He could then share his knowledge of firefighting and fire equipment and fit in with the scene where he could be the center of attention. ... Aaron had already killed five people in one of his fires. He rationalized the deaths as he did everything. It wasn't his fault. The people just acted stupidly, and their deaths had nothing to do with the fact that he set the fire" (PO 3 – 6).

In my opinion, this excerpt from Orr's novel shows unconscious guilt about the conflict between his external behaviors and his internal outlook. For his entire career, his motto had been that fire prevention was the mission of all fire-fighting stations. In his external life, he actively promoted fire prevention. He conducted training for fire fighters. He wrote articles for fire-fighting journals. He arranged fire patrol activities to alert residents to fire risks on their properties. In his internal life, he harbored a compulsive need that he could only satisfy in contradiction to all his fire-fighting principles. His high IQ score did not help him resolve the conflict between his fire-fighting and his fire-setting. He acknowledged that the character of the protagonist in his novel, Phil Langtry, was modeled on his own investigative style, while claiming that the antagonist, Aaron Stiles, was modeled on arsonists he had arrested. The investigators, the prosecutors and the jury all saw through the conflict upon which Orr had built the fragile façade of his life. To help readers understand the relationship that Orr had with serial fires, I provide background information about his life in the next section, and information about pyromania in the following section.

Background Information about John Orr

John Orr was born in April 1949 in the city of Glendale, the youngest of three boys in a middle-class family. They grew up in the adjacent community of Highland Park, where their father, Joe, was a machine manufacturer, and their mother, Leora, was a secretary in a dental office. John Orr's earliest memories were at age 5 or 6 when, over a short period of time, he watched fires damage three homes that were within walking distance from his home. An excellent student, he graduated from Eagle Rock High School in 1967 with his sights set on becoming either a policeman or a firefighter. In his memoir, Orr described his parents as excellent providers and caregivers. He recalled them taking the family camping and on hunting expeditions. Describing his parents as a good team, he credited them with raising three normal boys who were sometimes spanked when they deserved it, but who were not beaten.

When John was 15 years old, he got his first job as a cook at a local Jack-in-the-Box. One day, he arrived home from work to find a note his mother had left for his father. She abandoned her family to be with a former boyfriend she had left in Missouri, with the explanation that family life did not suit her anymore (BPM 44). Father Joe was devastated, but teenaged John did not see his mother's departure as being significant. Looking back, he called his mother's departure beneficial to all involved and expressed the view that it left no emotional scars (BPM 44). I wonder about John's assessment of family life. If family life was normal, why was his mother's departure beneficial? He and his brothers were teenagers, at the stage in life when young men are taking interest in relationships with young women. Did his mother's abandonment of the family have no emotional impact on the boys' outlook on relationships? Or was John not emotionally equipped to discern the impact? At the point in time when he wrote his memoir, which referenced his mother's departure, Orr was in his fourth marriage. His elder brother, Patrick, viewed the family situation differently. Patrick identified his mother's departure as the point in time when the whole family fell apart and the three brothers went in different directions.

In his last year of high school, John met Jody who would later become the first of his four wives. At age 17, he joined the Air Force as a trainee firefighter. Before leaving for an assignment in Spain, he and Jody got married. Early in the marriage, his behavior took on a destructive pattern. Whenever he and Jody disagreed about anything, he would simply leave home. Instead of trying to resolve an issue, he would walk out at the first sign of disagreement. Often away from home, he spent his time womanizing (BPM 48). Unable to get him interested in activities like going to church or going bowling, Jody left Spain and returned to the United States alone. Orr was not enjoying his job in the Air Force. On his own, he began reading about firefighting, and adopted a philosophy that fire prevention was the mission of all fire departments (BPM 48). Successful fire prevention reduces the need for firefighting, saves lives and protects property. He volunteered for fire inspection work. On assignment in Montana, he was preparing for discharge from the Air Force when the couple realized Jody was pregnant. Rather than put himself at a disadvantage of having to stay a few more months in a job he disliked, he chose to put his wife and unborn child at a disadvantage. He went ahead with his decision to discharge, leaving Jody without the prenatal care that would have been available had he stayed a few more months in the Air Force. Although he enjoyed fire inspection work, he disliked being told what to do, where to go and how long he could be away. Although he had the insight to recognize that his resentfulness toward authority arose from his insecurities, he did not appear to have been interested in doing anything about it.

Hoping to get a job in the Los Angeles Police Department (LAPD), as one of his friends had done, Orr studied and prepared for the civil service test (BPM 51). He passed the written examination, the physical agility examination, and the oral interview examination. What remained was the Minnesota Multiphasic Personality Inventory (MMPI) test. It is a psychological test designed to categorize personality traits for identification of emotional problems. He failed the psychological test. The doctor who conducted the test noted that Orr had anxiety about relationship with women and authority figures. In summary, the doctor stated that Orr was passive, resentful, suspicious, confused about his sexuality and unsuitable for a career in law enforcement (BPM 53). Devastated, Orr appealed, but his appeal was denied. He took a job as manager of a Kentucky Fried Chicken franchise located in La Canada Flintridge, where he resented his customers for being educated, wealthy young people on their way to bigger and better opportunities.

During Independence Day celebration in 1973, Orr lit illegal fireworks that got out of control and set a hillside on fire. When the firefighters arrived, he asked Jody not to tell them that he was throwing firecrackers because that would jeopardize his hope of getting a job as a firefighter (BPM 56). Unable to satisfy the psychological qualification to become a policeman, Orr decided to become a firefighter. He prepared for an application to the Los Angeles Fire Department (LAFD). He passed the examination, but failed the test for physical agility (BPM 60). Still holding out the hope of becoming a firefighter, Orr later applied for a position in the Glendale Fire Department, where he was accepted. In 1974, he progressed from training as a recruit to full-time firefighter. To increase his earnings, he got a second job as a security guard at Sears. He enjoyed the opportunity to make arrests like a policeman, and the camaraderie of his fellow firefighters, but he did not like taking orders from his superiors. He believed they insulted his intelligence. He enjoyed spending time with fellow firefighters in the den at the fire station, because it was a home away from home ... away from the responsibilities of being a father and husband (BPM 61).

In 1975, Orr abandoned his family. He communicated his decision to abandon his wife and two young daughters by leaving a letter, just as his mother had done. Following the divorce, the children went to visit their father and his current girlfriend about one weekend per month. In his memoir, Orr stated that he found it difficult to spend time with his daughters because he felt guilty when he left them after each visit (BPM 66). His way of handling that discomfort was to distance himself from his daughters, rather than spend more time with them. Later that year, he married his second wife, Sheila. His relationship with Sheila was not much different from the relationship with Jody. Soon, Orr was avoiding home by spending more time at Sears and the Glendale Fire Department (BPM 67). Girardot describes Sheila's recollection of having sex with Orr. He liked to tie her wrists and ankles to the bed and rip off her clothing as if to simulate rape. He would wear a bandana folded diagonally to cover his face, while there would be candles burning in the background (BPM 71). Orr also liked sex outdoors because it heightened his experience. Sheila never saw her husband drink to excess, and she never saw him take drugs. Sheila always knew him to have two sides: a public face that was warm and charming, and a private face that was a woman chaser and borderline abusive (BPM 73). The relationship between Orr and Sheila was not good, and it worsened when he asked to have an open marriage. After a year of marriage, they were divorced, but remained on friendly terms.

In addition to fire prevention and firefighting, Orr took an interest in fire investigation techniques (BPM 69). At Sears, he was developing detective techniques, like spotting a crook, getting suspects to talk during interviews, and surveillance of suspects. However, his superiors disapproved of some of Orr's techniques, like carrying a gun when firefighting, being unkempt in appearance even when he was not working undercover, and using blue light with siren when apprehending suspects (BPM 82). In Orr's mind, he was providing a valuable service to the community. However, policemen ridiculed him as someone who failed the test to become a policeman, but who desperately wanted to be part of the police fraternity (BPM 85).

By 1979, Orr was promoted from fire patrol, which involved checking on the maintenance of water sprinklers and fire extinguishers, to provisional fire investigator, which involved determining the points of origin and the causes of fires (BPM 88). He enjoyed being outdoors doing investigations on his own. In 1980, he arrested 40 suspected serial arsonists (BPM 89). To become a full-fledged fire investigator, Orr had to take an MMPI test, the same psychological test he failed when he applied to become a policeman. This time he passed the psychological test and was installed as Glendale's first official arson investigator (BPM 93). More financially stable now, he left his job at Sears and prepared to marry his third wife, Sherry (BPM 93). Orr's skills as a fire investigator were increasing and he was getting favorable reports about his performance. In his 1985 performance review he was reprimanded for not letting his supervisor know when he was out of the Glendale area (BPM 112). In addition to his role as fire investigator, Orr was writing journal articles about fire investigation for trade publications such as "American Fire Journal" (BPM 113). Believing that his experiences would make good fiction, Orr also started writing a novel. The protagonist was an ethical fireman named Phil Langtry, while the antagonist was an arsonist named

Aaron Styles (BPM 103).

In the mid-1980's, there was a series of brush fires around Los Angeles County in the areas of Glendale, Pasadena and Burbank (BPM 94). That was followed by another series of fires which involved buildings. At one building, firefighters found a hand-made device composed of cigarette, matches, and yellow writing pad paper (BPM 94). Investigators set up a regional task force and created a database to share information as they searched for evidence, perpetrators and motives (BPM 95). Several agencies, hoping to reduce the rapid increase of arson, created a task force they called Fire Investigators Regional Strike Team (FIRST) (BPM 103). By 1984, there were several waves of fires that resulted in damaged property, lawsuits and insurance claims (BPM 104). As the FIRST team proceeded with investigations of many fires in the Los Angeles area, investigators began to accumulate evidence that pointed to one of their own ... John Orr. One investigator noticed that fires tended to break out in cities where the Fire Fighting Association had their annual meetings. He suspected that the arsonist might be a firefighter, but he could not explore that suspicion because his superior refused permission to obtain fingerprints of the attendees at the meetings. When Orr conducted training about fire investigation, he would use pictures to illustrate investigative techniques. While attending Orr's training, one firefighter noticed that Orr showed pictures of a building before the fire started, during the blaze, and after the fire was put out. That firefighter wondered how Orr knew that building was going to be set ablaze before the fire started. At the scene of a fire that had just been put out, Orr arrived to help investigators. They noticed that he went directly to the point of origin of the fire without having to search the scene. They wondered how he could be so surefooted in his investigation. When Orr gave copies of his novel *"Points of Origin"* to colleagues in 1991, he became a suspect.

At one of the scenes, investigators found a home-made incendiary device made up of matches tied together with a rubber band, and attached to a cigarette. They figured that the slow-burning cigarette would give the arsonist a few minutes to get away from the scene before the fire started. At that scene, they also found a partial fingerprint on a piece of yellow paper from a lined, writing pad. That partial fingerprint did not match any fingerprint in the database of criminals. One investigator compared the partial fingerprint on the paper from the yellow writing pad with the fingerprints of people who had applied to become fire-fighters. There was a match. It matched John Orr's fingerprint. When investigators arrived at Orr's house to arrest him for arson, Orr casually told his wife Janie that it was all a mistake, that the charge would soon be cleared to reveal his innocence. A federal jury found him guilty of multiple counts of arson. A California jury found him guilty of multiple counts of murder in relation to arson. After being released from federal custody in 2002, Orr began serving concurrent life sentences in California State Prison, where he will spend the rest of his life without the possibility of parole.

Background Information about Pyromania

Experienced fire investigators point to six motives for setting a destructive fire (BPM 95). They are fraud, covering up crime, rioting, revenge, vanity and pyromania (BPM 95). Pyromaniacs are people who derive sexual gratification and godlike feelings of power when they watch an out-of-control fire (BPM 99). Pyromania is a disorder in which a person's inability to manage their impulse results in the compulsive setting of fires due to emotional motivations that are not connected to the fire. Sometimes, they set fires to release anxiety or tension, other times they set fires for sexual arousal. The Diagnostic and Statistical Manual of Mental Disorders (DSM-5) defines pyromania as an impulse control disorder evidenced by a person's inability to resist the urge to set fires. The cause of pyromania is unknown. Contributing factors may include emotional stressors, a history of abuse or neglect, chemical imbalance in the brain, genetic make-up, or deficits in social skills. By Orr's account, his fire setting involved sexual satisfaction. In his novel "Points of Origin" which prosecutors regard as a confession, he wrote in detail about how the antagonist achieves sexual satisfaction by setting and watching fires.

The Los Angeles basin is a geographic area surrounded by mountains on three sides. When the plumes of a fire go up in the air, it is visible from anywhere in the basin. That gives an arsonist a sense of power to be able to see their handiwork on a large scale (BPM 99).

Arson presents the arsonist with many opportunities to exhibit great power over large numbers of people and godlike powers over nature (BPM 100). In 1980, the FBI declared arson a national epidemic. FBI psychologists separated arsonists into five groups (BPM 101). They are unintentional fire starters who are young or mentally retarded, delusional types who set fires because they hear voices, revenge seekers, mischief makers, and erotic fire starters who are sexually aroused by fires. The FBI indicated that sexual deviants were especially worrisome when it came to starting large wildfires because many were using their blazes as a conversion of a sexual impulse into a special substitutive excitement (BPM 101).

While Orr was in United States of America (USA) federal custody, serving time for arson, the International Association for Analytical Psychology (IAAP) was having their 2001 Congress in the United Kingdom (UK), where psychologists were debating opposing definitions of archetype. At that time, investigators, biographers, forensic analysts, and journalists were proposing ideas about how to interpret the life of John Orr. Since then, there has been a profusion of televised documentaries, and publications about Orr's life viewed from various perspectives. My contribution is from a psychological perspective. More specifically, I write about Orr's life in terms of the containment model, viewed in the context of two definitions of archetype. Psychologists Wilfred Bion and Duncan Cartwright built the containment model on the principles of projection and introjection. Because projections occur when archetypes are activated, I describe the relationship between Orr and serial fires as mediated by an archetype. To do that, I rely on the two definitions of archetypes that were debated at the IAAP in 2001. The first definition is in the context of archetype-as-biological-entity. The second definition is in the context of archetype-as-emergent-phenomenon.

Context of Archetype as Biological Entity: Projection & Introjection

This section is about the interaction that John Orr had with serial firesetting in the context of archetype-as-biological-entity. When an archetype is viewed as a biological entity, it is regarded as an ancestral heritage of human experience accumulated over many generations and located in collective unconsciousness. When psychologists define an archetype as a biological entity, the processes they identify for converting experience to meaning are projection and introjection. Projection is an evacuation of unconscious content from the psyche due to an unbearable state of mind. John Orr's projection was an evacuation of an unbearable state of mind about the conflict between his motto of protecting his community from fire, and his pyromaniacal activities that resulted in deaths and property damage. Introjection is a transformation of an unbearable state of mind to a bearable state of mind, followed by its integration into conscious content of the psyche. Orr did not have the benefit of a container capable of introjection, because his projection was cast onto a series of inanimate fires.

Earlier in this chapter, I characterized Orr's interaction with serial fires as an autistic mode of containment, based on my interpretation of the Bion-Cartwright containment model. One reason for describing the relationship as an autistic mode of containment is that the containment involved a projection, not to the mind of another, but to inanimate fires. Orr was not actually interacting with the fires, he was observing them through binoculars, from afar. He was in an autistic mode of containment with the exterior aspects, or the surface areas, of the fires. A second reason for calling this an autistic mode of containment is that there was no psychological growth for Orr. As it turns out, the projection had a profound effect on his life, one of psychological harm. Orr, the community-minded fire-fighter turned into a pyromaniac obliged to spend the rest of his life in prison. He has continued to claim innocence, even after the hard evidence persuaded a federal jury and a state jury of his guilt. Orr's projection was about setting fires for sexual arousal and a desire for power. It is useful to ground the description of a projection in the relevant archetype. According to psychologist Marie-Louise von Franz, a projection always originates in an archetype (PRJ 24). Orr's projection emerged from the anima archetype. In Analytical Psychology, the anima represents the inner feminine side of a man. Initially, it is about the emergence of a man's object of desire. When a projection first emerges from the anima archetype, its content is about attraction to the opposite sex, romantic love and fascination with objects of desire. As the man matures psychologically, the content of later projections shifts to topics of insight and sagacity. The anima makes up the unconscious, feminine, psychological qualities that a man possesses. The anima makes itself known by influencing a man's attitude toward the opposite sex. Anima development is about a man opening up to his emotionality, and expanding his consciousness to include love, creativity, intuition and imagination.

Orr's projections were not cast to physical, flesh-and-blood women. His projections were cast onto images of blazing fires. In the language of autistic containment, Orr's projections were cast onto surfaces of fires. His goal was not biological sexual intercourse for establishing intimate relationships by getting to know any woman. His goal was autistic interaction, that is surface interaction, with views of blazing fires for the immediate purposes of sexual arousal and performance. In his effort to construct and sustain a coherent sense of self, he set fires, watched them blaze and took photographs of them. Unfortunately, his projections onto the fires amounted to projection onto inanimate surfaces that were incapable of providing containment.

When the anima archetype is activated, it is important to distinguish its influence from reality. When Orr became interested in fires, he was oriented to service to his community. Later, when he developed a fascination with fires for sexual gratification, the anima archetype was activated. He was captivated by the power of the fire. Fire-setting gave him power over people, as well as power over acres of brush and property. He found images of the flames seductive. Orr was not deprived of feminine companionship. He had four wives and acknowledged his philandering ways to his colleagues, but he had difficulty establishing emotional connections with women. He had more control over fires. To satisfy his passion he set fires, enjoyed the sexual thrill while they blazed, then he went to the scene of the fire to help the investigators find the points of origin and identify the causes. His projection was cast onto the ongoing series of fires that he set to obtain the sense of power over others and achieve the thrill of sexual gratification. Although fires consume oxygen and move along the ground, fires are inanimate entities. Orr derived his sense of power and sexual gratification from interacting with the surface of the fires. His means of interacting with surfaces of the fires were binoculars and cameras.

The anima plays a role in social life as well as a role in personal life. The anima archetype makes it possible for a man to regard his experience as being personal. Anima is the archetype which gives personification to the way a man forms a bridge between the outer world and his inner world. The more conscious role of the anima is turned toward social life, while the less conscious role is turned inward and experienced as personal interiority. Orr's projection arose from the anima archetype at the unconscious end of the bridge and was cast onto fires at the social end of the bridge. By his projection of seductress onto the surfaces of fires, Orr obtained a satisfaction he was unable to obtain from women. He could control fires. He decided where to set them, when to set them, how to set them, how to watch the blaze through binoculars, and from what distance to photograph them. The women in his life were not as controllable as the fires.

A man's psychological maturity involves developing an awareness of how the anima forms a bridge between collective unconsciousness and personal consciousness. As a personification of the unconscious aspect of the psyche, the anima has both a positive and a negative side. The anima can enliven a personality with development and creativity, or it can make a person's outlook hardened and compulsive. With the anima archetype activated, Orr's behavior was becoming compulsive. For him, control was more important than interaction, and fires were more controllable than women. He was in search of the thrills of sexual arousal, without the demands of person-to-person interactions. Searching for experiences of arousal to make him feel alive and energized, he settled for interactions with images of fires, rather than developing meaningful interactions with actual women. He engaged in a stream of fire-setting to find serial sexual arousal, rather than build a multi-faceted relationship with a real woman. He was constantly looking for the next arousal from the next fire as an escape from the reality of his unsatisfying serially married life. Unable or unwilling to connect with another at an intimate level, he sought a source of stimulation that would bring him pleasurable satisfaction without the burden of having to satisfy another. He sought an experience that the moment can bring as an escape from reality. In his search for sexual fulfillment, he went from one fire to another, seeking one feature that satisfies the desire for escape, but not the full range of romantic features of a full-blown containment. He appreciates the initial arousal based on physical appearance, and progresses to marriage, but does not move on to engaging the mind of the other.

For years, Orr managed to balance his respectable outer life with a shameful inner life. He was trying to keep his impulses hidden, but he was not trying to control them. He lost his ability to manage boundaries, as seen in his inclusion of pre-fire photographs in his training. The self-disclosures in his novel were not obvious to him, but investigators and the jury saw through them. He was willing to justify killing other people by blaming them for being stupid for not getting out of the way of the fires. He rationalized his fire-setting behaviors. His willingness to tie himself to one-dimensional relationship with fire suggests a poor self-esteem. He lost himself in the pursuit of sexual pleasure, sacrificing himself for the images of his desire. He gave in to his autistic side because he could not control his impulses. The fascination with fire gave way to obsession, and the obsession overwhelmed him. His passion led him to neglect his own well-being, his career, his family and his marriages. Overcome by the impulse to conduct a steady stream of fires, he neglected his reputation as a respectable fire investigator and his responsibility to protect his community. Since fires are inanimate; they are not capable of being carriers of projections. However, they are convenient vehicles for compulsive fire-setting behavior because the hidden identities and unknown motivations enable pyromaniacs to illude investigators. Having no mind, the fires were unable to help Orr to construct meaning from the content of his projection. The fires could not metabolize his unprocessed emotional states and structure them into useful thoughts. Up to the point in time when he was imprisoned, his projection was not broken. Despite the evidence, Orr continues to maintain a stance of innocence. There was no introjection because fires are inanimate entities, which are not capable of mind-to-mind interaction. The containment failed.

The anima was activated at a critical stage of Orr's life. The first recording of his fire-setting activity began in the mid 1980's. At the time, he was in his third marriage, which he found not much different from his first two marriages. He did not derive much satisfaction from being a husband or being a father. So, he spent many of his waking hours at the den of the fire station, or chasing women for casual, sexual encounters.

Although he was being promoted at the fire station, he wanted more recognition. He studied fire prevention, wrote journal articles about fire science and conducted training for other fire fighters. At his stage of psychological development, the capacity for emotional interaction between contained and container had not yet fully formed, or was shut down. As a substitute, he chose to set blazing fires as the psychic surfaces on which to focus an effort to hold his sense of self together. Attention to development of the interior aspect of psychic life was either inadequate or evaded, so phantasies that would, in the form of a projection, be cast onto another mind as a means of communication, are not transmitted to another mind. Instead, the projection is transmitted to the psychic surface of fires. Projection relies on communication to an internal mental space. Fires have no internal mental space. In the autistic mode of containment, ideas or conceptions about an internal mental space bring about anxiety and contribute to fragmentation of the sense of self. In the autistic mode of containment, sensations, thoughts and emotions are used to block mind-to-mind connection, or relating to another. The result is a diminishment of vitality in the experience of life. For Orr, the fires are inanimate surfaces used to wall off the experience of his emotions.

According to Duncan Cartwright, emotion is the fabric which animates contained-container relations (CSM 152). Containment is a way of relating that is driven by reliance on projection into the interior, that is, the mental space of another. For Orr, the purpose of the projection was evaded. Instead of projecting onto another mind, Orr had phantasies of sticking to the surface of inanimate fires in an effort to achieve a coherent biographical narrative. He clung to the three-dimensional fires because he regarded them as his own production, things he could control. Fires he could control. Wives he could not control. Clinging to fires not only blocked encounter with his own internal world, but also blocked entry into a containing – thinking – mind. He adopted a repetitive strategy of reducing relationship to interaction with a sensory surface. With that obsessive action, he blocked the processing of experience that would otherwise be jointly constructed in a containment that involves another person. Genuine interaction between contained and container could not occur because it was limited by the level at which his psyche operated.

Orr looked to fires for opening up his emotionality. He admired the beauty of the fires through his binoculars. He devoted time to going to the scenes where he had set fires on the pretense that he was helping local firefighters determine the origins of fires. He wrote a novel in which fire setting was central to the relationship between the protagonist and antagonist. When people died in his fires, he warded off emotions like sympathy and remorse by rationalization that they were too stupid to get out of the way. Overcome by the impulse to produce a steady stream of fires, he neglected his reputation as a fire fighter, and his responsibility to protect his community. In 1992, a federal jury convicted Orr of arson (BPM 235). In 1998, a California state court convicted him of 4 murders related to arson. He was sentenced to 4 concurrent terms of life without parole. Orr's projection was not broken. He continues to claim innocence by rationalizing his arson activities. He does not believe he did anything wrong. He believes the people who died in the fires he set were at fault for not getting out of the paths of the fires. The narrative he constructed for his life is fragile and based on defense mechanisms. His narrative would crumble if he were to acknowledge that he did something wrong. A crumbled narrative would leave his life meaningless, so he clings to his rationalizations. In this section, I described Orr's interaction with fires in the context of archetype-as-biological-entity. In the next section, I will describe the interaction in the context of archetype-as-emergent-phenomenon.

Context of Archetype as Emergent Phenomenon: Appropriation & Internalization

This section is about the interaction that Orr had with serial fires viewed in the context of archetype-as-emergent-phenomenon. In this context, an archetype is an emergent property of a dynamic, developmental system that is made up of human brains, human activities, society's external environment and the narrative competence of humans in the society. In viewing archetype as an emergent phenomenon, the means for converting life's experience to meaning are appropriation and internalization. Appropriation is an adoption of conscious content from social and cultural sources in the external environment. Orr's appropriation was an intellectual preoccupation with the science of fire, combined with an emotional connection to the control of fire. Internalization is the incorporation of a cultural appropriation into one's mental model. Without a mind-to-mind connection with a container capable of helping him process the appropriation, Orr was unable to internalize anything useful in his mental model.

For readers who are unfamiliar with the processes of appropriation and internalization, they can be observed in the way that children acquire language skills. At first, children appropriate language from social and cultural sources in the external world, then, with the help of adults, they internalize language into their mental models. Children are then able to use the language constructs for composing sentences. I offer that well-known example as a segue into discussion of John Orr's interaction with serial fires in the context of archetype as emergent phenomenon. Orr's behaviors in relating to the fires, and his communications about the fires, were those of a man enthralled with fires. He studied to become a firefighter. His failure in the examination was disappointing, not just because he had put so much effort into preparation for the examination. It was also because he had no other goal. After a stint of earning an income at other jobs, he tried again. When he passed the examination, he was so thrilled, the science of fire became a preoccupation. Having already appropriated fire-fighting techniques from the culture of fire-prone California, he made additional appropriations in the areas of fire science: fire prevention and fire investigation. He earned the respect of his colleagues and a promotion to fire captain in the Glendale Fire Department.

While Orr was intellectually preoccupied with the science of fire, his emotional connection to fire was emerging. His fascination with fires so consumed him that he began to set fires for the thrill of watching his creation develop into a blazing glow. This fascination took hold of him and outweighed all the fire science he had appropriated, indicating that the anima archetype was activated. His limited impulse control gave way to the enormity of the satisfaction he derived from watching the result of his fire-setting. The fires were his creations. He had complete control over all aspects of his fires. He chose the location, the means of incineration, the time of day to set the fire, the type of building, the best angle from which to watch the fire as it developed, and when to take photographs as supplement for the fire-training classes he conducted. He was aware of the sexual gratification he derived from watching his fires. He understood that he harbored opposing motivations: a fire-prevention motivation to protect his community and a fire-setting motivation to satisfy his pyromaniac impulses. He understood them well enough to write a novel about the opposing motivations of a protagonist who engaged in fire-prevention, as opposed to an antagonist who engaged in fire-setting. Although the novel was a mirror for his behaviors, it was not enough to influence a change in his behavior. Instead of changing his behavior, he rationalized his behavior by holding the people who died in his fires responsible for their own deaths. With such rationalization, he set up a defense mechanism to shield himself from guilt. What broke the stranglehold that fires had over him was his arrest, but the arrest only put an end to his fire-setting. His appropriation was not dissolved. Confronted with evidence of his fire-setting, he resolutely denied setting fires. The autobiographical narrative that he constructed for his life was so tightly wound around his identity as a fire-prevention professional that he could entertain no variation of that narrative. To do so would render his life's narrative devoid of meaning. To sustain his fragmented sense of identity, he held on to his autobiographical narrative of innocent fire-fighter throughout his trials and well into his incarceration. Orr had not been able to engage the mind of another. Without another mind to function as a container, he did not have the kind of dialogue that would enable him to use the content of his appropriation to construct meanings from his life experience. On an intellectual level, he knew enough about his life story to write a novel about it, but he was not able to establish a mind-to-mind connection with anyone who could help him construct meaning from his narrative and internalize them into his mental model of relationship with someone of the opposite sex. Orr appropriated a warped view of female-male relationship from his cultural environment. For him, fire became an enchantress, so appealing that instead of seeking help for his diminishing impulse control, he took refuge in rationalizations. The autistic mode of containment in Orr's relationship with fire brought him psychological harm. He avidly pursued an interest in the science of fire as preparation for his roles in firefighting, fire investigation and fire prevention. Those were his conscious strivings. Those were the roles that he chose to incorporate into his mental model. He did manage to function in those roles, long enough to earn the respect of his community. However, the fabric of his emotional development was not adequate to animate the contained-container interaction necessary to sustain those roles for the betterment of himself or his community.

Converting Experience to Meaning: Symbolization

Regardless of whether psychologists define containment in terms of projection or appropriation, they regard the capacity for symbol forma-tion as being useful in the achievement of psychological growth during a containment. Duncan Cartwright, who defines containment in terms of projection, points out that at the symbolic level of organization of the psyche, symbols have the property of generativity, that is, symbols become containers of meaning, allowing the verbal communication of a shared meaning system (CSM 15) between contained and container. Warren Colman, who defines containment in terms of appropriation, explains that a symbolic capacity in the ego enables affective states to be understood and enriched by the fact that symbolic forms can take on multiple meanings (AIE 228 – 229). Emotion and symbolic thought go hand in hand since higher levels of emotion require robust forms of thought to contain them while symbolic thought promotes a greater range and depth of emotional sensitivity in relationships (AIE 230). So, I researched the available verbal communications by and about John Orr. That involved scrutinizing written materials as well as a video documen-tary for indications of symbolic thought.

In my reading of biographies, investigative reports, and news articles about John Orr, I searched for the emergence of a symbol in his com-munications. I did not find anything that fit the definition of symbol in "A Critical Dictionary of Jungian Analysis". In that dictionary, Andrew Samuels and his fellow psychologists define symbol in terms of concept, intent, purpose and content. In my opinion, the connection between Orr and the serial fires did not accrue any symbolic meaning. Although Orr insists that his novel "Point of Origin" is a work of fiction, it reveals a close biographical parallel because it is a story of a man's internal con-flict between the fire-fighting protagonist and the fire-setting antago-nist. However, the interaction between them plays out on a literal level without the subtleties or the emotional turmoil that drives symbol formation. The novel helped Orr to construct a story that resembles an autobiographical narrative, but it did not help him achieve the degree of narrative competence necessary for symbol formation.

Call To Action: Take Away A Portable Understanding

This chapter is about the life of a man who created a successful career as a skilled firefighter in the external world, but who knew little of his internal world. He built a career as a public servant, became a respected professional in fire science, married four wives and fathered two daughters. He demonstrated great capability in crafting his outer life, but his inner life was unknown to him until he was arrested. Until he was found guilty of arson, he did not realize, and may still not realize, that he has a psychological disorder. This chapter is a call to action for readers to take away a portable understanding of the autistic mode of containment. To help readers, I offer the following summary as a reminder of how John Orr came to realize that his fire setting had come to an end.

- **Mode:** There was an autistic mode of containment involving Orr and the serial fires that he set in California.
- **Roles:** In this containment, Orr was the contained and the serial fires were his attempt to find a container.
- **Symmetry:** In this asymmetrical relationship, Orr was a human while the serial fires were inanimate entities.
- **Psychological Frame:** Orr created an outdoor psychological frame for his autistic containment. The sunken geography of the Los Angeles basin surrounded by mountains formed the space boundary of the frame for fire setting and fire watching. The time boundary of the frame covered about seven years, from 1984 to 1991, when Orr is believed to have set roughly 2,000 fires. The purpose of the frame was to obtain sexual gratification and satisfy his desire for power, while hiding his pyromania, an impulse control disorder. The means of interacting with the fires were binoculars and cameras.
- **Dialectical Narrative:** The first narrative was Orr's construction of his life story about secretly setting fires to satisfy a pyromaniac impulse he could not control. His novel was a

substitute for a coherent autobiographical narrative that he strove to assemble. There was no second narrative. Since fires are inanimate, they neither compose narratives, nor function as containers. The third narrative is supposed to be the result of a dialectical interaction between contained and container. Since Orr's projection was cast onto fires, or inanimate entities, which are incapable of responding to a projection, there was no contained-container dialogue, and therefore no third narrative. There was no dialectical narrative.

- **Psychological Growth / Harm**: The interaction between Orr and the serial fires resulted in psychological harm for him. The external reality of the interactions between Orr and the serial fires resulted in nothing meaningful. Instead, it brought him loss of job, loss of respect of his community, loss of emotional support from his daughter Lori, and loss of his freedom. The internal reality is that he did not recognize that his fire setting had become an addiction, which he could no longer control. He continued to maintain his innocence years after the investigation revealed evidence which tied him directly to the fires.

After the Containment Ended

The containment ended when Orr was incarcerated. He could no longer set fires. In 1992, a federal jury convicted Orr of multiple counts of arson. In 1998, a California state court convicted him of four arson-related murders, and sentenced him to concurrent terms of life without parole. After being released from federal custody in 2002, Orr began serving concurrent life sentences in the California State Prison. While in prison, Orr continues to maintain his innocence.

The A&E Network featured the investigation of John Orr's case in an episode of "*Diary of a Serial Arsonist*" that aired in 1995. John Orr's novel "*Point of Origin*" was made into a movie of the same name and released by HBO in 2002. After several years of believing her father's insistence that he is innocent, Orr's daughter, Lori Orr Kovach, came to regard her father as guilty. She discontinued communication with him and pooled her effort with journalist Frank Girardot Jr. in co-authoring a 2018 publication titled "*BURNED: Pyromania, Murder, and A Daughter's Nightmare*".

Sources

My sources of information about John Orr are:
- "*Into the Fire: Forensic Interview with John Orr: The Most Prolific Arsonist of the 20th Century*" by Anthony Meoli
- "*BURNED: Pyromania, Murder, and a Daughter's Nightmare*" by Frank C. Girardot, Jr. with Lori Orr Kovach
- "*Points Of Origin*" by John Orr
- Documentary HLN Original Series: "Very Scary People" "The Firestarter: A Wall of Flames" "The Firestarter: Chasing a Pyromaniac"
- "*Sex Addiction 101*" by Robert Weiss
- "*Containing States of Mind*" by Duncan Cartwright
- "*Projection and Re-Collection in Jungian Psychology*" by Marie-Louise von Franz.

CHAPTER 17

A Pseudo-containing Mode of Containment Involving: Michael Cohen & Donald Trump

"I reveled in Trump's approval as I gave sycophancy a new dimension."

— Michael Cohen

He was doing all the things that his generation strives to do: earn a university degree, build a career, invest some money for the future, get married and raise a family. He was successfully navigating his way through life. He had a thriving career, a happy family life and was a multi-millionaire. His success in the external world did not protect him. His psychological neediness drew him into the orbit of a celebrity. Biologically mature and intellectually mature, he was psychologically less than mature. His psyche needed to attach itself to something bigger than itself. He perceived what he thought were strong convictions in the celebrity. So great was his psychological neediness that the content of the convictions did not matter. His legal training gave him a clear sense of what is legal and what is illegal. Yet, he was willing to engage in illegal behavior in exchange for being in the shadow of the celebrity's power, and basking in the reflected celebrity status. He dreamed of a time when heads would turn as he walked into a room. When journalists would shove microphones into his face to get his opinions about issues of the day. When photographers would jostle to take his picture. Then one day, as he was purchasing condominiums for his extended family, he met the son of a celebrity. He recognized the name of the celebrity as a real estate mogul frequently seen in New York social circles. A few days afterwards, the celebrity reached out to the lawyer for assistance in a legal matter. Eagerly, the lawyer agreed. So thrilled was he to be in contact with a celebrity that he provided his legal service without charging a fee. That led to another request. And another request. Soon, the lawyer was on the celebrity's payroll as his personal lawyer. Years into their relationship, the lawyer proudly announced his loyalty in public by stating that he would 'take a bullet' for the celebrity. That was long ago. Today, people's heads turn when the former lawyer appears in public. TV anchors invite him to appear on the evening news. They invite him to express views on the many lawsuits filed against the celebrity he once looked up to as a leader. A cult leader, that is. With candor, Michael Cohen, now stripped of his lawyer's license, declares on national TV that he was a sycophant who was initially blind to the manipulations of celebrity Donald Trump.

In 2020, Michael Cohen published his book "*DISLOYAL*" about the relationship between himself and Donald Trump. The book is my main source of information about their relationship. Cohen is remarkably clear-headed about his complicity in his own downfall. The book's credibility does not come from Cohen, the author. It is public knowledge that Cohen is now a disbarred lawyer and a convicted felon. The book gets its credibility from being consistent with information that came from Trump himself in televised interviews with TV News anchors, in press briefings with journalists at the White House, and in televised campaign rallies.

My interpretation is that Michael Cohen and Donald Trump had a relationship with a pseudo-containing mode of containment during the period 2006 to 2018, when Cohen served as Trump's personal lawyer. I see their relationship as having a pseudo-containing mode of containment because it circumvented the emotional turmoil that is a natural part of the contained-container interaction. Cohen, the contained, and Trump, the container, mimicked the containment and perverted its role. While joining efforts to wield power against others, their interaction barely entered a psychological containment since they were not disposed to feel the benefits of holding or being held in the mind of another. To help readers understand the relationship between Cohen and Trump, I offer some background information in the next two sections. The information is about their early lives leading up to their decision to work together.

Background Information about Michael Cohen

As a boy, Cohen had a middle-class Jewish family life. He was born in 1966 in New York, where he went to school at Woodmere Academy. His father was an ear-nose-and-throat doctor, and his mother a surgical nurse. They were financially comfortable and had tight relationships with other Jewish families in New York. Their Jewish identity derived more from cultural, rather than religious practices. Cohen discovered his taste for power and wealth through his uncle Morty, a medical doctor and playboy bachelor, with whom he frequented a popular, social gathering spot, El Caribe, a country club with pool, restaurant and bar. There, Cohen obtained a part-time job and was exposed to the behaviors of mobsters and gangsters, the art of intimidation, and the philosophy of loyalty-over-ethics. Cohen went on to earn a law degree from Western Michigan University, Cooley Law School in 1991. While at university, he drove a Porsche. In 1994, he and Laura Shusterman were married at The Pierre, an upscale hotel in Manhattan. They later had two children. He made himself a multi-millionaire partly by practising law as an injury attorney, and partly by acquisition of New York taxi medallions. Cohen enjoyed a luxurious lifestyle.

Michael Cohen and Donald Trump were both residents of New York where they had met each other occasionally, but 2006 was the year they decided to work together. While purchasing a condominium in Trump World Tower, Cohen noticed that some condominium owners were trying to get the Trump organization removed as property manager. Cohen looked into the dispute and assisted Trump in retaining the property management role. Cohen impressed Trump who complained that his own lawyers failed to help him keep control of the building, and Trump hired Cohen as an executive of the Trump Organization and as his personal counsel.

Background Information about Donald Trump

The year 2016 was an election year in the U.S.A. In early 2016, *The Washington Post* assigned reporters, fact-checkers and editors to research the lives of the two likely nominees for president of the United States: Donald Trump and Hillary Clinton. The reporters and editors who researched Trump travelled to Germany, Scotland, New York, Philadelphia, New Jersey, Panama, Russia and Azerbaijan to speak with Trump's family, friends, competitors, business partners, executives, employees and Trump himself. The book *"TRUMP REVEALED"* is the result of the research about Donald Trump's life. This book is my source of information about Donald Trump's background.

Trump was born in 1946 in New Yok, where his parents were German immigrants of Christian faith. His father Fred had acquired wealth by developing apartment buildings for a modestly priced real estate market (TR 32). His mother Mary was a homemaker, who enjoyed social gatherings and was devoted to charitable work as well as volunteering at the local hospital (TR 37). With the benefit of his big athletic frame, young Trump excelled at sports in the private Kew-Forest School. He performed well in baseball, basketball and football, but his academic grades suffered and his behavior earned him many detentions (TR 35). Fred's fatherly advice to Donald was that he needed to become a 'killer' in all his activities (TR 37). It is not clear if young Donald took this admonition literally, or if he was collecting switchblades because of his admiration of the popular play *"Westside Story"*. When Fred discovered the collection of switchblades, he was alarmed and decided to send young Donald to New York Military Academy, a strict boarding school. It was 1959 and young Trump was 13 years old (TR 38). Life at the boarding school entailed a major adjustment. At home, he had his own bedroom and bathroom. At the academy, he had to get accustomed to sleeping in barracks and sharing a bathroom with other boys (TR 38). It might not have been any consolation to Trump that the academy's motto carved at the main entrance was 'Courageous and Gallant Men Have Passed Through These Portals' (TR 40). He was able to balance his dissatisfactions with accomplishments and pleasurable activity. During his years on campus, he rose from private to corporal and later to sergeant (TR 41). As he grew older and taller, he became known as a Ladies' Man because of the attractive, expensively dressed young women who came to visit him on campus (TR 41).

As Trump grew older, he had many achievements in quick succession. By 1968, he obtained a bachelor's degree in economics from the Wharton School of the University of Pennsylvania. In 1971, he became president of The Trump Organization, his father's real estate business, to which he later added skyscrapers and golf courses. The year 1982 marked his first appearance on the Forbes list of wealthy people. His estimated net worth was $200 million dollars. He wrote *"The Art of the Deal"* which became a New York Times best seller in 1987. Between 1977 and 2005, Trump serially married three wives and fathered five children. In 2004, he co-founded Trump University for offering real estate training to the public. He hosted a reality TV show called '*The Apprentice*' which started in 2004 and ran for 15 seasons. Trump hired Cohen as a vice-president of the Trump Organization and his personal counsel.

Wilfred Bion and Duncan Cartwright built the containment model on the principles of projection and introjection. Because projections occur when archetypes are activated, I describe the relationship between Cohen and Trump as mediated by an archetype. To do that, I rely on the two IAAP definitions of archetype. In the next two sections, I describe the Cohen-Trump relationship first in the context of archetype-as-biological-entity, then in the context of archetype-as-emergent-phenomenon.

Context of Archetype as Biological Entity: Projection & Introjection

This section is about the Cohen-Trump relationship viewed in terms of archetype-as-biological-entity. When an archetype is viewed as a biological entity, it is regarded as an ancestral heritage of human experience accumulated over many generations and located in collective unconsciousness. When psychologists define an archetype as a biological entity, the processes they identify for converting experience to meaning are projection and introjection. Projection is an evacuation of unconscious content from the psyche due to an unbearable state of mind. There was a projection from the mind of Cohen to the mind of Trump.

Cohen's projection was an unconscious, unbearable state of mind about assuming the role of sycophant while idealizing a celebrity businessman. Introjection is a transformation of an unbearable state of mind to a bearable state of mind, followed by its integration into conscious content of the psyche. There is no indication that Trump became a container for Cohen's projection, so there was no introjection.

The behaviors and communications between Cohen and Trump were related to their roles as sycophant and celebrity. A couple of months after being employed to Trump, Cohen found himself taking pride in bullying others on behalf of Trump ... with disregard for the legal framework combined with an utter lack of conscience (DM 42). This is how Cohen described his role as sycophant to Trump:

> *"I reveled in Trump's approval as I gave sycophancy a new dimension."*
> — Michael Cohen (DM 275)

That declaration indicates that the sycophant archetype was activated. The sycophant archetype is made up of an ancestral heritage of human experience about mindless servitude offered to a celebrity of great wealth and power, in the hope of basking in reflected glory and influence. In the context of archetype-as-biological-entity, the sycophant archetype is located in the collective unconscious aspect of the psyche. Activation of the sycophant archetype indicates that there was a forceable evacuation of a projection from Cohen's mind to Trump's mind. The content of Cohen's projection was raw experience of unprocessed emotions, images and memories ... an idealization of a celebrity businessman. The raw experience was incomprehensible to Cohen and was therefore evacuated as an unbearable state of mind. Trump's mind was not engaged as a carrier of Cohen's projection. Trump was not able to help Cohen metabolize unprocessed emotional and cognitive experience. My opinion is that the conscious part of their communication consumed the relationship, leaving little room for the unconscious communication that is involved in the structuring of raw experience into useful thoughts.

The sycophant archetype was activated at a critical stage of Cohen's life cycle. He was moving from a role as private professional to a role that put him in the public eye. He was in pursuit of something he felt was missing from his life. He found an opportunity in his role as 'fixer' for Trump who was a well-known real estate mogul, host of the popular reality TV show 'The Apprentice', author of bestselling book 'The Art of the Deal', with a regular appearance on Forbes magazine's list of wealthiest people. Trump also indulged in occasional musings about the possibility of running for office as President of the United States of America. Cohen and Trump seem to have gravitated to their relationship, each filling a need in the other. Cohen describes Trump as a cult leader. To have been drawn into Trump's orbit, and to have stayed there for years, suggests that Cohen must have been in need of a cult leader to be his guide. Trump needed Cohen to be a 'fixer' who is willing to use his lawyer's knowledge to cover up legally questionable deeds ... someone Trump could bend to his will. The fact that they stayed in each other's orbit for so many years, indicates that each satisfied a need in the other. Cohen's wife and children begged him to stop working for Trump; they did not like him being continuously at Trump's beckon call. That was an intrusion in their family life. At age 15, Cohen's daughter observed that he displayed symptoms of Stockholm Syndrome (feelings of trust and affection that a victim has toward a captor) in his relationship with Trump. At the time, Cohen did not see it. It was much later that Cohen noticed his own behavior, and still later before he acted on it. As events unfolded, it was prison time that eventually forced him to reflect on his own behavior.

The meeting of Cohen and Trump activated the archetype of sycophant. A projection arising from the sycophant archetype was cast from the mind of sycophant Cohen to the mind of celebrity Trump. With candor, Cohen informs his readers that he was a sycophant in his relationship with Trump (DM 275). A sycophant is a yes-man who insincerely flatters a famous or powerful leader to gain some advantage, such as social status or authority. Cohen presented himself as legal enforcer to ensure that Trump's wishes were satisfied by means of threat, intimidation, or bluff. A narcissistic celebrity, Trump rewarded Cohen's flattery because it helped Trump maintain his inflated self-image. Totally loyal to Trump, Cohen carried out his leader's wishes without question, and regardless of whether they fell in the range of acceptable norms or legal behavior.

Aware that he held his position entirely at Trump's whims, Cohen was totally committed to the execution of Trump's demands. He stayed in Trump's orbit, putting his legal career in jeopardy. Cohen was intimidated by Trump. A lawyer, Cohen was on the payroll to produce plausible legal rationalization for Trump's decisions, especially since Trump was more inclined to deal-making than to legal strategy. As a narcissist who lacks impulse control, Trump is prone to issuing demands that are impulsive. Cohen created explanations and justifications for Trump's impulsive demands, with little regard for what is appropriate or legal. When Trump announced his candidacy for President of the U. S. A. in 2015, his need for protection of sensitive information about his lifestyle took on an urgency which heightened Cohen's power as enforcer of the candidate's wishes. Trump won the 2016 election and was inaugurated in January 2017. Cohen did not receive a position in the Trump administration, but he remained Trump's personal lawyer.

Cohen points out that he has something in common with the evangelicals who support Trump, in spite of his non-evangelical outlook and lifestyle. Cohen believes that Trump has a genius for attracting to his world, people who are sycophants and loyal yes-men. Cohen offers the observation that politicians and evangelicals, who are drawn to Trump, all desire something that matters to them more than public service and morals. The evangelicals' desire is that Trump stacks the courts with judges who are opposed to topics like civil rights and planned parenthood. Politicians, knowing the magnetic hold Trump has on his base, desire the favor of Trump supporters in their own upcoming (re-)election bids. They align themselves to Trump, because they want his support and they fear his wrath. Cohen admits that, while he was Trump's personal attorney, he too desired Trump's praise and feared Trump's anger.

Over the years, Trump had performed and directed what Cohen calls dirty deeds. Cohen had loyally covered up the dirty deeds. About the time of the 2016 election, the dirty deeds started coming to the attention of the public ... and the attention of the court in the Southern District of New York. Cohen gives examples of what he covered up. Throughout the 2016 elections, Cohen covered up Trump's active pursuit of the opportunity to build Trump Towers in Moscow. Cohen covered up Trump's alleged marital infidelities by arranging hush money payments. Cohen covered up Trump's lack of interest in creating jobs for the Midwesterners. Cohen covered up Trump's disdain for evangelicals. According to Cohen, Trump is disdainful of evangelicals because they place their confidence in prayer. Knowing that the evangelicals are a significant segment of voters, pro-choice Trump pretends to be pro-life so he can court the evangelicals, who want a president to stack the courts with pro-life judges. The fact that evangelicals support Trump by overlooking his public, un-Christian behavior speaks not only to Trump's lack of a moral compass, but also to the expedience of the evangelicals' moral compass. Knowingly, Cohen had made himself an instrument of Trump's manipulation of evangelicals.

In the 2016 election, much of Trump's support came from working-class, white people who live in the Midwest. Many of these people feel disenfranchised and left behind because technology automated their jobs and globalization relocated their factories overseas. Many have deep-seated anger that the government failed them. So mistrustful of the government were they in 2016, that they chose to place their confidence in Trump, who never held public office, and whose vociferous bravado they interpreted as strength in a leader. In Cohen's view, Trump is a master manipulator, who was quick to leverage their anger into enthusiastic support by persuading them that he cares about them. Cohen states that Trump does not care about them. Cohen's opinion is borne out not only by Trump's poor record in creating jobs for the Midwesterners, but also by the fact that he chooses to have his Trump neckties and Trump suits manufactured overseas. Cohen sees his own sycophantic allegiance to Trump reflected in sycophantic behavior in the Midwestern segment of the population. Midwesterners threw their support behind Trump when he promised to bring back factories to the U.S.A. Despite his not having done much about that, many Midwesterners still support him. They look to Trump as a strong leader and a savior. So gullible are they, that they follow him where common sense would not go. When people were dying from COVID-19 infections, supporters followed him to crowded campaign rallies without masks and without social distancing ... while he stayed at a distance behind a podium surrounded by protective Secret Service and sometimes surrounded by bullet-proof glass.

Early in Trump's presidency, and shortly before the relationship with

Cohen unraveled, 27 psychiatrists and health care experts took the unusual step of publishing a collection of warnings in a book titled "*The Dangerous Case of Donald Trump*" which was edited by Bandy Lee, Assistant Clinical Professor in Law and Psychiatry at Yale School of Medicine. It was an unusual step because psychiatrists have a professional code of ethics about avoiding diagnosis of public figures they have not personally examined. They made the exception because they believed their moral and civic 'Duty to Warn' the American public is more important than their professional neutrality. Here are some of their warnings about Trump: pathological narcissism, paranoia, impulsivity in terms of extreme hedonism, risk of using Twitter technology to send a nuclear Tweet that endangers the population, failure to recognize that his behavior is at odds with the Law and the Constitution, an untrained mind bereft of information, being married to stratospheric self-confidence, denial of the shadow which is projected outward to others, propensity to attract followers who absorb his claim to omnipotence while shutting down reason and conscience, tendency to appeal to segments of the population for which he represents all their denials and thwarted greatness. The characteristics that the psychiatrists attribute to Trump offer some indication of why the pseudo-containing mode of containment applies to the relationship he had with Cohen. There was not enough psychological maturity to support a containment. Cohen's unbearable state of mind related to the desire for reflected glory in the proximity to power and celebrity status was not metabolized. A container can only help a contained to metabolize what he or she has already successfully metabolized. The psychiatrists' descriptions of Trump indicate a rather limited maturity, not up to the task of helping another mind to convert experience into meaning.

Cohen's book "DISLOYAL" has so many nuanced details that I have to wonder if Cohen had been keeping detailed records for years. Many people construct a narrative of their life as a way of sustaining a sense of continuity in their lives. Some people construct the narratives in their heads, others keep journals. Cohen states, in hindsight, that he had entered a Faustian bargain with Trump. He must have had some idea that it was heavily weighed against him, and probably suspected he would one day need contemporaneous notes to protect himself. If he had such a fear, it was confirmed when the Federal Bureau of

Investigation (FBI) first appeared at his home with a warrant to seize property for their investigation. With a search warrant, the FBI raided Cohen's office and apartment in April 2018. The raid took Cohen by surprise, but he cooperated with the FBI. In his view, he had nothing to hide. Besides, he had been the president's loyal, personal attorney for several years, so he expected that Trump would use his presidential power to support him, if necessary. During the raid, Cohen placed a call to Trump at the White House. When Trump called back, he asked about Cohen's family, characterized the raid as a 'witch hunt' and expressed verbal support for Cohen. That conversation left Cohen feeling that if he stayed loyal to Trump, then Trump would be loyal to him (DM 348). Later that day, Cohen watched Trump speaking at a press conference. While condemning the FBI raid, Trump referred to Cohen as **one** of his personal attorneys (DM 348). One of his personal attorneys. Trump was distancing himself from Cohen. That was the first crack in Cohen's projection. Cohen began to question his conviction that Trump, whom he had idealized as a celebrity leader extraordinaire, would be loyal and supportive. When he learned he was being indicted for tax evasion, lying to Congress and misrepresentation to a bank, Cohen was perplexed because he had never filed a late tax return, never been audited, and never received a letter from the IRS (DM 351 – 352). He also wondered how he could be charged with misrepresentation to a bank regarding the use of a line of credit when the bank had never asked him what he was doing with the money (DM 354). He had two choices: plead guilty or be indicted. He was also being charged with campaign finance fraud for payments he made to an adult film star and a playboy bunny. After years of working as Trump's loyal personal lawyer, Cohen was convicted for tax evasion, campaign finance violation, false statements to a feder-ally-insured bank, and payments to silence two women who otherwise planned to speak out publicly about their alleged romantic affairs with the presidential candidate. For a collection of charges, Cohen was sen-tenced to 36 months in prison and assigned to Otisville Federal Satellite Camp in upstate New York, where he began his incarceration in May 2019 (DM 357). When the COVID-19 virus started spreading through the prison, inmates' confinement was converted to home detention. When news that Cohen was writing a book leaked out, his lawyer was served with a Cease and Desist letter from the Trump Organization (DM 359 – 360). That was the last crack in Cohen's projection. The demolition of Cohen's idealization of Trump as a celebrity leader was complete ... the psychological projection was broken.

Throughout his book, Cohen repeatedly refers to himself as 'sycophant'. This is hindsight. He was not as clear-eyed about himself while he worked for Trump. The media spotlight and FBI investigations forced him to reflect on his behavior. After much reflection, Cohen takes responsibility for his crimes, and he is remorseful about the impacts his actions had on others, but there is a residual sentiment of justice being miscarried. He still wonders why he went to prison for committing crimes directed by Trump for Trump's benefit, while Trump himself enjoyed the comfort and protection of the White House. In this section, I described the Cohen-Trump relationship in the context of archetype-as-biological-entity. In the next section, I describe the relationship in the context of archetype-as-emergent-phenomenon.

Context of Archetype as Emergent Phenomenon: Appropriation & Internalization

This section is about the Cohen-Trump relationship viewed in terms of archetype-as-emergent-phenomenon. When considering archetype as an emergent phenomenon, it is seen as an emergent property of a dynamic, developmental system that is made up of human brains, human activities, society's external environment and the narrative competence of humans in the society. In viewing archetype as an emergent phenomenon, the means for converting life's experience to meaning are appropriation and internalization. Appropriation is an adoption of conscious content from social and cultural sources in the external environment. Cohen appropriated characteristics of a sycophant drawn from the external world where celebrity status attracts high flattery and large followings. Internalization is the incorporation of a cultural appropriation into one's mental model. Cohen did not find a container in Trump. The containment effort was thwarted by Trump's inability to function as container, so there was no internalization.

For those readers who may be unfamiliar with the processes of appropriation and internalization, they can be observed in the way that children acquire language skills. At first, children appropriate language from social and cultural sources in the external world. Then, with some coaching from adults, children internalize language into their mental models. Children then use the internalized language constructs to compose sentences. Cohen appropriated an idealization of a celebrity leader from the external world. The behaviors and communications between Cohen and Trump were related to their expectations that Cohen would use his legal skills to be a loyal 'fixer' for sustaining the celebrity status of the 'Boss' Trump. By his own account, Cohen had become a sycophant, reveling in the reflected glory and power of Trump. Their meeting activated the sycophant archetype, which emerged from a complex system that is made up of society's attitude to celebrity status, the cultural environment in which celebrities achieve their status, and the narratives that people compose about their lives as sycophants and celebrities. In the context of archetype-as-emergent-phenomenon, the sycophant archetype has no specific location; it is pervasive across society's sycophant-celebrity relationship habits and institutions in the cultural environment. Activation of the sycophant archetype indicates that Cohen had an emotional appropriation of the sycophant from the external world. The content of Cohen's appropriation was conscious experience made up of emotions, thoughts, images and memories about a sycophant's role drawn from the adulation of celebrity leaders in the cultural environment ... fawning, public statements of flattery, and eagerness to take advantage of privileges not available to ordinary citizens.

Although Cohen and Trump enjoyed an ongoing 2-way dialogue for years, their communication was not used to construct meaning from the content of Cohen's appropriation. Their mental models remained unchanged over the duration of their relationship. It is clear from news reports and books written about the Trump administration that Cohen had an appropriation, but there is no indication that Trump was engaged in addressing Cohen's appropriation. It is as if their communications were all about conscious matters. Cohen looked to Trump as a celebrity leader and Trump accepted Cohen's loyal support, but the two do not appear to have had the kind of mind-to-mind connection that enables psychological growth. The construction of meaningful thoughts and emotions from the appropriation was simply not a part of their interaction. Trump never stepped up to the role of container in the sense of guiding Cohen in the emotional turmoil of a containment. Their relationship was about using Cohen's legal skills to whitewash Trump's activities. Throughout their engagement with the social-symbolic world of business and politics, they were not able to transform unprocessed emotional states into processed emotional states and structure them into useful thoughts. The sycophant archetype was activated at the level of psychic complexity where Cohen was transitioning from providing legal injury-related service for individuals in a private forum, to becoming a provider of legal counsel to a celebrity with constituents in a public forum. The containment did not get off the ground. Its intent was thwarted by a would-be container practised in the art of manipulative scaffolding, but unable to provide psychological scaffolding. Their relationship did not have the kind of emotional bond that could foster a psychological containment.

The pseudo-containing mode of containment bypasses the emotional turmoil that is a natural part of the interaction between contained and container. Instead of engaging the emotional turmoil that makes a containment possible, Cohen and Trump adopted the outward appearance of a containment, while perverting its purpose. The unmetabolized experience that had not been processed was communicated with an assured and righteous sense of clarity. Cohen and Trump wielded their power to intimidate others into compliance with their demands, as if the righteousness of the law supported those demands. For example, Cohen used his perceived sense of his own power to threaten legal action against a university if they published Trump's grades, even as Trump was publicly claiming that his academic performance was excellent. Unassimilated mental states are not only attached to chaotic emotion, they can also be overly reasoned forms of thought. For example, Cohen used his unassimilated mental state about his own power to give legal cover to Trump's rationale that he could not disclose his tax returns because he was being audited by the IRS, a procedure not confirmed by the IRS. Both emotional overload and calculated thought are linked to unmetabolized experience in the pseudo-containing mode, where contained and container resist containment and psychological growth. In the pseudo-containing mode, the rigid and apparently well-reasoned person subtly resists entering a containing relationship and is unable to feel the benefits of being held in mind by another. Cohen and

Trump worked together to rationalize their activities, but they barely entered into a containment. Their mental activities were directed outward. Containment involves mental activities being directed inward as one mind helps another mind to convert experience to meaning. In the pseudo-containing mode, the narrative of the contained is not derived from raw experience that seeks transformation, but is generated by mimicking the unconsciously perceived intentions, needs or functions of the container. This is seen in Cohen's mimicking of Trump's autocratic style of functioning, with little regard for what is legal. The result was a great deal of pseudo-intelligence and story-making that did not allow genuine components of thought to emerge from the containment. Because the pseudo-containing mode short-circuits the processing of unresolved states of mind, the contained is left with no sense of managing unassimilated thoughts and feelings. There is a marginal idea that thoughts can be explored or developed, but a perversion of the containment prevents that. Their containment was nullified because Trump failed to respond to Cohen's need to identify with power. Cohen's voracious envy of power prevented his becoming dependent on a container. Consequently, he could not have the experience of being held in the mind of another. Without there being any tolerance for difference between contained and container, the possibility of a containment disappears from the mind of the contained. This explains why Cohen appeared to be going along reasonably well without a need of containment, until the relationship was interrupted by sudden deteriorations that appear to come from nowhere. For a time, Cohen was holding his sense of self together, until the relationship became untenable. Because there was no difference between contained and container, Cohen felt trapped in a world where he could not have a separate containing mind. For him, the connection between physical reality and psychical reality was tenuous. Cohen's raw thoughts and feelings about his own power were not based on evidence, they were based on pseudo-mentalization, which gave him a terrifying sense that underlying his attempts to achieve power was a sense of nothingness. The emotional content of Cohen's appropriation did not undergo real transformation. Instead, the pseudo-containing relationship generated a façade that prevented real psychical experience. To function as a container, Trump would have had to adopt the opposite approach to Cohen's need for power, and help Cohen to convert his raw experience into meaning appropriate for

Cohen. What might have appeared to be reasoned and mature thinking on Trump's part was actually made up of communication about physical things rather than real thoughts that convey understanding or meaning. This pseudo-containment occurred because the reality of difference, separateness, and the nature of another's mind were limited by defensive strategies that did not allow Cohen and Trump to actually enter into a containment.

Converting Experience to Meaning: Symbolization

The frequency and durations of their interactions as personal attorney and celebrity-businessman-politician provided ample opportunity for symbol formation, but my research yielded no evidence of symbol formation in the interaction between Cohen and Trump. Their biographies do indicate voluminous behaviors and communications in each other's company, but I found no instance of the emergence of any symbol as defined in "A Critical Dictionary of Jungian Analysis" where a symbol is made up of a concept, an intent, a purpose and content. Their relationship did not achieve the kind of emotional bonding and shared reverie that would support a psychological containment. Trump did not have the wherewithal to provide the mental scaffolding for Cohen to benefit from either a projection or an appropriation. In the same way that Cohen was functioning according to his appropriation about the role of sycophant, Trump was functioning according to his appropriation about the role of celebrity.

In the 2020 publication of his memoir 'DISLOYAL' Cohen discloses:

> "I confess I never really did understand why pleasing Trump meant so much to me, and others. To this day I don't have the full answer. In a matter of a couple of months, I had started falling under the spell of Donald Trump. ...
> Nor did I consider that Trump was testing my fealty and submissiveness, the way a gang leader assesses a new recruit, giving the wannabe small crimes to commit to see if he will act without question or concern for his own well-being. Donald Trump was like a mafia don, in a sense, and I wanted

to be his soldier in the worst way. And I was ready to pass any test put in my path. ...

I gradually gave up my mind to Trump" (DM 42 - 43).

In working together, Cohen became habituated to Trump's lifestyle. It was the lifestyle of a celebrity accumulating wealth and influence in society. In my view, Trump provided a scaffolding about survival in the business-political world, but not a scaffolding about psychological growth for Cohen. While not becoming a carrier of Cohen's psychological projection, Trump responded to Cohen by sharing those skills which he had honed and used to move himself up the celebrity ladder. He could manipulate the media. He could bend legal norms. He had published a book on the art of the deal. Those were the skills that he found useful in carving out a life for himself. That was the kind of scaffolding he provided Cohen, who eagerly embraced whatever cemented his place in Trump's orbit, where he derived satisfaction from the reflected power of Trump's status, first as a real estate mogul and later as the President of the United States of America.

The interaction between Cohen and Trump was not dialectical. Their interaction affected their external world much more than their internal worlds. The eventual impacts on their external reality were illegal activities that resulted in Cohen's imprisonment and Trump's impeachment. The changes in their internal reality are somewhat different. If Cohen's book *'DISLOYALTY'* is an indicator, his internal reality changed to the extent that he now accepts responsibility for his illegal actions while he was Trump's 'fixer' and he is remorseful about the impact his behavior had on the lives of other people. His televised interviews about Trump indicate that he holds on to the view that justice was served unevenly because he went to prison for work that was directed by Trump for Trump's benefit, while Trump was not held accountable for his role. Trump's televised interviews and campaign rallies indicate that his internal reality has not changed. He dissociates himself from Cohen, he dismisses his two impeachments as hoaxes, and he has publicly announced his candidacy for the U. S. presidency in the 2024 election, with no discernable change of outlook, political or otherwise.

Call To Action: Take Away A Portable Understanding

This chapter is not just to tell a story of the relationship between Michael Cohen and Donald Trump, both of whom lead very interesting lives. I hope readers find this chapter informative about the pseudo-containing mode of containment. The Cohen-Trump interaction was a toxic relationship that ended with Cohen going to prison for assuming that his connection with Trump's power placed him beyond the reach of the U. S. justice system, while Trump was impeached for abusing the power bestowed on him for service to the American public. This is a call to action for readers to take away a portable understanding of the pseudo-containing mode of containment. To help readers, I offer the following summary as a reminder of what drew these two people into each other's orbits, and the outcome of their interaction.

- **Mode:** Cohen and Trump had a pseudo-containing mode of containment.
- **Roles:** As the contained, Cohen was the sycophant whose projection was cast onto Trump, the celebrity-businessman-politician. There is no indication that Trump played the role of container.
- **Symmetry:** Cohen and Trump had an asymmetrical relationship. There was a gradient of power between them. Cohen was the younger man, offering a professional service in a subservient role. Trump was the celebrity with more resources at his disposal ... celebrity status, financial resources, business acumen, and later political clout. Cohen was dispensable to Trump. Trump was Cohen's employer. Although Cohen has the legal skills to be financially independent, he depended on Trump as a cult leader, for approval, public recognition, and notoriety that secured compliance from others when Trump wanted to bend legal norms.
- **Psychological Frame:** This attorney-client relationship created a privacy that could have served the purpose of a psychological frame. Cohen and Trump both had offices in the Trump Organization and their attorney-client relationship lasted twelve years. That made it possible for them to engage in emotional bonding and overlapping reveries between the contained and container. However, their bonding appears to have occurred

on a conscious level, without the benefit of the unconscious communication necessary for a psychological frame. Their emotional bonding was so fragile that Trump distanced himself from Cohen right after the FBI raided Cohen's home. The opportunity for a psychological containment was lost, partly because the emotional bonding was too weak to sustain a containment, and partly because Trump did not step up to the role of container.

- **Dialectical Narrative:** Cohen contributed the contained's narrative which was about his need to satisfy his sycophant's desire for the reflected power of a celebrity. Trump contributed the container's narrative about wielding power as a celebrity by bending others to his will. Since Trump did not become a useful container for Cohen's unprocessed emotions and thoughts about celebrityhood, there was no third narrative. They did not have the kind of dialectical interaction that would make a third narrative possible. Cohen's narrative and Trump's narrative were so closely aligned that there was no room for dialectical interaction between them.

- **Psychological Growth / Harm**: In the absence of a dialectical interaction, there was no psychological growth. The relationship ended with Cohen being incarcerated for illegal activity regarding campaign funding regulation, among others. While Cohen accepts responsibility for his illegal actions, he characterizes his actions as having been carried out at the direction of, and the benefit for, Trump. The relationship left Trump as it found him, with neither psychological growth nor harm.

After the Containment Ended

Cohen was disbarred by the Appellate Division of the New York Supreme Court in 2019. His law license was revoked and he can no longer practise law. In 2020, Cohen was convicted for lying to Congress and for covering up illegal activities he performed on Trump's behalf. He received a 3-year prison sentence for lying to Congress, campaign finance violations and paying hush money to women who alleged affairs with Trump. In 2021, Cohen along with other prisoners, were released early from New York's Otisville prison and allowed to spend the rest of their sentences under house arrest, due to the spread of the COVID-19 epidemic.

After completing his sentence, Cohen became the host of a Podcast named *'Mea Culpa'* established with a mission to right the wrongs he perpetrated when he worked with Trump. Cohen also published a book titled *'DISLOYAL: A Memoir'* to tell what he calls the true story of the former personal attorney to President Donald J. Trump. The book indicates that Cohen takes responsibility for his crimes, and he is remorseful about his wrongdoings. However, he still harbors a residual feeling of justice being miscarried, because he went to prison for committing crimes directed by Trump, while Trump escapes accountability.

During his 4-year term in office, the U. S. House of Representatives voted to impeach Trump twice. The December 2019 impeachment was for abuse of power and obstruction of Congress. On the second occasion, in January 2021, the charge was incitement of an insurrection. Trump does not accept responsibility for any of the charges leveled at him in either of the two impeachments. He calls the impeachments witch hunts. Trump campaigned for a second term as president of the United States in 2020, but lost his bid for re-election. Although the election results were certified at multiple levels of government, by both Republicans and Democrats, Trump maintains the unsupported stance that the election was stolen from him.

As I am writing this book in springtime of 2023, I watch TV News coverage of four concurrent court cases involving Trump. In one case, he is being investigated for possible interference in election laws in the state of Georgia during the 2020 U. S. A. election. In a second case Trump is being investigated for possible unlawful possession of classified documents found in his home in Florida after he left office as president. The third case is an investigation into Trump's involvement in the storming of the U. S. Capitol on January 6, 2021. The fourth case is an investigation of whether any campaign funding law was broken by hush money payments made to an adult film star and a playboy bunny who are alleged to have engaged in sexual encounters with Trump. Under oath, Cohen has testified multiple times about his involvement in the payments. Trump declined the District Attorney's invitation to testify.

Sources

The sources of information that I used in preparing this chapter are:

- *"DISLOYAL: A Memoir"* by Michael Cohen
- *"TRUMP REVEALED: The Definitive Biography of the 45ᵗʰ President"* by Michael Kranish & Marc Fisher
- *"The Dangerous Case of Donald Trump"* by Bandy Lee (editor)
- *"The Cult of Trump"* by Steven Hassan
- *"Containing States of Mind"* by Duncan Cartwright
- *"Projection and Re-Collection in Jungian Psychology"* by Marie-Louise von Franz.

CHAPTER 18

A Reflexive Mode of Containment Involving: Dante Alighieri & Beatrice Portinari

> *"Behold, a deity stronger than I; who coming, shall rule over me."*
>
> – Dante Alighieri

The literature about psychological containment usually depicts a projection as going from one mind, the contained, to the mind of another, the container. Sometimes, the contained and container engage in a sustained dialogue that enables the content of the projection to be processed for the psychological benefit of one or both. On other occasions, there may be a failure of one mind to engage the other mind. It is rare for a mind to engage itself in processing its own projection. My opinion is that the Italian poet, Dante Alighieri had such a rare mind. My interpretation is that the containment model developed by Wilfred Bion, and enhanced by Duncan Cartwright, does not have a mode of containment suitable for a mind relying on itself to process a projection. So, with all the respect due to Bion and Cartwright, I take the liberty of proposing that a new mode of containment be added to the Bion-Cartwright model: the reflexive mode of containment. This is a mode of containment that applies to someone who finds themself in isolation, whether enforced or self-imposed, and who becomes a container for himself / herself. Instead of depending on containment by another mind for psychological growth, the person processes their own projection through reflexion. Dante's isolation was enforced. He was exiled from his beloved home city of Florence by political foes. I believe that Dante processed his projection to Beatrice by a reflexive mode of containment.

Dante fell in love with Beatrice Portinari during their first meeting at a May Day Fair in the year 1274. They were both approximately nine years old. He later described the impact of the meeting by making a declaration that reveals how he experienced the power of his projection:

> "Behold, a deity stronger than I; who coming, shall rule over me" (LS 56).

He saw her again nine years later, walking with two companions on a road that runs alongside the Arno River in Florence. An oil painting by artist Henry Holiday shows Dante's right hand holding onto the Santa Trinita Bridge as if for stability, while his left hand clutches his beating heart. He stares at her. She acknowledges him. Each goes on to marry someone else. When Beatrice dies at age 24, a distraught Dante retreats into himself and writes an anthology of poems titled 'La Vita Nuova' (The New Life) to honor her memory. Beatrice's death removed any possibility of Dante's projection making a connection with Beatrice's mind. Yet, Dante's projection lingered. An image of her stayed with him for the rest of his life. He later created a literary device to process the emotional upheaval of his own projection. It is as if Dante turned the emotional power of his projection into a reflexive force. In this chapter, I explain my view that Dante demonstrated that a person can withdraw a projection, process the emotional upheaval that gives it power, and convert the relevant experience to meaning, without reliance on another mind.

My interpretation is that what began as medieval style courtly love between Dante and Beatrice became a reflexive mode containment for Dante. The projection from his mind to Beatrice did not meet with a response from her. There was no mind-to-mind connection between them. She did not become a container for his projection. However, he continued to carry an image of her in his mind long after she died. First, he sustained the projection during his time of grief, then withdrew it while transforming his fascination into a muse, who inspired him and influenced his creative sonnets and prose for the remainder of his life. In the next two sections, I provide some background information about the lives of Dante and Beatrice.

Background Information about Dante Alighieri

When he was born in 1265, Dante Alighieri entered a family with a history of involvement in the politics of Florence. Dante's mother, Bella, died in 1272, when he was seven years old. His father, Alighiero II, married again and had two more children. In his ninth year, Dante attended a neighborhood celebration that he would remember for the rest of his life. Annually, the city of Florence celebrates the arrival of Spring on the first day of May when the beautiful Tuscan flowers are blooming. In 1274, the prestigious Portinari family held a celebration for their neighbors and that is when Dante met Beatrice, who was dressed in what he recalled as the noble color of crimson (DAL 23 - 24). Later he would claim that 'many times in my childhood' he sought out Beatrice by going to the little church in Santa Margherita, where Beatrice's mother brought her to pray (DAL 25). He would sit a few feet away and gaze at Beatrice in admiration.

When Dante was 12 years old, his father arranged for him to be officially betrothed to Gemma Donati, the daughter of a friend who was an influential banker. At that time, it was customary to arrange a betrothal at a young age. Dante and Gemma married several years later and had at least four children. Dante's father, Alighiero II, died in 1280 (DAL 19) when Dante was fifteen years old. At age 22, Dante enrolled at the University of Bologna where he studied Tuscan poetry and influenced the development of Italian literature. Two years afterwards, he enlisted in the Florentine army and participated in the Battle of Campaldino. Then he served a term in city government, as one of six priors, known for putting the welfare of the community above all other considerations (DAL 11). Because of the thriving community in Florence, the collection of merchant guilds, the impressive architectural structures of gates and towers around the city, and the bridges across the Arno River, Florentines took pride in their city, and Dante regarded it as the ideal place to live (DAL 6 - 10). This idyllic setting provided small comfort for Dante when Beatrice died in 1290. Stricken with grief, Dante immersed himself in the study of philosophy and the writing of *La Vita Nuova* (*The New Life*) which he published in 1294. This book of sonnets reflects his first efforts to depict Beatrice as an abstract model of love and beauty. He believed that his experience of loving Beatrice at-a-distance had a divine and mystical quality to it.

Dante's family was of modest means and belonged to the Guelph political party, which believed in the separation of church and state. At the time, the city of Florence was experiencing political conflicts between two political parties, the Guelphs and the Ghibellines, about the balance of leadership between church and state (DAL 3 - 11). The Guelph party supported the pope as ruler of the Catholic Church, but rejected his involvement in secular affairs. The opposing political party, the Ghibellines, believed a pope should rule both secular and religious matters. Dante's opposition to the pope's interference in matters of the state brought him into conflict with Pope Boniface VIII. When his political adversaries made allegations against him, Dante became fearful about his safety. When he failed to appear in court to answer the false criminal charges of financial fraud, his property was confiscated, and he was sentenced to be burned at the stake. He was exiled by the leaders of the Black Guelphs in 1302, after which he never returned to Florence (DAL 11).

While in exile, Dante had no one to mirror his life ... no other mind available to provide mental scaffolding for psychological growth. So, he had to rely on himself. Since he was capable of symbolic thought, he was able to construct meaning from his life experience. During the period of exile (1301 – 1321), he published his trilogy serially, Inferno in 1314, Purgatorio in 1316 and Paradiso in 1321. Dante invented a rhyming scheme that sets up a cadence for a new way of writing poetry. His rhyming scheme is the terza rima verse form. The Italian expression 'terza rima' translates to English as 'third rhyme'. It is a rhyming verse form in a poem which has 3-line stanzas, with an interlocking rhyme scheme. The last word of the second line in one stanza provides the rhyme for the first and third lines in the following stanza. The structure he set up for *Commedia* is a rhyme with a pattern aba, bcb, cdc, and so on. The letters a, b and c represent words in the lines of the poem. Avoiding Latin, the language of the intellectually sophisticated in his lifetime, Dante formulated an Italian vernacular set in rhyming verses for laypeople to access his poetry easily.

Dante arranged *Commedia* in three parts - Inferno, Purgatorio and Paradiso, that is, Italian for Hell, Purgatory and Paradise. These three components are like the three parts of a well-proportioned building that is majestic and awe-inspiring. They are the linguistic equivalent of a psychological frame ... a fitting frame for the dialogical interaction that he established by separating his mental activity into two parts that functioned in parallel. Dante-the-poet maintained a dialectical interaction with Dante-the-protagonist throughout the composition of *La Commedia*. He wrote while living a nomadic lifestyle roaming among cities that included Bologna, Padua and Verona. He had time for reflexive reverie because the relatives and friends he had in Florence were no longer a part of his day-to-day life. His wife and children were in Florence. He no longer had the political role that occupied him in Florence. Without family, friends and political colleagues, he had time for a reflexive reverie that enabled him to process his own projection.

Background Information about Beatrice Portinari

At Beatrice Portinari's birth in 1269, she entered a wealthy family living in the city of Florence in northern Italy. Her father was Folco Portinari, a respected banker in the community. Beatrice met Dante when she was about nine years old. Their first meeting took place at a May Day party being held by the Portinari family for friends and neighbors. Nine years later, while walking with two companions along a street next to the Arno River, Beatrice exchanged a cursory greeting with Dante. He was standing at the Ponte Vecchio bridge which crosses the Arno River.

In 1287, Beatrice married Simone dei Bardi, an influential banker in Florence. She died in 1294. She is believed to have died while giving birth to their first child. Even though she was physically dead, her image remained with Dante for the remainder of his life. While Beatrice is not identified explicitly in Dante's autobiographical *La Vita Nuova*, her death inspired the sonnets. He wrote of her in the style of courtly love, that is, intense passion for a woman who is not available for a relationship. After writing *La Vita Nuova* in 1294, Dante vowed to write nothing more about Beatrice until he could "*say of her what was never said of any woman*" (DAL 61). In the next two sections, I describe the interaction between Dante-the-poet and Dante-the-protagonist first in the context of archetype-as-biological-entity, then in the context of archetype-as-emergent-phenomenon.

Context of Archetype as Biological Entity: Projection & Introjection

This section is about Dante's infatuation viewed in terms of archetype-as-biological-entity. When an archetype is viewed as a biological entity, it is regarded as an ancestral heritage of human experience accumulated over many generations and located in collective unconsciousness. When psychologists define an archetype as a biological entity, the processes they identify for converting experience to meaning are projection and introjection. Projection is an evacuation of unconscious content from the psyche due to an unbearable state of mind. Dante's projection was an unconscious evacuation of an unbearable state of mind about his idealization of womanhood cast onto Beatrice at their first meeting. Introjection is a transformation of an unbearable state of mind to a bearable state of mind, followed by its integration into conscious content of the psyche. Dante did not have the opportunity to interact with Beatrice, so there was no introjection initiated by her. However, I propose that Dante was able to process his unbearable state of mind by engaging in a reflexive mode of containment.

The method of Dante's internalization was accomplished by what I am proposing as a reflexive mode of containment. I use the word 'reflexive' as defined in the book "*Conversations About Reflexivity*" edited by Margaret Archer. 'Reflexive' refers to an internal conversation that involves self-monitoring and self-control in a paradoxical dialogue conducted as a form of modelling one's own thinking, with an expectation of generating new thought processes (CR 145 - 147). 'Reflexive' describes the practice of folding the mind back on one's own thinking process, in a self-referential loop of seeing and changing how one interacts with the world. It involves observing one's own state of mind, while engaging in a critical examination of one's own thoughts in an iterative interaction.

The anima archetype was activated when the sight of young Beatrice in her crimson dress triggered a projection from Dante. The content of Dante's projection was an unprocessed emotional experience about the opposite sex. In their book "*Transforming Sexuality*" Ann and Barry Ulanov explain that the activation of the anima archetype is recognized by the numinous quality of Dante's encounter with Beatrice. Numinous describes the awe-inspiring, spiritual, mysterious feeling that Dante experienced as if in the presence of divinity when he meets Beatrice. He expressed the awe-inspiring effect of meeting Beatrice with the words: "*Behold, a deity stronger than I; who coming, shall rule over me*" (LS 56). Dante's projection to Beatrice consumed and threatened to overpower him. I believe that Dante's projection was broken at the time when he decided to include Beatrice as a character in *La Commedia*. That is the point in time when Beatrice was transformed, in Dante's mind, from an abstract model of love and beauty to an inspiring muse.

Although the conscious aspect of the encounter between Dante and Beatrice was just a simple, social greeting, the activation of the anima archetype awakened an unconscious response. It opened up in Dante an interior space in his psyche and marked the beginning of an inner dialogue. His inner dialogue was all he had because Beatrice was not available to engage in a person-to-person dialogue, or become container of his projection. His interior dialogue involved two entities, Dante-the-poet and Dante-the protagonist. Dante-the-poet was the flesh-and-blood person. Dante-the-protagonist was a fictional character in the poem *Commedia*. These two entities participated in an ongoing dialogue in his psyche for decades after Beatrice's death. Dante had created a literary device of separating his mental activity into Dante-the-poet and Dante-the-protagonist, which enabled him to engage in a dialogue for processing the content of his projection. Dante-the-poet and Dante-the-protagonist engaged in a dialectical interaction that resulted in the withdrawal of the projection, and the conversion of its content from the emotional turmoil of his experience into meaning that inspired the composition of *Commedia*, a notable literary work that has inspired generations. In this section, I described the relationship between Dante-the-poet and Dante-the-antagonist, in the context of archetype-as-biological-entity. In the next section, I will explain the relationship in the context of archetype-as-emergent-phenomenon.

Context of Archetype as Emergent Phenomenon: Appropriation & Internalization

This section is about Dante's infatuation viewed in terms of archetype-as-emergent-phenomenon. When considering archetype as an emergent phenomenon, it is seen as an emergent property of a dynamic, developmental system that is made up of human brains, human activities, society's external environment and the narrative competence of humans in the society. When viewing archetype as an emergent phenomenon, the means for converting life's experience to meaning are appropriation and internalization. Appropriation is an adoption of conscious content from social and cultural sources in the external environment. Dante's appropriation was an idealization of womanhood drawn from the cultural environment of 14th century Italy where courtly love was a natural part of life. Internalization is the incorporation of a cultural appropriation into one's mental model. Since Beatrice was unavailable for a relationship, Dante could not have a mind-to-mind connection with her. In her absence, he chose to set up a reflexive mode of containment, where Dante-the poet could have a dialogue with Dante-the-protagonist. The reflexive mode of containment served the purpose of internalization.

For readers who are unfamiliar with the processes of appropriation and internalization, they can be observed in the way that children acquire language skills. At first, children appropriate language from social and cultural sources in the external world, then, with the help of adults, they internalize language into their mental models. That well-known example of appropriation provides a segue into a discussion of Dante's appropriation. The content of Dante's appropriation was an unrepresented state of mind about the courtly love he felt for Beatrice. Dante's appropriation was drawn from his 14th century world where the dynamic developmental system included human mental activity in the external environment's mix of courtly love, politics and religion, plus the narrative competence of the people in that society. Dante's internalization was achieved in what I propose as a reflexive mode of containment. My use of the word 'reflexive' is taken from the definition by sociologist Margaret Archer in the book "*Conversations About Reflexivity*". The word 'reflexive' refers to an internal conversation that involves self-monitoring and self-control in a paradoxical dialogue conducted as a form of modelling one's own thinking, with an expectation of generating new thought processes (CR 145 - 147). So, a reflexive mode of containment involves observing one's own state of mind, while engaging in a critical examination of one's own thoughts during an iterative interaction. Exile from Florence imposed on Dante an isolation that forced him to look inward. In doing so, he crafted a literary technique that enabled a reflexive mode of containment. He separated his mental activity into two parallel trains of thought. One train of thought belonged to the flesh-and-blood Dante-the-poet. The other train of thought belonged to Dante-the-protagonist, that is a character in the trilogy *La Commedia*. The internalization of his appropriation was accomplished by an ongoing dialogue between Dante-the-poet and Dante-the-protagonist. The evidence for this internalization can be seen in Dante's explanation that Love dictates to him from within (LS 46). In the next section, I use Dante's comment about Love dictating to him from within, epitomized in Andrew Frisardi's expression 'Love's dictation' to describe the symbolization that I believe occurred during the dialogue between Dante-the-poet and Dante-the-protagonist.

Converting Experience to Meaning: Symbolization

Regardless of whether psychologists define containment in terms of projection or appropriation, they regard the capacity for symbol formation as central to psychological containment. Mental activity in projection and introjection disrupts unbearable states of mind, thereby enabling symbolic meaning to be achieved through language communication. Duncan Cartwright, who defines containment in terms of projection, describes symbol formation as the capacity to generate psychic representations, without which people struggle to understand affective experience (CSM

246). The ability to generate meaning demands that an encounter be subjected to a series of transformations of lived experience that are unfolding at the cusp of awareness (CSM 3). This involves transforming raw, unassimilated experience into mentation through building meaningful commentaries about the self in the interaction (CSM 4) between the containment pair.

At the symbolic level of organization of the psyche, symbols have the property of generativity – at that level, symbols become generators of meaning, allowing the verbal communication of a shared meaning system (CSM 15) between contained and container. Warren Colman, who defines containment in terms of appropriation, describes Bion's one-to-one emotional containment by pointing out that humans cannot develop to maturity without a socio-cultural context within which meaning can be formulated (AIE 224). A flexible symbolic capacity in the ego enables affective states to be apprehended and enriched by the multi-dimensionality of symbolic form (AIE 228 – 229). Emotion and symbolic thought go hand in hand since higher levels of emotion require robust forms of thought to contain them, while symbolic thought also promotes a greater range and depth of emotional sensitivity (AIE 230).

In my reading of the literature by and about Dante, I found a number of possible symbols. The symbol I chose for analysis is one that I regard as consistent with the definition of symbol that I found in "A Critical Dictionary of Jungian Analysis" where three psychologists define symbol in terms of concept, intent, purpose, and content. The symbol I chose is captured in Dante's words in Purgatorio XXIV.52-54. Here is an English translation:

> "I am one who, when Love inspires me, takes note,
> and the way that He dictates [to me] within,
> I write it" (LS 46).

Andrew Frisardi, author of "Love's Scribe: Reading Dante in the Book of Creation" characterizes that remark as Dante's response to Love's dictation (LS 46). The expression 'Love's dictation' resonates with Dante's expression 'the way He dictates [to me] within'. Dante received Love's dictation from within. He found Love's dictation overpowering. He did not understand it, but he wrote it down. Although he does not know specifics of what Love's dictation will become, or how it will affect his life, he prepares to understand it by writing it down. Applying the definition of a symbol as having a concept, intent, purpose, and content, this is how I interpret Dante's symbol captured in the expression Love's dictation:

- **Concept:** The concept embodied in Dante's symbol of Love's dictation was an intuitive idea that Dante had about courtly love being more than just a source of anxious admiration for a beautiful woman. The intuitive idea was not fully formulated, but it seemed to hold promise because it gripped him intensely.

- **Intent:** The intent behind Dante's symbol of Love's dictation was to discover a goal that he believed to be in existence, but which he found difficult to verbalize. The goal was about a transition from his current path of courtly love to a different path. It seemed unlikely that the transition could be worked out from a rational perspective. Instead, a more nuanced perspective seemed to be necessary for the transformation of courtly love to a more satisfying experience.

- **Purpose:** The purpose served by Dante's symbol of Love's dictation was to resolve an existing conflict about courtly love. He could not possess Beatrice because she was dead, but he could not get her out of his mind. The purpose of the symbol was to resolve the anxiety invoked by the conflict.

- **Content:** The content of Dante's symbol of Love's dictation was courtly love expressed in his uniquely individual terms, but which also had a potential for expression in collective terms and universal imagery, as seen at the end of *La Commedia*, where Beatrice has moved from the role of individual to the collective role of bringer of blessings for all of humanity. The meaning of Dante's symbol of Love's dictation can be found in the images that emerged about courtly love. When he reflected upon the images, he found them influential in controlling, ordering and giving new meaning to his life. This is seen in the new meaning he created by transforming his life from exiled politician-cum-pharmacist to poet extraordinaire.

When Dante wrote *La Vita Nuova*, I believe he was not aware that his image of Beatrice could be a projection of his own inner life, or an appropriation from the external environment. He indicated his view that Beatrice was like a deity by stating: "*Behold, a deity stronger than I; who coming, shall rule over me.*" In *La Vita Nuova*, he was convinced that what he saw in Beatrice were truly attributes of Beatrice. *La Vita Nuova* is a combination of prose and poetry describing Dante's meetings with Beatrice, her beauty and her goodness. He also described his own intense feelings for her and his reactions to her graciousness. In addition, *La Vita Nuova* described his anguish when informed of her death. Although he does not identify Beatrice explicitly in *La Vita Nuova*, the poetry focuses on the effects that his love for her has on him. After expressing his grief about her death, Dante decided that from then onward he would speak only in praise of her. He aimed to portray higher forms of love in his future poetry. In 1294, he published *La Vita Nuova* to express his grief, his unrequited love and his emotional autobiography. At the end of *La Vita Nuova*, Beatrice appeared to Dante in a vision. She appeared just as he had seen her in their first meeting: a nine-year-old girl in a crimson dress. Dante informed readers that he felt inadequate to write of her as she deserved and he vowed that, after devoting himself to further study, he would in future: "*write of her that which has never been written of any other woman*".

In the eight years between publishing *La Vita Nuova* and being exiled, Dante was a significant player in the Florentine community: a politician, a husband, a father, and a householder. In 1302, his political opponents made false allegations of financial fraud against him. Since he refused to answer the charges in court, he was exiled. Threatened with being burned at the stakes, he left Florence. In exile, he wandered from city to city surviving at the generosity of acquaintances in Bologna, Padua and Verona. Without the political and familial roles to occupy him, he composed *La Commedia* which he serializes in three parts: Inferno, Purgatorio, and Paradisio (Hell, Purgatory and Paradise). The separation of *La Commedia* into three realms of Inferno, Purgatorio and Paradisio, might be interpreted as three stages of Dante-the-poet's processing his projection. Inferno is the realm where he recognizes that his feelings for Beatrice are actually about images of his inner world being projected out into the external world. Purgatorio is the realm where he withdraws the projection after going through the terraces where he engages others who relate their own transgressions, affording him the opportunities to reflect on his own transgressions. When he enters Purgatorio, an angel uses the tip of a sword to carve the letter 'P' seven times on his forehead. 'P' stands for 'piaghe' which is Italian for wound and is derived from 'peccati' which means sin. The implication is that Dante must cleanse seven wounds. As he leaves each terrace in Purgatorio, an angel cleanses a wound on his forehead by removing a letter 'P'. The word 'sin' implies a religious interpretation. I propose a psychological interpretation that the cleansing of the wounds implies that Dante gradually withdraws the content of his projection and accepts that the projection was really about his interior life. Paradisio is the realm where he experiences relief from having processed the emotional turmoil of his projection and is ready for a more psychologically mature approach to life.

In the absence of a container, Dante composed La Commedia as a way of processing his emotional turmoil in the projection that had been cast onto Beatrice. La Commedia is a poetic trilogy about 3 tiers of Christian afterlife. La Commedia has been interpreted from many perspectives, including linguistic, religious, political, spiritual, and historical. My interpretation is psychological. Exile from Florence eliminated his normal activities leaving a gap in Dante's life. He treated this as an opportunity to fulfil his promise that he would write of Beatrice as no other woman had ever been portrayed. This is where the activated anima, clothed in the image of Beatrice, began to lead him in a journey through his inner life. He began to fill the gap in his life with writing. He gave his poem the title 'La Commedia' which translates to the English word 'Comedy' because it has a happy ending. I honor Dante by using the title he chose: La Commedia. The expression Divine Comedy was composed by others. In his imagination, Dante developed a cast of characters, the main ones being Virgil and Beatrice. He imagined Beatrice looking down on him from heaven and being sorry for him in his state of exiled despair. He composed a story about her sending Virgil to rescue him. The story formed a psychological frame for him. Dante metabolized his unprocessed internal experience by setting up a psychological frame for a reflexive mode of containment. The containment is reflexive because he played the roles of both contained and container. In other words, he becomes his own container. The sustained dialogue between Dante-the-poet and Dante-the-protagonist enabled him to recognize that his image of Beatrice was either a projection of his inner life, or an appropriation from the external world. Dante-the-poet was able to metabolize the unbearable state of mind that he experienced as unrequited love for Beatrice by parsing out his emotions and reflecting on their psychological implications while Dante-the-protagonist was being guided through Inferno and Purgatorio by Virgil.

The establishment of a dialogue between Dante-the-poet and Dante-the-protagonist demonstrates a reflecting ego that uses the imagination to represent internal and external reality. My interpretation is that while Dante-the-protagonist was experiencing a spiritual journey through Purgatorio, Dante-the-poet was experiencing a parallel psychological journey. To be able to write *La Commedia*, Dante-the-poet must have understood how to manage a psychological projection, or a psychological appropriation, even if he did not use psychological terms to describe it. *La Commedia* starts with Dante-the-poet experiencing a revival of the emotional upheaval that disturbed him when he first met Beatrice. Since she died, she was not available to become container of his unprocessed state of mind. Her death had not diminished the enormity of the turmoil of his feelings for her. In keeping with his calling as a poet, he composed poetry to express his feelings. His need was to manage his unprocessed emotion of love. *La Commedia* is a poetic medium for managing his state of mind. He composed a story about a fictional version of himself engaged in an inward-looking journey through levels of the afterlife, where he learns a great deal about the shades of love by listening to the penitents in Purgatorio describe their earthly behaviors that led them to Purgatorio. They are in Purgatorio due to sins of pride, envy, wrath, sloth, avarice, gluttony and lust. While Dante-the-protagonist focuses on a religious classification of human experience in terms of sinfulness, Dante-the-poet focuses on a psychological classification of love: perverted love, deficient love, and excessive love. Perverted love is about taking actions that are harmful to others. Deficient love is about neglect of loved ones. Excessive love is about undue attachment to people, things, pleasures and possessions.

At the end of *Paradiso*, Dante-the-poet and Dante-the-protagonist become one again. Dante no longer presents himself as a protagonist in a story. Instead, he is a poet sitting in his study after completing his journey and returning from Inferno, Purgatorio and Paradisio. He is trying to remember the experience (Paradiso 33, ll. 60–84), and struggling to put what he could remember into words. Dante suggests that this fictional story is not a fiction after all, as he merges the protagonist with the poet. This disclosure confers on the poet the knowledge of one who, as the protagonist, had actually experienced this journey. Dante-the-poet structures human experience in layers of emotions that use dialectical exercise of the intellect to tame the emotions through periods of penance, while going through the seven terraces of Purgatorio, where the emotions are sublimated and refined in preparation for souls to move on to Paradisio. While experiencing the pull of opposites at each terrace in Purgatorio, Dante-the-protagonist gradually transforms his fevered love for Beatrice into a transcendent love for humanity. When they meet in Paradisio, Beatrice and Dante are emotionally neutral towards each other. It is no surprise that Beatrice is neutral. She only saw him on a few occasions during her life, and she had not developed feelings for him. Dante's feeling for her was an unrequited love. What is noteworthy is that, when they meet in Paradisio, Dante is emotionally neutral toward Beatrice. After all, he had been infatuated with her ever since he met her. I interpret his emotional neutrality to mean that he had withdrawn his projection, or dissolved his appropriation. What is even more noteworthy is that Dante was able to recognize and withdraw his projection without relying on the mind of another. He created a literary device that enabled him to engage in a reflexive mode of containment, rely on his own mind, recognize his projection or appropriation, and over a period of years, transform it.

With the literary device of separating his mental activity into two parallel streams of thought, Dante was able to make the psychological transition from regarding Beatrice exclusively in terms of an emotional cauldron of courtly love, to bringing out what Frisardi calls the public, civic function of Beatrice. There was a transformation of courtly love from an erotic, individual experience to a collective metaphysical and theological experience. She was no longer just one person; she became a 'bringer of blessings to all' (LS 42). Dante-the-poet made the transition from a love-smitten, politician-cum-pharmacist in exile, to creator of the great Italian poem La Commedia which has been an inspiration to generations since it was first published in the Middle Ages.

Call To Action: Take Away A Portable Understanding

In this chapter, I use the life of Dante to explain my view that it is possible for a person to process their own unassimilated state of mind, and re-direct its energies from an individual purpose to a humanitarian purpose. Significant factors in a reflexive mode of containment appear to be a high tolerance for isolation, combined with the ability to focus on one's own mental processes over a prolonged period of time, plus a determination to re-direct energy from one area of life to another. This chapter is a call to action for readers to take away a portable understanding of the reflexive mode of containment. To help readers, I offer the following summary as a reminder of how Dante engaged in a reflexive mode of containment by taking advantage of his isolation to compose the poetic trilogy La Commedia.

- **Mode:** Dante-the-poet and Dante-the-protagonist had a reflexive mode of containment.
- **Roles:** The mind of Dante played the role of contained as Dante-the-poet, while at the same time playing the role of container as Dante-the-protagonist.
- **Symmetry:** Dante-the-poet and Dante-the-protagonist had a symmetrical relationship. The two roles were played by the same mind, which created the narratives for both roles.
- **Psychological Frame:** Dante set a psychological frame with a purpose of composing poetry that would be worthy of Beatrice. He wanted to fulfill the promise he made after writing La Vita Nuova, that he would write no more until he could write about Beatrice what had never been written of any woman. The spatial boundary of the psychological frame was defined in Dante's imagination as a literary architecture of Hell, Purgatory and Paradise. The terraces and tiers reveal the spatially structured frame where Dante-the-poet and Dante-the-protagonist engaged in the journey through Hell, Purgatory and Paradise. The time boundary of the psychological frame spans the period of exile from Florence in 1302 to his death in Ravena in 1321. The timing frequency of the dialectical interaction between Dante-the-poet and Dante-the-protagonist is unknown since it was internal, however, it appears to be reflected in the cadence of the 'terza rima' rhyming scheme that he invented as a way of

writing poetry in the Italian vernacular. The psychological frame has a linguistic counterpart. The terza rima rhyming scheme forms a pattern of words (aba, bcb, cdc, and so on). The literary cadence of that rhyming scheme resonates with the back-and-forth dialogue that accompanied the resolution of opposites which occurred in his reflexive mode of containment.

- **Dialectical Narrative:** What gives this containment its reflexive nature is that Dante is both the contained and the container. The first narrative came from Dante-the-poet who wrote *La Commedia* with the aim of fulfilling the vow he made to himself after *La Vita Nuova*: that he would write of Beatrice as had been written of no other woman. The second narrative came from the literary character Dante-the-protagonist who makes a spiritual pilgrimage through Inferno, Purgatorio and Paradisio, with Virgil and Beatrice as guides. The third narrative came from the mental space where Dante-the-poet and Dante-the-protagonist engage in dialectical interactions that produce results in Dante's internal reality as well as in his external reality. In his internal reality, Dante learns to process his unassimilated state of mind, by making the journey through Inferno, Purgatorio and Paradisio. Externally, he produces the creative poetry in *La Commedia*, now regarded as the pre-eminent work in Italian literature, and one of the greatest works of world literature. The third narrative was inspirational poetry for humanity. The dialectical narrative produced the internationally acclaimed epic *La Commedia*, a literary accomplishment that may also be viewed as a psychological accomplishment. The three realms of Inferno, Purgatorio and Paradiso might be interpreted as three steps in the psyche's maturity, Inferno demonstrating the recognition of a projection, Purgatory the withdrawal of a projection, and Paradise the psychological maturity that follows.
- **Psychological Growth / Harm:** The dialectical interaction between Dante-the-poet and Dante-the-protagonist produced psychological growth in the sense that it ended with Dante having processed his unassimilated state of mind about courtly love. When he met Beatrice in Paradise, the energy from the emotional turmoil of his courtly love of her had been harnessed and re-purposed to create poetry for the benefit of humanity.

Viewed in the context of archetype as biological entity, Dante learned to process his projection by conducting his own introjection. From the perspective of archetype as emergent phenomenon, he learned to internalize his own appropriation. To do that, he constructed a literary device which enabled him to contribute the first narrative in his role as Dante-the-poet, as well as the second narrative in his role as Dante-the-protagonist. By sustaining a dialectical interaction between those two roles for about two decades, Dante generated a third narrative that gave the world *La Commedia*.

After the Containment Ended

Dante does not mention his wife Gemma Donati in any of his writings, nor is there any indication of discontent in the relationship between them (DAL 27). When Dante was exiled from Florence in 1301, Gemma and her children remained in Florence.

Around the time that he was completing *La Commedia*, Dante contracted malaria. Dante's daughter, Antonia, went to Ravenna to nurse him during his illness. Overwhelmed by the fever that accompanied malaria, Dante died in Ravenna in 1321. After he died, Antonia entered a convent in Ravenna, and took the name of Sister Beatrice (DAL 165). After Dante's death, Gemma relocated to Ravenna where she also entered a convent.

Paradisio, the third part of the *Commedia* trilogy was published posthumously. Despite Dante's status of being exiled from Florence for allegation of fraud, the trilogy *La Commedia* was well received when published in Italy, and has become a source of literary inspiration internationally.

Sources

The sources of information that I used in this chapter are:
- *"Dante: A Life"* by R. W. B. Lewis
- *"Love's Scribe: Reading Dante in the Book of Creation"* by Andrew Frisardi
- https://digitaldante.columbia.edu

- *"Containing States of Mind"* by Duncan Cartwright
- *"SYMBOLIZATION: Representation and Communication"* by James Rose (Editor)
- *"Conversations About Reflexivity"* by Margaret S. Archer (Editor)
- *"Projection and Re-Collection in Jungian Psychology"* by Marie-Louise von Franz
- *"Transforming Sexuality: The Archetypal World of Anima and Animus"* by Ann & Barry Ulanov.

CHAPTER 19

A Reflexive Mode of Containment Involving: Ludwig Van Beethoven & The Immortal Beloved

"My angel, my everything, my very self. ... Oh, wherever I am, you are with me, I talk to myself and to you, arrange [it] that I can live with you – what a life!!! As much as you love me, I love you even more deeply ... you know my faithfulness to you, never can another own my heart, never – never. ... What yearning with tears for you – you – you – my life – my everything. Farewell — oh continue to love me – never misjudge the most faithful heart of your Beloved L.

forever thine

forever mine

forever us"

– Ludwig van Beethoven

When Ludwig van Beethoven died in 1827, a letter to his unnamed 'Immortal Beloved' was found among his personal possessions. For the next one hundred and thirty years, biographers, researchers, and musical historians drove each other to distraction speculating and counter-speculating about the identity of his Immortal Beloved. While they speculated, Beethoven collectors hoarded a variety of items related to his life. The collector who broke the speculation was a Swiss physician named Hans Conrad Bodmer, owner of the largest private Beethoven collection. For decades, Bodmer hoarded Beethoven artifacts including furniture, legal documents, music sheets, conversation notebooks and letters. Protective of the privacy of his collection, Bodmer would not allow researchers to read Beethoven's letters. In his last will and testament, Bodmer bequeathed his collection to the Beethoven-House Association in Bonn, Germany, Beethoven's birthplace. The collection was made available to the public in 1957. Among the many letters found in Bodmer's collection were drafts of thirteen letters that Beethoven wrote to Countess Josephine von Brunsvik. Those letters had been obtained from Josephine's descendants. The similarity in wording to the Immortal Beloved letter convinced many researchers that Josephine was his Immortal Beloved. In addition, letters from Josephine to Beethoven supported the notion that she was his Immortal Beloved. The diary of Josephine's sister, Therese, further corroborated the relationship between Josephine and Beethoven. There were no records of Beethoven having any other romantic interest from 1812, when he wrote the 'Immortal Beloved' letter, up to 1827 when he died. At the time when Beethoven wrote the Immortal Beloved letter, he was hopeful that Josephine would initiate divorce proceedings against her estranged husband and marry him. He gave up that hope when he later realized that Josephine's estranged husband was an intermittent member of the marital household. Biographers, researchers, and musical historians have now found a new topic about which to speculate. Nine months after the Immortal Beloved letter, when Beethoven and Josephine are believed to have met accidentally in Prague, Josephine delivered a baby girl, whom she named Minona. Since Josephine and Beethoven were together on the date calculated for conception, while her estranged husband was living in a different country, the speculation is about whether Beethoven is Minona's father. Speculators point out that Minona bore a striking resemblance to youthful images of Beethoven. Like young Beethoven, the child Minona was musically gifted. Since she did not marry and had no children, there is no bloodline available for conducting a DNA test of paternity.

My interpretation is that Ludwig van Beethoven had a reflexive mode of containment during the 4-year period between 1812, when he wrote the 'Immortal Beloved' letter, and 1816 when he composed the Song Cycle 'Faraway Beloved'. Both the letter and the song cycle were intensely emotional communications. He kept the letter hidden in a desk drawer for the rest of his life. He published 'Faraway Beloved' in 1816. These two emotion-laden communications mark a period in Beethoven's life when he retreated from society into a self-imposed isolation that was, at the same time, a source of psychological distress and a period of fevered new musical composition. During the period from 1812 to 1816, Beethoven isolated himself from social interaction and refrained from piano concerts. Having no one to be a container, he became a container for himself. In what I describe as a reflexive mode of containment, he created an ongoing dialogue between the mental activity of Beethoven-the-lover and the mental activity of Beethoven-the-musician. An eventual outcome from that dialogue was a calm acceptance of the reality that Josephine would never be his wife. Another outcome was that he harnessed the energies which he had been pouring into romantic emotions and developed a resolution to apply those energies to an exploration of his full potential as an artist. Gradually, he shifted his attention from his personal life to focus on exploring his musical capabilities for the benefit of humanity. In his self-imposed isolation, there was no one to mirror his life … no other mind to provide mental scaffolding for psychological growth. So, he relied on himself. By developing a capacity for symbolic thought, he was able to construct meaning from his life experience. In the next two sections, I provide some background information about the lives of Beethoven and Josephine.

Background Information about Ludwig van Beethoven

Jan Caeyers is a conductor, a musicologist, and an expert on Beethoven. He wrote the biography "BEETHOVEN: A Life" which I found a useful source of information because it combines a knowledge of music with expertise about Beethoven. This biography is my main source of information about Beethoven. The Beethoven family was one of middle-class, respected musicians, when Ludwig van Beethoven was born in December 1770 in the city of Bonn, Germany. Grandfather Beethoven was Kapellmeister, court musical director, and father Beethoven was court musician. Young Ludwig was expected to become a musician. Biographers have not been able to find any record of a birth date for baby Ludwig. There is record of a Catholic baptism, dated 17 December. In the 18th century, it was customary to baptize a child one or two days after birth. So, his birthday may be a couple days before 17 December. There was speculation about the circumstances of Beethoven's birth. Since there is no record of his birth in Bonn, the speculation is that he was illegitimate, which might explain why it appears that Beethoven's father never fully accepted him. His mother had been away from Bonn months prior to his birth, and he had no middle name. These are contributing factors surrounding speculation of his illegitimacy.

Ludwig's parents, Johann and Maria, had seven children, three of whom lived beyond infancy: Ludwig, Karl and Johann. Their family life was difficult. It was his mother who was head of the household. A hardworking woman, she raised the children in a frugal manner, and took little joy in life. She held the view that marital bliss is short-lived, and marriage is prone to misery (BAL 16 – 17). Ludwig's father adopted a very disciplined approach to his music lessons, often boxing his ears and rapping his fingers when he made mistakes at the keyboard (BAL 17). Maria died of tuberculosis in 1787 when she was forty years old and Ludwig was seventeen. According to biographer Caeyers, Ludwig's father had a successful early career as a musician, but experienced decline when he lost his job as court musician, after which he projected his own failed musical ambitions onto his gifted son (BAL 10 - 11). Beethoven enjoyed playing the piano, but he preferred free improvisation which conflicted with his father's more disciplined approach (BAL 17). Ludwig's education went no further than primary school where pupils were instructed on basic principles of mathematics, literacy, religion and Latin (BAL 18).

The Beethoven's were commoners and they had no delusions about their station in life, nor about the availability of formal education for commoners. They understood that the best path in life for them was to pass accumulated skills from each generation to the next. Grandfather Louis had passed his musical skills onto father Johann, who passed on what he knew to son Ludwig. Ludwig's progress at the keyboard was so rapid that his father arranged his first public appearance when he was just seven years old. That was followed by regular private performances for music lovers in Bonn. These early successes must have had a large impact on the psyche of shy, introverted Ludwig (BAL 20). When Ludwig was ten years old, he dropped out of primary school to study music, beginning with church organist Christian Neefe as tutor. Ludwig had dedicated but mediocre musical teachers. His musical education lacked the technical background and a proper foundational structure, because his teachers were selected from those who happened to be available near the Beethoven residence in Bonn (BAL 21). Beethoven's instructors in Bonn had good academic intentions, but their approach was less scholastic and more improvisational, which explains how Beethoven learned to trust his imagination, which later became an essential ingredient in his compelling artistry (BAL 21 - 22).

Ludwig travelled from Bonn to Vienna in 1784, probably to get musical lessons from Mozart, or from the network of composers at the court in Vienna (BAL 43). He returned to Bonn in 1787, the year his mother died of consumption (BAL 46). At age seventeen, he took over responsibility for his two younger brothers because his father was too prone to alcoholism to be a functional father to his sons. In 1789, the father was forced to retire from his job at the Court in Bonn, due to his alcoholism, and there was an order that half of his pension be paid directly to Ludwig for support of the family. Ludwig contributed further to the family's income by teaching piano lessons. He did not like teaching, but it was necessary to support the family. Caeyers reports that commentators have expressed a view that the father experienced psychological problems, which may have originated in the contempt his own father had shown him (BAL 13). Although Ludwig bravely took responsibility for bringing up his brothers, there was always friction in his relations with them.

With help from musician Joseph Haydn in Vienna and some local Bonn citizens, Ludwig relocated to Vienna in 1792 to expand his musical horizon (BAL 63). He was twenty-one years old. Vienna was a modern, wealthy city whose population consisted of two layers: commoners and aristocrats. The commoners included merchants, lawyers, craftspeople, tradesmen, and civil servants, while the aristocrats included princes, barons, and counts (BAL 73). In Vienna, Haydn was Beethoven's tutor, and Viennese nobility became his patrons. He supplemented his income by offering piano lessons. Vienna is where he was professionally trained, and it is the city where he later established himself as Ludwig van Beethoven, the virtuoso pianist, and still later as a great composer during the transition from the Classical era to the Romantic era. Realizing that the Viennese attach great importance to appearance and attire, Beethoven bought himself some new clothing and a piano when he arrived in Vienna (BAL 77). He obtained accommodation in the home of Count Karl von Lichnowsky who would later become his first patron (BAL 79). While in Bonn, Beethoven's ambition had been to become Kapellmeister, court musical director, like his grandfather, but Vienna proved to be a competitive arena in spite of the fact that Vienna's famous musician, Mozart, had recently died (BAL 97 - 98). Beethoven developed his skills to become a respected concert pianist mainly for an audience of Viennese nobility. He also composed sonatas, string quartets and symphonies, which he dedicated to his patrons.

In May of 1799, Beethoven began giving piano lessons to the daughters of Hungarian Countess Anna von Brunsvik. Although he had an aversion to teaching, he enjoyed the company of Therese and Josephine. During this time, he fell in love with the younger daughter, Josephine. Countess Anna was a widow who had brought her daughters to Vienna to learn piano music from the well-known concert pianist Beethoven, as a way of increasing the girls' marriage prospects. Her interest was in finding wealthy aristocrats for sons-in-law. When the countess noticed an infatuation developing between Beethoven and Josephine, she quickly arranged for Josephine to be married to Count Joseph Deym, who ran a gallery trading in classical art works and wax portraits. Beethoven was disappointed, but he remained a friend of the Brunsvik family.

For six years leading up to 1802, Beethoven had been experiencing a gradual loss of hearing. This was a serious concern to him because hearing is the sense a musician needs most. According to his physician, Johann Schmidt, Beethoven had succumbed to a combination of internal and external pressures, to demons both physical and metaphysical (BAL 174). Schmidt recommended at least six months away from the city. On that advice, Beethoven decided to spend a six-month retreat, from April to October 1802, at a health spa in the Austrian town named

Heiligenstadt, where he tried to come to terms with his situation. During that time, he wrote the Heiligenstadt Testament, a letter to his younger brothers Carl and Johann. The letter reveals that Beethoven considered suicide, but instead made a resolution to devote his life to his art for the benefit of humanity. The letter was not delivered; it was found among documents hidden in his desk after his death. Beethoven stated his determination in the expression that he would 'seize Fate by the throat; it shall certainly not crush me completely'. Here are excerpts from the Heiligenstadt Testament taken from the web site ABC Classic:

> *"The Heiligenstadt Testament*
>
> *To my brothers Carl and [Johann] Beethoven*
>
> *Oh you men who think or say that I am malevolent, stubborn, or misanthropic, how greatly do you wrong me. ... (F)or six years now I have been hopelessly afflicted, ... Yet it was impossible for me to say to people, "Speak louder, shout, for I am deaf." Ah, how could I possibly admit an infirmity in the one sense which ought to be more perfect in me than others. ... But what a humiliation for me when someone standing next to me heard a flute in the distance and I heard nothing ... Such incidents drove me almost to despair; a little more of that and I would have ended me life - it was only my art that held me back. Ah, it seemed to me impossible to leave the world until I had brought forth all that I felt was within me. ... Divine One, thou seest my inmost soul thou knowest that therein dwells the love of mankind and the desire to do good. ... I declare you two to be the heirs to my small fortune ... Recommend virtue to your children ... Thanks to it and to my art, I did not end my life by suicide. Farewell and love each other ... With joy I hasten towards death. Come when thou wilt, I shall meet thee bravely.*
>
> Ludwig van Beethoven, Heiligenstadt,
> October 6th, 1802"
> – ABC Classic

While at Heiligenstadt wrestling with psychological distress over the loss of his hearing, Beethoven experienced a flash of insight that he called 'the new way' without having any explicit understanding of the expression. That insight guided him out of his distress and pointed him in a new direction. During six months of introspection at the 1802 retreat in Heiligenstadt, it dawned on him that 'the new way' for him would be about spending more energy on musical composition and less on performance as a concert pianist. Beethoven's hearing loss did not prevent him from composing music, but it made playing at concerts — an important source of income at that phase of his life — increasingly difficult. It also contributed substantially to his withdrawal into social isolation. Beethoven's return to Vienna from Heiligenstadt was marked by a change in musical style, that is characterized by 'a new way' in which he composed original works on a grand scale. An early major work employing this new style was the Third Symphony 'Eroica' (Hero). He composed the symphony between 1803 and 1804, based on the idea of creating a symphony about the career of Napoleon whom he regarded as a hero at the time. Beethoven, sympathetic to the ideal of the heroic, revolutionary leader, originally gave the symphony the title 'Bonaparte', but disillusioned by Napoleon declaring himself Emperor in 1804, he scratched Napoleon's name from the manuscript's title page, then published the symphony in 1806 with the title 'Eroica' (Hero) and the subtitle 'to celebrate the memory of a great man'. Eroica was longer and larger in scope than any previous symphony. When it premiered in early 1805, it received a mixed reception. Some listeners objected to its length or misunderstood its structure, while others viewed it as a masterpiece. Beethoven's Fifth Symphony 'Schicksals-Sinfonie' (Fate Symphony) was set in the style of emotions that arouse the kind of yearning that was central to romanticism. By 1810, Beethoven was regarded as one of the great composers in the era of Romanticism, on par with Joseph Haydn and Wolfgang Mozart. Some of his early patrons gave him annual stipends in addition to commissioning works for special occasions.

Josephine became a widow when Count Deym died in 1804. Beethoven began to visit her and resumed a romantic correspondence. Although he seemed to understand that Josephine did not wish to marry him, he continued writing letters to her even after she relocated to the Brunsvik family home in Budapest. Eventually, he accepted her refusal in an 1807 letter where he stated: 'I thank you for wishing still to appear as if I were not altogether banished from your memory'. As the connection between Beethoven and Josephine was fading, the European political scene was becoming hostile. While France was invading Austria in 1809, the Viennese nobility was leaving the city. That meant reduced income for Beethoven and disruptions to the publication of his musical compositions. During the occupation, Beethoven's output was reduced and his health suffered. In need of another retreat in summer of 1812, Beethoven decided to go to Teplitz (BAL 327). This initiated another period of psychological distress for Beethoven. The four-year period of psychological distress began in early July 1812 when, at the advice of his doctor, Beethoven retreated to Teplitz, a Bohemian spa town, for health reasons. He was going deaf, suffering from ill health, and worried about his finances. The doctor ordered him to take a restorative cure. For recuperation, he chose Teplitz where there are a natural lake, a forest and hot springs. On his way to Teplitz, he stopped in Prague for business. While in Prague, he accidentally encountered Josephine, who was there to meet with in-laws from her first marriage. The encounter must have rekindled their infatuation, because days afterwards, while in Teplitz, Beethoven wrote the impassioned 'Immortal Beloved' letter, while entertaining great hope of marrying Josephine as soon as she divorced her estranged husband. He did not mail the letter. He kept it until his death fifteen years later. The letter was found among documents hidden in his desk drawer. A comparison of that letter with other letters obtained by collectors from Brunsvik descendants revealed the identity of the Immortal Beloved as Josephine. Here is an excerpt from the letter, taken from "The Immortal Beloved Compendium" by John Klapproth:

> "My angel, my everything, my very self. ... Love demands
> everything and completely, and with good reason, that is how
> it is for me with you, and for you with me. ... Oh, wherever I
> am, you are with me, I talk to myself and to you, arrange [it]
> that I can live with you – what a life!!! As much as you love
> me, I love you even more deeply ... you know my faithfulness
> to you, never can another own my heart, never – never. ...
> Be patient, only through quiet contemplation of our existence
> can we achieve our purpose to live together. What yearning
> with tears for you – you – you – my life – my everything.

Farewell — oh continue to love me – never misjudge the most faithful heart of your Beloved L.

forever thine

forever mine

forever us."

— Ludwig van Beethoven (IBC 11 - 16)

Soon after writing the Immortal Beloved letter, Beethoven's hope of marriage to Josephine evaporated when he realized that she had resumed her relationship with her estranged second husband. Nine months after the meeting in Prague, when Josephine gave birth to a daughter, Beethoven must have realized he could be the father — a father who could not acknowledge his child because of fear of scandal. The lost opportunity for marriage to his beloved and the arrival of a daughter he could not acknowledge must have been severe blows to his masculine pride, that further eroded his emotional wellbeing. Those events contributed to Beethoven's further isolation of himself from society. Having nobody functioning as a container for him, he became a container for himself. He divided his outlook into two perspectives that enabled him to sustain a 4-year dialogue in a reflexive mode of containment. The two perspectives were those of Beethoven-the-lover and Beethoven-the-musician.

In early 1813, Beethoven went through a difficult emotional period, and his compositional output dropped. He was almost completely deaf by 1814, and so he gave up public performance as a concert pianist and as a conductor. His brother Kaspar died from tuberculosis in November 1815, after which Beethoven became involved in a legal dispute with Kaspar's wife, Johanna, about custody of their nine-year-old son, Karl. Kaspar had written in his will that his brother and his wife should have joint custody of Karl. That legal responsibility drained Beethoven emotionally and financially before he was able to remove Karl from Johanna's custody in January 1816, and enroll him in a private school. Beethoven's efforts at being a good uncle were often experienced by Karl as overbearing behavior.

Beethoven made his last public appearances as a soloist in May 1814.

From that time onward, he used ear-trumpets to amplify sound for the purpose of conversation. In 1815, he continued musical composition, but his interest and his energy flagged because he was finding himself at odds with the customs of traditional classical music. Because of his deafness, Beethoven began to use what he called 'conversation books' for communicating with others. These notebooks provide a rich source of information about his life after he became deaf. They contain discussions about music, business, and personal life. They are also a valuable source for his contacts and for investigations into how he intended his music to be performed, also of his opinions of the art of music.

Four years after the Immortal Beloved letter, Beethoven wrote a Song Cycle titled 'An die ferne Geliebte' (Faraway Beloved). That Song Cycle is regarded as autobiographical because it is about Beethoven's emotion-driven need to make changes in his life. One change related to Josephine. His expectations of her were changing from fevered desire for her as a marriage partner to a calm acceptance of her as a platonic friend. A parallel change was the direction of his musical artistry. The dialogue between Beethoven-the-lover and Beethoven-the-musician enabled a gradual shift from being in a rut where he was limited to embellishments of traditional classical music, to a larger sphere of musical options where he created original classical music. Throughout the 4-year period, Josephine stayed on the periphery of Beethoven's life. She did not become a container for him. Instead, he became a container for himself by separating his mental processing into two perspectives. By making that distinction, he was able to engage in a reflexive dialogue between the two perspectives. In 1816, his dialogue about his psychological distress revealed some insight embodied in the Song Cycle (Faraway Beloved). In his summary of the six songs, musicologist Caeyers offers a succinct expression that, in my opinion, captures a symbol for Beethoven's insight in Song Cycle ... 'bridge the gulf of distance and time'. The gulf between Beethoven and Josephine would now take a back seat, while the gulf between Beethoven and humankind would take a front seat. He would accept the loss of love and re-direct his energies toward using his art as a communication to humanity.

Beethoven started the year 1821 with health issues of jaundice and rheumatism. As the year progressed, other issues arose. Josephine died in

March that year and he grieved the loss of his Immortal Beloved. By the autumn of 1821, he had additional problems. Financially, he was doing badly because the aristocrats who used to support him had left Vienna, and the commoners had little interest in his music (BAL 145). Another source of worry was conflict with his brother and his nephew. He further isolated himself from society, while he struggled to finish musical compositions in time for scheduled publication dates. He neglected his personal grooming. His appearance was so unkempt that the police arrested him believing him to be a tramp. Although he told the police he was Beethoven the famous musician, they did not believe him. Next day, the musical director of Wiener Neustadt identified Beethoven and police released him (IBC 125).

Years before, in Heiligenstadt, Beethoven had decided to accept a life of personal suffering and devote himself to his highest potential as an artist. In the intervening years he produced sonatas, symphonies, an opera, string quartets and works of chamber music (BAL 146). After ten years of striving for the highest potential in his art, he thought of his work as being closer to mediocrity than anything approaching genius. A commission offered by the Philharmonic Society of London, at the end of 1822, improved Beethoven's financial situation. In November, the Society offered him a commission for a symphony. He was grateful because he thought the Society would be an appropriate home for the Ninth Symphony (Ode To Joy) on which he was working. Beethoven's 'Ode To Joy' premiered in Vienna in 1824 (BAL 482). It was known as the Choral Symphony, because unlike other symphonies, it has a choir singing lyrics at the end of the composition. Michael Umlauf was the conductor at the premiere performance. In spite of his diminished hearing, Beethoven insisted on participating. As a courtesy, Umlauf agreed to include Beethoven on stage, but he made a prior arrangement with the orchestra that they should follow him regardless of what Beethoven did during the performance (BAL 486). The performance went well, but when the orchestra stopped playing, Beethoven continued to wave his arms about as if conducting. Unable to hear the music, he was unaware that it had stopped. A soloist walked up to him and turned his body around so he could see the audience applauding wildly (BAL 486). That was the last public concert for Beethoven.

In December of 1826, illness struck Beethoven. His symptoms included fever, swollen limbs, coughing and breathing difficulties. There was an abnormal build-up of fluid in his abdomen and his feet (BAL 533). Abdominal punctures and drainage were not enough to save him (BAL 533). As the news of Beethoven's diminishing health spread, friends and colleagues sent tributes and gifts. The Philharmonic Society in London sent a case of expensive wine of excellent vintage from Schotts. When the wine arrived, a bedridden Beethoven murmured "*Pity – too late*." On 24 March, a priest was summoned to administer last rites (BAL 537). Beethoven died on 26 March 1827 at the age of 56 (BAL 538 – 539). An autopsy indicated that Beethoven had liver damage, possibly due to his alcohol consumption. There was also damage to his auditory nerves. Beethoven's funeral procession in Vienna on 29 March 1827 was attended by an estimated ten thousand people. Six years after Josephine's death in 1821, Beethoven's assistant Anton Schindler chose to have him buried next to Josephine's grave at Wahring Cemetery, because Beethoven had developed a habit of spending time at her grave (IBC 125).

Throughout his life, Beethoven developed musical themes that depict the human struggle in both the external world and the internal world. He was a transitional figure from the era of Enlightenment into the era of Romanticism, where there was a focus on viewing personal life and art as an organic whole. Biographer and musicologist Caeyers regards Beethoven as having elevated musical composition from craftsman level to artist level (BAL xxi).

Background Information about 'Immortal Beloved' – Josephine von Brunsvik

Josephine von Brunsvik was born into a family of Hungarian aristocrats in March 1779. Her parents, Anton and Anna, were raising their family in a castle named Martonvasar near Budapest. When Count Anton died in 1792, Countess Anna was left to take care of four children: Therese, Franz, Josephine and Charlotte. Their ages ranged from 17 to 10 years. Countess Anna kept up the tradition of private education for the children in literature, languages and music. Interested in securing wealthy aristocratic sons-in-law, she took her daughters Therese and Josephine to Vienna to study piano for improving their marriage prospects. For a piano teacher, Countess Anna chose Beethoven, who was a well-known pianist in 1799. Beethoven developed a friendship with the Brunsvik family and often stayed longer than the time scheduled for piano lessons. Soon, it came to Countess Anna's attention that there was an infatuation developing between Beethoven and Josephine. She quickly arranged for her daughter to marry Count Joseph Deym, who was about twice Josephine's age. It turns out that Count Deym had misrepresented his financial affairs, but he and Josephine settled into a comfortable relationship. When Josephine was pregnant with their fourth child, Count Deym died of pneumonia in January 1804.

Josephine felt overwhelmed by the combined responsibilities of pregnancy, education of the children, operation of a gallery, and management of their real estate portfolio. She reached out to her friend Beethoven who rushed to her side to comfort her by offering musical solace. Beethoven wanted to marry her, but Countess Josephine declined because she would lose custody of her aristocratic children if she married a commoner. Other reasons for declining were that she could not envision Beethoven being a stepfather to her children, and the Brunsvik family pressured her to avoid marriage to him (BJB 53 - 56). To explain her feelings, Josephine wrote a letter to Beethoven informing him that platonic affection and respect at a distance were all she could offer. Here is an excerpt from the letter written by Josephine in response to Beethoven in 1805 (IBC 213):

> "My heart you have won long ago, dear Beethoven ... The greatest proof of my love ... my respect you receive, by this confession, by this my trust! ... It is what ennobles you the most. — The fact that you appreciate it – that you know the value of the possession, the most precious possession of my self, which I hereby assure you – you will show to me – if you are satisfied with this – Do not tear my heart apart — — Do not further insist – My love of you is unspeakable – like a pious mind loves another one – Are you not capable of such an alliance? — I am not now susceptible to any other kind of love" (IBC 213).

In 1809, Josephine hired Estonian Baron Christoph von Stackelberg, a proponent of the popular Pestalozzi method of educating children by involving head, hand and heart. About a year after taking on the role of educator of her children, Stackelberg declared that he could continue the education of her sons only as Josephine's husband, because he loved her (BJB 79). The Brunsvik family was opposed to such a marriage because he was not a Catholic, he was a stranger to them, and of lower social status. It turns out that Josephine was already pregnant with his child, having been seduced by him. Josephine kept her pregnancy secret and gave birth to Maria in December 1809. Countess Anna reluctantly approved the marriage so that Maria would have a father. In 1910, the wedding was arranged in a remote Hungarian town. There were no guests at the wedding. The marriage produced a second daughter, Theophile, in 1811. The marriage was a disappointment from both spousal and educational perspectives (BJB 80 – 81). As a spouse, Stackelberg was egocentric, tyrannical, short-tempered, and a poor manager of finances. As an educator, he was inclined to theorize about abstract concepts instead of providing practical guidance to the children. Overall, he had an oppressive effect on the entire household. Although Stackelberg gave the impression of striving to live up to his Protestant principles, Josephine's sister, Therese, experienced his influence as a lack of God's blessing upon the whole house (BJB 80). Josephine suffered emotionally and grew sickly. The marital relationship was strained due to arguments about the education of the children and about the family's financial situation. When Stackelberg failed to pay his share in a joint financing for a purchase of real estate, it resulted in a significant loss for Josephine, and the hardship that followed strained the marriage to the point of separation. According to biographer Tellenbach, Josephine later stated that she never loved Stackelberg, and never wanted to marry him, but that he had forced her to give herself to him through tricks of seduction (BJB 78). In 1812, there was a separation. Some biographers believe that Josephine kicked him out of the residence, while others believe he abandoned her because Josephine refused to give him money for his personal use.

In July of 1812, Josephine took a trip to Prague to request financial help for her children. She went to see Deym in-laws from her first marriage. She also planned to see the emperor who, on the death of her first husband, had promised to help her. While in Prague, she encountered Beethoven, who was there on business. When they accidentally met, they got together to catch up on each other's lives. Beethoven wanted her to start divorce proceedings against her estranged husband and marry him. There is no indication of her being willing to marry him. However, nine months later, Josephine gave birth to a baby girl whom she named Minona. Since her husband was estranged at the time of conception, Josephine hid the pregnancy from society and gave baby Minona to her sister Therese for childcare. In her diary, Therese noted that Minona was entrusted to her care soon after birth. Because Josephine showed no interest in the child, Therese had to obtain a goat from a local farm to get milk for Minona.

There is justified speculation that Beethoven may be the father of Minona. When they met accidentally in Prague, Beethoven and Josephine may have given in to their infatuation for each other. In a romantic romp, they may have conceived a child. She might have considered herself free from marital vows due to estrangement from her husband. Beethoven might have thought that the estrangement would be followed by divorce. My thought is that Minona was not a love child. If Minona had been a love child, Josephine would have cherished the child. Since Josephine took no interest in the child, my guess is that Beethoven probably forced himself on her in the hope of claiming her as his own and precipitating a divorce. The 1812 encounter in Prague had been his third attempt to convince her to marry him. She had already explained that she would not marry him because she would lose custody of her children.

Stackelberg returned to Vienna in 1814 to ask Josephine to go with him to live in Estonia. When she refused, he left Vienna. The following year, when Stackelberg acquired an inheritance from a deceased relative, he returned to Vienna to persuade Josephine to relocate to Estonia. Again, she refused. Angrily, Stackelberg filed a police report accusing her of being an unfit mother, and claiming that there was incestuous activity among her children. On the grounds of those claims, he obtained help from the Viennese police to remove his three children from Josephine's house. The Brunsvik family thought he had taken the children to Estonia, his country of origin. Left to take care of the four Deym children on her own, Josephine rented out rooms in the large Deym house to earn income. For education of the children, she hired Baron von Andrian-Werburg (BAL 122). She succumbed to his charms, became pregnant, and gave birth to her eight child, Emilie, in September 1815. During her pregnancy, she hid in a hut to avoid a scandal about an illegitimate child. Josephine dismissed Andrian, and handed over his illegitimate daughter Emilie to his care. Andrian accepted the responsibility, however, little Emilie died of measles before reaching her second birthday.

Deacon Franz Leyer in Bohemia wrote Josephine in December 1815 to inform her that he had her three young daughters in his custody, and that Stackelberg had left the children at his parsonage without providing money for their support. Josephine and sister Therese quickly arranged to collect the children from the parsonage, but they arrived too late. Stackelberg's brother removed the children before the sisters could collect them. The fact that he deposited the children in a parsonage implies that taking the children from their home was an act of vengefulness … Stackelberg was not interested in the education or care of the children. According to Tellenbach's research, the children were housed in the woods, where they spent their time learning and playing the piano. Stackelberg did not take them to his family home in Estonia. He also tried to take from Josephine's care the children from her first marriage, but the Brunsvik family intervened to prevent their removal.

Josephine became sick, bedridden and lonely in 1820. Her teenage children from her first marriage had left home to pursue their interests. Her brother Franz stopped sending her money. Her loyal sister Therese withdrew. Her mother, Countess Anna, was judgmental about what she considered to be Josephine's unfortunate life choices. Josephine died on March 1821 and was buried without any ceremony at Wahring Cemetery (IBC 125). She was forty-two years old. There was no headstone to mark her grave, nor any inscription to inform history of her existence. The Brunsvik family imposed their wishes to avoid including her in a family plot. The archive of the Brunsvik family tree does not list Josephine among her siblings.

The containment model is built on the principles of projection and introjection. Because projections occur when archetypes are activated, I describe the relationship between Beethoven and Josephine as mediated by an archetype. To do that, I rely on the two definitions of archetypes: first in the context of archetype-as-biological-entity, then, in the context of archetype-as-emergent-phenomenon.

Context of Archetype as Biological Entity: Projection & Introjection

Viewed as a biological entity, an archetype is regarded as an ancestral heritage of human experience accumulated over many generations and located in collective unconsciousness. In the context of archetype as a biological entity, the processes that psychologists identify for converting life's experiences to meaning are projection and introjection. Projection is an evacuation of unconscious content from the psyche due to an unbearable state of mind. There was a projection cast from Beethoven's mind to Josephine's mind. The content of the projection was an idealization of womanhood. The projection arose from the anima archetype. Introjection is a transformation of an unbearable state of mind to a bearable state of mind, followed by its integration into conscious content of the psyche. Although they bonded on a shared interest in music and they kept in touch over several years, Beethoven and Josephine did not have a containment. She kept him at a platonic distance. After years of trying to get her to become his wife, he came to accept that, in the interest of keeping custody of her children, who were aristocrats, she would not consider marrying him, a commoner. Without a container for his projection, Beethoven divided his mental process into two perspectives that enabled him to engage in what I propose as a reflexive mode of containment.

Activation of the anima archetype was initiated by Beethoven's infatuation with Josephine. Josephine did not become a container of his projection, due to a number of factors. One factor was that the Brunsvik family pressured her to avoid a relationship with Beethoven because they were aristocrats and he was a commoner. Another factor was that Josephine could not imagine him as a stepfather to her children because his temperament was overbearing, erratic, and eccentric ... characteristics that are not conducive to good parenting. Josephine valued education, which was not one of his strengths. Beethoven's formal education ended at primary school. His education was limited compared with what she wanted for her children. The most important factor contributing to her refusal of his marriage proposal was that she would lose custody of her children if she married Beethoven. Josephine explained her feelings in a letter to Beethoven informing him that platonic affection and respect at a distance were all she could offer. Her explanation that she loves him 'like a pious mind loves another one' is an indication that she was not emotionally engaged, but he continued to hope. His projection lingered.

I believe Beethoven became a container for himself. All the modes of containment in the Bion-Cartwright model involve two minds, two people. In conducting the research for this book, I have come to believe there are some people who can function as their own container. To include those people, I propose adding a reflexive mode of containment to the model, while acknowledging my respect to Bion and Cartwright. On reading the literature about Beethoven, I observed that he separated his mental activity into two parallel streams. In one stream, his outlook was that of Beethoven-the-lover. In the other stream, his outlook was that of Beethoven-the-musician. Beethoven-the-lover and Beethoven-the-musician engaged in a sustained dialectical interaction that enabled a shifting of energy from the projection to the composition of original classical music. In a reflexive mode of containment, he managed his own unbearable state of mind. He identified his projection, withdrew it and harnessed the energy for creative musical composition. The four years between writing 'Immortal Beloved' and composing 'Faraway Beloved' marked a period of introjection for Beethoven. By separating his mental processing into two roles he was able to conduct an ongoing dialogue about opposite points of view: pay attention to the unavailable Immortal Beloved or pay attention to his art. I believe Beethoven-the-lover and Beethoven-the-musician engaged in a reflexive dialogue to consider what he would do with his life going forward. The result of the introjection was a shift of attention from his personal life to his professional life. In the interval between his writing the 'Immortal Beloved' letter and his composition of the 'Faraway Beloved' song cycle, Beethoven withdrew his projection from Josephine, harnessed the energy of his desire for her and channeled it into musical creativity. He functioned as his own container. Seen from the perspective of archetype as biological entity, Beethoven's projection was transformed from romantic disappointment to a creative development in his career. The turning point is noticeable in the Song Cycle which represents a process of change. I believe Beethoven's projection was broken during the writing of the Song Cycle. In a later section, I use the 'Immortal Beloved' letter and the 'Faraway Beloved' song cycle to describe the symbolization that I believe occurred during the dialogue between Beethoven-the-lover and Beethoven-the-musician.

Context of Archetype as Emergent Phenomenon: Appropriation & Internalization

In the context of emergence, an archetype is viewed as an emergent property of a dynamic, developmental system that is made up of the human body including the brain, the society's external environment and the narrative competence of the humans involved. Viewed as an emergent phenomenon, an archetype does not exist in any particular location; it is pervasive across the cultural environment. When psychologists define an archetype as an emergent phenomenon, the processes they identify for converting experience into meaning are appropriation and internalization. Appropriation is an adoption of conscious content from social and cultural sources in the external environment. For example, the acquisition of language is an appropriation. Children appropriate the language of the culture in the environment where they grow up. When adults travel to a new country and become emersed in a new culture, they appropriate the language of the culture in the new environment. Beethoven's appropriation from the external environment was an idealization of womanhood. In the Viennese culture, an ideal woman was a beautiful, educated aristocrat, who is appreciative of classical music, speaks more than one language, and is a gracious hostess. Josephine fit Beethoven's appropriation of womanhood from the Viennese culture. Internalization is the incorporation of a cultural appropriation into one's mental model. Beethoven's appropriation was not compatible with his mental model. He and Josephine belonged to different social classes, at a time when inter-class marriage between commoners and aristocrats was not considered acceptable. Her family pressured her to avoid a romantic relationship with him because of the difference in status. She was educated by private tutors, while his formal education ended at primary school level. She lived in a castle with servants, while he took his meals in public cafes. Her family had financial resources to support their luxurious lifestyle, while he had to depend on the patronage of Viennese nobility. Beethoven's appropriation did not fit into the mental model of his existence. His appropriation was based on a desire that was unattainable.

Beethoven was simultaneously hopeful and fearful. He hoped that his beloved would not walk away from him. He was fearful because his fate was in her hands. He grappled with opposites of hope and fear about a situation that he could not control. His fear was realized when she did not file for divorce and her estranged husband returned to the marital household. Beethoven was burdened by a desire for a beloved who had passed up yet another opportunity to share a life with him. This may have reminded Beethoven of an earlier time in his life when he grappled with the opposites of life and death. At that time, he had retreated to the health spa in Heiligenstadt, to contemplate what to do with his life as a musician who was losing his hearing. His despair was so great he had considered suicide. At the time, Beethoven grappled with opposite sides of his dilemma. If he committed suicide, he would end his suffering, but he would lose the opportunity to develop his full capabilities as a musician. If he continued to live, he would suffer the loss of hearing and isolation from society, but he would have the opportunity to exercise his artistic capabilities to the fullest extent. After fighting with the opposite sides of that dilemma for 6 months in Heiligenstadt, he learned an important lesson. He learned that he could harness energy from a major setback and turn it to his advantage. Instead of giving up on life, he decided to transition from a career as a concert pianist to a musical composer. For the next 10 years, from 1802 to 1812, he produced a flurry of traditional classical compositions.

In 1812, Beethoven was experiencing another setback. He lost the love of his life and he was chafing under the rules of traditional classical composition. This time, he took a health retreat to the town of Teplitz. Since he had no one to be a container for him, I believe that he engaged in a reflexive mode of containment where a sustained dialogue between Beethoven-the-lover and Beethoven-the-musician processed his unbearable state of mind. Between 1812 and 1816, he harnessed the energies of the disappointment about not being able to marry Josephine and turned it to his advantage in his career development. The activation of the anima archetype inspired him to turn his disappointment with the beloved into energies that fueled a career transformation. Up until that time, Beethoven had been building his musical career according to the rules of traditional classical music, with some embellishments. After the 1812 – 1816 period, he departed from traditional classical music and gave himself the liberty of creating a 'new musical grammar' for the composition of contemporary classical music. By the end of the 4-year period, he had harnessed his disappointment in love and channeled his energies to fashion a new, original way of composing classical music. One example of his creativity after 'Faraway Beloved' was his 'new musical grammar' which he used to compose classical music in a contemporary style consistent with the approaching era of Romanticism. Another example of creativity after the 4-year period bracketed by 'Immortal Beloved' and 'Faraway Beloved' was that he developed the ability to use his mind's ear to compose music while deaf. He composed his Ninth Symphony 'Ode To Joy' without hearing it played by instruments. Intentionally, he gave up the pleasures of the company of society, retreated from public performances, isolated himself and exercised his art for the benefit of humanity. Seen from the perspective of archetype as emergent phenomenon, Beethoven's appropriation was transformed from romantic love to a creative development in his career. The turning point is noticeable in the Song Cycle which represents a process of change. I believe Beethoven's appropriation was dissolved during the writing of the Song Cycle. In the next section, I use the 'Immortal Beloved' letter and the 'Faraway Beloved' song cycle to describe the symbolization that I believe occurred during the dialogue between Beethoven-the-lover and Beethoven-the-musician.

Converting Experience to Meaning: Symbolization

Psychologists in both archetype-as-biological-entity and archetype-as-emergent-phenomenon camps agree that the capacity for symbolic thought is essential to a successful containment, that is, a containment in which psychological growth occurs. The letters between Beethoven and Josephine provide access to direct communications that occurred between them. "Beethoven: A Life" by Jan Caeyers and "Beethoven and His 'Immortal Beloved' Josephine Brunsvik" by Marie-Elisabeth Tellenbach are my sources for letters between Beethoven and Josephine.

During the period 1812 through 1816, Beethoven experienced a life-changing transition in his outlook The trend to that conclusion was clear. He loved her with desire for a union when she was single, but her mother intervened. His love was rekindled when she became a widow, but their difference in social status and pressure from the Brunsvik family prevented a union. His love was re-animated when her second husband was estranged, but again circumstances prevented a union. His terminology indicates that his thoughts about her changed. In 1812, she was his 'Immortal Beloved'. By 1816, she had become his 'Faraway Beloved'. In 1816, Beethoven no longer harbored the illusion of perfect love with his ideal woman (BAL 404). His projection to Josephine was broken when he finally accepted that his beloved did not want him as a life partner. The treatment of Josephine as his Faraway Beloved seems to say that his acceptance of the situation freed him from a consuming romantic passion, enabling him to accept her as a platonic friend. This turning point in his relationship with Josephine is seen in the Song Cycle "An Die Ferne Geliebte" (To The Faraway Beloved). The Song Cycle was composed by a medical student named Alois Jeitteles and believed to be commissioned and later personalized by Beethoven (BAL 405).

There is a web site, JSTOR (Journal Storage), that is a digital library for journals in the humanities. At that web site, I found an article which provides information about the meaning of the expression 'Song Cycle' during Beethoven's lifetime. The article is "The Antecedents of Beethoven's Liederkreis" was written by Luise Eitel Peake. She explains that the 19th century use of the German word 'Liederkreis' was a social circle or a club of people who get together to sing. Since Lieder means poems as well as songs, Liederkreis can refer to a literary salon or musical group. Peake also states that in Beethoven's lifetime, a Song Cycle was a collections of poems or songs written for the 'furtherance of sociability'. In a Song Cycle, all the songs relate to the same topic, but the tempo changes across songs. A Song Cycle was written as a single musical composition, with the motif present in the first song returning in the last song, thereby closing the circle. Beethoven is credited with using the song cycle to break new ground by setting a model of composition for Romantic composers, such as Schubert and Brahms (BAL 405). All six songs of 'Faraway Beloved' are linked together in a transitional arrangement, where all of the melodies are derived from motifs present in the first song (BAL 406). The initial imagery of the first song returns in the song at the end of the cycle.

Beethoven's Song Cycle was composed in April 1816. Biographer Caeyers sees the Song Cycle as an ending of a 4-year period when Beethoven changed his outlook from one of harboring hopes of becoming husband to Josephine, his ideal woman, to an outlook of mutual, amicable, platonic friendship (BAL 404). My reading of the Song Cycle is that it shows Beethoven grappling with opposite ends of a dilemma, where he relinquishes hope for a passionate love interest by refashioning his unspent romantic energies into a novel approach for composing music. Here is Caeyers' prose summary of the six songs in the Song Cycle 'Faraway Beloved' (BAL 405):

> "The cycle's subject matter speaks for itself: after first lamenting the separation from, and subsequent longing for the absent beloved, the devoted poet goes on in the second song to measure the distance between them in terms of mountains, valleys and forests. The third song is an entreaty to the birds, clouds, and rivers to communicate his aching and painful longing to her; in the fourth, he begs the same birds, clouds and rivers to transport him instead, that he might embrace her himself. Although the month of May unifies all things living (and loving – such as the birds), the fifth song tells of how this joy is denied him. Lastly, the poet dispatches the songs themselves to his beloved in the hopes that she will sing them and thus bridge the gulf of distance and time by which they are separated" (BAL 405).

I think Caeyers' expression 'bridge the gulf of distance and time' captures the symbol that arose in the dialogue between Beethoven-the-lover and Beethoven-the-musician, during the writing of the Song Cycle. The bridge is neither literal nor logical. It is about change. It points in a direction that is unknown at the time Beethoven wrote the Song Cycle ... it is a vague notion of bridging an unspecified gulf. In time, that bridge turned out to have two meanings. One is about the gulf of distance and time between him and Josephine. The other is about the gulf of distance and time between him and humanity. A comparison of the 'Immortal Beloved' letter and the 'Faraway Beloved' song cycle reveals a changing state of mind. The letter is a fevered, emotion-laden hope for an event – marriage – that faces insurmountable obstacles. The song is a grace-ful, dignified acceptance of an existing gulf between an outlook that is being transformed from the personal to the humanitarian. The bridge in 'Faraway Beloved' could not be summoned. Nor calculated. Nor ratio-nalized. Rather, the symbol of the bridge emerged during the dialogue between Beethoven-the-lover and Beethoven-the-musician. The notion of bridging the gulf was a symbol pointing in the direction of change, without any specifics of what the change might entail. The notion of bridging the gulf expressed itself in the images of the Song Cycle.

In "A Critical Dictionary of Jungian Analysis" psychologist Andrew Samuels and others explain that symbols are captivating pictorial statements ... enigmatic portrayals of movement stirring the psyche. From the point of view of Analytical Psychology, a symbol is defined in terms of concept, intent, purpose and content. The symbol emerged during Beethoven's transition from unbearable to bearable state of mind, while he was com-posing the Song Cycle. Here I explain the symbol in terms of concept, intent, purpose and content.

- **Concept:** The expression 'bridge the gulf of distance and time' embodies a concept about transformation. In Beethoven's life-time, a song cycle pointed to an advance in ideas ... a change in thinking ... a furtherance of sociability. The change across the songs was more important than the words of any of the six songs. The process of change was primary. At first, Beethoven did not know what bridging the gulf would turn out to be. The bridge was not something he could summon, rather it emerged out of the dialogue between Beethoven-the-lover and Beethoven-the-musician. The concept that underpins 'bridge the gulf of distance and time' came to be expressed in Song Cycle images that emerged from his dissatisfactions with his love life, and his musical career. The images took the form of messages being carried in song form by birds across forests and rivers and mountains. He needed a change. The symbolic process began with Beethoven feeling stuck with an unsatisfying love life and an uncertain career, then gave way to transformation. When the symbol emerged, it pointed a way to get out of being stuck. The symbol was not an instrument of rationality; it was an encapsulation of Beethoven's psychological situation at that point in time. His drive to find a way to 'bridge the gulf of distance and time' guided the direction of his emotional life from a failed husband-to-be to a platonic friend. It also guided his career from a rule-bound traditional classical musician to a creator of a new musical grammar. The Song Cycle indicates that he placed his confidence in Fate or Divine Providence to help him construct a bridge for the gulf in distance and time.

- **Intent:** Behind the symbol 'bridge the gulf of distance and time' was an intent to redefine his identity and his lifestyle. Fate was forcing him to give up being a failed husband-to-be, but he was not sure what he would become instead. He had a general hope of being able to continue a musical career, because he did not believe he had exercised all his musical capabilities. The intent behind the symbol was to find a way of exploring the musical capabilities he had not used yet. It took four years of dialogue with himself to realize he did not have to comply with the rules of traditional classical music. Fate pushed him in a new direction ... improvisation by creating a new grammar for musical composition.

- **Purpose:** The symbol 'bridge the gulf of distance and time' served the purpose of releasing Beethoven from the pain of longing for a marital relationship that would not become a reality. It also released him from the pain of being stuck in a role of compliance with rules of traditional classical music. The purpose that the symbol served was not merely to come up with an alternative point of view. Nor was the purpose of the symbol to work out a logical derivation of a solution to the conflict. The purpose that the symbol served was to reveal a new musical role through the back-and-forth dialogue of opposing sides of traditional classical music versus a desire to explore new capabilities. That dialogue led him to a new musical grammar.

- **Content:** The content of the symbol 'bridge the gulf of distance and time' included a new order of priorities and a new meaning of life for Beethoven. It dislodged him from feeling stuck in his roles of lover without his beloved and musician without his hearing. He no longer lived with the dwindling possibility of ever sharing a life with Josephine. It also dislodged him from the limitations of performing in public according to the rules of traditional classical music. The content of the symbol opened up to him in the dialogue between Beethoven-the-lover and Beethoven-the-musician and was articulated in the subtlety of the Song Cycle. According to the dictionary of terms in Analytical Psychology, a symbol is 'pregnant with meaning' that presents a challenge to thoughts and feelings. A way of discerning the meaning is to examine the symbol as it is expressed in images that control, order and give meaning to people's lives. The isolation that Beethoven imposed on himself, due to his loss of hearing, provided the psychological frame to put time and effort into introspection about the possibility of a viable future as a deaf musician. During that introspection, he composed the Song Cycle 'Faraway Beloved' whose imagery formed the symbol of bridging the gulf of distance and time as something without a literal name stirring in the psyche. It turned out to be an image that was instrumental in controlling, ordering and giving meaning to his future as a composer. The symbol 'bridge the gulf of distance and time' gave new order and meaning to Beethoven's life by being instrumental in the management of his unrepresented state of mind. Feeling rejected in love combined with being stalled in a career rut constituted an unrepresented state of mind, which he decided would not dictate his future state of mind. By sustaining the dialogue between Beethoven-the-lover and Beethoven-the-musician, he was able to re-purpose the energies of the activated anima archetype, by shifting his attention from disappointment about his Immortal Beloved to an exploration of his untested musical capabilities. The sustained dialogue moved him from feeling stuck as a rejected lover and spent musician to becoming one of the creative geniuses of his generation. Instead of relying on public performances as a source of income, he wrote and published original musical compositions. He also created a new grammar for contemporary classical music which later contributed to the new style of music in the Romantic Era. In addition, he created original compositions such as his Ninth Symphony (Ode To Joy), which the European Union later adopted as its anthem. The symbol 'bridge the gulf of distance and time' took the form of images that enabled Beethoven to give new meaning to his life by turning his attention from the personal to the humanitarian.

The psychological growth that Beethoven achieved can be seen in his behavior after the 4-year period of containment. His pursuit of Josephine subsided, indicating his projection was broken. His attention turned from a preoccupation with her embodiment of his idealized womanhood to a preoccupation with activities that expanded his consciousness to include intuition, imagination and creativity. To explore his artistic capabilities for the benefit of humanity, Beethoven relied on a psychological space that was more mental than physical. He relied more on his mind than his skill with instruments. His isolation from society was his workshop. According to Caeyers, Beethoven's ideas took shape and gradually developed into coherent music without any logical sequence of activity (BAL 186). During the 4-year period of isolation and introspection between 1812 and 1816, Beethoven was already deaf, as a result of which he stopped using the piano to explore new musical possibilities and used his mind instead. I see that 4-year period as the time of his reflexive mode of containment. The containment ended with his writing of the Song Cycle. After the Song Cycle, his musical output consisted of combinations of stored memories and a vision for the future (BAL 414). He also broke with traditional classical music. In the past, he had demonstrated a propensity for improvisational stylings in piano music, which was an embellishment of traditional, classical musical grammar (BAL 182). A change was noticeable. After the Song Cycle, he began composing original themes instead of embellishing well-known melodies. He replaced recurring themes with stepwise constructions that Caeyers compares with being gradually coaxed out of unconsciousness (BAL 183). Beethoven established himself as an independent artist by creating a new musical grammar. His transformation is noticeable in a comparison of his composition of symphonies before and after the Song Cycle. While the Song Cycle begins simply and with a minimal melodic element, the cyclic complexity is indicative of the direction that Beethoven later took with his masterpiece ... the Ninth Symphony (Ode To Joy).

The development of symbolic thinking is compatible with the principle of enantiodromia, according to which, a given conscious outlook eventually gives way to an opposing outlook that emerges from an unconscious source. The emergence of the new outlook gives the impression of a compensation at work. The conscious outlook is being balanced by an unconscious movement. The symbol 'bridging the gulf of distance and time' helped the transition from one path to the other, from focus on traditional classical music composition to focus on contemporary composition, facilitated by his creation of a new musical grammar. The symbol aided the transition, not by rationality, but by summarizing his psychological situation. The symbolic process began with Beethoven feeling that his personal life and professional life were in a rut, and believing that they were being obstructed by circumstances beyond his control. The symbolic process ended with his being able to see that he could tame his passion for Josephine, harness the energy of his activated anima archetype, and re-purpose the romantic energy for creating a new musical grammar. The diary Beethoven started in the summer 1812 provided a vehicle for introspection, for establishing structure and finding stability in his life (BAL 346).

Caeyers' view is that the Song Cycle is both a message to Beethoven's 'Faraway Beloved' and a message to all of humanity (BAL 405). The message to his 'Faraway Beloved' is about the taming of his romantic passion into an amicable, platonic friendship. That message spans a time of four years across the distance – Vienna to Budapest — that separated them. The message to all of humanity is an aspiration of making his art into a means of communication with the whole world. The Song Cycle is intended to be sung artlessly. That corresponds to Beethoven's shedding of the tradition of classical musical composition. The customary melodic, harmonic, tonal elements that were common in his early works were not present in the Song Cycle (BAL 405). When he was writing the Song Cycle, he did not yet know how to make his aspiration a reality, but people who live in the 21st century know that Beethoven fulfilled that aspiration. It is also common knowledge that humanity rewarded his achievement. He has been honored in documentaries, museums, monuments and university level studies. In 1977, samples of his music were included in two interstellar probes: Voyager 1 and Voyager 2. In addition, many religious organizations celebrate the ecumenical nature of the symphony "Ode To Joy". The Song Cycle was a turning point for Beethoven. The symbol that emerged during his 4-year period of reflexive dialogue — bridge the gulf of distance and time – led him in a new direction that enabled him to bridge the gulfs in his life: the gulf between him and Josephine, also the gulf between him and humanity. He achieved his aspiration to surmount his deafness by using his music to remain in touch with the outside world (BAL 405).

Call To Action: Take Away A Portable Understanding

This chapter is about Ludwig van Beethoven, a 14th century musician whose music still appeals to humanity in the 21st century. After establishing himself as a respected concert pianist, he lost his hearing. In a self-imposed isolation from society, with no one available to be an adequate container for his unassimilated state of mind, he took on the challenging task of becoming a container for himself. It appears that formal education is not a factor in reflexive containment, because Beethoven's formal education went no further than elementary school. Significant factors appear to be a high tolerance for isolation, combined with the ability to focus on one's own mental processes over an extended period of time, plus a determination to re-direct energy from one area of life to another. This chapter is a call to action for readers to take away a portable understanding of the reflexive mode of containment. To help readers, I offer the following summary as a reminder of how Beethoven used his deafness to create a self-imposed isolation in which he achieved psychological growth by composing contemporary classical music for humanity.

- **Mode:** Beethoven-the-lover and Beethoven-the-musician had a reflexive mode of containment.
- **Roles:** The mind of Beethoven-the-lover played the role of contained, while at the same time playing the role of container as Beethoven-the-musician.
- **Symmetry:** Beethoven-the-lover and Beethoven-the-musician had a symmetrical relationship. The two roles were played by the same mind, which created the narratives for both roles.

- **Psychological Frame:** The isolation that Beethoven imposed on himself, due to his loss of hearing, provided the psychological frame for containment. The purpose of the frame was to create a space to put time and effort into introspection about the possibility of a viable future as a deaf musician. The space boundary of the frame was his home in Vienna. The time boundary of the frame was the 4-year period from 1812 to 1816 when Beethoven-the-lover engaged in a sustained dialogue with Beethoven-the-musician.

- **Dialectical Narrative:** This containment had three narratives. The first was Beethoven-the-lover's narrative about his efforts to make Josephine his wife. The second was Beethoven-the-musician's narrative about his life as an artist. The interaction between those two narratives generated a third narrative, which had internal component and external components. The internal component was made up of the creativity and the self-confidence that the writing of the Song Cycle (Faraway Beloved) imbued with the symbol of bridging the gulf across distance and time. The external components were Beethoven's gifts to humanity ... a new musical grammar and contemporary classical compositions.

- **Psychological Growth / Harm:** The dialectical interaction between Beethoven-the-lover and Beethoven-the-musician produced psychological growth that is evidenced in how he processed the content of his own projection. A reading of his composition of the 'Faraway Beloved' Song Cycle reveals that Beethoven had withdrawn his projection, processed the unbearable state of mind associated with it, and integrated new knowledge into his consciousness. Josephine's role in his life had shifted from 'Immortal Beloved' to 'Faraway Beloved'. The emotional turmoil of his love for Josephine had been refined into a desire to make his artistry the best he could possibly make it — for the benefit of all humanity.

The relationship between Beethoven and Josephine does not fit any mode of containment in Wilfred Bion's model, or Duncan Cartwright's elaboration of the model. A mind depends on another mind for psychological growth — that is the theme of Duncan Cartwright's book

"Containing States Of Mind" (CSM 2), but my view is that Beethoven showed how one mind can achieve psychological growth without depending on another. After years of failing to get Josephine to respond to his projection, Beethoven separated his mind into Beethoven-the-lover and Beethoven-the-musician to help him through the psychological despair about his life. With that separation, he engaged in what I am proposing as a reflexive mode of containment. During the 4-year period of self-imposed isolation and introspection, from 1812 to 1816, Beethoven withdrew his projection, harnessed the anima inspired energy, and transformed it into his own creative style of classical music. Beethoven's story is an example of the way in which the psychological distress of a projection can influence the actions of an individual to achieve psychological growth. Ultimately, Beethoven demonstrated that one mind can be enough to triumph over the psychological distress of a projection.

After the Containment Ended

There is a museum named Beethoven House, located in the place of Beethoven's birth, central Bonn in Germany. The artifacts that Swiss collector, Hans Conrad Bodmer, bequeathed to the museum in 1956 are stored there for public viewing. The city of Bonn began hosting an annual musical festival, Beethovenfest, beginning in 1845. Years later, in 1985, the leaders of the European Union adopted Beethoven's Ninth Symphony 'Ode To Joy' as its anthem.

When Ludwig von Beethoven died in 1827, he had started work on his Tenth Symphony, but left it unfinished because of declining health. In a 2-year effort, Beethoven fans, musicologists and computer scientists, combined efforts to complete the symphony with the help of Artificial Intelligence. A recording of Beethoven's Tenth Symphony was published in 2020 as part of the celebration of the 250th anniversary of his birth. As a part of that celebration, Beethoven was designated Australia's favorite composer in 2019. On that occasion, ABC Classic commissioned actor John Bell to read the Heiligenstadt Testament, while Moonlight Sonata played in the background. See a link to the reading in the list of sources at the end of this chapter.

Sources

The sources of information that contributed to my analysis in this chapter are:

- *"Beethoven: A Life"* by Jan Caeyers
- *"The Immortal Beloved Compendium"* by John E. Klapproth
- *"Beethoven and His 'Immortal Beloved' Josephine Brunsvik: Her Fate and the Influence on Beethoven's Oeurve"* by Marie-Elizabeth Tellenbach
- John Bell reads Beethoven's Heiligenstadt Testament - ABC Classic
- *"The Psychology of Beethoven and The Eroica Symphony"* by Sean P. Harty, Rebekah K. Gohl, Dana J. Burhorn & Joshua S. Murano
- *"The Antecedents of Beethoven's Liederkreis"* by Luise Eitel Peake
- *"Projection and Re-Collection in Jungian Psychology"* by Marie-Louise von Franz
- *"Symbolization: Representation and Communication"* by James Rose (Editor)
- *"A Critical Dictionary of Jungian Analysis"* by Andrew Samuels, Bani Shorter and Fred Plaut.

CHAPTER 20

A Theistic Mode of Containment Involving: Charles Austin Miles & The Christian Son of God

"Under the inspiration of this vision I wrote as quickly as the words could be formed, the poem exactly as it has since appeared."

— Charles Austin Miles

A common theme across many religions is that people obtain relief from despair, woe, or anxiety, by turning to their deity. This is true for people of the Hindu religion, the Jewish religion, the Christian religion, among others. People have relationships with their deities. People derive satisfaction from those relationships because they experience containment, in the form of emotional support, mercy, forgiveness, advice and sometimes an adjustment of their outlook on life. The containment model built by Wilfred Bion and elaborated by Duncan Cartwright, does not include a mode of containment for the relationship between a person and their deity. With due respect to Bion and Cartwright, I am proposing a theistic mode of containment, in which a projection is cast from the mind of an adherent of a religion to their deity. A deity is an entity that adherents of a religion believe to be accessible for addressing human needs. As an example of the theistic mode of containment, I choose Charles Austin Miles' hymn "*I Come To The Garden Alone*" because it is well known in the Christian community. What the Christian Bibles have in common with the psychology of relationship and containment is the notion that a mind needs another mind to convert experience into meaning. Since adherents of theistic religions regard their deities as having powers greater than humans and the ability to carry humans to new levels of consciousness (GG 378), I treat a deity as having a mind. In this chapter, I regard the Christian Son of God as having a mind.

It was March in 1912 when Christians were preparing to celebrate Easter the following month. In a cold, dark, dreary basement in New Jersey, Charles Austin Miles reached for his Bible and it opened at his favorite passage, John 20: 1 - 18, which is about the morning when disciples went to look for Jesus at the tomb where He was buried. That is the morning of Jesus' resurrection. On reading the Bible verses, Miles experienced a vision that inspired him to write about his divine encounter in the form of a song, for which he later composed the music. The song so resonates with the Christian community that it found its way into the hymnals and gospel songs albums in several Christian denominations. "*I Come To The Garden Alone*" is the title of the song that became a hymn. I choose that hymn as an example of a theistic mode of containment because it is well known in the Christian world and it illustrates the concept of a psychological containment.

My interpretation of Miles' hymn is that he had a containment with his perception of the Christian Son of God. What the hymn depicts is a psychological containment in which there is an interactive dialogue during which he sought divine help in alleviating an experience of woe. By engaging in a dialectical interaction with the Son of God in his vision, Miles learned how to process the emotional turmoil he experienced in relation to the woe in his life. Psychologist Warren Colman explains Lucien Levy-Bruhl's definition of 'mystical' as the belief in forces and influences and actions which, though imperceptible to sense, are nevertheless real. Thus, belief in spiritual forces is an expression of affective states that have become symbolized via collective representations and thereby transformed to include taking on a social aspect (AIE 239). The word 'mystical' refers to an experience of direct communication with God. Such communications are less rational and more symbolic in meaning. I see Miles' experience as being mystical in the sense that it is a vision – a direct communication with the Christian Son of God – and it is about the Resurrection as a major event of renewal in which the Son of God redeems humanity. While the hymn was the result of a vision in Miles' personal life, I believe it takes on a social aspect for Christian believers in general, people who share his faith in the resurrection, that is, people for whom the appearance of the risen Son of God is an article of faith. To help readers understand the circumstance surrounding Miles' composition of the hymn, I provide background information about Miles in the next section, and the Christian Son of God in the following section.

Background Information about Charles Austin Miles

I found no biography of Charles Austin Miles, and the information available on the Internet is sketchy. He was an American songwriter, who lived in New Jersey from 1868 to 1946. He studied pharmacy at the University of Pennsylvania, and worked as a pharmacist. According to the web site Hymnary.org, he married Bertha Haagen and they had two sons named Charles and Russell. Miles gave up his career as a pharmacist in 1892 and started writing gospel songs. Initially, he submitted his songs to the Hall-Mack Company for publication. His gospel songs were well received, and he became curious about exploring other talents. When he was 44 years old, he experienced a vision while reading his Bible. It was March 1912 when Christians were preparing for Easter celebration. Miles was reading his favorite Bible passage, John 20:1 – 18. That passage is about the story of the morning when the resurrected Jesus appeared to his disciples just outside the tomb where he was buried. It is the story that marks the beginning of the Christian movement … the story of the risen Son of God on the first Easter morning. While reading the passage, Miles felt he was walking with the risen Christ in a garden on that morning. He experienced a vision during which a melody played in his mind. During the vision, he felt transported to an imaginary garden. He stood at the entrance of the garden looking down a winding path. There, the Son of God engaged him in a moving interaction and granted him a gift of a melody. Immediately after the vision, Miles quickly wrote down the words of the melody. Later that same day, he wrote the music to accompany the words. The vision brought him a quickening of mind that lifted him out of his everyday activities and motivated him to write down the song.

The web site Wikipedia.org reports a comment from Miles' great-grand-daughter, that the song was written 'in a cold, dreary and leaky basement in Pitman, New Jersey that didn't even have a window in it let alone a view of a garden'. The song was first published in 1912 and popularized during evangelistic campaigns of the early twentieth century. Soon after its publication, Miles expanded his career by taking on roles of musical editor and manager of the Hall-Mack Publishing Company. According to the Discipleship Ministries web site, between 1935 and 1936, Miles managed the merger of Hall-Mack Publishing Company and Rodeheaver-Ackley Company. The new company was named Rodeheaver-Hall-Mack Company. It pioneered the production of gospel song recordings in the early 20th century. Miles worked with the company for 37 years. He felt he was serving God better in the gospel song production than he had been in the pharmaceutical business. When he died in 1946, Miles had written over three hundred songs.

Background Information about the Christian Son of God

In Christian theology, the title Son of God is a reference to Jesus as part of the Trinity, which is made up of God the Father, Jesus the Son of God and the Holy Spirit. More than two thousand years ago, Jesus was born in Bethlehem, Israel where he grew up with earthly parents Mary and Joseph. God had produced a human son to live among humans, experience their suffering, atone for their sins, and offer salvation to believers. Jesus was both human and deity. When Jesus was born, there arose over Bethlehem a star, the sight of which attracted visitors from the East. These visitors understood the Bible's prophesy that a messiah would be born in Israel and would have an impact on the whole world. To avoid competition, the ruler of Israel at the time, King Herod, ordered the deaths of all newborn babies. Warned by an angel, Mary and Joseph took Jesus to live in Egypt. When King Herod died, the family returned to Israel, this time to live in Nazareth. When Jesus was twelve years old, his parents took him to Jerusalem to celebrate the Feast of the Passover. After the celebration, Jesus became separated from Mary and Joseph. Later, Jesus was found in the Temple, talking with adults who were impressed with Jesus' knowledge.

At about age thirty, Jesus began his ministry at the River Jordan, with a baptism by John the Baptist. After baptism, Jesus fasted in the desert for forty days. His three-year ministry began with a miracle performed at a wedding party in Canaan. The wedding party did not have enough wine for the guests. Jesus miraculously transformed water into wine. During the three-year ministry, Jesus called twelve disciples to his ministry, and trained them to serve the community by teaching them to pray and heal the sick. The four Gospels (Matthew, Mark, Luke and John) recorded over thirty miracles during Jesus' ministry. In the final year of the ministry, Jesus took disciples Peter, James and John up a mountain to witness a transfiguration. Jesus' face shone like the sun. His clothes became white. He conversed with prophets who were long dead. A bright cloud cast a shadow over them and a voice spoke through the cloud: "*This is my beloved Son, with whom I am well pleased; listen to him.*" (NAB Matthew 17, Verse 5).

Near the end of the three-year ministry, local religious leaders disputed Jesus' authority and plotted to kill him. Judas, one of the disciples, betrayed Jesus for thirty pieces of silver. Aware of his upcoming death, Jesus gathered his disciples for a Last Supper, where he established 'communion' which is the practice of sharing bread and wine under a covenant for the forgiveness of sins. Jesus' antagonists chose Calvary as the city where they nailed him to a cross. Jesus' body was placed in a tomb by two of his followers. The next morning, Mary Magdalene, Peter and John found the tomb empty (NAB John 20, Verses 1 – 18). Three days after death, Jesus was resurrected (NAB First Corinthians Chapter 15, Verse 20) and made several appearances to followers. After telling disciples to spread his teachings, Jesus ascended into Heaven (NAB Mark Chapter 16, Verses 19 – 20). In the next two sections, I describe the relationship between Miles and the Son of God, first in the context of the savior archetype as biological entity, then in the context of the savior archetype as emergent phenomenon.

Context of Archetype as Biological Entity: Projection & Introjection

This section is about the relationship between Charles Austin Miles and the Christian Son of God viewed in the context of archetype-as-biological-entity. When an archetype is viewed as a biological entity, it is regarded as an ancestral heritage of human experience accumulated over many generations and located in collective unconsciousness. When psychologists define an archetype as a biological entity, the processes they identify for converting experience to meaning are projection and introjection. Projection is an evacuation of unconscious content from the psyche due to an unbearable state of mind. Miles's projection was an evacuation of an unbearable state of mind about a personal woe, the specific nature of which is not identified in the hymn. The projection was from the mind of Miles to the Son of God, indicating that the archetype of savior was activated. Introjection is a transformation of an unbearable state of mind to a bearable state of mind, followed by its integration into conscious content of the psyche. Relying on his Christian faith, Miles turned to the Son of God when he needed help with his unbearable state of mind. Their interaction took the form of an introjection during which Miles experienced relief from his woe, over a period of time spent in the imaginary garden.

The garden is a psychological frame that Miles imagined for his encounter with the Son of God. He comes to the garden alone for dialogue with his deity. Miles' hymn does not articulate his specific need until near the end of the hymn, when he refers to woe. In the religious world, personal woe is on par with unbearable state of mind in the world of psychology. Miles does not write in the song what brings about his woe, but the urgency of the stanzas and the repetition of the refrain indicate that there is a sustained dialogue about the woe. Throughout the lyrics, Miles listens to the voice of his deity. With each refrain, Miles tarries with the Son of God. Miles' word 'tarry' translates to what would be 'reverie' in psychology. Miles and the Son of God have a shared reverie. On the social media platform, YouTube, there are many video recordings of "I Come To The Garden Alone" that show a background of a garden where the hymn is sung by a choir. I do not find those videos reflective of Miles' hymn because the vision is about one person's personal relationship with the Son of God. In my view, it is fitting that this hymn be sung by one person. The cheery renditions by smiling, cherubic faces on YouTube do not do justice to the hymn. The hymn is about woe. One performance I find fitting for words of the hymn is the YouTube video by Merle Haggard. The words of the hymn convey an intense communication about Miles' emotional despair. Here are the lyrics:

I COME TO THE GARDEN ALONE
By Charles Austin Miles, 1912

I come to the garden alone,
While the dew is still on the roses;
And the voice I hear, falling on my ear,
The Son of God discloses.

Refrain:
And He walks with me, and He talks with me,
And He tells me I am His own,
And the joy we share as we tarry there,
None other has ever known.

He speaks, and the sound of His voice
Is so sweet the birds hush their singing;
And the melody that He gave to me
Within my heart is ringing.

Repeat refrain

I'd stay in the garden with Him
Tho' the night around me be falling;
But He bids me go; thro' the voice of woe,
His voice to me is calling.

Repeat refrain

In the school of Analytical Psychology, there is an archetype for every typical situation in life. Miles' situation is that he is experiencing the burden of woe. In his time of need, Miles turns to his savior. The archetype of savior is activated in Miles' life. It is the view of psychologist Marie-Louise von Franz that a projection emerges from an archetype. Miles' projection emerged from the savior archetype. In the words of von Franz "... wherever known reality stops, where we touch the unknown, there we project an archetypal image" (PRJ 24). Miles' archetypal image of savior is projected onto the Son of God. In Christian theology, the Son of God, or Jesus, functions as both a human and a deity. In his human role, Jesus lived on earth during the first century AD. In the role of deity, the resurrected Jesus grants Miles a vision, in which he receives the gift of a melody.

My opinion is that the relationship between Miles and Jesus involves a theistic mode of containment with Miles as the contained and the Son of God as the container. The containment is initiated by an activation of the savior archetype which triggers Miles' projection. The projection emerges from the savior archetype, whose characteristics are compassion, sympathy and empathy for those in distress. The projection is involuntarily cast from the mind of Miles to his deity, the Son of God. The content of the projection is Miles' emotional turmoil pertaining to woe in some unspecified area of his life. I infer that the area of life in which he experiences woe is his career, because the change in life that occurs after the containment is in his career. He progresses from songwriter to editor-cum-manager of Hall-Mack Publishing Company. Although Miles does not state the cause of his woe, it is urgent enough for him to need a private encounter with the Son of God, who became the carrier of Miles' projection. Miles looks to the Son of God as a savior who will guide him in his state of anxiety. Miles' lyrics indicate that each encounter in the imaginary garden begins in the morning when the dew is still on the roses, and ends in the evening when the night is falling. He states his woe without going into details, and he listens to the voice of the Son of God. Below, I comment on the lines of the hymn. The bold text is Charles Austin Miles' lyrics. The italicized text is my interpretation of the hymn seen from the point of view of a theistic mode of containment.

I COME TO THE GARDEN ALONE
By Charles Austin Miles, 1912

I come to the garden alone,

Miles enters the psychological space in his imaginary garden, where he anticipates having a private encounter with the Son of God. He comes 'alone' because he wants to have a personal encounter with his savior. He does not find it necessary to state the nature of his personal woe because he knows that his savior already knows his distress. The imaginary garden is a spatial boundary of the psychological frame of the containment. The garden is where Miles' woe (mentioned later in the hymn) is projected unto his savior — the Son of God.

While the dew is still on the roses;

Dew on the roses indicates that Miles' encounter with the Son of God begins in the morning. The morning is part of the time boundary of the psychological frame of the containment.

And the voice I hear, falling on my ear,

Miles' projection invokes a response from his savior — a voice falling on his ear indicates that an introjection by the Son of God is underway.

The Son of God discloses.

Miles experiences his savior's assurance of being with him in the imaginary garden.

Refrain:
And He walks with me, and He talks with me,

Miles (the contained) is experiencing a containment by his savior (the container) in the imaginary garden. This line of the hymn conveys a dialectical interaction between Miles and the Son of God.

And He tells me I am His own,

Miles experiences the Son of God's introjection in the form of an assurance of a private space where his savior interacts with him individually.

And the joy we share as we tarry there,

> The word 'tarry' indicates that Miles lingers with his savior in a shared reverie from which Miles derives joy, that is, relief from his woe. The refrain expresses relief from the burden of raw emotions projected onto his savior.

None other has ever known.

> Miles experiences his savior relating to him in a personal encounter. This is Miles' statement about his felt containment in the psychological frame of the imaginary garden.

He speaks, and the sound of His voice

> This stanza expresses the effects of the introjection and shared reverie that metabolize the content of Miles' projection and give meaning to his experience.

Is so sweet the birds hush their singing;

> Miles so welcomes interaction with the Son of God that it drowns out the earthly pleasure of birds singing.

And the melody that He gave to me

> Miles receives the gift of a melody from the Son of God.

Within my heart is ringing.

> Miles' heart welcomes the melody as a means of transformation of his woe to joy.

Repeat refrain
I'd stay in the garden with Him

> Miles' desire to stay in the imaginary garden indicates he is deriving satisfaction from the containment.

Tho' the night around me be falling;

> *Night falling indicates that day's encounter is ending. The evening is part of the time boundary of the psychological frame of the containment.*

But He bids me go; thro' the voice of woe,

> *The purpose of the containment is being served as the Son of God's introjection helps Miles understand the content and meaning of his projection. Miles' current life experience is being mirrored by the vision. Easter, a commemoration of the resurrection, is approaching while Miles is reading John Chapter 20, which is about the resurrection. The vision consisted of images about how the disciples' crucifixion woe is transformed into resurrection joy. Buoyed by his Christian faith, the lesson Miles takes away from the containment is that his personal woe can be transformed into joy. After all, resurrection is about God's promise to intervene when humanity experiences despair.*

His voice to me is calling.

> *As he leaves the imaginary garden at the end of day, Miles is aware that the Son of God is calling him. He knows that he is being called, but not where he is being called. Not yet. The dialectical interaction will continue in the next encounter. The containment continues.*

Repeat refrain

Resurrection is about a promise to humanity that the Christian Son of God will intervene when life is weighted down by emotions such as despair, woe, grief or suffering. The refrain of the hymn repeats the shared reverie — 'and the joy we share as we tarry here' — of the containment. Repetition of the refrain after each stanza reflects a repetition of encounters between Miles and his savior, possibly over several days of dialogue in Miles' imaginary garden. The inspiration for Miles' vision was the passage in the Gospel of John that describes the appearance of the Jesus on the morning of resurrection. The Son of God was making His presence known in the roles of teacher and master ... as savior of humanity. Resurrection is about the uniqueness of the Son of God. Jesus' resurrection gives substance to the vague notion that humans will be resurrected. Miles knew that resurrection holds a promise that God will intervene in life's most difficult periods. I believe the projection was broken when Miles received the gift of a melody playing in his head. The fevered writing down of the song followed by same-day composition of music are about Miles' relief and gratitude for a precious gift ... a gift from the Son of God. In this section, I described the relationship between Miles and the Son of God in the context of archetype as biological entity. In the next section, I will describe the relationship in the context of archetype as emergent phenomenon.

Context of Archetype as Emergent Phenomenon: Appropriation & Internalization

This section is about the relationship between Miles and the Son of God viewed in terms of archetype-as-emergent-phenomenon. When considering archetype as an emergent phenomenon, it is seen as an emergent property of a dynamic, developmental system that is made up of human brains, human activities, society's external environment and the narrative competence of humans in the society. In viewing archetype as an emergent phenomenon, the means for converting life's experience to meaning are appropriation and internalization. Appropriation is an adoption of conscious content from social and cultural sources in the external environment. For example, the acquisition of language is an appropriation. Children appropriate the language of the culture in which they grow up. When adults travel to a new country and become emersed in a new culture, they appropriate the language of the new culture. In a manner similar to the appropriation of language, Miles has an appropriation of a career that is compatible with God's purpose. Although the hymn does not state the specific nature of Miles' woe, the change that occurred in his life after the vision, points to an appropriation about the availability of career options that are compatible with his desire to serve God. He had left his job as a pharmacist behind and taken up songwriting. Now he wanted more. His desire for a broader career was limited by his preference for an occupation that is in line with serving God's purpose. Internalization is the incorporation of a cultural appropriation into one's mental model. Having established a theistic mode of containment with the Son of God, Miles incorporated into his mental model a reinforcement of the story of resurrection. Resurrection is God's promise to humanity that there will be divine intervention when humans experience difficulties in life. Miles did not have to compose the melody because the Son of God gave it to him as a gift. All he had to do was write it down. Miles was able to internalize in his mental model, his savior's reassurance that his life would have a transition from woe to joy just as the disciples had during that first Easter weekend. In the next section, I use the hymn "*I Come To The Garden Alone*" hymn to describe the symbolization that I believe occurred during the dialogue between Miles and the Christian Son of God.

Converting Experience to Meaning: Symbolization

On that cold, dreary morning in March 1912, while the Christian community was preparing to celebrate the resurrection, Miles had opened his Bible and read about the resurrection. While reading, he experienced a vision that included the creation of a symbolic form which made it possible to understand his unrepresented state of mind and render it usable. Symbolization serves a cognitive function that reveals insight, new knowledge, or inspiration in a mental space where it can be examined and understood. Symbolic thinking involves a process of formulation which transforms felt emotion into perception. In my research about Miles and the hymn, the expression 'His voice to me is calling' – last line of the hymn — stands out as being consistent with the emergence of a symbol as described in "*A Dictionary of Jungian Analysis*" where psychologist Andrew Samuels and others define symbol in terms of concept, intent, purpose and content. Here is my application of that definition to Miles' expression 'His voice to me is calling':

- **Concept:** The concept of the symbol 'His voice to me is calling' is about being called into a new state of being, but without any specific information about the nature of the state, or any logical instructions on how to get there. For Miles, the concept of 'His voice to me is calling' was expressed in images of the vison granted to him by the Son of God. The symbol was not about rationality; it was a summation of the psychological situation in which Miles found himself. He was at a turning point in life. No longer satisfied with song writing, he wanted more, but he was not sure how to satisfy his need while keeping his career aligned to God's purpose.

- **Intent:** Behind the expression 'His voice to me is calling' was an intent to accomplish a change, but it was difficult to articulate because the end state was unknown. For Miles, there was a general intent to make a career change, but he did not know what would be next. He was already writing songs and publishing them, but the symbol pointed in a direction where there was more. The intent of 'His voice to me is calling' was to take on more than he had so far, that is, bring more into his portfolio of skills.

- **Purpose:** The purpose of the symbol was served by Miles' shift of attention toward a new outlook by expanding his role in the publishing world to include editing and management. The purpose the symbol served was not merely to come up with an alternative point of view. Nor was the purpose of the symbol to work out a logical derivation of a solution to the conflict. The purpose was to reveal a new outlook through the back-and-forth interaction of opposing sides of Miles' woe.

- **Content:** The content of the symbol of 'His voice to me is calling' turned out to be a new meaning of career that would expand Miles' professional capabilities. According to the dictionary of terms in Analytical Psychology, a symbol is 'pregnant with meaning' that presents a challenge to thoughts and feelings. A symbol is expressed in images that control, order and give meaning to people's lives. The symbol of 'His voice to me is calling' guided Miles' passage from an unprocessed state of mind about his career to a processed state of mind, which included publishing and management in the world of gospel music production.

Miles' new career was not logically deduced, by weighing alternatives. The symbol of 'His voice to me is calling' enabled a transition from the old to the new outlook in the music industry by navigating a back-and-forth movement until a synthesis of their opposing outlooks was achieved. When confronted with the uncertainty of the symbol, Miles' ego was freed from the knot of his woe, enabling him to reflect on new possibilities from which to choose a new outlook. The symbolic process started with Miles 'feeling stuck' in his career as songwriter. The symbolic process ended with Miles being relieved of 'feeling stuck'. A loosening of the knot of conflicted expectations that had obstructed his career gave way to a feeling that his dissatisfaction with his psychological situation had cleared. He had created a new way of working in the publishing world that fit with his expectations of a satisfying career. Miles had reached out to his savior in the hope of changing his career without having a prescribed goal, and without the means of achieving a goal. The outcome was an elaboration of his involvement in the publishing of gospel music. The symbolic process ended with Miles being relieved of his personal woe. His spiritual and psychological distress were alleviated.

Call To Action: Take Away A Portable Understanding

This chapter is about a pharmacist-turned-songwriter who had what I characterize as a theistic mode of containment with his deity, the Christian Son of God. This chapter is not just a story of how Miles came to write a beloved hymn. It is also informative about the nature of a theistic mode of containment. This chapter is a call to action for readers to take away a portable understanding of the theistic mode of containment. To help readers, I offer the following summary as a reminder of how Miles obtained his savior's support in alleviating emotional distress, expanding his career and publishing the hymn "*I Come To The Garden Alone*".

- **Mode:** Charles Austin Miles and the Christian Son of God had a theistic mode of containment.
- **Roles:** Miles, the contained, was a believer whose projection was cast onto his savior, the Christian Son of God, the container.
- **Symmetry:** This was an asymmetrical relationship. Miles was a mortal human being, while the Son of God is a deity in Christian theology.
- **Psychological Frame:** The psychological frame creates a privacy in which the contained and container can have overlapping reveries. The frame has a purpose, a time boundary and a space boundary. The psychological frame for this containment is a garden, which is a fantasy in Miles' mind. The imaginary garden forms a space boundary for the psychological frame. The time boundary of an encounter in the garden is bracketed by the

morning, when 'the dew is still on the roses', and the evening, when 'the night around me be falling'. The repetition of the refrain supports the notion that there was a dialectical interaction between Miles and the Son of God, over a period of days.

- **Dialectical Narrative:** The first narrative is Miles' communication about his personal woe. The second narrative is the Son of God's introjection in a voice that lightens Miles' burden of woe. While the reader of the hymn has no specifics of that divine response, it is clear that Miles experiences relief from his burden of woe through his interaction with the Son of God in the imaginary garden. The interaction between Miles and his savior generated a dialectical narrative that is partly internal and partly external. Internally, Miles' outlook about his unbearable state of mind was transformed to a bearable state of mind by the dialogue with his savior, and by the mental gift of a melody, whose delivery — as Easter approached — was a reminder that the resurrection extends to humanity a promise that God will intercede when life's burdens are too much to bear. An external outcome of the dialectical narrative was the production of the hymn "*I Come To The Garden Alone*" which became a source of inspiration to the Christian segment of humanity, a message of hope and a salve for the psyche of all Christendom. Another external outcome of the dialectical narrative was an expanded musical career for Miles as editor and manager of a publishing company for gospel music, a relatively new industry at the time.

- **Psychological Growth / Harm**: The containment ended with psychological growth for Miles. He overcame the psychological distress associated with his personal woe, in a manner that had a transformative effect on his life. Evidence of his psychological growth is seen in his learning a new way of functioning and adapting to new circumstances in his life. He made the transition from songwriter to musical editor. He also learned to function as a manager of a music publishing company. Miles acquired the confidence and the skills to expand his career from song writer to editor-cum-manager of Hall-Mack Publishing Company.

After the Containment Ended

The vision that Miles had during the containment inspired him to write the hymn "*I Come To The Garden Alone*" whose resonance with the Christian psyche made it a popular inclusion in hymnals of several denominations of Christianity. That resonance is also noticeable in the musical albums of many gospel singers, who over the years, have sung the hymn according to their own musical stylings, but kept the original words intact. After the theistic mode of containment between Miles and the Son of God, Miles expanded his songwriting. At the time of his death in 1946, Miles had written over 300 hundred songs of which "*I Come To The Garden Alone*" became his best known.

Sources

The sources of information that I used in writing this chapter are:
- "*I Come To The Garden Alone*" by Charles Austin Miles
- C. Austin Miles | Hymnary.org
- In the Garden (1912 song) - Wikipedia
- Discipleship Ministries | History of Hymns: 'I Come to the Garden... (umcdiscipleship.org)
- Merle Haggard - He Walks With Me - YouTube
- "*The New American Bible*" by Catholic Book Publishing
- "*SYMBOLIZATION: Representation and Communication*" by James Rose (editor)
- "*Containing States of Mind*" by Duncan Cartwright
- "*Projection and Re-Collection in Jungian Psychology*" by Marie-Louise von Franz.

CHAPTER 21

A Theistic Mode of Containment Involving: Prince Arjuna & The Hindu Lord Krishna

"One cannot reach the real point of factual knowledge without being helped by the right person, who is already established in that knowledge."

— Bhagavad Gita

Religions play a significant role in society because people derive spiritual and psychological benefits from relationships with their deities. As sources of guidance about the conduct of life, religions provide opportunities for psychological containment. In encounters with their deities, adherents of religions experience emotional support in the form of hope, joy, mercy, relief from despair, and sometimes a new outlook on life. This is true for adherents of the Hindu religion from which I selected the sacred scripture *Bhagavad Gita* as an example of the relationship between a human, Prince Arjuna and Lord Krishna, who is both a human and a deity. I am proposing that they had a theistic mode of containment in which a projection was cast from the mind of Arjuna to Krishna. I choose the *Bhagavad Gita* because it is a well-known example of Hindu scripture. What the *Bhagavad Gita* has in common with the psychology of containment is the notion that a mind needs another mind to convert experience into meaning. Adherents of theistic religions regard their deities as having powers greater than humans along with the ability to carry humans to new levels of consciousness (GG 378). In the *Bhagavad Gita*, Lord Krishna engages Prince Arjuna in a mind-to-mind interaction that carries him to new levels of spiritual and psychological growth.

Although the *Bhagavad Gita* is a portion of the Hindu epic *Mahabharata*, it functions as an independent spiritual guide. In the *Bhagavad Gita*, Arjuna's mind leans on the mind of Lord Krishna to process the emotional turmoil he experiences about whether to wage a righteous war with a risk of great casualty. The *Bhagavad Gita* begins on the battlefield of Kurukshetra, where warrior Arjuna sits with his war counsellor Krishna in a chariot surveying the two armies being assembled. At the beginning of the *Bhagavad Gita* , Arjuna does not know that Krishna is a deity. Arjuna is caught between two opposites: his emotional attachment to the community and his duty as a warrior. Although a skilled warrior, Arjuna is reluctant to fight because he is aware that, however righteous, this war would kill many people who are important to his life ... family members, friends, mentors, and community leaders. He is attached to these people because they have been the social network of emotional support throughout his life. He shares his dilemma with Krishna, who offers counselling. Words about attachment and non-attachment. Words about the three gunas: sattva, rajas and tamas. Words about karma. Words about the duty of a warrior. Words. Words. Words. Informative and wise, but not persuasive to Arjuna in the face of his emotional dilemma.

Their interaction reaches a turning point when Arjuna, mentally drained, shifts the focus of their intense dialogue from his dilemma to Krishna's credentials as a war counsellor. Arjuna demands to know who is this Krishna in whom he places such confidence about matters of life and war. Arjuna is not satisfied with the wisdom of Krishna's communications. He asks Krishna for a manifestation from Brahman. In the Hindu religion, Brahman is the Supreme Being, the divine power that is invisible and animates the whole universe. Krishna blesses Arjuna by granting him a vision. Arjuna suddenly experiences a blazing flash of light in which multiple images merge into a single underlying unity. From the vision, Arjuna realizes that people may see themselves as individuals in the external world, but at an unconscious level, all are part of the single unity of the Ultimate Reality that permeates everything in the universe. In granting the vision, Krishna offered Arjuna a temporary glimpse of divine insight. Arjuna begins to see Krishna in his true form, an avatar, that is, an earthly incarnation of a Hindu deity. The vision has a profound effect on Arjuna, for whom the resolution to his dilemma now appears within reach. This is the turning point in the dialogue between them. This is when Arjuna is able to see a clear decision-making path through his emotional turmoil about war and life. Arjuna also realizes that his charioteer is not merely a human war counsellor, but Lord Krishna, a worldly incarnation of Lord Vishnu, who is part of the Hindu trinity: Shiva the destroyer, Brahma the creator, and Vishnu the preserver. Together, they create, protect and transform life in the universe.

What I interpret from the *Bhagavad Gita* is that Prince Arjuna and Lord Krishna had a relationship that involved a theistic mode of containment. As the contained, Arjuna needed help to process the emotional turmoil of having to decide whether to wage a righteous war. The dilemma for him was that on the one hand, he was a warrior with a duty to fight, but on the other hand, he was reluctant to fight because war would result in the deaths of many people to whom he had strong attachments. Krishna, in his role as the container, took on the responsibility of being war counsellor who informs Arjuna of the relevant Hindu scriptural considerations. Over a series of discourses, the dialectical interaction between Arjuna and Krishna continuously informs and reshapes the dilemma until it burned off the mental fog, leaving a clear decision about whether to fight the righteous war. I propose that their relationship had a theistic mode of containment because of the psychological growth that Prince Arjuna achieved in his interaction with Lord Krishna. My main sources of information about the *Bhagavad Gita* are "*Perennial Psychology of the Bhagavad Gita*" by Swami Rama, and "*GITA: A Timeless Guide For Our Time*" by Isaac Bentwich. The interpretations about a theistic mode of containment are mine.

A theistic mode of containment occurs when there is a projection cast from a person's mind onto their perception of a deity. Psychologist Warren Colman explains the notion of 'mystical' as a belief in forces and influences and actions which, although they are not perceptible to the senses, they are nevertheless real. So, belief in spiritual forces is an expression of affective states that have become symbolized and transformed through collective representations, and this includes taking on a social aspect (AIE 239). While the discourses in the Gita are about Krishna's instructions to Arjuna, who is one individual, I believe it takes on a social aspect for Hindu devotees in general, that is, people for whom the path of renunciation, the three gunas and the principle of attachment are part of their belief system. This means that people can grow psychologically from their relationship with their perception of deity. The word 'mystical' refers to an experience of direct communication with God. Such communications are less rational and more symbolic in meaning. I see Arjuna's experience as being mystical in the sense that it involves a vision, in a direct communication with Lord Krishna. It is also about communicating to Arjuna through the symbolic imagery of Lord Krishna's expression 'you are only the instrument in My work'. To help readers understand the circumstances leading up to the discourses between Prince Arjuna and Lord Krishna, I provide background information about them in the next two sections.

Background Information about Prince Arjuna

The *Bhagavad Gita* is commonly translated as *The Song of God*. It is a part of the Hindu scripture *Mahabharata* which is estimated to have been composed over five thousand years ago. In the *Mahabharata*, two sides of a family, the Pandavas and the Kauravas are cousins who fight each other over the kingdom of *Kurukshetra*. The *Bhagavad Gita* is a portion of the history of the *Mahabharata*. In the *Bhagavad Gita*, the Pandavas and the Kauravas are preparing for war over the kingdom of Kurukshetra. A member of the Pandavas side of the family, Arjuna is a young prince of the Hindu warrior caste. The Pandavas have been exiled from the kingdom of Kurukshetra for several years and robbed of their rightful heritage by their cousins in the Kauravas branch of the family. The Bhagavad Gita begins with the story of the Pandavas' struggle to reclaim the kingdom, which requires that Arjuna wage war against his own relatives.

Arjuna is well known and respected for his warrior skills, especially his archery. The *Bhagavad Gita* opens with Arjuna in crisis about the questionable justice of engaging in a war that would result in high casualty of people to whom he has emotional attachments. He obtains a resolution to his crisis through a series of discourses with Krishna, who gradually helps him find a way out of the confusion in his unprocessed state of mind, regarding his duty as a warrior. Arjuna represents an archetypal warrior. The *Bhagavad Gita* begins with Arjuna in a state of intense doubt, when he asks charioteer Krishna to position the chariot in the battlefield so he can survey the armies while they are being assembled.

Background Information about the Hindu Lord Krishna

Lord Krishna is a deity in the Hindu religion. He is an earthly incarnation of the deity Vishnu, god of protection, love and compassion. As a popular Hindu deity, Krishna appears in many religious texts outside the *Bhagavad Gita*. Sometimes he is pictured playing a flute. Prior to the start of the *Bhagavad Gita*, Krishna offers his assistance to the two groups of cousins who are about to fight. He offers either his army or his war counselling. The Kaurava cousins choose Krishna's army. The Pandava cousins choose Krishna as their war counsellor. The story of the dialectical interaction between Arjuna and Krishna begins when Krishna steers the chariot onto the battlefield at Arjuna's request. The battlefield is the location where they engage in the eighteen discourses that enable a decision about whether to fight the war. In the next two sections, I describe the relationship between Prince Arjuna and Lord Krishna from the context of the warrior archetype, first as a biological entity, then as an emergent phenomenon.

Context of Archetype as Biological Entity: Projection & Introjection

This section describes the relationship between Prince Arjuna and Lord Krishna within the context of archetype-as-biological-entity. As a biological entity, an archetype is seen as an ancestral heritage of human experience accumulated over many generations and located in collective unconsciousness. When psychologists define an archetype as a biological entity, the processes they identify for converting experience to meaning are projection and introjection. Projection is an evacuation of unconscious content from the psyche due to an unbearable state of mind. Prince Arjuna's projection was an evacuation of an unbearable state of mind regarding a conflict about whether to fight a righteous war whose casualties would include his relatives and friends. The content of Arjuna's projection was an idealization of a warrior. The projection was cast onto Krishna who functioned as war counsellor for Arjuna. Introjection is a transformation of an unbearable state of mind to a bearable state of mind, followed by its integration into conscious content of the psyche. Prince Arjuna obtained help from Lord Krishna in metabolizing his unbearable state of mind and coming to a decision about whether to wage a war. Lord Krishna's way of helping Arjuna was to engage in a series of iterative discourses during which he listened to Arjuna's communications about his state of mind, and responded with spiritual advice about how to function as a warrior dealing with life's moral decisions. Arjuna's projection was broken after Krishna granted him a Cosmic Vision.

The Kurukshetra battlefield represents a psychological frame where Prince Arjuna and Lord Krishna engage each other in a theistic mode of containment. They sit in their chariot on the battlefield, where they have private, long-running conversations about Arjuna's dilemma. They engage in dialogue that consists of eighteen discourses in which Lord Krishna shares Hindu principles to educate Prince Arjuna. What follows are highlights of the topics of dialogue in the eighteen discourses between Prince Arjuna and Lord Krishna. Readers who are familiar with the *Bhagavad Gita* may wish to skip my summaries of the eighteen discourses.

First Discourse: Arjuna's Despondency
Conflicted about fighting a war that will likely result in enormous casualty of people about whom Arjuna cares deeply, he asks his charioteer Krishna to position the chariot in the battlefield, where he surveys the armies. Arjuna confides his moral conflict to Krishna. On the one hand he could fight the battle and regain the kingdom of Kurukshetra that rightfully belongs to him and his brothers. It a battle that would involve killing people who are his relatives, friends and former instructors. On the other hand,

he could refuse to fight and avoid killing people he cares about, but then he would be forfeiting the kingdom that belongs to his family and he would be considered a disgraced warrior. Both armies had gathered. Leaders, including Arjuna, had blown their celestial conches, indicating readiness for war. Arjuna raised his bow. Unwilling to fight, he lowered his bow and turns to Krishna for counselling (PPB 13 – 40).

Second Discourse: The Way of Self-Knowledge

Krishna begins to make Arjuna aware of his inner strength, by reminding him of his proud ancestry of wise individuals as well as his status as a skillful warrior and a true seeker of enlightenment. Krishna awakens Arjuna to three distinct levels of understanding and approaching life. At the first level, there is a dependence on external resources. The Kauravas function at this level where the focus is on the physical strength of their army. Their perspective is materially oriented. At the second level, there is a reliance on the strength of a person's inner life, such as the individual courage of a warrior. At the third level, the focus is on the immortal Atman which is a vital force that animates the individual. Arjuna's despondency arises from his attachments to the kingdom, the family, and the society, all of which are destabilizing his mind and diminishing his courage to act. He is concerned about the external world and not sensitive to his interior life (PPB 43). Arjuna is torn between a fear of being victorious and a fear of being defeated. He has lost his sense of discrimination, which renders him indecisive and unable to fight the battle of life (PPB 47). Krishna explains to Arjuna that his duty is important because it is the means of fulfilling the purpose of his life. That which supports the fulfillment of one's duty is called dharma. Arjuna is a warrior who specializes in the art and science of war, but he is conflicted about his dharma (PPB 71). Krishna explains to Arjuna that while he has the right to perform his duty, he does not have the right to expect specific fruits of his labor. Neither duty performed with the motivation to acquire the fruits of one's action nor attachment towards inaction is helpful (PPB 82).

Third Discourse: The Yoga of Knowledge and of Action

Krishna explains that there are two means for attaining the state of tranquility: yoga of knowledge and yoga of action. Yoga of knowledge is the path where essential values are non-attachment and renunciation. Yoga of action is the path where performance of one's duties skillfully and selflessly and with non-attachment are the pre-requisites. Both paths are equally valid. Followers of the path of knowledge (jnana nishtha) believe in having a firm conviction that one can attain the highest state of liberation through knowledge alone. Followers of the path of yoga of action (karma nishtha) believe in performing their duties with non-attachment as a means of self-unfoldment (PPB 125). To attain a state of non-attachment, one must abandon longing for externals that have been left behind. Non-attachment is also love for duty, rather than indifference or disinterest. Non-attachment is a virtue that is helpful in both yoga paths (PPB 126).

Fourth Discourse: Renunciation and Wisdom

Attachment is an intense form of desire (PPB 184) and the emotion associated with attachment has the power to disturb thought and distort one's ability to take action (PPB 189). Krishna instructs Arjuna to light the fire of knowledge which alone has the power of reducing attachment to ashes. The fire of spiritual knowledge burns impurities, all evil thoughts of the mind are reduced to ashes and the mind is freed from impurities (PPB 198). Arjuna wonders whether he should fight the war or follow the path of renunciation. Since non-attachment is an essential pre-requisite for renunciation, he considers escaping from his life as a warrior to live a different life, but realizes that true renunciation is not escapism.

Fifth Discourse: Renunciation and Action

Arjuna asks Krishna for information about the paths of renunciation and of action, so he can be clear in his thinking as he chooses a path (PPB 206). Krishna responds by explaining that both paths are valid. Then he recommends a path of action for Arjuna for a number of reasons (PPB 206). Arjuna is full of grief because of attachment to his relatives. Arjuna is leaning toward renunciation, but that is just an escape because he does not have the courage to process the mental conflict he experiences. He is being selfish thinking only about himself and his position. He is thinking of renouncing his role as warrior, but that is a clear sign of cowardice for a warrior (PPB 206). Refusing to fight a just war and running away from the battlefield would have nothing to do with renunciation (PPB 206).

Sixth Discourse: The Path of Meditation

Krishna encourages Arjuna to practise silence to gain control over his mind. Until one experiences perfect silence, he is not aware of the profound difference between leading a life in the external world and treading the path of the inward journey. The systematic method that leads to the deepest state is meditation (PPB 232). In the deep state of meditation, the whole personality is transformed. Through meditation, the mind attains a state of tranquility. Meditation leads to mastery of the mind, leaving no desire for sense pleasures, while enabling mastery in the performance of actions. Arjuna also learns that loneliness and silence are two different states of mind. In silence, one has the company of an inner dweller, but in loneliness one is all alone (PPB 233). As the *Bhagavad Gita* teaches it, meditation is about being in the center of consciousness, while performing actions selflessly with non-attachment. Meditation centers the mind by bringing scattered attention to a single point of full attention. Reliance on external resources, that is, search for sources outside of himself, such as multiple shrines or going from one teacher to another leaves the disciple's inner thirst for silence unquenched (PPB 234). When one gets into his inner world, he gradually realizes that which he was seeking outside is actually within (PPB 236). The *Bhagavad Gita* encourages a distinction between the lower self and the higher self. One who has successfully conquered the lower self with all its desires and appetites attains the highest state of uninterrupted peace, and he is above the influences of pairs of opposites such as pain and pleasure, heat and cold (PPB 238).

Seventh Discourse: Knowledge of the Absolute in its Entirety

Krishna prepares Arjuna to receive knowledge of the Absolute through spiritual practice (sadhana). First, Arjuna should set a goal for acquiring knowledge, then he should devise a method of spiritual practice for achieving that goal (PPB 269). With these two aspects of knowledge, an aspirant can tread the path of and obtain perfection, that is, samadhi. After attaining the state of perfection, there still remains to be attained the highest state: Self-realization, which is the highest goal that an individual is capable of achieving (PPB 269). The last step is total expansion of the knowledge he has attained, so that he becomes one with the whole universe (PPB 270). Krishna explains that the external world is made up of constituents such as earth, water, fire, air, space, mind, intellect and ego. These constituents make up the lower being. They are the phenomena of life. There is a higher being that includes originator, sustainer, and annihilator of the whole universe. This is the driving force behind the phenomena of life. When Arjuna applies his resources with full devotion, he will grasp the knowledge of that driving force. To attain that knowledge and expand his consciousness, Arjuna must examine his capabilities and devise a method of spiritual practice (PPB 271). The sacred word OM (A-U-M) is a universal sound that is an important theme of Hindu scripture. The three syllables (A, U, M) personify the waking, dreaming and sleeping states. There is a fourth syllable that is silent: turiya, which is a state of being beyond waking, dreaming and sleeping. This is the state where the essential nature of universal consciousness is established in individual consciousness (PPB 272). The spiritual practice of meditation leads the aspirant from an awareness of the gross constituents of his lower being to an awareness of the subtle constituents of a higher being, after which the aspirant can achieve union with the divine (PPB 273).

Eighth Discourse: Knowledge of the Eternal

In response to Arjuna's questions about Brahman, Krishna explains that it is the liberated state of consciousness where divinity resides. Brahman is the highest of all spiritual principles.

Brahman is Absolute Reality, and pure Consciousness (PPB 288). Krishna encourages Arjuna to prepare for his last hour of departure from this world by remembering a mantra, which can be a word, a syllable, or set of words. When a mantra is remembered consciously, it is recorded in the aspirant's unconsciousness. It creates a bridge between conscious life and unconscious life. At the point of departure from earth, the prominent thoughts are the deciding factor about whether one's voyage into the unknown will be pleasant or unpleasant. Whatever state an aspirant habitually remembers is the same state he attains after leaving his body. He who habitually remembers worldly pleasures will continue to long for those pleasures after leaving the body. Because those desires cannot be fulfilled in the state between death and birth, he will suffer. In that state there are no senses and no objects. He who habitually remembers a mantra, and who is a meditator, will achieve a deep state of tranquility leading up to rebirth (PPB 290 - 291).

Ninth Discourse: Knowledge of Mysticism

To help Arjuna understand his internal organization, Krishna shares knowledge of the Hindu scriptures and teachings of the sages. He explains the non-intellectual knowledge of mysticism (PPB 303). The power of mysticism resides in every human, as being subtle, invisible, and cannot be grasped by sense perception. Arjuna needs to practise meditation, contemplation and self-surrender to achieve a union and absorption into the divine. The result is like a river that meets the ocean and becomes part of the ocean (PPB 318). These practices will take him beyond the pairs of opposites of Arjuna's dilemma, enabling him to learn how to extend his individual consciousness to the universal consciousness. By doing so, he will establish himself in his true nature and attain Self-realization. When a mind is not allowed to roam around, but becomes focused by meditation, it becomes purified, one-pointed and can attain union with the divine (PPB 307).

Tenth Discourse: Manifestations of Divine Reality

The conversations with Krishna gradually help dispel Arjuna's doubts. They diminish his identification with qualities of the mind or the personality. He learns that those are mental creations that manifest from his karma (PPB 323). The qualities that emanate from an all-pervading mind are wisdom, truth and contentment. The aspirant who understands the difference will retain a tranquil mind in situations of happiness and misery, success and failure, fame and infamy. He who remains in union with the divine remains fearless (PPB 323). To control a dissipated mind, the novice meditator should focus his mind on the flow of his breadth and be aware that all creatures of the universe are sustained by the same vital force, breadth. The aspirant should also become aware that there is only one force which sustains the entire universe. With that awareness, he learns to love all as he loves himself. Eager to know the practical way of meditation, Arjuna learns from Krishna that the path to meditation is guided by a profound knowledge of the universe in all its forms ... manifestations of Divine Reality in the sun, moon, stars, oceans, as well as things animate and inanimate (PPB 332 – 333).

Eleventh Discourse: The Vision of the Cosmic Form

Arjuna is not fully satisfied with understanding and believing what Krishna teaches. Arjuna makes a request to see a manifestation of the Brahman. Krishna blesses Arjuna by granting him a Cosmic Vision, in which Arjuna is overwhelmed by a view of the entire universe in a single glance (PPB 336 - 337). Astonished by the multiplicity of images that merge into its underlying oneness in a blazing flash of light, Arjuna bows with praying hands that indicate he is aware that the union of individual consciousness and universal consciousness is the purpose of human life (PPB 339). Arjuna recognizes in the vision both the potential for mercy and the potential for annihilation. Arjuna becomes aware that, when the mind turns inward, the manifestation of diversity only has one source. He also realizes that his grief and despondency are self-created because of his attachments to objects and relationships of the mundane world (PPB 346). However, Arjuna's dilemma remains. He is finding it difficult to decide whether to engage in war. Lord Krishna responds by telling Arjuna 'you will only be an instrument of My work' (*Bhagavad Gita* 11:33). That becomes a turning point for Arjuna.

Twelfth Discourse: The Path of Devotion

Arjuna's Cosmic Vision was a temporary glimpse into divine insight. As he returns to ordinary reality, he asks Krishna how to conduct himself in the external world where he exists. Should he follow a Path of Devotion, or a Path of Knowledge? Is it better to cultivate devotion or strive to know absolute reality? Krishna recommends a Path of Devotion because it is more accessible. Krishna advises Arjuna to concentrate on an object for meditation ... an object that has qualities which will lead him to reverence and devotion (PPB 360 - 361). In the Path of Devotion, there is no duality, no pair of opposites. This path is a conscious dissolution of one's individuality in devotion to God (PPB 370).

Thirteenth Discourse: The Field and its Knower

Krishna encourages Arjuna to become aware of the distinction between the Field and Knower of the Field. The Field is the individual human made up of ego, mind, intellect, and organs of the body, all of which are useful in attaining the purpose of life (PPB 372). The Field is body plus the mind, governed by the ego. The Knower is the individual immortal soul dwelling in the body (PPB 371 - 372). The Knower is not the human body. The Knower's gaze is turned inward toward a divine identity. When an aspirant learns there is no difference between himself and the universal form of the Lord, he realizes that he is Atman and that the whole universe is his field. Krishna explains that the Field is the human being, while the Knower of the Field is the immortal soul dwelling in the aspirant's body.

Fourteenth Discourse: Knowledge of the Three Gunas (Three Attributes of Nature)

Krishna explains to Arjuna that the entire universe is a drama enacted by the three gunas: sattva, rajas and tamas (PPB 390 – 391). When sattva is predominant, the aspirant remains serene and happy, with elevated thoughts that are helpful for maintaining mental and emotional equilibrium. When rajas predominates, the aspirant is continually pursuing attractions or attachments to objects and people in the world, but the aspirant is never satisfied and is always seeking new sources of pleasure. That can lead to hypertension and other diseases because the aspirant functions under the sway of unconscious habits, without understanding his behaviors. When tamas is predominant, sloth and inertia prevail. The aspirant is controlled by negative emotions and life becomes burdensome (PPB 390 - 391). The gunas dwell in every human mind, one being predominant while the others are inactive. When the aspirant learns to keep the gunas under control, he can make progress on the path of meditation and contemplation (PPB 392). Arjuna asks how to recognize someone who has gone beyond the three gunas? How does such a person behave? Krishna explains that such a person is aloof and emotionally balanced, unaffected in all situations (PPB 397).

Fifteenth Discourse: Supreme Reality

The *Bhagavad Gita* portrays the universe as a manifestation of one supreme, imperishable reality. Yet, this universe is transitory because all objects in the external universe constantly change as a result of the three gunas. In human life, the body changes but not Atman. Without Atman, the body cannot exist; the body exists only because of the existence of Atman (PPB 400). Those aspirants who have examined the phenomenal world know that they are caught by the snare of deaths and births. When they understand the basis of their bondage, they also realize they can cut themselves free from their entanglements with the powerful weapon of non-attachment. By cultivating non-attachment, the aspirant becomes free from bondage created by charms, temptations, and attractions to objects of the world (PPB 401). When the aspirant attains freedom from egotism, pride, delusion and attachments, then he becomes content within. Free from all desires, he attains wisdom and finally the highest state of knowledge of Supreme Reality (PPB 402).

Sixteenth Discourse: Destiny of the Wise and the Ignorant
Krishna explains to Arjuna that he is the architect of his destiny ... the composer of the life he lives (PPB 411). He also explains that there are essentially two categories of people in the world. In one category, there are people who have knowledge of an orderly creation in the power of the Lord. In the other category, there are people who are ignorant of any orderly creation behind the world. Knowledgeable people are able to renounce harmful habits of selfish desire, anger and greed. They use the scriptures as their guide and they are not afraid of dying. The ignorant people remain inflated and deluded, lead a materialistic life and are constantly competing with others. They pursue allurements in the external world, but are never satisfied. Such ignorant people are afraid of dying. The aspirant should avoid the company of such people because their influence could be injurious (PPB 414 - 417).

Seventeenth Discourse: Three Types of Conviction
Arjuna asks Krishna to explain the types of conviction. Krishna replies that conviction, or faith, depends on which guna is predominant in one's life. (PPB 420). People who are of sattvic conviction perform religious rites according to the scriptures. They engage in charitable works without expecting rewards or recognition. People who are of rajasic conviction worship with the desire to fulfil selfish ends. They engage in charitable works with the expectation of rewards for the fruits of their labor. People who are of tamasic conviction do not do much. Although they have expectations and desires, they prefer to depend on others (PPB 420). Krishna recommends close reflection on one's own behavior to determine the type of one's own conviction.

Eighteenth Discourse: Liberation through Renunciation
Arjuna asks Krishna: What is true renunciation? (PPB 433). The goal of the renunciate is to systematically fathom one after another of the various stages of consciousness that lead to the innermost One. The renunciate directs all effort toward Self-realization. He does not waste time or energy pursuing desires based on self-interest. The renunciate's journey is inward rather

than toward the external world. The renunciate is not involved with objects because they have been consciously renounced (PPB 436). Krishna tells Arjuna that one should not renounce his duty under the influence of either rajas or tamas. Instead, one should do one's duty because the duty (dharma) carries samskaras (mental impressions or psychological imprints) from previous lives. It is those latent tendencies within himself that create his duties (PPB 438 - 440).

There are differing interpretations about the outcome of the discourses between Arjuna and Krishna. Some interpretations make Krishna the decision-maker about whether to fight the war. In those interpretations, Arjuna completely surrenders to Krishna, offers his allegiance to Krishna and asks Krishna to tell him what to do. Other interpretations make Arjuna the decision-maker. In these interpretations, Arjuna applies the scriptural knowledge obtained from Krishna to resolve his conflict about war. My interpretation makes neither Arjuna nor Krishna the decision-maker. In my opinion, the discourses are dialectical interactions in which Krishna, in his role as container, mediated an introjection to help Arjuna process his projection. Arjuna and Krishna produced an outcome that was the result of starting with a position, then negating it, then modifying it, in repeated cycles until they arrived at a joint decision. In other words, they sustained a dialectical interaction about Arjuna's unassimilated state of mind until they reached a workable decision.

By granting Arjuna a Cosmic Vision, Krishna revealed himself to be not just a human counsellor, but also a deity. Prince Arjuna's projection was broken after he experienced the Cosmic Vision. Their decision to follow the path of action and fight the battle was not based on rationality. It was the result of the dialectical interaction between them. The decision involved a number of factors. One factor was that Arjuna's duty as a warrior is to fight. The decision was not just to regain the kingdom, nor to demonstrate superior war strategy. Rather, the decision was for Arjuna to perform his duty as a warrior, taking into account his dharma, the principle of non-attachment, and the three gunas. The decision was also for Arjuna to take his place as warrior by making a serious effort to perform his duties selflessly, by putting in the effort to be of service to others. The overall goal of the decision was to seek the level of consciousness where duties are performed without attachment because that is a viable path to renunciation (PPB 148).

The Kurukshetra battlefield was a psychological frame for this reflexive mode of containment. While the physical battlefield of Kurukshetra was being prepared for a physical war, there was a battlefield in Arjuna's mind where he struggled with a spiritual battle and a psychological battle. The *Bhagavad Gita* captures the essence of a warrior dealing with life's moral decisions. The intense conversations illuminate the moral dilemma that Arjuna faced. During the interaction between warrior Arjuna and his charioteer Krishna, the *Bhagavad Gita* presents Hindu themes that explain the human knowledge and actions necessary to overcome life's difficult decisions. Although the discourses were conducted in a spiritual context, they can also be viewed in a psychological context. In the study of Analytical Psychology, there is an archetype for every typical situation in life. In Arjuna's life, the warrior archetype was activated. According to Swiss psychologist Marie-Louise von Franz, a projection emerges from an archetype. Arjuna's projection emerged from the warrior archetype. In the words of von Franz "... wherever known reality stops, where we touch the unknown, there we project an archetypal image" (PRJ 24). Arjuna's behavior and communication indicated that his known reality stopped at his aptitude for war. He had the physical skills of a warrior, but he needed help with determining the conditions for applying his skills. His projection had emerged from the warrior archetype, whose characteristics are courage, integrity, a knowledge of war and an aptitude for war. With help from his war counsellor, Arjuna grappled with his mental conflict about whether to fight the battle. Prince Arjuna's projection was broken after he experienced the Cosmic Vision granted by Lord Krishna. In this section, I described the relationship between Prince Arjuna and Lord Krishna in the context of archetype as biological entity. In the next section, I will describe the relationship in the context of archetype as emergent phenomenon.

Context of Archetype as Emergent Phenomenon: Appropriation & Internalization

This section is about the relationship between Prince Arjuna and Lord Krishna viewed in terms of archetype-as-emergent-phenomenon.

Considering archetype as an emergent phenomenon involves viewing the archetype as an emergent property of a dynamic, developmental system that is made up of human bodies, human activities, human minds, society's external environment as well as the narrative competence of humans in the society. When viewing archetype as an emergent phenomenon, the means for converting life's experience to meaning are appropriation and internalization. Appropriation is an adoption of conscious content from social and cultural sources in the external environment. For readers who are unfamiliar with appropriation, a common example of appropriation is seen in the acquisition of language. Children appropriate the language of the culture in which they grow up. They adopt communications from social and cultural sources in the external environment. They internalize those communications into their mental models. Then, the children use the internalized language constructs to compose sentences of their own. In a similar way, Arjuna had a conscious appropriation from his culture. His appropriation was a combination of habits and practices drawn from the Eastern culture in which he lived. His appropriation included considerations about one's duty as a member of the warrior caste, karma from previous lives, emotional attachments to relatives and friends, a sense of familial pride about recovering the land that belonged to his family, and the scriptural considerations of life as a member of the Hindu religion. Internalization is the incorporation of a cultural appropriation into one's mental model. Having established a theistic mode of containment with Lord Krishna, Prince Arjuna incorporated into his mental model a refined sense of duty to function as a warrior without expectations about the fruits of his effort. Prince Arjuna was also able to internalize into his mental model, the importance of giving priority to his dharma in the interest of emancipation from the cycles of life that underpin reincarnation.

The theistic mode of containment was initiated by an activation of the warrior archetype which triggered an appropriation. The appropriation left Arjuna in a confused state of mind. When Arjuna confided the appropriation to his war counsellor Krishna, the response was a series of discourses about scriptural concepts. With Krishna's help Arjuna achieved an internalization that incorporated the scriptural concepts to achieve a new outlook on his situation. The Cosmic Vision preceded a turning point for Arjuna. After the vision, he was still finding it difficult to decide whether to engage in war. In his role as deity, Lord Krishna responds by telling Arjuna 'you will only be an instrument of My work' (*Bhagavad Gita* 11:33). That becomes the turning point for Arjuna. Lord Krishna's remark does not tell Arjuna what to do. It does not make the decision for him, but the remark reduces the burden of Arjuna's responsibility for war. It points out that the weight of the decision does not rest solely with Arjuna because he functions in the context of a universe where divinity creates the setting for humanity. In the next section, I use the expression 'you will only be an instrument of My work' to explain the symbolization that I believe occurred during the dialogue between Prince Arjuna and Lord Krishna.

Converting Experience to Meaning: Symbolization

Arjuna's dilemma occurs at a critical time in his life when he is making the transition from one level of maturity to a higher level of maturity. At the start of the *Bhagavad Gita*, he functions at the same level as his Kauravas relatives. At that level, the focus is on the physical strength of their army, and their perspective is materially oriented. Arjuna is at the threshold of a higher level of maturity where there is a reliance on the strength of a person's inner life, which includes an individual's courage as a warrior. To help Arjuna over the threshold, Krishna tells him that one should not renounce his duty under the influence of either rajas or tamas. Instead, one should do one's duty because the duty (dharma) carries samskaras (mental impressions or psychological imprints) from previous lives. It is those latent tendencies within himself that create his duties (PPB 438 - 440).

In my research about the interaction between Prince Arjuna and the Bhagavad Gita, I noticed that the images of the Cosmic Vision so overwhelmed Arjuna that he turned to Krishna with astonishment, praised him and requested forgiveness for having doubted his capability as war counsellor. However, Arjuna's dilemma remained. He was still finding it difficult to decide whether to engage in war. In his role as deity, Lord Krishna responds by telling Arjuna 'you will only be an instrument of My work' (*Bhagavad Gita* 11:33). That becomes a turning point for Arjuna. Lord Krishna's response does not instruct Arjuna on whether to fight.

The response does not present Arjuna with a readymade decision. The response lightens the burden of Arjuna's responsibility for war. Krishna's response, 'you will only be an instrument of My work', makes it clear that the full weight of the decision does not rest solely with Arjuna because he functions in a universe where divinity creates the setting for humanity. Lord Krishna's response stands out as being consistent with the emergence of a symbol as described in "*A Dictionary of Jungian Analysis*" where psychologist Andrew Samuels defines symbol in terms of concept, intent, purpose and content. This is how I apply the dictionary definition of symbol to Lord Krishna's expression 'you will only be an instrument of My work':

- **Concept:** The concept of the symbol 'you will only be an instrument of My work' is about being called into a new state of being, but without any specific information about the nature of the new state, or any logical instructions on how to achieve that state. For Arjuna, the concept was a distillation of the images of the Cosmic Vision granted to him by Lord Krishna. The symbol was not rationally composed; it was a summing-up of Arjuna's psychological situation.

- **Intent:** Behind the expression 'you will only be an instrument of My work' was an intent to bring about a change of outlook. The symbol pointed in the direction of a conclusion, but did not state the nature of the conclusion. The intent of the symbol pointed him in a new direction for seeing his role of warrior from a different perspective.

- **Purpose:** The purpose of the symbol was to reveal a new outlook through the back-and-forth interaction between Arjuna and Krishna regarding two sides of the dilemma of whether to wage a righteous war.

- **Content:** The content of the symbol of 'you will only be an instrument of My work' turned out to be a new meaning of his role as warrior. The symbol guided Arjuna out of his unprocessed state of mind to a processed state of mind about his function as warrior. Processing his state of mind was not just about making a decision on whether to wage a war. It was also about shaping his life according to principles of attachment, and the mix of the three gunas in his life. More important, it helped him choose a path of renunciation that is appropriate for his life.

At the end of the *Bhagavad Gita*, Arjuna is able to understand that his duty is important because it is the means of fulfilling the purpose of his life. That which supports the fulfillment of one's duty is called dharma. Arjuna was a warrior who specialized in the art and science of war, but he was conflicted about his dharma (PPB 71) when he chose Lord Krishna as charioteer. At the end of the discourses, Arjuna was able to take into account that while he has the right to perform his duty, he does not have the right to expect specific fruits of his labor. He had learned that duty performed with the motivation to acquire the fruits of one's action is not helpful. He also learned that inaction due to attachment is not helpful either.

Symbolization serves a cognitive function that reveals insight, new knowledge, or inspiration when unprocessed states of mind are drawn into a mental space where they can be viewed and understood. Symbolic thinking involves a process of formulation which transforms felt emotion into perception. Examination of the symbol, in that shared mental space where Arjuna and Krishna interacted, brought the realization that the weight of the decision does not rest solely with Arjuna because he functions in the context of a universe where divinity creates the setting for humanity.

The theme of the Bion-Cartwright containment model is that a mind depends on another mind to grow psychologically. The *Bhagavad Gita* seems to have a similar outlook, which is expressed in chapter 1 verse 43 whose English translation is:

> *"One cannot reach the real point of factual knowledge without being helped by the right person, who is already established in that knowledge."*
> — Bhagavad Gita 1:43

That observation applies to Arjuna, who reached a point of factual knowledge with the help of his human war counsellor, who turned out to be a deity, Lord Krishna. I believe that psychological growth can be achieved by the interaction between a human and a deity. In proposing a theistic mode of containment, I offer the relationship between Arjuna and Krishna as an example. During their discourses on the battlefield, Krishna provided the psychological and spiritual scaffolding for Arjuna to manage his unprocessed state of mind regarding his role as warrior. I propose that this relationship involved a theistic mode of containment, with Arjuna as contained and Krishna as the container. By learning the Hindu principles that Krishna taught him and participating in the dialectical discourses, Arjuna achieved the psychological growth necessary to process the emotional turmoil that plagued him at the beginning of the *Bhagavad Gita*. The psychological growth also gave him the courage to fight the Kurukshetra War free of the attachments that initially rendered him unable to make a decision.

The symbolic process began with Arjuna feeling that his path in life was being obstructed, because he was torn between two prongs of a dilemma about engaging in war. The symbolic process ended with Arjuna being relieved of the obstruction when he realized that he was only an instrument in the greater context of the universe. His unassimilated state of mind was processed and he obtained clarity in the spiritual and psychological aspects of his situation. Spiritually, he learned that divinity creates the setting of the universe in which humanity functions. Psychologically, he moved to a new level of consciousness where his outlook became one of an individual who transcends group attachment. Arjuna was no longer tethered to the attachments of his community.

Call To Action: Take Away A Portable Understanding

This chapter is about a dialogue between Prince Arjuna, a young warrior, and his Hindu deity, Lord Krishna, in what I call a theistic mode of containment. It is not just a story about how Arjuna obtained advice from his war counsellor. The dialogue between them enabled Arjuna, not only to process his unassimilated state of mind, but also to situate his human decision-making in the knowledge that divinity creates the setting of the universe in which humanity functions. Psychologically, the dialogue helped Arjuna move to a new level of consciousness where his outlook became that of a more mature individual, who was no longer tethered to the attachments of his community. In a call to action, I invite readers to take away a portable understanding of the theistic mode of containment. To help readers, I offer the following summary as a reminder of how Lord Krishna provided the mental scaffolding for Prince Arjuna to overcome his anxiety about fighting a righteous war:

- **Mode:** Prince Arjuna and Lord Krishna had a theistic mode of containment.

- **Roles:** Arjuna was the human contained, while Krishna was the human container, who turned out to be a deity.

- **Symmetry:** Arjuna and Krishna had an asymmetrical relationship. Arjuna was a young warrior, who had selected Krishna as an experienced war counsellor. Arjuna was a mortal human being, while Krishna was an earthly incarnation of a deity in Hindu theology.

- **Psychological Frame:** The psychological frame of sitting in the chariot in the battlefield of Kurukshetra created a privacy that made it possible for Arjuna and Krishna to have overlapping reveries. The frame has a purpose, a time boundary and a space boundary. The psychological frame of the containment in the *Bhagavad Gita* serves the purpose of creating a setting for the dialogue that enables a resolution of Arjuna's conflict about war. Different interpreters offer differing time boundaries for the dialogue. In my primary source of information, "*Perennial Psychology of the Bhagavad Gita*" the dialogue between Arjuna and Krishna is made up of eighteen discourses that cover a period of eighteen days, one for each chapter of the *Bhagavad Gita* (PPB 97). The space boundary of the psychological frame is the arena of the battlefield of Kurukshetra where two armies were preparing for war (PPB 12).

- **Dialectical Narrative:** The first narrative was Arjuna's disclosure of his conflicts regarding whether to fight a righteous war. His ego made an effort to compose a narrative that he could control, without making his dilemma an either-or decision. The second narrative was Krishna's responses in counselling Arjuna on self-transformation and his duty as a trained warrior. The third narrative of the containment had both an internal result and an external result. The internal result of the dialectical interaction between them was that Arjuna experienced a series of self-transformations about his outlook on war and life. The external result of their interaction was the celestial Song of God which became known as the *Bhagavad Gita,* a sacred text in the Hindu religion.

After the Containment Ended

After engaging in the *Bhagavad Gita*'s eighteen discourses with Krishna, Arjuna fights the Kurukshetra War and wins, thus regaining the kingdom that rightfully belongs to the Pandavas, that is, his side of the family. Krishna moves on to later events in the *Mahabharata,* where, in a human incarnation, he was killed accidentally by a hunter.

Sources

The sources of information that I used in preparation of this chapter are:
- "*Perennial Psychology of the Bhagavad Gita*" by Swami Rama
- "*GITA: A Timeless Guide For Our Time*" by Isaac Bentwich (translator)
- "*Containing States of Mind*" by Duncan Cartwright
- "*SYMBOLIZATION: Representation and Communication*" by James Rose (editor)
- "*Projection and Re-Collection in Jungian Psychology*" by Marie-Louise von Franz.

APPENDIX A

Hotlines for
Psychological Support

This Appendix offers some telephone numbers for national organizations that provide psychological support in the United States of America.

Drug Abuse and Addiction
Telephone (844) 289-0879

National Domestic Violence Hotline
Telephone (800) 799-7233

National Eating Disorder Association Information and Referral Helpline
Telephone (800) 931-2237

National Institute of Mental Health Information Line
Telephone (800) 647-2642

National Violence Domestic Hotline
Telephone (800) 799-7233

Pyromania and Addiction
Telephone (844) 640-0175

Shoplifters Anonymous
Telephone (800) 848-9595

Social Media Addiction Solutions and Treatment
Telephone (866) 291-6226

Substance Abuse and Mental Health Services Administration (SAMHSA)
National Helpline
Telephone (800) 662-4357

APPENDIX B

Characterizations of Archetype By Jung, Stevens, Bion, Knox, Hogenson, and Colman

This Appendix offers some highlights of the characterizations of archetype by Carl Jung, Anthony Stevens, Wilfred Bion, Jean Knox, George Hogenson and Warren Colman. These views cover the period from 1919 when an archetype was regarded as an innate sensing mechanism to 2016 when an archetype came to be regarded as an emergent phenomenon.

Carl Jung (archetype as biological entity: 1919 – 1961)

The inspiration for Jung's thoughts about archetypes was his observation of the behavior of patients at Burgolzli Hospital and his Word Association Test (APC 52). Having noticed patterns of behavior in both situations, he postulated that there might be an underlying influence, but was not sure about it at the time. When he wrote "Transformations" he postulated that there might be a theory of archetype and that its manifestation could be in the symbolic world of the human psyche (APC 53). In that book, he indicates that under certain circumstances, the human mind produces typical patterns of ideation and representation, but Jung did not articulate them.

Two notions that crop up repeatedly in Jung's discussion of archetypes are 'a priori' and the notion that they are linked with instincts. These notions appear along with his first use of the term 'archetype' in his 1919 paper "Instinct and the Unconscious" giving the impression that he sees archetypes in terms of biological inheritance (AIE 20). Later, in his 1947 essay "On The Nature of the Psyche" Jung distinguishes between two poles of an archetype: the instinctual pole and the spiritual pole. The poles suggest that he was shifting his opinion of archetypes from a purely biological inheritance toward a partly metaphysical view. During collaboration with physicist Wolfgang Pauli, Jung appeared to be trying to ground his archetypal hypothesis more in physics and less in biology. He seems to be striving to give his archetypal hypothesis a basis in empirical science (AIE 21). When Jung was writing, the notion of emergence was not well known in the scientific world. The idea that an archetype may be an emergent phenomenon does not appear in his archetypal hypothesis.

In "Symbols of Transformation" Jung wrote that symbols are not allegories and are not signs; they are images of content which transcend consciousness (Collected Works 5, Paragraph 114). The withdrawal of a projection involves a reconciliation that is not accomplished rationally, but symbolically. Jung used the expression 'transcendent function' to refer to this symbolic process. Since a projection emanates from an archetype, Jung was making a connection between his pre-existent archetype and the symbolization that occurs in his transcendent function.

Anthony Stevens (archetype as biological entity: 2003)

In the Glossary of his book "Archetypes Revisited" Anthony Stevens defines archetypes as biological entities: Archetypes are "innate neuropsychic centers possessing the capacity to initiate, control and mediate the common behavioral characteristics and typical experiences of all human beings irrespective of race, culture or creed" (AR 352). As biological entities, they have a natural history and are subject to the laws of evolution. He argues that archetypes evolved through natural selection (AR 17). Stevens also states that "Archetypes ... (are) the neuropsychic centers responsible for coordinating the behavioral and the psychic repertoires of our species in response to whatever environmental circumstances we may encounter ..." (AR 17). His argument is that archetypes correspond to genetically defined need that must be fulfilled if humans are to develop successfully. Archetypes are an inherited mode of functioning. They are collective in the sense that they embody general characteristics of groups of individuals rather than the peculiarities of specific individuals.

Stevens points out that under certain circumstances the psyche transcends reason and the rules of logic because it is capable of the simultaneous perception of incompatibilities (AR 278). In making that point, he establishes that the psyche offers the opportunity for psychological growth because it is capable of processing symbolic forms.

Wilfred Bion (archetype as either biological entity or emergent phenomena: 1960 - 1970)

James Grotstein was a professional colleague and friend of Wilfred Bion. After Bion died, Grotstein wrote the book titled "*A Beam of Intense Darkness: Wilfred Bion's Legacy to Psychoanalysis*" to explain Bion's work for a general audience. That seems to me a rather forbidding title for a book intended for a general audience, but I find it more accessible that Bion's own work. Grotstein reports that archetypes found an enthusiastic reception in Bion's thinking. Beta elements, or unbearable states of mind, emerge from archetypes that exist in unconsciousness before they undergo transformation by the alpha function to become alpha elements, that is, bearable states of mind (BID 135 – 136). Because Bion uses the words 'projection' and 'introjection' (words commonly used by Jung and Stevens) it gives the impression that he favored the pre-existent definition of archetype. Although Grotstein describes the containment model without mentioning emergent phenomenon explicitly, he writes about containment as if it occurs in a context of emergence. For example, Grotstein explains that from the incubation of emotions which occurs in containment, there "*emerges spontaneously a 'selected fact' that gives coherence to the entirety of the communication*" between contained and container (BID 156). That implies an emergent phenomenon. I found that Bion's model is compatible with both the pre-existent and the emergent definitions of archetypes.

Jean Knox (archetype as emergent phenomenon: 2001 & 2003)

In her book "*Archetype, Attachment, Analysis*" psychologist Jean Knox's theme is that archetypes emerge out of the earliest stages of psychic development and forms the foundation for development of core meanings as people gradually construct mental models of the world around them, organizing day-to-day experience into patterns which can then guide their future expectations of life in all its aspects, including expectations of relationships (AAA 10 – 11). Knox expresses the view that core symbolic meanings cannot possibly be inherited because the human genome has turned out to be far too limited to carry such complex information (AAA 49). She explains that is because there are about 30,000 genes in the human genetic code, and given the complexity of the human body and mind, it would be impossible to store the necessary volume of information in the genes. She espouses another way which does not involve any form of innate structure. Her research demonstrates that, rather than being pre-given, psychic structures are emergent through the interaction with the environment (AIE 42). While Knox rejects the claim that archetypes are innate structures, she preserves the fundamental idea of archetypes as abstract, organizing frameworks combined with core meanings (AIE 43). She argues that their apparent universality is due to the commonalities of human experience. Knox's internal models are not about psychological material passing from one person's mind to another's mind, as in a projection. Her internalization is a description of the consequences in interpersonal experiences, but it is also an account of the information-processing which goes on within one person's mind as a result of a two-person interaction. Knox believes that humans have minds which are capable of creating and storing complex symbolic mental representations, the symbolic kind of representation that is demonstrated by human speech, writing and drawing (AAA 43). These activities involve semantic and symbolic representations such as an awareness of self, the ability to remember the past and imagine the future (AAA 44).

George Hogenson (archetype as emergent phenomenon: 2001 & 2004)

The book "*Analytical Psychology: Contemporary Perspectives in Jungian Psychology*" is a collection of essays edited by Joseph Cambray and Linda Carter. I draw on Chapter 2 "*Archetypes: Emergence and the Psyche's Deep Structure*" written by George B. Hogenson. Hogenson argues that the key to understanding archetypes is to see them as emergent phenomena (APC 32 – 55). From his perspective, an archetype is an emergent property of the dynamic developmental system that is made up of brain, environment and narrative (APC 46). Archetypes do not have a property of location because they permeate the cultural environment. Hogenson's conclusion is that archetypal influences are more about the dynamic force of psychic systems than about the particularities of individual archetypes (APC 37).

Warren Colman (archetype as emergent phenomenon: 2016)

Warren Colman wrote the book "*Act and Image: The Emergence of Symbolic Imagination*" in which he expresses the view that archetypes are not merely a hypothesis, they are a living reality that provides orientation and meaning for life in general (AIE 3). He points out that people are shaped by social factors as well as psychological factors (AIE 3 – 4). Writing in 2016, Colman states "*Over the past fifteen years or so, archetype theory has been reconfigured in terms of emergence theories, notably by Jean Knox and George Hogenson*" (AIE 4). He argues that the social organization and material environment play a role in the construction of symbolic thought and imagination. Colman thinks that Jung's archetypal hypothesis has outlived its purpose, and researchers should direct their attention to the actual phenomena that archetypes were introduced to explain ... symbolic imagination, that is, symbols and their meanings (AIE 50).

The human mind is not simply a cognitive apparatus for high-level problem-solving, but an embodied emotional responsiveness deeply intertwined with its cultural environment (AIE 80). It is only through the use of symbols that anything like archetypes come into existence (AIE 86). In the evolution of biology, the chief instruments of transmission and change are the genes (in organic structures). In the evolution of society, the chief instruments of transmission and change are symbols (AIE 88). Culture does not arise from ideas in the mind, but out of social and material practices which become embedded in symbols as carriers of meaning that can be transmitted to subsequent generations and trans-formed by future circumstances. So, although ideas cannot be inherited, symbols can be, not biologically, but through the medium of culture, the true medium for emergence of the psyche (AIE 89).

Colman shares Vygotsky's account of how children acquire language. They first encounter language in the world around them and use it in social interaction. Only gradually does language become appropriated for use as a means of private thought. Colman's way of image formation reverses the notion of projection in Jung's formulation that unconscious content appears first in projection (AIE 161). Rather than assuming that what is discovered in the world is simply a model for something that already exists unconsciously in the psyche, Colman uses the notion of appropriation to argue that it is only through activity in the world with things and other people that we are able to develop psychic lives at all (AIE 161 – 162). For humans, emotion is differentiated through symbol-ization (AIE 165). Material symbolization is necessary for the imaginal world to be realized (AIE 166). Mind is emergent from the symbols we use when we imagine; without symbols, there can be no imagina-tion, and without imagination, there can be no human mind. (AIE 168). It is only through symbolization in a cultural context that psychic life can emerge as a distinct domain of human experience. In this respect, psyche, imagination, spirit, and self-reflexive consciousness are all linked aspects of the same process … symbolization. Symbolization not only enhances consciousness, but also creates it, or brings it forth. In the process of being represented, emotional states are reformulated and thus constituted in a different, a more reflexively conscious way (AIE 185 – 186).

Colman references Wilfred Bion in describing the construction of mean-ing from life experiences. The creation of meaning is an important theme in Bion's containment model (AIE 222). The model describes processes whereby bodily, affective states are transformed through relationships between people. The model locates the origin of the symbolic world of cultural experience in the intermediate area of shared experience between contained and container, initially via transitional phenomena that are neither created (imagined) nor found (already existing). In the light of emergence theory, it is now recognized that Bion was referring to something emergent. Symbolic meaning has to be scaffolded by the container's communication, enabling the contained to enter a world of meaning (AIE 222). Emotion and symbolic thought go hand in hand since our higher levels of emotion require robust forms of thought to contain the emotions and to communicate them, while symbolic thought also promotes a greater range and depth of emotional sensitivity (AIE 230). Symbolic imagination emerges from collective social living and the intersubjective aspects of relationship. The more humans lived in social groups, the more developed their emotional lives became and the more symbolic language was needed both to reflect this and to organize it (AIE 256).

Sources

The sources of information that shape my thinking in this appendix are:
- *"Symbols of Transformation"* by Carl Jung
- *"Archetype Revisited: An Updated Natural History of the Self"* by Anthony Stevens
- *"Containing States of Mind"* by Duncan Cartwright
- *"Archetype, Attachment, Analysis: Jungian Psychology and the Emergent Mind"* by Jean Knox
- *"Archetypes: Emergence and the Psyche's Deep Structure"* by George Hogenson in *"Analytical Psychology: Contemporary Perspectives in Jungian Psychology"* edited by Joseph Cambray & Linda Carter
- *"Act and Image: The Emergence of Symbolic Imagination"* by Warren Colman
- *"A Critical Dictionary of Jungian Analysis"* by Andrew Samuels, Bani Shorter & Fred Plaut.

Glossary

WORD	MEANING
Alpha Elements	Expression used by Wilfred Bion when referring to components of a bearable state of mind.
Alpha Function	Expression used by Wilfred Bion when referring to the process of transforming an unbearable state of mind to a bearable state of mind.
Analytical Psychology	A school of psychology that was developed by Carl Jung. It studies both the conscious and unconscious aspects of the human psyche, and promotes a quest for individuation.
Appropriation	An appropriation is made up of processed experience about meaningful thoughts of emotions, images and memories that are adopted from the cultural environment.
Archetype-as-biological-entity	Psychologists who wrote in the 20th century defined archetype as an ancestral heritage of human experience accumulated over multiple generations. For those psychologists, archetype is a biological entity, which influences human behavior and communication when unconscious projections are cast from the internal world of the psyche.

WORD	MEANING
Archetype-as-emergent-phenomenon	Psychologists who write in the 21st century are defining archetype as an emergence from a complex system that is made up of human actions, the cultural environment and people's narratives. For these psychologists, archetype is an emergent phenomenon, which influences human behavior and communication when conscious appropriations are drawn from the culture of the external world.
Autistic Mode of Containment	An attempt at interaction between a person and another person, a place or a thing. The containment fails because there is no mind-to-mind interaction, and some of the mental operations of the contained are shut down. For example, John Orr (firefighter) had an autistic mode of containment with serial fires.
Beta Elements	Expression used by Wilfred Bion when referring to components of an unbearable state of mind.
Bifurcation	A separation of something into two branches.
Carrier	A person (or entity) in the external world who provides a hook for a psychological projection.
Chaos Theory	The interdisciplinary science which states that although complex systems may appear to be random and unpredictable, they have underpinning patterns from which novel phenomena can emerge.
Cognitive Psychology	A school of psychology founded by Ulric Neisser. It focuses on the conscious aspect of the human psyche often by noting sensory input, applying stimuli and analyzing subsequent behavioral changes.
Collective Unconscious	That part of the psyche which contains experiences shared by all humanity.
Commensal Mode of Containment	An interaction between two people who engage in an iterative interweaving of narratives, based on their emotional bond. The container provides the mental scaffolding for the contained to transform an unbearable state of mind. For example, Hermann Minkowski (mathematician) provided the mental scaffolding for Albert Einstein (theoretical physicist) to achieve a bearable state of mind about how to prove his intuition regarding the theory of relativity.

WORD	MEANING
Complex	A word that Carl Jung used to mean a core pattern of emotion arranged around a common theme and located in the personal unconscious aspect of the human psyche.
Contained	In a containment pair, the contained is the person whose narrative reveals an unprocessed state of mind.
Container	In a containment pair, the container is the person who provides the mental scaffolding which helps the contained to transform an unprocessed state of mind to a processed state of mind. Sometimes the container is an inanimate object upon which the contained's projection is cast. Since an inanimate object cannot function as a container, such a containment fails.
Containment Model	An interactional model created by psychologists to categorize human interaction in terms of processing unassimilated states of mind.
Ego	That component of the human psyche which mediates interaction between consciousness and unconsciousness.
First Narrative	Conscious and unconscious communications contributed to a psychological containment by the contained, that is, the person whose projection / appropriation initiates the containment.
Individuation	A life-long process for psychological development that differentiates an individual from all others and things.
Internalization	Internalization is an interaction between a contained and a container, aimed at the construction of meaning from the content of a conscious appropriation drawn from the culture in the external world.
Introjection	Introjection is an interaction between a contained and a container, aimed at the construction of meaning from the content of an unconscious projection cast from the internal world of the psyche.

WORD	MEANING
Narrative Dialogue	A narrative dialogue is an iterative process in which a story is created first by one person (contained), and then taken over and retold by another (container) on a new level (AAA 147 – 148). The container holds the storyline while the contained gradually internalizes the meaningful connections made for him / her. Over time, the contained acquires an awareness of a sense that their mind is an agent of change (AAA 148). The narrative is then taken over by the contained. A successful narrative dialogue is one that can become meaningful to the contained so that he / she can take it over, use it for himself / herself and adapt it to establish a sense a connection between their intrapsychic experience and the external world.
Parasitic Mode of Containment	An interaction between two people where one person feeds off the meaning-making resources of the other. Lacking adequate resources to process their own intolerable emotional and cognitive experience, the contained attempts to parasitize the meaning-making resources of the container. For example, Ted Bundy (serial killer) and Elizabeth Kendall (girlfriend) had a parasitic mode of containment.
Personal Unconscious	That part of the psyche which contains repressed or forgotten experiences of an individual.
Projection	A projection is made up of raw experience about emotions, images and memories that are incomprehensible and so are evacuated as an unbearable state of mind.
Pseudo-containing Mode of Containment	An interaction between two people whose behaviors run counter to a containment and therefore preclude the opportunity for psychological growth. The communications between them involves pseudo-intelligence and story-making that prevents the processing of unassimilated thoughts and feelings. For example, Michael Cohen (personal lawyer) and Donald Trump.(real estate entrepreneur and politician) had a pseudo-containing mode of containment.
Psyche	The collection of processes and content that pertain to both consciousness and unconsciousness.

WORD	MEANING
Psychological Frame	A psychological frame has a goal, a space boundary and a time boundary. The goal is an agreement between the contained and container to process an unassimilated state of mind. The space boundary is the private psychological space where the contained and contained engage in communication. It may be a physical or a virtual space. The time boundary is defined by the frequency and duration of their communication.
Reflexive Mode of Containment	An interaction between two mental roles – contained and container — played by the same person. The person depends on their own mind for containment, by turning their attention to thinking about their own mental processes. For example, Dante-the-poet and Dante-the-protagonist in *La Commedia* (Divine Comedy) had a reflexive mode of containment.
Second Narrative	Conscious and unconscious communications contributed to a psychological containment by the container, that is, the person whose introjection / internalization mediates a dialectical interaction during the containment.
Sociality	Sociality is what distinguishes the biological definition from the emergent definition of archetype. Sociality refers to individuals living in social groups for cooperative efforts.
Symbiotic Mode of Containment	Interaction between two people who engage in a mutual dependence that limits the opportunity for psychological growth. The connection between contained and container is one of emotional turmoil that is dampened by each seeing the other as an extension of themselves. Each becomes a receptacle for the other's sense of identity. For example, Carl Jung and Sigmund Freud had a symbiotic mode of containment.
Symbolic Imagination	Symbolic imagination is a way of thinking and feeling suited to the expression and representation of emotional aspects of experience. It is about deriving meaning from life experiences where there is a heightened level of affectivity. It is a non-rational form of apprehension suited for the arts, religion, myths, dreams, psychology, rituals, and human creativity.

WORD	MEANING
Symbolization	The definition of symbolization is taken from "*A Critical Dictionary of Jungian Analysis*" where psychologist Andrew Samuels defines symbol in terms of concept, intent, purpose and content. Symbolization is the processing of images that control, order and give meaning to human experience
Theistic Mode of Containment	Interaction between a person and a theistic god who gets involved in human affairs. The person and the deity bond on a religious belief system. The person presents an unassimilated state of mind to the deity and obtains relief in the form of a blessing, a punishment, or a restitution. Adherents of theistic religions regard their deities as having powers greater than humans, along with the ability to carry humans to new levels of consciousness (GG 378). For example, Arjuna (a human prince) and Krishna (a Hindu god) had a theistic mode of containment.
Third Narrative	A third narrative is the result of the dialectical interaction between contained (first narrative) and container (second narrative) during a containment. The result can be internal, such as a change of mental outlook. The result can also be external, as in the creation of a physical product.

Bibliography

Abedin, Huma
    "BOTH/AND: A Life in Many Worlds"
    Scribner, 2021

Andersen, Christopher
    "Barack and Michelle: Portrait of An American Marriage"
    William Morrow, 1st edition, 2009

Archer, Margaret S.
    "Conversations About Reflexivity"
    Routledge, 1st edition, 2013

Bair, Dierdre
    "Jung: A Biography"
    Back Bay Books, 2004

Bentwich, Isaac
    "GITA: A Timeless Guide For Out Time"
    Harmonia Publications, 2019

Bernstein, Carl
    "Chasing History: A Kid In The Newsroom"
    Henry Holt & Company, 2022

Bion, Wilfred
    "Attention and Interpretation"
    Rowman & Littlefield Publishers, Inc.: Revised edition, 1995

Caeyers, Jan
"Beethoven: A Life"
University of California Press, 1st edition, 2020

Carlisle, Al
"The 1976 Psychological Assessment of Ted Bundy"
Carlisle Legacy Books, LLC; Illustrated edition, 2020

Cartwright, Duncan
"Containing States of Mind"
Routledge; 1st edition, 2009

Catholic Book Publishing
"The New American Bible"
Catholic Book Publishing Company, 1st edition, 2011

Cohen, Michael
"DISLOYAL: A Memoir"
Skyhorse Publishing, 1st edition, 2020

Colman, Warren
"ACT AND IMAGE: The Emergence of Symbolic Imagination"
Spring Journal, Inc., 2016

Davies, Kevin
"Editing Humanity"
Pegasus Books, 2021

DePaolo, Robert
"BUNDY: A Clinical Discussion of the Perfect Storm"
Abuzz Press, 2020

Donn, Linda
"Freud and Jung: Years of Friendship, Years of Loss"
CreateSpace Independent Publishing Platform, 2011

Freud, Sigmund
"The Interpretation of Dreams"
W. W. Norton, 1980

Frisardi, Andrew
"Love's Scribe"
Angelico Press, 2020

Galison, Peter
"Minkowski's Space-Time: From Visual Thinking To The Absolute World"
https://projects.iq.harvard.edu/sites
Historical Studies in the Physical Sciences, Vol 10, (1979):85-119

Girardot, Frank C. & Kovach, Lori Orr
"BURNED: Pyromania, Murder & Daughter's Nightmare"
WildBlue Press, 2018

Grotstein, James
"A Beam of Intense Darkness: Wilfred Bion's Legacy to Psychoanalysis"
Routledge, 1st edition, 2007

Hogenson, George
"Archetypes: Emergence and the Psyche's Deep Structure"
In *"Analytical Psychology: Contemporary Perspectives in Jungian Psychology"* Edited by Joseph Cambray & Linda Carter
Brunner-Routledge, 1st edition, 2004

Hogenson, George, B.
"Jung's Struggle With Freud"
Chiron Publications, 2013

Isaacson, Walter
"EINSTEIN: His Life and Universe"
Simon & Schuster, 2008

Isaacson, Walter
"The Code Breaker"
Simon & Schuster, 2021

Jaffe, Aniela
"Memories, Dreams, Reflections"
Vintage, Reissue edition, 1989

Jung, Carl
"The Archetypes and the Collective Unconscious"
Collected Works of C. G. Jung, Volume 8, Part 1
Pantheon Books, 1959

Jung, Carl
"The Psychology of Transference"
Princeton University Press, 10th printing edition,1969

Kendall, Elizabeth
"The Phantom Prince: My Life With Ted Bundy"
Harry N. Abrams, 2020

Klapproth, John E.
"The Immortal Beloved Compendium"
CreateSpace Independent Publishing Platform, 2017

Knox, Jean
"Archetype, Attachment, Analysis: Jungian Psychology and the
Emergent Mind"
Routledge, 1st edition, 2003

Kranish, Michael, & Fisher, Marc
"TRUMP REVEALED: Definitive Biography of 45th President"
Scribner, 1st edition, 2016

Launer, John
    "Sex vs. Survival: The Life and Ideas of Sabina Spielrein"
    Lulu.com, 2011

Lee, Brandy
    "The Dangerous Case of Donald Trump"
    St. Martin's Press, 2017

Leonnig, Carol, & Rucker, Philip
    "I Alone Can Fix It"
    Penguin Press, 2021

Lewis, R. W. B.
    "Dante: A Life"
    Penguin Books, 2009

Lipsey, Roger
    "Make Peace Before The Sun Goes Down"
    Shambhala, 2015

Littleton, C. Scott
    "Gods, Goddesses, And Mythology"
    Marshall Cavendish, 2005

Meoli, Anthony
    "Into the Fire: Forensic Interview with John Orr"
    CreateSpace Independent Publishing Platform, 2017

Mott, Michael
    "The Seven Mountains of Thomas Merton"
    Houghton Mifflin Company, 1986

Obama, Barack
    "A Promised Land"
    Crown, 1st edition, 2020

Obama, Michelle
"Becoming"
Crown, 2018

Ogden, Thomas H.
"Reverie and Interpretation: Sensing Something Human"
Routledge, 1999

Orr, John
"Points Of Origin"
Infinity Publishing, 2021

Rama, Swami
"Perennial Psychology of the Bhagavad Gita"
Himalayan Institute Press, 1ˢᵗ edition, 2007

Rose, James (editor)
"SYMBOLIZATION: Representation and Communication"
Routledge, 1ˢᵗ edition, 2019

Rule, Ann
"The Stranger Beside Me"
Sphere, 2019

Samuels, Andrew, Shorter, Bani, & Plaut, Fred
"A Critical Dictionary of Jungian Analysis"
Routledge, 1ˢᵗ edition, 1986

Stevens, Anthony
"Archetype Revisited"
Routledge, 2015

Tellenbach, Marie-Elizabeth
"Beethoven and His 'Immortal Beloved' Josephine Brunsvik"
CreateSpace Independent Publishing Platform, 2014

Ulanov, Ann & Barry
> "Transforming Sexuality: The Archetypal World of Anima and
> Animus"
> Shambhala, 1994

Von Franz, Marie-Louise
> "Projection and Re-Collection in Jungian Psychology"
> Open Court Publishing Company, 1985

Weiss, Robert
> "Sex Addiction 101"
> Health Communications, Inc., 2015

Wesley, Matthew
> "Barack and Michelle Obama: Biography of the Ultimate Power
> Couple"
> Independently published, 2019

Whitebook, Joel
> "FREUD: An Intellectual Biography"
> Cambridge University Press, 2017

www.ingramcontent.com/pod-product-compliance
Lightning Source LLC
Chambersburg PA
CBHW050559270326
41926CB00012B/2116